The TOWN of SHERBURNE in the ISLAND of NANTUCKET.

Second and Enlarged Edition

EARLY SETTLERS OF
Nantucket

THEIR ASSOCIATES AND DESCENDANTS

COMPILED BY

LYDIA S. HINCHMAN

ILLUSTRATED WITH PHOTOGRAPHS AND WITH DRAWINGS BY
MARGARETTA S. HINCHMAN

**Southern Historical Press, Inc.
Greenville, South Carolina**

This volume was reproduced
from a personal copy located in
the Publishers private library

All rights reserved. No part of this publication may be reproduced,
stored in a retrieval system, transmitted in any form, posted
on the web in any form or by any means without the
prior written permission of the publisher.

Please direct all correspondence and book orders to:
SOUTHERN HISTORICAL PRESS, Inc.
1071 Park West Blvd.
Greenville, SC 29611

Copyright 1906 by:
  Lydia S. Hinchman
ISBN #978-1-63914-637-6
Printed in the United States of America

FULL-PAGE PLATES.

THE TOWN OF SHERBURNE, . . . Frontispiece.

	OPP. PAGE
SANKATY HEAD,	2
ABRAHAM QUARY,	8

The last native representative of Indian blood on Nantucket; died in 1854.

PROFESSOR MARIA MITCHELL,	12
PORTLEDGE,	24

The Coffin Manor House in England.

ELIZABETH, WIDOW OF RICHARD COFFIN, ESQ.,	26

"Portlinch;" born 1651.

THE TRISTRAM COFFIN HOUSE, Newburyport, Massachusetts,	28
DRESSER IN THE TRISTRAM COFFIN HOUSE,	29
ADMIRAL SIR ISAAC COFFIN, Baronet,	41
THE JOHN SWAIN HOUSE, Nantucket,	66
MRS. E. D. GILLESPIE,	69
BIRTHPLACE OF MARIA MITCHELL, Vestal Street, Nantucket,	73
PROFESSOR HENRY MITCHELL,	76

"Shearing Day,"	100
The Old Grist Mill, ...	109
Watching for Whaleships, ...	111
Timothy Folger, ...	114
Photographed from a painting by George Fish, after Copley.	
John Richardson's Meeting, . . .	120
A Nantucket Street, ...	133
A Nantucket Garden, ...	135
"The Order and Manner of Seating and Placing of the Parishnours and Inhabitance of the Parish of Brixton anno Domini 1638," .	306
Copied from the Original Coffin School Medal, .	313
Richard Coffin, Esq., of Portledge, . . .	314
Sheriff of Devonshire in 1699.	

To my Children
IN WHOSE INTEREST THIS WORK WAS UNDERTAKEN
AND
To my Sister
MARY A. ALBERTSON
WHOSE ASSISTANCE IN GENEALOGICAL WORK HAS BEEN OF GREAT VALUE

This Book is affectionately Dedicated

PREFACE.

It has not been the plan of the compiler of this book to make an exhaustive history of Nantucket, or a complete genealogy of its various families.

Several histories and genealogical books of individual families have been prepared, and are a great help in a work like this.

It is not necessary, however, to the islanders that complete genealogies be put at their disposal, since the town, court and Friends' records are unusually complete and well preserved, and may be consulted if one really " wants to know."

There are matters which, to the people of Nantucket, who have one hundred or more years of family record on the island, are of common interest.

It must be remembered that very few of the early settlers came directly from the old world to Nantucket. Settlements were located on the " main land," and family alliances made which are now interesting to note; and in the few instances where the families are brought down to the present time, it is intended to show the cropping up wherever one may go of descendants of the quiet Quaker people whose beginnings were so humble, but whose influence has been so widespread.

If some names are mentioned of those who have attained prominence, it is not with the view of passing others by. Perhaps the credit may be due not to him who has made his mark, but to the earnest parent who in his far-off island home has toiled

> To save all earnings to the uttermost,
> And give his child a better bringing up
> Than his had been, or hers.

The early settlers were pioneers in every sense of the word, and had more of family history than of this world's goods with which to begin life. The American ancestry of Nantucketers is not alone on the little island, which it is our pleasure to honor, but may be found in several States.

The purpose of this volume is to follow to some extent the wanderings and the manner of life, not only of the early settlers themselves, but of their associates and descendants.

The compiler would express her appreciation of the valuable information given by members of the several families whose lineage is herein set down.

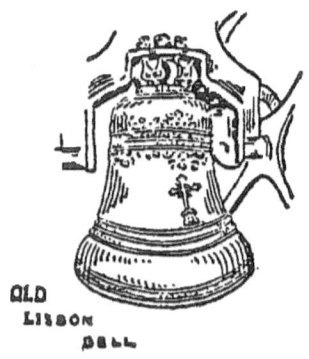
OLD LISBON BELL

CHAPTER		PAGE
I.—DEEDS OF PURCHASE AND SETTLEMENT OF THE ISLAND,		1

Discovery—Names of Purchasers—Ten Proprietors Added—Houses Built—Town Named.

II.—THOMAS MACY, ... 14

Arrival in America—His Record in Salisbury, Massachusetts—Violation of Laws in Religious Matters—Admonition—Apology—Departure for Nantucket.

III.—EDWARD STARBUCK, ... 19

Settlement at Dover, New Hampshire—Possessions in Dover—Profession of Anabaptism—Joins Thomas Macy on his Voyage to Nantucket—Name of Starbuck Associated with his Former Possessions until 1716—Deed of Conveyance to Nathaniel Starbuck.

IV.—TRISTRAM COFFIN, ... 24

Birth—Marriage—Arrival in America—Early Ancestry—Coffin Home in Normandy and England—Life and Services at Nantucket—Commission as Chief Magistrate of Colony—Sketch of his Children.

V.—ADMIRAL SIR ISAAC COFFIN, Baronet, . . 41

His Early Life in Boston—Interest in Nantucket—Services for the King—Story of his Whaling Experience—Marriage and Death in England.

VI.—STEPHEN GREENLEAF, WITH SOME ACCOUNT OF HIS FATHER, EDMUND GREENLEAF, . . 46

Origin of the Family—Arrival in America of Edmund Greenleaf and Family—Public Service—Extract from Will—STEPHEN GREENLEAF as Proprietor of Nantucket—Military and Civil Services—Death.

VII.—CHRISTOPHER HUSSEY, ... 50
    Baptismal Record—Marriage—Arrival in Boston—Settlement at Hampton, New Hampshire—Public Services—STEPHEN HUSSEY—Account of Stephen Batchelder and John Wing.

VIII.—OTHER PROPRIETORS, ... 60
    ROBERT PIKE—Settlement at Salisbury—Relations with Nantucket—Public Life—THOMAS COLEMAN as Proprietor—THOMAS AND ROBERT BARNARD—Proprietors of Nantucket and Record at Salisbury and Amesbury—RICHARD SWAIN—Connection of his Family with Weare Family, of Hampton, New Hampshire—JOHN SWAIN as Proprietor—His House.

IX.—PETER FOLGER, ... 67
    Origin of Folger Family—Peter Folger's Arrival in America—Life and Missionary Work at Martha's Vineyard—Cotton Mather's Description of Him—Settlement at Nantucket—His Family—Benjamin Franklin and his Descendants in Philadelphia—Walter Folger—Maria Mitchell—Jacob Barker—Thomas Prence—William Collier—William Allen Butler—Charles James Folger.

X.—THOMAS GARDINER, AND HIS SONS RICHARD AND JOHN GARDNER, ... 79
    Settlement in America—Life at Cape Ann and Salem—Removal of RICHARD GARDNER to Nantucket—Richard as Magistrate—JOHN GARDNER as Magistrate on Nantucket, Judge of Probate, and Captain of "F'foot Company."

XI.—SAMUEL SHATTUCK, ... 86
    Association of Name with Nantucket—Persecution—Banishment from America—Samuel Shattuck's Return to America with the King's Mandate.

XII.—THOMAS MAYHEW AND THOMAS MAYHEW, JR., 96
    Thomas Mayhew as Proprietor of Nantucket—His Life at Martha's Vineyard—Missionary Work of Thomas Mayhew, Jr., among Indians—Children and Descendants of Thomas Mayhew, Jr.

XIII.—CUSTOMS, DOCUMENTS AND INCIDENTS OF NANTUCKET, 100

XIV.—NANTUCKET IN THE REVOLUTION, . . . 111
    An Explanation of the Neutral Position of Nantucket during the Revolutionary War.

XV.—EXTRACTS FROM JOURNALS OF THOMAS CHALKLEY, JOHN RICHARDSON AND THOMAS STORY, GIVING SOME ACCOUNT OF THE RISE OF FRIENDS ON NANTUCKET, ... 120
    Establishment of Friends' Meeting—Present Condition of the Society on the Island.

XVI.—AN IMPARTIAL JUDGMENT, ... 133

Detail of Descent from Proprietors and Settlers.

XVII.—The Mitchell Family, ... 141

XVIII.—The Russell Family, ... 149

XIX.—The Swain Family, ... 152

XX.—The Barker Family, ... 155

XXI.—Family of Lucretia Mott, . . . 160

XXII.—Families of Thomas Earle and John Milton Earle, ... 166

XXIII.—The Swift Family, ... 169

XXIV.—Family of William Rotch, . . 176

XXV.—Wing and Hathaway Connection with Nantucket Families, ... 183

XXVI.—Newhall Connection with Nantucket Families, ... 189

XXVII.—Family of Abraham Macy, . . . 195

XXVIII.—Family of Josiah Macy, of New York, . 203

XXIX.—Cornell Connection with Nantucket, . 211

XXX.—The Coggeshall Family, . . . 216

XXXI.—Stanton Connection with Nantucket Families, 221

XXXII.—Connection of The Waterman Family with Nantucket, ... 224

XXXIII.—The Wadley, or Wadleigh, Family, . 227

XXXIV.—Family of Coffin Colket, . . . 231

XXXV.—John Greenleaf Whittier, . . 234

XXXVI.—The Nathan Bunker Family, . . . 237

Appendix I., ... 243

Appendix II., ... 307

Names of Ministers of the Society of Friends and their Companions Who Visited Nantucket from 1664 to 1847, . . . 317

Early Settlers of Nantucket
Their Associates and Descendants.

CHAPTER I.

DEEDS OF PURCHASE AND SETTLEMENT OF THE ISLAND.

BELKNAP, in his Biography of Biron,* says, "An Icelander of the name Herioff and his son Biron * made a voyage every year to different countries for the sake of traffic.

"About the beginning of the eleventh century (1001) their ships were separated by a storm. When Biron * arrived in Norway he heard that his father was gone to Greenland, and he resolved to follow him; but another storm drove him to the southwest, where he discovered a flat country, free from rocks, but covered with thick woods, and an island near the coast."

When on his return to Greenland his discoveries became known, Lief, the son of Eric, Earl of Norway, equipped a vessel, and " taking Biron * for his pilot sailed (1002) in search of the new country."

Belknap says, " Biarne's * description of the coast is

---
* Bjorne.

very accurate and in the island situate to the eastward (between which and the promontory that stretches to the eastward and northward Lief sailed) we recognize Nantucket. The ancient Northmen found there many shallows." There is little doubt that Nantucket was visited by *Englishmen* very early in the seventeenth century (1602).

In the biography of Gosnold, Belknap says, " The shoal water and breach which he calls Tucker's Terror corresponds with the shoal and breakers called Pollock's Rip. . . . To avoid this danger, it being late in the day, he stood so far out to sea as to overshoot the eastern entrance of what is now called the Vineyard Sound.

" The land which he made in the night was a white cliff on the eastern coast of Nantucket now called Sankaty Head.

" The breach which lay off Gilbert's Point I take to be the Bass Rip and the Pollock Rip with the cross ripplings which extend from the southeast extremity of that island.

" Over these ripplings there is a depth of water from four to seven fathoms, according to a late map of Nantucket, published by Peleg Coffin, Esq., and others." *

Some one has said, " He only has the credit of discovery who locates." Captain Weymouth was the first to give the geographical position of Sankaty Head in 1605.

It is difficult to imagine any native of Nantucket

---

*American Biography. By Jeremy Belknap, D.D. With Additions and Notes by F. M. Hubbard. Published by Harper & Brothers in 1843.

Sankaty Head.

who would not be interested in facts relating to its history, whether geographical, historical, geological, or genealogical; but the practical interest for us of the present day dates from 1659, when it was finally settled by sturdy men, ancestors to so many in this broad land that a brief detail of the public services of those pioneers cannot fail to be of value to their descendants.

Tradition assigns two causes for the sudden departure of Thomas Macy and Edward Starbuck from Salisbury, Massachusetts.

Many of their descendants have believed that persecution on account of the harboring of Quakers led those early settlers to leave an already established home, to seek another upon a desolate, bleak island, where skulking Indians, added to its isolated position, made a most inhospitable landing-place.

On the other hand, most historians attribute the journey of Thomas Macy and Edward Starbuck in 1659 to a business negotiation between them and Thomas Mayhew in regard to the purchase of the island of Nantucket.

Benjamin Franklin Folger, one of the well-known genealogists of Nantucket, has stated that early in 1659 Tristram Coffin went on a voyage of investigation, first to Martha's Vineyard, where he secured the services of Peter Folger as interpreter, thence to Nantucket, "his object being to ascertain the temper and disposition of the Indians and the capabilities of the island that he might report to the citizens of Salisbury what inducements for emigration thither were offered."

Thomas Mayhew, some years before, had received a grant of the islands off the southeast coast of Massachusetts from William, Earl of Sterling, and Sir Fernando or Ferdinand Gorges, as is shown by the records in the secretary's office at Albany, New York, Nantucket having belonged to New York until about 1690.

In 1659 the island or the patent of it was still in the possession of the Mayhews.

F. B. Hough's book says, "In 1659 the elder Mayhew admitted nine others to a joint partnership in the Island of Nantucket, reserving a small part to himself, and in February following it was agreed that each Partner might admit another to an equal share in Power and Interest, not being justly excepted to by the Rest."

We find on record that in July of 1659 a deed was given by Thomas Mayhew, confirming the sale of the island of Nantucket to nine purchasers,—viz.:

TRISTRAM COFFIN.

RICHARD SWAIN, or SWAYNE.

PETER COFFIN.

STEPHEN GREENLEAF.

WILLIAM PIKE.

THOMAS MACY.

THOMAS BARNARD.

CHRISTOPHER HUSSEY.

JOHN SWAIN, or SWAYNE.

NOTE.—In 1641 Nantucket appears to have been under the control of William, Earl of Sterling, and Sir Fernando or Ferdinand Gorges, as "during this year the Elizabeth Islands, Caparrock or Martha's Vineyard, Nanticon or Nantucket and Tuckanuck or Tuckanuckett" were "graunted unto Thomas Mayhew at Watertowne, Merchant, and to Thomas Mayhew his sonne."

The consideration named in the deed of Nantucket was "that Thomas Mayhew and Thomas Mayhew his sonne or either of

Copy of Deed of Nantucket to Nine Purchasers (dated July 2, 1659).

"Recorded for Mr Coffin and Mr Macy afores^d ye Day and Year afores^d.

"Be it known unto all Men by these Presents that I, Thomas Mayhew of Martha's Vineyard, Merchant, doe hereby acknowledge that I have sould unto Tristram Coffin, Thomas Macy, Christopher Hussey, Richard Swayne, Thomas Bernard, Peter Coffin, Stephen Greenleafe, John Swayne and William Pike that Right and Interest I have in ye Land of Nantuckett by Patent; ye wch Right I bought of James Fforrett, Gent. and Steward to ye Lord Sterling and of Richard Vines, sometimes of Sacho, Gent., Steward-Gen^{rll} unto Sir Georges Knight as by Conveyances under their Hands and Seales doe appeare, ffor them ye aforesaid to Injoy, and their Heyres and Assignes forever wth all the Privileges thereunto belonging, for in consideration of ye Sume of Thirty Pounds of Current Pay unto whomsoever I ye said Thomas Mayhew, mine Heyres or Assignes shall appoint.

"And also two Beaver Hatts one for myself and one for my wife.

"And further this is to declare that I the said

---

them or their Assignes doe render and pay yearly unto the Honble the Lord Sterling, his Heyres and Assignes, such an acknowledgment as shall be thought fitt by John Winthrop Esqr the Elder or any two Magistrates in the Massachusetts Bay, being Chosen for that End and Purpose by the Honble the Lord Sterling or his Deputy and by the said Thomas Mayhew and Thomas Mayhew his Sonne, or their Assignes." This deed was dated October 13, 1641.

Thomas Mayhew have received to myself that Neck upon Nantucket called Masquetuck or that Neck of Land called Nashayte the Neck (but one) northerly of Masquetuck, ye aforesaid Sayle in anywise notwithstanding. And further, I ye said Thomas Mayhew am to beare my Part of the Charge of ye said Purchase above named, and to hold one twentieth Part of all Lands purchased already, or shall be hereafter purchased, upon ye said Island by ye afores^d Purchas^{rs} or Heyres and Assignes forever.

"Briefly: It is thus: That I really sold all my Patent to ye aforesaid nine Men and they are to pay mee or whomsoever I shall appoint them, ye sume of Thirty Pounds in good Marchantable Pay in ye Massachusetts, under wch Governm^t they now Inhabit, and 2 Beaver Hatts, and I am to beare a 20th Part of ye Charge of ye Purchase, and to have a 20th Part of all Lands and Priviledges; and to have wch of ye Necks afors^d that I will myselfe, paying for it; only ye Purchasers are to pay what ye Sachem is to have for Masquetuck, although I have ye other Neck.

"And in witness hereof I have hereunto sett my Hand and Seale this second Day of July sixteen hundred and fifty-nine—(1659).

"Per me

"Tho. Mayhew.

"Witness   John Smith

"Edward Searle."

By this deed it will be observed that a share of the island was retained by Thomas Mayhew, and in this way he became one of the proprietors who are said in all histories of the place to have founded the settlement.

On May 1st, 1901, Mr. Henry B. Worth, who is authority on old Nantucket records, sent to the *Inquirer and Mirror* * a copy of a deed by which a portion of Nantucket was conveyed by the Indians to Thomas Mayhew; this deed antedates that previously published as the first deed, and is confirmatory of the theory that business negotiations between Thomas Macy and his friends, and Thomas Mayhew were pending for a considerable time before the deed of July 2d, 1659, was executed.

Mr. Worth says that " the deed seems to have remained in the possession of Mayhew and his family until the Indians appealed to the General Court to recover their lands, when the owner found the old deed and placed it on record," March 26th, 1731, Book 4, p. 93.

" The record is accompanied by a plan which plainly indicates the section covered by the deed."

COPY OF THE DEED OF " TWENTYETH OF JUNE, 1659."

" ' This doth witness that we, Nickanoose of Nantucket, Sachem, and Nanahumo of Nantucket, Sachem, have sold unto Thomas Mayhew of the Vineyard the plain at the West end of Nantucket, that is, according to the figure underwritten, to him, his heirs and assigns forever. In consideration whereof we have received by earnest of the said Thomas Mayhew the sum of

---

* A weekly paper of Nantucket.

twelve pounds answerable to Peage at 8 a penny; also the said Sachems have sold the said Mayhew of the Vineyard the use of the Meadow and to take wood for the use of him the said Mayhew, his heirs and assigns forever.

"'In witness hereof we the Sachems aforesaid have hereunto set our hands this twentyeth of June 1659. The pond Acamy lieth north and by east and south and by west or near it.'

"The deed is signed by the marks of the two Sachems and is witnessed by Mr. Harry, also by John Coleman, Thomas Macy and Tristram Coffin; it is therefore clear that these witnesses were at that date in Nantucket."

The records indicate that in February, 1659, months before the execution of the deed of conveyance of Thomas Mayhew to nine purchasers, "the associates in Salisbury, Massachusetts, were enacting rules and regulations concerning the method of governing Nantucket."

Thomas Macy and his friends appear to have lost no time after the business arrangement between Mr. Mayhew and the Indians was completed, the purchase being effected within two weeks after the transaction with Nickanoose and Nanahumo.

The following deeds prove that notwithstanding the purchase of the island from Thomas Mayhew, a business negotiation was made with the Indians also, and that the land was fairly bought from them:

Abraham Quary.

*The last native representative of Indian blood on Nantucket.
Died in 1854.*

DEED OF WANACKMANACK.

"This witnesseth that I, Wanackmanack, Chief Sachem of Nantucket, hath sold unto Mr. Tristram Coffin and Thomas Macy their heirs and assigns that whole neck of land called by the Indians Pacummohquah,* being at the East end of Nantucket, for and in consideration of five pounds to be paid to me in English goods, or otherwise to my content by the same Tristram Coffin aforesaid at convenient time as shall be demanded.

"Witness my hand or mark this 22 of June 1662.
                                        WANACKMAMAK.

"Witness hereto, Peter Folger and Wawinnesit whose English name is Amos."

"Copy of Indian deed of Nantucket, Recorded for Mr. Tristram Coffin and Mr. Thomas Macy, ye 29th of June 1671 aforesaid.

"These P^{r}sents Wittness y^t I Wanackmamack Head Sachem of ye Island of Nantuckett, have Bargained and sold, and doe by these Presents Bargaine and Sell unto Tristram Coffin, Thomas Macy, Richd Swayne, Thomas Bernard, John Swain, Mr Thomas Mayhew, Edward Starbuck, Peter Coffin, James Coffin, Stephen Greenleafe, Tristram Coffin Junr, Thomas Coleman, Robert Bernard, Christopher Hussey, Robert Pyke, John Smyth, and John Bishop these Islands of Nantucket, namely, all ye west end of ye afores^d Island unto ye Pond comonly called Waquittaquay and from ye Head of that Pond to ye North side of ye Island

---
* Pocomo.

Manamoy; Bounded by a Path from ye Head of ye Pond aforesaid to Manamoy; as also a Neck at ye East End of ye Island called Poquomock,* wth the Property thereof, and all ye Royaltyes, Priviledges and Immunityes thereto belonging, or whatsoever Right I ye afores^d Wanackmak have, or have had in ye same: That is, all ye Lands afore menconed and likewise ye Winter sseed of ye whole island from ye End of an Indyan Harvest untill Planting Time, or ye first of May, from yeare to yeare forever, as likewise Liberty to make use of Wood and Timber on all Parts of ye Island; and likewise Halfe of ye Meadows and Marshes on all Parts of ye Island wthout or beside ye afores^d tracts of Land Purchased; And likewise ye use of ye other Halfe of ye Meadows and Marshes, as long as ye aforesaid English their Heyres or Assignes live on ye Island; And likewise I the aforesaid Wanackmamack doe sell unto ye English afore menconed ye propriety of ye rest of ye Island belonging unto mee, for and in consideracon of fforty Pounds already received by mee or other by my Consent or Ord.

"To Have and to hold, ye afores^d Tracts of Land, wth ye P'riety, Royaltyies, Immunityes, Priviledges, and all Appertenances thereunto belonging to them ye afores^d Purchas^{rs} their Heyres and Assignes forever.

"In witness Whereof I the afores^d Wanackmamack have hereunto sett my Hand and Seale ye Daye and Yeare above written.

"The Sign of Wanack-Mamack.

"Signed, Sealed and Delivered
  in ye p^{r}sence of

---

* Pocomo.

" Peter Foulger,
" Eleazer Foulger,
" Dorcas Starbuck." *

RECEIPT OF WANACKMAMACK.

(*Nantucket Records, Old Book, Page* 27.)

" Received of Tristram Coffin of Nantuckett, the just sume of five poun, which is part of the seven poun that was unpaid of the Twenty poun Purchase of the Land that was purchased of Wanackmamack and Neckanoose, that is to say from Monomoy to Waquettaquage pond, Nanahumack Neck and all from Wesco westward to the west end of Nantucket, I say Received by Me Wanackmamack of Tristram Coffin, five pounds Starling the 18th 11 M 1671

" The Mark × of Wanackmamack.

" Witness hereunto
  " RICHARD GARDNER.
  " ELEZER FOLGER."

The following Associates were chosen by the first Proprietors:

TRISTRAM COFFIN, JR.	JOHN SMITH.
ROBERT PIKE.	ROBERT BARNARD.
THOMAS COLEMAN.	EDWARD STARBUCK.
NATHANIEL STARBUCK.	THOMAS LOOK.
JAMES COFFIN.	THOMAS MAYHEW, JR.

---

* Dorcas Starbuck was a daughter of Edward Starbuck. Eleazer Foulger was a son of Peter Foulger.

NOTE.—The official records of these deeds are in the office of the Secretary of State, Albany, New York.

They purchased or were given a half-interest in the original apportionments, making at a very early date twenty landed proprietors.

Among these were men of varied experience and marked executive ability, evinced by their embracing every opportunity for the advancement of the settlement, and soon an interesting society was established upon the island.

The first houses were built at the northwest, not far from a small harbor now called Maddequet Harbor.

Later the larger harbor on the north side of the island offered decided advantages, and the town was finally located there and named Sherburne, in compliance with written orders of Governor Lovelace, of New York, recorded in Albany in the Secretary's office in Book of Deeds III., p. 85. Many of the houses were moved from their original sites to the new town.

Numbers at first were so small that intermarriages among these families were very common, and it is not infrequent for a descendant to find the same settler in his family tree several times.

These intermarriages made relationships so close that until the latter half of the nineteenth century, when new people began more and more to move to the island, nearly all natives of Nantucket were cousins through a common ancestry.

An amusing incident was related to the writer by Maria Mitchell, who during her residence in the observatory at Vassar College, received and entertained many guests; on one occasion she was greeted with "Miss Mitchell, I met a cousin of yours the other day." "Where?" was the natural question; "on

Professor Maria Mitchell.

Nantucket," the expected reply. Miss Mitchell quickly said, " Oh, very likely; I have five thousand cousins on Nantucket." At that time five thousand covered the entire population of the island.

The population increased steadily until about 1849, when the California gold fever led many to seek wealth on the Pacific Coast, and later, the final decline of the whale fisheries compelled the younger men to find means of support elsewhere, and in comparatively few years the population decreased from nearly ten thousand to less than five thousand.

CHAPTER II.

THOMAS MACY.

NEAR the town of Salisbury, in Wiltshire, England, in the Parish of Chilmark, resided ("prior to his embarkation for America, probably in 1635") Thomas Macy.

The name of the vessel upon which he came to America is not recorded, but he arrived not later than 1639.

Thomas Macy was among the original settlers of Salisbury, Massachusetts, and is in "The first or Original list of ye townsmen of Salisbury in ye booke of Records."

Among those to whom lots of ground were granted in Salisbury we find the names of Thomas Macy, Robert Pike and Phillip Challis. There is no date to the paper or document giving this list, but it is indexed 1639.

Merrill's map of Amesbury locates most of the lots on the "Circular Road." Macy's lot is given on the "road to the neck."

In 1650 "Phillip Challis, Robert Pike and Tho. Macy" were included in a list of Commoners, and at the same meeting at which they were so enrolled we find "it was ordered y^t all whose names are here under written shall be accomp^{t}ed townesmen & Comoners & none butt them to this p^{r}sent." *

---

* Hoyt, pp. 8-9 and 11.

We find also recorded that he was "a merchant, planter,* one of the select-men of the town, a juryman, and, withal a preacher."

The Massachusetts laws passed in 1656 and 1657 were a great drawback to freedom of worship.

Several persons were prosecuted for violating the law of 1657 which prohibited entertaining Quakers. Among these was Thomas Macy, who was fined thirty shillings, notwithstanding his "explanation and apology," and was ordered to be admonished by the governor.

It is a matter of record that he sheltered Edward Wharton, William Robinson, merchant of London, and Marmaduke Stephenson, of Yorkshire, England. The two last named were hanged in Boston the 27th of October, 1659.

The following letter from General Court files is a copy of a reply to a summons to appear at court to answer for his violation of the law in this particular:

"This is to entreat the honored Court not to be offended because of my non-appearance. It is not from any slighting the authority of this honored Court, nor from feare to answer the case, but I have bin for some weeks past very ill, and am so at present, and notwithstanding my illness, yet I desirous to appear, have done my utmost endeavour to hire a horse but cannot procure one at present.

"I being at present destitute have endeavoured to purchase, but at present cannot attaine it, but shall relate the truth of the case as my answer should be to y^e

---
* A farmer.

honored Court, and more cannot be proved, nor so much.

"On a rainy morning there came to my house Edward Wharton and three men more, the said Wharton spoke to me saying that they were travelling eastward and desired me to direct them in the way to Hampton, and asked me how far it was to Casco Bay.

"I never saw any of ye men afore except Wharton neither did I require their names, or who they were, but by their carriage I thought they might be Quakers and told them so, and therefore desired them to passe on their way, saying to them I might possibly give offence in entertaining them, and as soone as the violence of the rain ceased (for it rained very hard) they went away and I never saw them since.

"The time that they stayed in the house was about three quarters of an hour, but I can safely affirm that it was not an houre.

"They spake not many words in the time, neither was I at leisure to talke with them, for I came home wet to ye skin, immediately afore they came to the house and I found my wife sick in bed. If this satisfie not the honored Court I shall subject to their sentence.

"I have not willingly offended. I am ready to serve and obey you in the Lord.

"THOS. MACY."

He was a Baptist, and on the Sabbath frequently exhorted the people; this, too, was in violation of the Massachusetts law which prohibited all but the regularly ordained from such service.

Tradition says that immediately after his sentence Thomas Macy removed to Nantucket.

In the "Macy Genealogy" it is related that "in 1659 he embarked at Salisbury in a small boat with his wife and children and such household goods as he could conveniently carry, and in company with Isaac Coleman and Edward Starbuck set sail for Nantucket." *

The same papers say, "because he could not in justice to the dictates of his own conscience longer submit to the tyranny of the clergy and those in authority."

It appears from the above detail that Thomas Macy satisfied the requirements of the law and paid his fine, but undoubtedly he believed he could lead a more peaceful and independent life at Nantucket, and may have preferred voluntary exile to possible banishment.

Thomas Macy must have returned to Salisbury, as he is recorded as living there in 1664.

Before his removal to Nantucket he was commissioner, and representative to the General Court from Salisbury, and the citizens of that town bore testimony of their sympathy with him by electing his friend and defender Robert Pike as his successor.

That he again, at a later date, removed to Nantucket is evident from old records, Register's office, in which it will be found that October 1, 1675, he was commissioned chief magistrate of the town.

He was the first recorder appointed on the island, and a portion at least of the first Book of Records in the office at Nantucket was written by him.

He died April 19, 1682, aged seventy-four. His

---

* James Coffin, son of Tristram, Sr., is said to have accompanied the three named.

wife, Sarah (Hopcot) Macy, who came with him from Chilmark, survived him for nearly a quarter of a century.

JOHN MACY, son of Thomas and Sarah Macy, born at Salisbury July 14, 1655, married Deborah Gardner, daughter of Richard and Sarah (Shattuck) Gardner, and died at Nantucket, October 14, 1691, at the early age of thirty-six; through him alone the name has descended to posterity.

NOTE.—In 1637-38, GEORGE MACY appears to have been prominent in the settlement of Taunton, Massachusetts. Savage (vol. iii., p. 142) says he was in 1643 lieutenant in King Philip's War, and representative in 1672 and for six years; also among the inhabitants of Taunton in 1668 there was a Samuel Macy, who is supposed to have been a son of George and to have died single prior to the death of his father; of this Taunton family there is no further record, nor of any others of the name excepting Thomas and his descendants.

The only reasons for supposing George Macy was of the same family as Thomas are the name and the date of his emigration to America.

The name Macy signifies mace or staff.

CHAPTER III.

EDWARD STARBUCK.

EDWARD STARBUCK was born in 1604, and came from Derbyshire, England, to Dover, New Hampshire, with his wife, Katharine * (Reynolds), of Wales, about 1635.

"He is first mentioned as receiving 1643 a grant of forty acres of land on each side of the Fresh River at Cutchechoe . . . and also one platt of Marsh above Cutchechoe great Marsh, that the brook that runs out of the river runs through, first discovered by Richard Walderne, Edward Colcord, Edward Starbuck, and William Furber.

"He had other grants at different times, one of Marsh in Great Bay in 1643, one of the Mill privilege at Cutchechoe 2nd Falls (with Thomas Wiggins) and one of timber to 'accommodate' in 1650 and various others.

"Indeed Edward owned considerable land and was evidently a man of substance as to possessions as tradition says he was in body.

"He was a representative in 1643 and 1646, was an elder in the church and enjoyed various other tokens of respect given him by his fellow citizens.

"In fact he might have lived comfortably at Dover

---

* Some authorities give "Eunice."

and died in the midst of his family, respected and contented but that he embraced Baptist sentiments." *

In " Provincial Papers of New Hampshire," we find the following:

"Oct. 18, 1648.—The Court being informed of great misdemeanor Committed by Edward Starbuck of Dover with profession of Anabatism for which he is to be proceeded against at the next Court of Assistants if evidence can be prepared by that time & it being very farre for witnesses to travill to Boston at that season of the year, It is therefore ordered by this Court that the Secretary shall give Commission to Capt. Thomas Wiggan & Mr Edw. Smyth to send for such persons as they shall have notice of which are able to testify in the sd. cause & to take their testimony uppon oath & certifie the same to the secretary so soon as may be, that further proceedings may be therein, if the cause shall so require."

It is not to be wondered at that Edward Starbuck was quite ready to leave Dover under existing conditions. He was fifty-five years of age when he joined Thomas Macy in his voyage from Salisbury to Nantucket; he spent the winter there and in the spring returned to Dover for his family, who accompanied him to the island excepting his daughters Sarah (Austin) and Abigail (Coffin), who had married and settled in Dover. "Dover lost a good citizen" and Nantucket gained a much respected one; " he was a leading man on the Island and at one time a Magistrate;" * he is described as " courageous and persevering."

---

* N. E. Hist. and Gen. Reg., vol. viii., p. 68.

In "Landmarks in Ancient Dover" mention is made of Starbuck's Brook in 1701 as a boundary of property which Peter Coffin (son-in-law of Edward Starbuck) conveyed to John Ham. Starbuck's Marsh was granted to Elder Starbuck August 30, 1643, and Starbuck's Point and Marsh, now called Fabyan's Point, were granted to Edward Starbuck in 1643, and are again mentioned in 1662, 1702, and 1716 in conveyance of property, since which time the usual desire to change ancient names has destroyed what might be valuable historical landmarks.

One son only lived to perpetuate the name,—Nathaniel, who married Mary (daughter of Tristram Coffin), the ancestor of all American Starbucks.

Edward Starbuck died in 1690.

Other children of Edward Starbuck and Katharine Reynolds were:

Jethro, who died at the age of twelve.

Sarah, who married, first, William Story; second, Joseph Austin; third, Humphrey Varney (as second wife).

Dorcas, who married William Gayer.

Abigail, who married Peter Coffin.

Esther, who married Humphrey Varney (as first wife).

The original of the following conveyance of property from Edward Starbuck to his son, Nathaniel Starbuck, is in the rooms of the Historical Society of Nantucket:

"To all Chriftian peopole to whome this writing fhall Come, I, Edward ftarbuck, fend gretting.

"Know ye that I, the said Edward ftarbuck, as well

for the Indemnity, discharg and faving harmlefs my sonn Nathaniell ftarbuck his heirs Executors and adminiftrators and Every of them, and from all maner of Bond, and writtings obligatory what fo ever whare^{in} the faid Nathaniell Starbuck is and Standeth bond for me the faid Edward ftarbuck in any sum or sums of money to any perfon or perfons what so ever as alfo for divers other good causes and confiderations me heare vnto Espeafially moving, have given, granted Bargained and sold & Confirmed and by this prefents doe give grant, Bargain, fell and Confirm vnto the faid Nathaniell Starbuck al and fingular my goods & Chattells what fo ever, as well real as perfonall of what ever kind natuer quallity or Condition fo ever and to be in what plase or plasis the fame fhal or may be found as well in my owne Costody or poffefsion of any other perfon or perfons what fo ever to have and to hold all and fingular, the faid goods and Chattells, and al other premifes with the appurtenansis to the a fore fd Nathanell ftarbuck his heirs, Executors, Admineftrators and afsignes to his and there proper vfe & be hoofe for ever, and I, Edward Starbuck have dilevered vnto the fd Nathanell Starbuck one baffon * a part for the whole at the day of the Infeolling of this prefents and to the true performance where of I have heare vnto fet my

---

* In all such bills of sale previous to 1700 some object was delivered to the buyer to bind the bargain; to-day a sum of money is advanced as a "part for the whole."

In transfers of real estate the usual form was by "turf or twig, a part for the whole."

The Edward Starbuck transfer included household goods, and some household utensil was made to do duty as security; basson was the old spelling for basin.

hand feall this eighteenth day of marsh one thoufand fix hundred eighty five.

"EDWARD ſTARBUCK. (Seal.)"

Nathaniel Starbuck was a wealthy man for his times, and the supposition * is that he had given bonds for his father in some business transaction, and that this bill of sale was given as security.

Miss Susan E. Brock, curator of the Nantucket Historical Society, says there is scarcely a doubt that the deed in their possession is an original paper, and in reference to it she quotes from Mr. Henry Worth as follows: "Mr. Worth has examined it, and assures me that it is authentic without a doubt. He knew and recognized all the signatures, and said it would be impossible for them to be copied so perfectly as to deceive anyone who was familiar with them, especially that of Edward Starbuck himself."

---

* Edward Starbuck's daughters were well married and comfortably settled, and it is not improbable that he made the above-named conveyance in pursuance of the old English plan of conveying all property to the eldest son, to him who would perpetuate the name.

NOTE.—The name Starbuck is from the Norse, and signifies great or grand.

CHAPTER IV.

TRISTRAM COFFIN.

So MUCH information concerning Tristram Coffin has been developed and published in connection with the Coffin Reunion at Nantucket in 1881, that a very brief sketch is sufficient here.

He was so important in the early history of the settlement that at the risk of repeating much that has already been written, some notice of him and his interesting family will not be out of place.

Tristram Coffin, the founder of the family line of Coffins in America, signed his name "Coffyn."

He was born in Brixton, Devonshire, England, in 1605. He married Dionis Stevens, daughter of Robert Stevens, of Brixton.

In 1642 he came to America with his family and his widowed mother Joan, and resided first at Newbury, later at Haverhill and Salisbury, until 1660, when he settled at Nantucket.

The first of the name of whom there is any record is Sir Richard Coffin, who removed from Normandy to

---

NOTE.—Coffin is a word of Hebrew origin signifying a small basket. In the "Century Dictionary" may be found various meanings for the word, but in most cases it represents a receptacle of some kind.

In Wyclif's translation of the Bible, Mark 6 : 43, may be found: "And thei token the relifs of broken metis twelve coffinsful and of the fisches."

Portledge, The Coffin Manor House.
England.

England in 1066; he entered the English army, had lands granted to him, and was knighted by the king.

From Prince's "Worthies of Devonshire" we learn that "the Ancient family of the name settled at Portledge by the seaside in the Parish of Alwington five miles from Biddeford and flourished there from the Conquest, and that from the time of King Henry the First unto the age of King Edward the Second" for two hundred years each successive heir of this family bore the name of Richard.

Within a short distance of Fallaise, a town of Normandy, stands the old château of Cortiton, once the home of the Norman Coffins.

The last Miss Coffin married a Le Clerc late in the eighteenth century, since which time the Le Clerc family has occupied the Norman estates. When last visited, the château, though ancient, was in good repair.

Members of the family are mentioned in history often associated with royalty from 1066 to the latter part of the sixteenth century, since which time the lines of descent are complete.

Tristram lived at Northam,* near Capaum Pond, Nantucket, and died Tenth month 2d, 1681, aged seventy-six years.

He was the first chief magistrate of Nantucket. The

Coffin also appears to have been at one time synonymous with coffer; there are occasional records where the cofferer was a treasurer, an official servant in charge of a receptacle in which valuables and money were placed for transportation from place to place.

In Bowditch's "Suffolk Surnames" the name Tristram is spoken of as having been a surname.

* Northam was the first name of Dover, New Hampshire.

following is a copy of his commission, taken from Mr. F. B. Hough's book, compiled from official records at Albany.

"*Commiſſion Granted to Mr. Tristram Coffin, Senr., to be Chiefe Magiſtrate in and over the Iſlands of Nantuckett and Tuckanuckett.*"—[*Deeds III., 62, Secretary's Office, Albany, New York.*]

"Francis Lovelace, Esq., &c.: Whereas upon Addreſs made unto mee by Mr. Triſtram Coffin and Mr. Thomas Macy on ye behalfe of themſelves and ye reſt of ye Inhabitants of Nantuckett Iſland concerning ye Manno^r and Method of Governmn^t to be uſed amongst themſelves, and having by ye Advice of my Councell pitcht upon a way for them; That is to ſay That they be Governed by a Person as Chiefe Magiſtrate, and two Aſſiſtants, ye former to be nominated by myſelfe, ye other to bee chofen and confirmed by ye Inhabitants as in ye Inſtructions ſent unto them is more particularly Sett forth. And having conceived a good Opinion of ye ffitneſs and capacity of Mr. Triſtram Coffin to be ye p^{r}sent Chiefe Magiſtrate to manage Affayres wth ye Ayd and good Advice of ye Aſſiſtants in ye Islands of Nantuckett and Tuckanuckett, I have thought fitt to Nominate, Constitute, and Appoint and by these P^{r}fents doe hereby Nominate Constitute and Appoint Mr. Triſtram Coffin to be Chiefe Magiſtrate of y^e ſaid Iſlands of Nantuckett and Tuckanuckett. In ye Managem^t of wch ſaid Employm^t, hee is to uſe his beſt Skill and Endeavour to p^{r}ſerve his Maties Peace, and to keep y^e Inhabitants in good Ord^r. And all Persons are hereby required to give y^e ſaid Mr. Tristram Coffin fuch

Elizabeth, widow of Richard Coffin, Esq.,
"*Portlinch,*" *born 1651.*

Refpect and Obedience as belongs to a Perfon invefted by commiffion from Authority of his Royall Highnefs in y^e Place and Employm^t of a Chief Magistrate in y^e Iflands aforefaid. And hee is duely to obferve the Orders and Inftructions wch are already given forth for ye well governing of ye Place, or fuch others as from Time to Time fhall hereafter bee given by mee: And for whatfoever ye faid Mr. Triftram Coffin fhall lawfully Act or Doe in Profecution of ye Premifes, This is my Commiffion wch is to bee of fforce untill ye 13th day of October, which shall bee in ye Yeare of our Lord 1672, when a new magiftrate is to enter into the Employm^t fhall bee his sufficient Warrant and Difcharge.

"Given under my Hand and Seal at fforte James in New Yorke, this 29th day of June in ye 22^d Yeare of his Maties Reigne, Annoq. Dni. 1671.

"FRAN: LOVELACE."

The following is a list of children of Tristram Coffin:

HON. PETER COFFIN was born in England in 1631; he married Abigail Starbuck, daughter of Edward and Katharine Starbuck, of Dover, New Hampshire. He was one of the original purchasers of Nantucket, but resided there for a short time only. He was made a freeman in 1666 at Dover.

In 1675 he was a lieutenant on service in King Philip's War. In 1672-73 and again in 1679 he was a representative in the legislative branch. In 1690 he removed to Exeter, New Hampshire. From 1692 to 1714 he was at different times associate justice and chief justice of the Supreme Court of New Hampshire, and a member of the Governor's Council. He died at Exeter, March 21, 1715.

TRISTRAM COFFIN, JR., was born in England in 1632. He married in Newbury, Massachusetts, March 2, 1652, Judith Somerby, widow of Henry Somerby and daughter of Edmund and Sarah Greenleaf. He was made freeman April 29, 1668, and died in Newbury, February 4, 1704, aged seventy-two. He was a merchant tailor and filled many positions of trust. He lived in the Coffin mansion in Newbury, which still continues in the family; whether he or his wife's former husband built it is uncertain.

It is said that Tristram Coffin, Sr., lived in this old mansion before he removed to Nantucket.

ELIZABETH COFFIN was born in England about 1634-35; and married in Newbury, November 13, 1651, Captain Stephen Greenleaf, son of Edmund Greenleaf; she died at Newbury, November 19, 1678.

JAMES COFFIN was born in England, August 12, 1640. He married, December 3, 1663, Mary, daughter of John and Abigail Severance, of Salisbury, Massachusetts, and died at Nantucket, July 28, 1720, aged eighty years. He was one of the associate proprietors, and filled several important offices at Nantucket, among them judge of Probate Court, and is said to have been the first judge of probate on the island, appointed in 1680.*

---

* Massachusetts Civil List, pp. 112-114.

The Tristram Coffin House,

Newburyport, Massachusetts.

Dresser in Tristram Coffin House,
Newburyport, Massachusetts

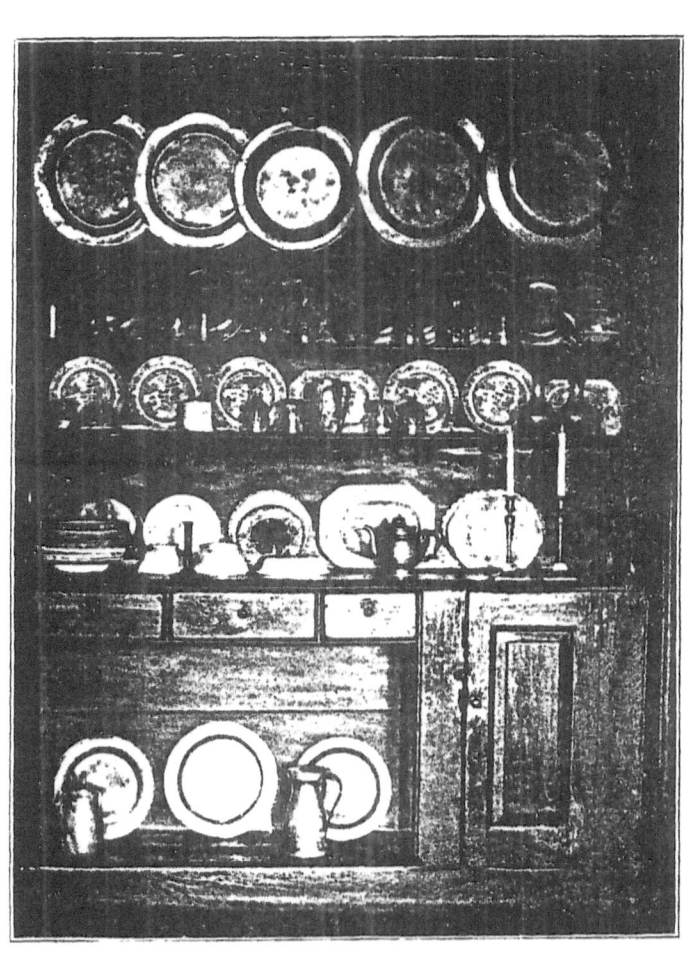

JOHN and DEBORAH, who died in infancy.

MARY COFFIN, seventh child of Tristram Coffin, Sr., was born in Haverhill, February 20, 1645. She was married in 1662, at the age of seventeen, to Nathaniel, son of Edward and Katharine (Reynolds) Starbuck.

The first book of births, marriages, and deaths for the town of Sherburne (page 11) says "Mary Starbuck departed this Liffe y^e 13 day of y^e 9^o_m 1717 in y^e 74 year of her age and was decently buried in Friends burying ground." Her husband, Nathaniel Starbuck, Sr., died in 1719.

She was a remarkable woman, anticipating by two centuries the advanced views of women of to-day. She took an active part in town debates, usually opening her remarks with "My husband and I, having considered the subject, think, etc."

In 1701, at the age of fifty-six, she became interested in the religious faith of the Friends, and held meetings at her house. She was a minister in the Society, as were also several of her children, her grandsons Elihu and Nathaniel Coleman, and her granddaughter Priscilla Bunker.

Elihu Coleman published one of the earliest protests against slavery in New England.

Mary Starbuck was "as distinguished in her domestic economy as she was celebrated as a preacher."

The following copy of a letter from Mary Starbuck to her granddaughter Eliza Gorham, who had suffered loss by fire, gives evidence of her interest in domestic matters.

"NANTUCKET 17th of 1st mo 1714.

"DEAR CHILD E. G.

"These few lines may certify thee that thou art often in my remembrance, with thy dear husband and children, with breathings to the Lord for you, that you may find rest in all your visitations and trials; As also that there is a trunk filled with goods which is intended to be put on Eben Stewards vessel, in which are several small tokens from thy friends which thou may particularly see by the little invoices here enclosed, and by some other marks that are upon the things.

"Thy Aunt Dorcas in a new pair of osnaburg sheets, thy Aunt Dinah in a pair of blankets, Thy Grandfather intends to send thee a bbl. of mutton, but it is not all his own, for Cousin James Coffin sent hither 17 pieces. Cousin James said he intended to send thee two or three bushels of corn.

"There is likewise sent from our women's meeting £7 which thy uncle Jethro said he would give an order for, for thee to take to Boston.

"Sister James told me she intended to send thee two bushels of corn and some wool and likewise that Justice Worth said he would send thee some corn.

"More meat and corn will be sent which will be in greater quantities, which thy uncle Jethro Starbuck will give thee an acct. of or to thy husband.

"I should have been glad if he had come over with Steward, but I hope we shall see him this summer, if not both of you.

"So with my kind love to thee and thy husband, children and to all our frds. committing you to the protection of the Almighty who is the wise disposer of all things and remain thy affectionate Grandmother

"MARY STARBUCK.

"Thy Grandfather's love to you all and Uncle Barnabas's, Susanna is well and her love to you also."

Nathaniel Starbuck was by no means a man of small ability, but his wife seems to have taken the lead in most matters.

LIEUTENANT JOHN COFFIN was born at Haverhill, October 30, 1647; he married Deborah, daughter of Joseph and Sarah (Starbuck) Austin. After his father's death he removed to Martha's Vineyard, and died there September 5, 1711.

Authority for his commission as lieutenant of militia will be found in Part First of Vol. XXXIV., and on page 21 of the New York Colonial Manuscripts in the custody of the Regents of the University in the State Library at Albany, and recorded by the Secretary of the Province of New York among memoranda of several military commissions, directed by Governor Thomas Dongan to be issued, and reads thus:

"Mr. John Coffin a Commission to be Lieu. of said Company at Nantucket June 5th 1684 all the first forme."

STEPHEN COFFIN was born at Newbury, May 10, 1652. He married Mary, daughter of George and Jane

(Godfrey) Bunker, about 1668, and died at Nantucket November 14, 1734.

He remained upon his father's estate, and to him was given the management of his father's business, on agreement " to be helpful to his parents in their old age."

It is not surprising that the descendants of Tristram Coffin still bearing the name are so numerous when we find that of his nine children five out of the seven who married were sons; that Peter had nine children, that Tristram, Jr., had ten children and left one hundred and seventy-seven descendants, that James had fourteen children, that Lieutenant John had eleven children, and that Stephen had ten.

The two daughters, Mary Starbuck and Elizabeth Greenleaf, each had ten children, adding in two centuries many more descendants to the list, although not of the name.

The Nantucket *Inquirer* of July 22, 1826, says, " The House * in which Tristram Coffin resided is still standing, and has been the residence of seven generations of the same name.

" The names of more than twelve thousand descendants of Tristram Coffin can be ascertained, some of whom are found in England, in all the British Dominions and in every state in the Union."

---

* At Newbury.

NOTE.—Savage says, " Twenty-six of Tristram's descendants graduated in 1828 at New England colleges, fifteen at Harvard alone."

The above was written by Joshua Coffin,* Newburyport, and is signed " Jam satis."

The following copies of the wills of the father, grandfather and great-uncle of the emigrant Tristram Coffin were extracted from the original records in England for Mr. C. Howard Colket, of Philadelphia, and by his courtesy placed at the disposal of the writer, and we believe are now for the first time published in full in America:

Extracted from the District Registry Attached to the Probate Division of the High Court of Justice at Exeter.

IN THE ARCHDEACONRY COURT OF TOTNES.

In the name of God Amen the twelveth day of September in the eleaventh yeere of the Raigne of our Sovraigne Lord James by the grace of God of England Frannce and Ireland and in the forty and seaventh yeere of Scotland Kinge Defend^r of the Fayth &c Anno Dni 1613 I *Nicholas Coffyn* of Buttlers wth in the pysh of Brixton in the Countye of Devon Husbandman beinge weake of bodye but pfect in minde thankes bee therefore given to Allmightie God do make this my last

---

* Joshua Coffin, antiquarian and historian, descended from Joshua Coffin[5], son of Joseph[4], Nathaniel[3], Tristram, Jr.[2], Tristram Coffin[1].

Joshua[5] was born in Newbury December 30, 1702, married July 15, 1725, Margaret Morse, dau. Benjamin Morse, also of Newbury. Joshua[5] died Sept. 12, 1773. The children of Joshua[5] and Margaret (Morse) were Sarah, Enoch, Mary and Joshua[6], born Jan. 9, 1731, married January 21, 1775, Sarah Bartlett; died March 30, 1774.—N. E. Hist. and Gen. Reg., Vol. xxiv., p. 313. (Edition 1890.)

Will and Testam^t contayning my whole minde and intent in mann^r and forme following First I do wth a free heart and willing minde render and give againe into the hands of my Lord God and Maker my Soule wch he of his Fatherly Goodness gave unto me nothing doubting but that he will receive it amonge his heavenly Angels And my body I bequeath to Christian buriall when & where it shall please God to appoint Itm I give and bequeath to Ann Meader the Daught^r of Eliner Meader five shillings Itm I give and bequeath to Peter Coffyn my eldest Sonne my greatest brasse pann and my minde is that my Wief shall have the use thereof during her lief. Itm I give & bequeath to Tristram Coffyn my Sonnes Sonne one yearling bollock Itm I give & bequeath to Johun Coffyn my Sonnes Daught^r one sheepe Itm I give and bequeath to every of my God-children twelve pence apeece Itm I give & bequeath to Johan Coffyn my Wief one bay nag wch we use to call Rowse Itm I give bequeath will and devise unto Nicholas Coffyn my Sonne All such right terme of yeeres intrest and demand as I myself my Executors or Assignes now have or here after may or ought to have of & in one tenem^t with his app^{r}tennce sett lying and being in Plimton Earle in the Countye of Devon aforesaid wherein one

---

There must have been a generation between Joshua[6] and the historian, as he was born in the old Coffin Mansion in Newburyport Oct. 12, 1792; he died June 24, 1864.

He was one of the twelve persons who, together with William Lloyd Garrison and others, formed the first anti-slavery society in New England. He was for many years a teacher, and numbered among his pupils men who attained high position in after years.

Thomas Spurwill there now dwelleth togith^r three
closes or pcells of land thereunto belonging whereof the
first is called or knowen by the name of Fortie Acres
the second Wallford als Woodpke and the third the
Meadow belowe the waie all wch recited p^{r}misses I have
and hold of and by the demise & grante of Willm Moulton of Plimton Earle aforesaide Gent. To have & to
hold All & singuler the said tenem^t & three closes of
land with th appurtennce unto the said Nicholas Coffyn
his Execut^{rs} administrators and assignes and to every of
them imediatly from and after my death for and during
all such time & tearme of yeeres as shall be then to
com and unexpired of and in the same Tenem^t & closes
of land by and under the yeerly rents suits & services
and all other covenants and condicons which I myself
myne Execut^{rs} administrators and assignes or any of us
stand chargeable for to yeeld pay and prforme for the
same during the tearme therein that shall be to come
after my death And in consideracon hereof my Will
and intent is that my said Son Nicholas Coffyn shall
within one whole yeere after my decease well & truely
content and paie unto my Daugh^r Ann Coffyn thirteene
pounds sixe shillings and eight pence of lawfull money
of England wch said some of XIII$^£$ VI^s VIII^d I do
hereby give and bequeath unto my said Daugh^r Ann
Coffyn And likewise the said Nicholas my Sonne shall
after my decease paie unto my Sonne John Coffyn eight
shillings yeerely during there naturall lives or as longe
as they two shall live togither. The residue of all my
goods and chattles moveable and unmoveable as well
quickstuffe & corne as implem^{ts} of household & all
other goods of what quality soever the same bee not be-

fore by these presents given nor bequeathed I give & bequeathe to the foresaid Nicholas Coffyn & John Coffyn my Sonnes whome I make & ordaine to be my ioynt Executors of this my last Will & Testam^t Provided allwaies that my Wief shall have the bed steed bedd & bedd clothes thereunto belonging wherein I do usually lie one brasse pann & one brasse crock to use the same duringe her lief and after her decease the same shall remaine to my said Executors And I do heereby appointe & entreat my well beloved Friends Bartholomew Clevanger & Nicholas Edwards to bee the overseeres of this my said last Will & Testam^t praying them to bee an aide to myne Executors herein & to see the same faythfully and truely prformed And I do revo°ke & annull all & every other & former Wills and Testam^{ts} legacies & bequeaths by me formerly made pronouncing this to be my p^{r}sent last Will & Testam^t In wittnes whereof I the said Nicholas Coffyn have hereunto sett my hand & seale yeven the daie and yeere first above written in the presence of those whose names are hereunder written. — Sealed & signed in the presence of us viz. ———

———Teste me — ROB^{TO} BICHFORD. ———
——— The signe of NICHOLAS EDWARDS. ———
This Will was proved on the third day of November 1613 by the Executors. ———

In the name of God Amen the VIth day of November in the year of our Lord God 1601. I *Tristram Coffing* of Butlers in the Pish of Brixton being sick of body but pfect of remembrance thankes be geven unto Almighty God do make this my last Will and Testament in manner and form following that is to saye First I geve and bequeath my Soule unto Almighty God my Maker and Jesus Christ my Redeemer through whose death & passion I hope to be saved First I geve & bequeath unto the poore men box of Brixon V^s Item I geve & bequeath to Johan Coffing the Daughter of Nicolas Coffing II brass pannes the greatest & the lest and on coverlett of draught work Item I geve and bequeath unto Tristram Coffing the Sonne of Philip Coffing forty shillings Item I geve and bequeth unto Philip Coffing XX^s Item I give unto Richard and Johan Coffing the children of Lionell Coffing VI^s VIII^d Item I geve to the children of Thomas Coffing each of them III^s IIII^d Item I geve more to Johan Coffing the Daughter of Nicolas Coffing V$^£$ Item I geve to An Coffing the Daughter of Nicolas Coffing the right and titell of such ground as I have from Robert Chember or eles the som of X$^£$ more I geve to the sayd An II brass pannes and on coverlett Item I geve to foure children of Nicolas Meader each of them III^s IIII^d Item I geve to John Coffing the Sone of Nicolas Coffing one bullock of the age of on year the resydue of my goodes & cattells movable or immoveable I geve and bequeath to Nicolas Coffing the Sone of Nicolas Coffing whome I make to be my whole Executor to pay my debts and to discharg my Legacies as far as bill bond or speciallitie is to shewe moreover I doe appoint Nicolas Coffing and James Coule to be my overseers to see Will and Testament to be pformed. ———

This Will was proved on the 16th day of October 1602 by Nicholas Coffine the Father of Nicholas Coffine a minor the Executor, during his minority. ———

In the name of God, Amen, ye 21th day of December in ye third yeare of the raigne of our Sovraigne Lord Charles of Greate Britaine France and Ireland Kinge Defender of ye Faith &c. I *Peter Coffyn* of the Parish of Brixton in ye County of Devon being sicke of body but in perfect minde and memory (thankes be to God) doe make and ordaine this my last Will and Testament in manner and forme followinge Impr^s I give and bequeath my Soule to Allmighty God my Maker and Redeemer and my body to the Earth to be decently buried. Item I give and bequeath to ye poore people of the Parish of Brixton XX^s in money to be delivred unto them according to the discretion of my Executrix hereafter mentioned. Item I give and bequeath unto Tristriam Coffyn my Sonne one feather bedd pformed my best brasen panne and my best brasen crocke Item I give and bequeath unto Johan Coffyn my Wife ye issues pfitts and comodities of all my lands tenements & hereditaments wth in ye sayd Parish of Brixton dureing her widdowhood she yeelding & payinge therefor yearly unto the sayd Tristriam my Sonne his heirs and assignes the summe of Fifty shillings of lawfull English money at ye four most usual feasts of the year and also sufficient meat drinke & clothes and convenient lodgings unto ye sayd Tristriam according to his degree and callinge dureing her Widdowhood onely And if it happen ye sayd yearly rent of Fifty shillings or any part thereof to be behinde and unpayd that then and from thenceforth itt may and shall be lawfull to and for the sayd Tristriam Coffyn his heirs and assignes into all and singular the said p^rmisses to enter and distraine and the distress so there taken from thence to lead drive carry away & empound and impound to detaine and keepe untill ye sayd rent of Fifty shillings with the arrearages of the same (if any bee) shall bee to him or them fully answered and payd. And further it is my Will that if the sayd Johan my Wife shall happen to marry that she shall immediately thereupon loose all ye pfitts comodities and right of that one tenement called Silferhey lying in Butlers in ye parish of Brixton aforesayd which dureing her Widdowhood by my Will she is to have and ye same to redound & be immediately in the possession of my Sonne Tristriam his heirs and assignes Item I doe give and bequeath unto my Sonne Tristriam All my lands rents reversions services & hereditamts with the appurtenances whatsoever sett lying & being wth in the sayd Parish of Brixton or elsewhere wth in ye sayd County of Devon To have and to hold ye same and every part and parcel thereof to ye sayd Tristriam Coffyn his heirs and assignes for ever to ye only use pfitt & behoof of the said Tristriam Coffyn his heirs and assignes to be holden of the cheife Lord and Lords of the Fee thereof by the rents and services therefor yearly due and payable and my Will farther is that if the said Tristriam my Sonne shall chance to dy without an heir male lawfully begotten or to be begotten of his body that then all the prmisses last mentioned & given to him shall redound unto John Coffyn my Sonne his heirs and assigns accordingly and in y^e same manner that it should to y^e said Tristriam my Sonne Item I doe give and bequeath unto Johan Coffyn Deborah Coffyn Eunice Coffyn and Mary Coffyn my four Daughters to each of them severally Thirty pounds in money that is to say amongst them CXX$^£$ to bee payd when they or each of them severally shall be of the full age of twentie years Itm I give and bequeath unto John Coffyn my Sonne Fourty pounds in money to be payd him when hee shall be of the age of twenty years Item I give and bequeath unto the child of my Wife now goeth withal the sume of Thirty pounds in money to be payd when he or she shall be of the age of twentie years. Provided always & my minde & will is that if either Johan Coffyn Deborah Coffyn Eunice Coffyn Mary Coffyn John Coffyn or ye child my Wife goeth withal happen to dy before he she or they doe come to ye age of twenty years that then his her or their portion or portions shall be equally divided amongst the survivors Item All ye rest of my goods chattels and cattells nor before given nor bequeathed I doe give and bequeath unto Johan Coffyn my Wife whome I make constitute and ordaine my full and whole Executrix of this my last Will and Testament And for ye better pformance hereof I doe intreat my well beloved in Christ my brother in law Phillip Avent and my Brother Nichas Coffyn to be y^a Overseers to see this my last Will & Testament pformed.

—— ARTHURE DURANT —— PHILLIP AVENT. ——

Proved on the thirteenth day of March 1627 by the Executrix. ——

Admiral Sir Isaac Coffin, Baronet.

CHAPTER V.

ADMIRAL SIR ISAAC COFFIN, BARONET.

THE following facts have been abridged from an account published in the Boston *Herald* within a few years.

On the easterly side of Harrison Avenue just above Kneeland Street, Boston, a trifle back from the avenue, stands a gambrel-roof wooden structure. This building was moved from its original site, corner of Beach Street and Oxford Place, to its present location nearly half a century ago. It was the residence of Nathaniel Coffin, one of the foremost adherents of King George, who at one time held the responsible position of collector of his Majesty's customs for the port of Boston. The house must have been built as early as 1750, and it was, on May 16, 1759, the birthplace of Isaac Coffin, who afterwards rose to be an admiral in the British navy. In the same house was born his brother John, who became major-general in the British army.

Sir Isaac retained an affection for the place of his birth, and coming from Nantucket stock he invested in 1827 the sum of £2500 in English funds for the establishment of a school on that island to be known as the "Coffin School."

Drake, in his "Old Landmarks of Boston," says that of this fund "the Mayor and Aldermen of Boston were made trustees for the distribution of the annual interest among five of the most deserving boys and as many girls of that school."

King George III., with whom Sir Isaac was a great favorite, gave him a grant of the Island of Magdalen in the Gulf of St. Lawrence, and in after years it was proposed to create him Earl of Magdalen; this proposition fell through, and the alleged reason was, that in establishing the Coffin School in Nantucket he was creating sailors who in mature age might fight against the crown.

At the present time the old house in Boston is used for manufacturing purposes.

Sir Isaac Coffin was the fifth generation in descent from Tristram, Sr., his father being Nathaniel, who married Elizabeth, daughter of Henry Barnes, of Boston. Nathaniel * was the son of William, who was the son of Nathaniel, who was the son of James, who was the son of Tristram Coffin, Sr.

The following extracts from an English biographical work on the life of Admiral Coffin are abridged from manuscript of the late Mr. George Howland Folger. This manuscript is now the property of the Historical Society of Nantucket.

Sir Isaac entered the navy in 1773, under the patronage of Admiral John Montague; he served as midshipman on board several ships, and in 1778 obtained a lieutenancy. In July, 1781, he was promoted to the rank of commander, and was in the "splendid battle" of April 12, 1782, which resulted in the capture of the

---

* N. E. Hist. and Gen. Reg., Vol. xxiv., p. 306, says Nathaniel Coffin (son of William) graduated from Harvard College in 1744, died in New York in 1780.

celebrated Comte de Grasse. In 1795, as commissioner, he resided in Corsica, where he remained until the evacuation of the island in 1796; here he twice narrowly escaped assassination. After passing through various fortunes of war, he was, in 1804, made rear-admiral. Soon after this he was raised to the dignity of baronet. In 1808 he was promoted to the position of vice-admiral, and in 1814 became full admiral, and in the general election in 1818 was chosen as representative to Parliament for the borough of Ilchester.

He married, in 1811, at the age of fifty-two, Elizabeth Brown Greenly, only daughter of T. Greenly, Esq. There were no children.

He crossed the Atlantic not less than thirty-one times, a circumstance more remarkable in the early part of the century than at present.

The following incident in his life, related by a relative, is somewhat amusing when told of one valiant in arms :

"Somewhere about 1824 the Admiral was in Philadelphia at the residence of his kinswoman, Anna (Folger) Coffin, widow of Thomas Coffin. To the company gathered to meet him he told that, being in command of a ship or fleet in the Pacific, an American whaler was spoken. The Admiral was curious to see the taking of a whale, and accordingly went on board the American vessel. Soon a whale was sighted; a boat was lowered, and the Admiral took his seat with the crew; the harpoon was thrown, and then came the rush of the boat through the water, which was walled on each side.

"'Cut the rope!' cried the Admiral. 'No, no;'

was the reply of the leader of the crew; 'you are not in command of this craft.'

"So Sir Isaac had to summon up what nerve he could and await his fate; he closed his story by saying he would infinitely rather have been at close quarters with a French seventy-four."

In the Nantucket *Inquirer* of September 2, 1826, may be found the following, copied from a Boston paper:

"According to previous appointment, the annual visitation of the public schools was attended on Wednesday last by the parents and friends of the pupils, and by several strangers of distinction. Admiral Coffin gave as a sentiment, 'The City of Boston.'

"He was replied to by one of the committee:

"'Our venerable and respected guest, Admiral Coffin, a native of our city and an alumnus of our ancient Latin school, who, though separated from us, in times of political dissension was generous and kind to his countrymen, who, amidst the honors and plaudits of a princely court, remembered with affection the land of his birth, and still bears testimony to the excellence of our civil and literary institutions.

"'May honorable fame ever attend him, and may his declining years repose in health and peace.'"

September 9, 1826.—"Honorary degree of M.A. was conferred on Admiral Sir Isaac Coffin at the annual commencement of Harvard University."

In the Nantucket *Inquirer* of date September 16, 1826, there is a notice of a visit of Sir Isaac Coffin to Nantucket, during which he spoke with affection of his native city, and attributed " all his attainments and renown to principles of knowledge imbibed in the public schools of Boston."

During his stay on the island he " visited principal places of resort, disregarded all court etiquette, and mingled freely with the inhabitants."

He died at Cheltenham, England, in 1839, aged eighty years.

CHAPTER VI.

STEPHEN GREENLEAF, WITH SOME ACCOUNT OF HIS FATHER, EDMUND GREENLEAF.

THE GREENLEAF FAMILY is supposed to have been of Huguenot origin; EDMUND, the first of the name who came to America, was born * in the Parish of Brixham. He married Sarah Dole, and, with several children, was among the early settlers of "Newbury, or Newberry, now Newburyport."

"Ould Newberry" was incorporated in 1635. In a list of first settlers to whom was granted "a house lot of at least four acres, with a suitable quantity of salt and fresh meadow," is found the name of Edmund Greenleaf.†

Edmund Greenleaf was ordered to be ensign for Newbury in June, 1639.†

From Colonial Records we learn that he was later made lieutenant, and removed to Boston.

Captain Johnson styles Edmund Greenleaf "an ancient and experienced lieutenant under Captain Gerrish in 1644."

The following is an extract from his will:

" . . . my will is being according to God's will and re-

---

* Hoyt says, page 183: "The Greenleaf genealogy gives baptism of Edmund Greenleaf January 2, 1574. This would make him ninety-seven years of age when he died. Another authority gives, Edmund, born 1590."

† James Edward Greenleaf's "Greenleaf Family."

vealed in his word, that wee must pay what we owe and live of the rest, unto whose rule the sons of men ought to frame their wills and actions therefore." This to show his correct principles. Another extract may be given, showing how absolute he considered his power over his wife, who evidently had a will of her own:

". . . Besides when I married my wife she brought me a silver bowl, a silver porringer, a silver spoon, she lent or gave them to her son-in-law, James Hill, without my consent."

This will is dated December 25, 1668.

STEPHEN GREENLEAF, son of Edmund, was born about 1628, and married, first: November 13, 1651, Elizabeth Coffin, daughter of Tristram Coffin and Dionis Stevens; second: In 1679, Esther (Weare) Swett, widow of Captain Benjamin Swett, and daughter of Nathaniel Weare or Wire (early in Newbury, afterward of Nantucket, where he died March 1, 1681).

Stephen Greenleaf was one of the original proprietors of Nantucket, and, authority says, a religious man.

In "Greenleaf Family" we find the first mention of Stephen Greenleaf as ensign, May 11, 1670. August 5, 1675, with others, he marched against the Indians in response to a call to the colonies from Swanzy, where shortly after "nine Indians were murdered," this being the first blood shed in King Philip's War.

In 1676 Stephen Greenleaf, with five others, was elected selectman, and in the same year was representative to the General Court.

In 1680 the "Town granted ensign Stephen Greenleaf permission to build a wharf."

He was ensign in 1686 and captain in 1690.

At a court held at Newbury in 1686, March 30, " David Pierce, Captain Thomas Noyes and Lieutenant Stephen Greenleaf are commissioned to be Magistrates by the Court."

" In the same year Lieutenant Stephen Greenleaf and Lieutenant Tristram Coffin, with others, are appointed a committee on laying out and dividing woodlands."

November 21, 1686, " deacon Nicholas Noyes, deacon Robert Long and deacon Tristram Coffin were, at the request of the selectmen, chosen standing overseers of the poore for the town of Newbury."

December 1, " Captain Daniel Pierce and Captain Stephen Greenleaf were added to the deacons as overseers of the poore," and any three of them had power to act.

May 6, 1689, " The Committee of Safety in Boston having desired us to send a man or men for consulting with them what may be best for the conservation of the peace of the country, Our inhabitants being met this 6th day of May, 1689, have chosen Captain Thomas Noyes and lieutenant Stephen Greenleaf sen. for the end aforesaid."

1690, Stephen Greenleaf, with nine others, was wrecked and drowned off Cape Breton.

A military spirit appears to have been transmitted to the third generation, the following story having been told of Stephen Greenleaf, Jr.:

March 5, 1696, Captain Greenleaf petitions the General Court for compensation for repulsing an Indian raid, in which he was wounded in his side and wrist.

His petition was read and forty pounds voted to be paid him out of the treasury of the province.

The house attacked by the Indians was John Brown's, and the following is the family tradition respecting it:

"The Indians had secreted themselves for sometime near the house, waiting for the absence of the male members of the family, who about three o'clock departed with a load of turnips. The Indians then rushed from their concealment, tomahawked a girl who was standing at the front door; another girl who had concealed herself as long as the Indians remained, immediately after their departure gave the alarm."

The coat which Captain Greenleaf wore in his pursuit of the Indians is still preserved by his descendants, together with the bullet which was extracted from his wound.

NOTE.—State Street in Newbury (now Newburyport) was formerly Greenleaf's Lane.

CHAPTER VII.

CHRISTOPHER HUSSEY.

CHRISTOPHER HUSSEY was baptized in Dorking, Surrey, England, and was son of John Hussey and Mary Wood.

This has been a tradition in the family, and is confirmed by the following extract from a letter written in 1880 by a New Bedford member of the Hussey family:

"I forgot to tell you about my visit to Dorking, where I went before leaving England. It is twenty-six miles from London, but took me an hour and a half by rail, but through a lovely country.

"It is a beautiful old town. They say the country about there is considered among the most picturesque in England.

"I went to the parish clerk; he had gone out, and his sister thought perhaps the vicar might know the book. So I went there and was shown into his study, a lovely old house and a very pretty room in summer, but a fire-place too small to half warm it.

"The vicar was a wonderfully handsome and gentlemanly person, who offered to do all he could for me, but said the clerk had the book. I at last found him, and we looked over it together.

"As I knew the exact date of Christopher's birth, it did not take long, although the writing was the same queer German text hand we saw at Hampton, which seemed to be the style then; but, strange to say, the book itself looked a hundred years younger than that, it had been kept so much more carefully, and was of parchment.

"We found Christopher, son of John Hussey, was baptized 18th of February, 1599, and, looking back a few years, found John Hussey and Marie (Moor or Wood) (I could not make out which) were married December 5th, 1593. Then John, son of John, baptized April 29th, 1594, and died November 8th, 1597. There is no other mention of any one of the name of Hussey that we could find in the book, and no person of that name is living there or has been known to live there. The vicar told me it was a Berkshire name, and John Hussey probably came there from some other place; and, as there seem to have been no other children that lived, no one of the name remains there. . . . All the English say it is not at all a common name; an 'old family'—but what family is not old?"

NOTE.—John Evelyn makes several interesting entries in his diary concerning the Hussey family, and, although his allusions to them are thirty-eight years after Christopher Hussey came to America, the fact that the shire named by Evelyn is the same in which John Hussey's family lived is significant.

September 17, 1670, Evelyn says: "To visit Mr. Hussey, who, being near Wotton, lives in a sweet valley, deliciously watered."

Again, 30th of August, 1681: "From Wotton I went to see Mr. Hussey (at Sutton in Shere), who has a very pretty seat, well watered, near my brother's.

"He is the neatest husband for curiously ordering his domestic and field accommodations, and what pertains to husbandry, that I have ever seen, as to his granaries, tackling tools, and utensils, ploughs, carts, stables, wood piles, wood house, even to hen roosts and hog troughs.

When a young man Christopher Hussey spent some time in Holland, where he solicited in marriage Theodate, daughter of Rev. Stephen Bachelor, who gave his consent to their union on condition that they would come to America with him; this condition was complied with, and they arrived in Boston in 1632 on the ship William and Francis or William Francis.

The fact that his eldest son Stephen Hussey was born in Lynn, and was the first child christened by Stephen Bachelor after the founding of the church, indicates that Christopher lived in Lynn with his father-in-law.

He was an early settler of the town of Newbury, and in 1636 was "chosen by papers" as one of the "seven men," as they were first called, then "townesmen," then "townesmen select," and finally "select men" as at present.

"They were fully empowered of themselves to do what the town had power to do, the reason whereof was the town judged it inconvenient and burdensome to be called together upon every occasion."

In 1638 he, with his father-in-law, Rev. Stephen

"Methought I saw old Cato or Varro in him, all substantial, all in exact order."

June 10th, 1685: "Mr. Hussey,* a young gentleman who made love to my late dear child, but whom she could not bring herself to answer in affection, died of the same cruel disease,† for which I am extremely sorry, because he never enjoyed himself after my daughter's decease, nor was I averse to the match, could she have overcome her disinclination."

February, 1695: "Our neighbor, Mr. Hussey, married a daughter of my cousin, George Evelyn, of Nutfield."

---

* Son of Peter Hussey, of Sutton in Shere, Surrey.

† Small-pox.

Bachelor, and others, settled the town of Hampton, New Hampshire, and in 1639 he was made Justice of the Peace, which office he held several years; he was also town clerk and one of the first deacons of the church.

In 1659 he became one of the purchasers of Nantucket; subsequently he was a sea-captain.

Orders were received from the king, September 18, 1679, "to erect New Hampshire into a separate government," under jurisdiction of a president and council to be appointed by himself; John Cutts was appointed president and Christopher Hussey, of Hampton, one of six councillors.

There are several theories concerning the death of Christopher Hussey. The fact that he followed the sea may have given rise to a belief that he was drowned at sea or eaten by cannibals. Joshua Coffin, however, says that he *died* at Hampton, New Hampshire, March 6, 1686, and Austin, in "One Hundred and Sixty Allied Families," states that "Town records of Hampton declare he was buried there March 8, 1686."

He had two sons and three daughters:

Stephen, married Martha Bunker.

John, married Rebecca Perkins.

Hulda, married John Smith and lived to be ninety-seven years old.

Mary.

Theodata.

His eldest son, Stephen, came to Nantucket and married Martha Bunker, October 8, 1676. He had lived at Barbadoes, had considerable property, and was a Friend before a Society was formed upon the island.

He was at one time representative to the General Court.

He died February 2, 1718, in his eighty-eighth year, and was buried in Friends' first burial ground at Nantucket. His children were Puella, Abigail, Sylvanus, Bachiller, Daniel, George, and Theodata.

John Hussey, second son of Christopher Hussey, was appointed member of Assembly before he removed from Hampton, New Hampshire, to Delaware in 1688, but, being unwilling to take oath, did not serve.

After his removal to Delaware he was appointed member of the Pennsylvania Assembly to represent New Castle County, at that time one of the "three lower counties of Penn," and as Pennsylvania Quakers were permitted to enter office without oath, he was duly enrolled in 1696.*

Rev. Stephen Bachelor † was born in England in 1561. He was well educated and had received orders in the Established Church, but was not in sympathy with its rites and institutions. His unwillingness to conform to its requirements had resulted in his being deprived of his ecclesiastical commissions.

He spent a few years in Holland, but returned to London. In some records we read that "his eldest daughter had emigrated to America and had settled in the new town of Saugus, now Lynn." Here came also Stephen Bachelor on June 5, 1632, and here he established the first Episcopal Church of Lynn, accord-

---

* Pennsylvania Archives, vol. ix., p. 673.

† The name is variously spelled in the old records, and not less variously at the present time by his descendants.

ing to his own ideas. Differences occurred from time to time, but finally, when a council of ministers was called, it was decided that, "although the church had not been properly instituted, yet the mutual exercise of their religious duties had supplied the defect."

His removal from Lynn was desired by those who differed with him, but where in that day did not religious difference lead to enmity?

On May 6, 1635, he was admitted a freeman and removed first to Ipswich, where he received a grant of fifty acres of land and proposed to locate; but he soon left Ipswich, and, with some friends, John Wing and others, went to Mattacheese, on Barnstable Bay, now Yarmouth, with a view to establishing a colony there. This enterprise proved impracticable, and he went next to Newbury, and on the 6th of July, 1638, received a grant of land from the town.

On the 6th of September the General Court gave him permission to settle a town at Hampton, a few miles from Newburyport, in New Hampshire.

In 1639 the town of Ipswich offered him sixty acres of upland if he would reside with them. This he declined.

On the 5th of July he sold his house and lands in Newbury, and, removing to Hampton, settled the town and established a church, of which he became pastor.

In 1640 Hampton granted him 300 acres of land, and he gave them " a bell for their meeting-house."

In 1647 he was at Portsmouth, where he remained three years.

At the age of eighty nine he married unfortunately,

and lived with this third wife a year only. In 1651 he returned to England and there died in his one hundredth year at Hackney, near London.

Freeman says of him: "From all that we gather out of much that was written of him by his contemporaries, we infer that he was learned, and in the judgment of charity a good man, but that his whole life was singularly complicated with incidents of trial."

Rev. Conway Phelps Wing, one of his descendants, from whose account of him much of the above has been gleaned, says: "In estimating his character we must take into consideration the peculiar spirit and agitations of the times, when the boldest innovations in opinion and practice were received on the one side with favor, and on the other, and especially on the side of the ruling powers, with intolerance and misrepresentation."

Mr. Prince says: "Mr. B. was a man of fame in his day, a gentleman of learning and ingenuity, and wrote a fine and curious hand."

His signature and seal appended to letters may be seen in Massachusetts Historical Collection, Vol. VII., fourth series.

His children were:

Deborah Bachelor, married John Wing.

Theodata Bachelor, married Christopher Hussey.

——— Bachelor, married ——— Sanborn.

Nathaniel Bachelor, married, 1656, (1) Deborah Smith; (2) Mary Wyman, of Woburn; (3) Elizabeth ———, and had seventeen children.

Francis Bachelor } who remained in London.
Stephen Bachelor

Henry Bachelor, who had a son Henry, who lived in Lynn.

Edwin L. Sanborn, LL.D., in his "History of New Hampshire," page 53, says: "The first churches were formed at Hampton and Exeter. Hampton claimes precedence in time. . . . The first pastor of this firstborn church of the new State, and the father of the town, was Rev. Stephen Batchelder, an ancestor on the mother's side of Daniel Webster."

"Susanna Batchelder, one of the descendants of Stephen's son Nathaniel, married, July 20th, 1738, Ebenezer Webster (born at Hampton October 10th, 1714), the grandfather of Daniel Webster." Lewis and Newhall's "History of Lynn," page 141, N. E.

Through Governor Winthrop's records, which come down to 1649, we learn that among the party which came with Rev. Stephen Bachelor in the William Francis were John Wing and his wife Deborah (Bachelor) Wing, and Edward Dillingham.

"JOHN WING was the original projenitor of nearly all who now bear the family name in America, so far as they are known to us." *

He not only settled at Saugus with Stephen Bachelor, but left it with him and went to Mattacheese, and though it was not a successful enterprise, he thereby became acquainted with the region afterwards called Cape Cod.

It could not have been fertility of soil or attractive country that afterwards induced John Wing and others

---

* Rev. Conway Phelps Wing's "John Wing, of Sandwich, and His Descendants."

to settle in a locality which without the people who later gave it attraction must have seemed inhospitable indeed. It was within the jurisdiction of the Plymouth colony, and the Indians in the vicinity were friendly to the English.

In the year 1637 Mr. Edward Freeman * and nine others who had lived in Saugus formed an association " to erect a plantation or town within the precincts of his Majestys General Court at Plymouth." The point selected was near the neck of land between Barnstable and Buzzard's Bay.

On the third day of April, 1637, a patent was granted the original association, giving it the right to form a town. Among the original " Ten Men of Saugus " appear the names of Edward Freeman and Edward Dillingham, and as the forty-fifth in the list of their associates, that of John Wing.

Nearly all were accompanied by their families, and strict rules, civil and religious, were laid down for their government.

In 1638 the General Court deputized Mr. Alden and Miles Standish " accurately to define the limits of each man's allotment of land with all convenient speed."

In 1639 an act of incorporation was granted, and the Indian name of Shawme became Sandwich.

Here John Wing and his descendants after him have lived until the present time.

John Wing was a quiet man, chiefly interested in his family and his lands, but his name may be found on court records as qualified for public business.

---

* Freeman's History of Cape Cod, vol. ii., pp. 15, 17.

From John Wing's son Daniel are descended those who by marriage were associated either with Nantucket or with the progenitors of Nantucket settlers.

In Bowden's "History of the Society of Friends in America" we learn that two English Friends named "Christopher Holden and John Copeland came to Sandwich on the 20th of Sixth month, 1657, and had a number of meetings."

In 1658 eighteen families in Sandwich recorded their names in one of the documents of the Society of Friends. The Sandwich Monthly Meeting was the first established in America, and its records extend back to 1672, and the Quarterly Meeting, held for many years alternately at New Bedford and Nantucket, was known as the "Sandwich Quarterly Meeting of Friends," having been an outcome of that organization.

The larger number of Friends at both New Bedford and Nantucket was a reasonable cause for changing the place of meeting.

CHAPTER VIII.

OTHER PROPRIETORS.

RECORDED details of the remaining proprietors are very brief; concerning some there appears to be little record excepting of their proprietorship.

ROBERT PIKE was one of the original settlers of Salisbury, Massachusetts, and shared the interest of Christopher Hussey as a proprietor of Nantucket. He continued his relations with the settlers of the island until his death, which occurred about forty years after the purchase. As has already been stated, he was the warm friend of Thomas Macy.

In 1637, on the 17th of May, in order to prevent the reelection of Sir Harry Vane as governor, and to strengthen the friends of Winthrop, ten men, among them Robert Pike and Thomas Coleman, went from Newbury to Cambridge on foot (forty miles) and qualified themselves to vote by taking the freeman's oath. Winthrop was chosen governor. (N. E. Hist. and Gen. Reg.)

Robert Pike was representative to the General Court in 1648-49 and 1658-59; captain and major in 1670; an assistant in 1682; and a member of the Council of Safety in 1689.

NOTE.—Davis's History of Bucks County says the Pike family of Bucks County, Pennsylvania, is said to descend from Robert Pike, of Massachusetts.

THOMAS COLEMAN must have removed to Nantucket prior to 1673, as on "October 20" of that year he is recorded as "drawn on the jury" there. From a newspaper clipping whose related facts have been deduced from a memorandum book of Nathaniel Coleman, great-great-great grandson of Thomas Coleman, we learn that Thomas arrived in Boston "June 3, 1635," came to Nantucket in 1680, and died in 1682.

Joshua Coffin, in his History of Newbury (p. 15), names Thomas Coleman among settlers of Newbury in 1635, and (p. 29) in a list of settlers of Hampton, with Stephen Bachelor, Christopher Hussey and others in 1639.

Although these records do not agree, even in facts given by the same authority, each may be entirely correct, as the settlers of Nantucket appear in several instances to have gone back and forth before their final settlement, and it is probable that this was the case in other localities.

From the same history (p. 298) we learn the following:

Thomas Coleman's first wife Susanna died November 17th, 1650, and in *that year* he removed to Hampton. He married Mary, widow of Edmund Johnson, July 11th, 1651; his second wife died in Hampton, Jan. 30th, 1663. He married a third time Margery —— (Ashbourne, say some authorities).

Children of Thomas Coleman were:
Benjamin Coleman, born May 1st, 1640.
Joseph Coleman, born December 2d, 1642.
Isaac Coleman, born February 20th, 1647.
(From above dates, children of first wife.)

Joanna Coleman.

Tobias Coleman, who was son of the third wife.

NATHANIEL COLEMAN was the only son of Barnabas Coleman and his first wife Elizabeth (Barnard).

Barnabas was son of John 3d, who was son of John 2d, who was son of John 1st, who was son of Thomas Coleman and Susanna ———.

Nathaniel Coleman was Register of Deeds for Nantucket from the " 3d of August, 1785, till the 20th of January, 1804."

He modestly enters in his memoranda the following record of his re-election: After stating that the number of votes cast was " 373 " " April 18, 1791," he says: " N. C. got 206; W. Folger got 70; S. Starbuck got 7."

His father, Barnabas Coleman, married as second wife Rachel Hussey, daughter of Sylvanus, who was son of Stephen, who was son of Christopher Hussey, and another entry among the memoranda of the above-named reads as follows: " Barnabas Coleman and Rachel his wife, the number of their children and grandchildren and great-grandchildren in 1796—children 13 grand children 113 great grand children 85."

THOMAS BARNARD, who settled in America about 1650, was one of the purchasers of Nantucket in 1659, and transferred one-half of his interest to his brother, Robert Barnard.

In Hoyt's " The Old Families of Salisbury and Amesbury," page 13, among signatures to " Articles of Agreement Between the Inhabitants of the Old Town and those of the New Town," May 1, 1654, we find Thomas Barnard, Phillip Challis, Thomas Macy, John Severance and others. Page 14, under "Divisions of Land, 1654," Thomas Barnard, Phillip Challis, Thomas Macy and others, and among "Amesbury Commoners" in 1667-8, Thomas Barnard, Sr. and Jr., and Lt. Phillip Challis.

Pages 20 and 21: "Jn° Barnard and Tho: Barnard" are named among citizens taking "Oath of Allegiance, Eamsbery," December 20, 1677.

Thomas Barnard is named as one of the "Brethren of Y^e Church." Page 49, Thomas Barnard, or Barnett, of Salisbury* and Amesbury, "planter or husbandman," born about 1612 (probably a brother of Robert), received land in the first division, 1640 and 1643, was one of the first settlers of Amesbury, received land there at various times, and a "township" for one of his sons in 1660.

His name appears in nearly all the early lists down to 1672. He married Helen or Eleanor ———.

The only explanation for the statement in an old record that Thomas Barnard "died abroad" lies in the fact that among old-fashioned people of Nantucket go-

---

* Hoyt says: "The plantation was first named Colchester, September 4, 1839, changed to Salisbury October 7, 1640."

NOTE.—Hoyt, in "The Old Families of Salisbury and Amesbury," page 18, says: "As early as 1642 the town of Salisbury ordered that thirty familes should remove to the west side of the Powow River (Amesbury) before 1645. Salisbury seems to have had about twice as many inhabitants as Amesbury soon after the formal separation. On Amesbury Records we find, dated March 19, 1654-5, in a list of the "present inhabitance and comenors heare in the new towne," Thomas Barnard and others.

ing out to an afternoon tea was "going abroad." Usually anywhere away from the island was "off" or "off island." This particular recorder certainly meant "off island" when he wrote "Thomas died abroad," as the records of Salisbury say he was killed by Indians about 1677.

His widow, Eleanor Barnard, administered on his estate. When it was settled, in 1679, there were nine children. (It is believed that some of these were children-in-law.)

In a list of inhabitants applying for "Amesbury Meeting House seats," July, 1667, is found the name of "Goodwife Barnard."

Eleanor Barnard, widow of Thomas, married, July 19th, 1681, George Little, of Newbury. She died November 27th, 1694.

ROBERT BARNARD, "husbandman," of Salisbury and Andover, removed to Nantucket in 1663, and died there in 1682. He married Joanna Harvey,* who died in 1705. He had a son, John Barnard, born 1642, who married Bethiah Folger, daughter of Peter Folger, and a daughter, Mary Barnard, who married her cousin, Nathaniel Barnard, son of Thomas and Eleanor Barnard.

Hoyt says: "Letters of administration on the estate of Robert Barnard, Senior, late of Andover, Yoeman, who died intestate, were granted to his grandson, Robert Barnard, February 1st, 1714-15. Stephen Barnard, son of the elder Robert Barnard, signed a statement

---

* Some authorities say daughter of ——— Harvey, of Plymouth Colony.

that he was incapable of acting by reason of age, and asking that his son Robert be appointed. James Bridges and Stephen Barnard were witnesses."

This administration was more than thirty years after the death of the intestate, and as a lawsuit with the State is mentioned in connection with the appointment of the administrator, it is probable that it was due to some claim made in behalf of the State.

Nathaniel Barnard, in his will, refers to "my father-in-law Robert Barnard," which leaves no doubt of the fact that Mary Barnard, daughter of Robert, was at one time his wife.

As he names no wife in said will it is a natural conclusion that he outlived her.

RICHARD SWAIN (Rowley, 1639) came to America in the Truelove 1635, aged thirty-four, settled at Hampton, and married, in 1658, Jane Godfrey Bunker, widow of George Bunker, of Ipswich. They removed to Nantucket. While living at Hampton he was "Selectman and Commissioner for Small Causes." In 1639 he had liberty to "settle small claims."

The children of Richard Swain were:

Francis, who married Martha ———.

William, of Hampton, N. H., who married Prudence Marston.

NOTE.—Nathaniel Barnard, son of Thomas, is by some said to have married Mary, daughter of John Lugg, but Savage says, vol. i., page 120: "High Nantucket authority claims that he came from England in 1650 with his uncle, Robert Barnard, whose daughter Mary he married." It is not impossible that he had two wives. Mary Barnard appears, from Nantucket records, to have been the mother of his children.

Dorothy, who married, first, Thomas Abbott; second, Edward Chapman.

Elizabeth, who married Nathaniel Weare.

John, who married Mary Wier or Weare.*

Richard Swain and his wife Jane (Godfrey) (Bunker) Swain had one son, Richard, who removed to New Jersey. Richard Swain, Sr., died in 1682.

JOHN SWAIN (the proprietor), son of Richard Swain, Sr., has left a record in his house, known as the oldest house on the island, which is still standing, although much out of repair. John Swain's wife, Mary Wier or Weare, was daughter of Nathaniel Weare (Savage, Vol. IV., p. 234). John Swain died in 1717. This family were members of the Society of Friends at a very early date.

---

* Nathaniel Weare, Newbury, son, perhaps, of Peter, ot the same, born in England about 1631, . . . became counsellor of N. H. . . . married Elizabeth, daughter of Richard Swain of Rowley." (Savage, vol. iv., p. 441.)

N. E. Hist. and Gen. Reg., vol. xxv., p. 246, says: "The family of Wier is one of good standing in Scotland, whose name is said to be the same as Vere.

"In early years in this country were persons spelling their name Weare, Weir, Weyer, Wier, Wire, Wyer, all probably intending the same name, and many, if not all, possibly belonging to one family.

"First was Robert Wyer, of Boston; next Peter Weare, who died in Newbury.

"There was a Nathaniel Weare or Wire early in Newbury, afterwards of Nantucket, where he died March 1st, 1681, who had a daughter Hester, wife of Benjamin Swett and Stephen Greenleaf, and a son Nathaniel, who married in Newbury December 3, 1656, Elizabeth Swain, moved to Hampton, was a Councillor and Chief Justice of New Hampshire, and died May 13, 1718, leaving sons Nathaniel and Peter," and, Savage says, " six others."

The John Swain House,

Nantucket.

CHAPTER IX.

PETER FOLGER.

BENJAMIN FRANKLIN, in his genealogical notes, infers that the Folger family was of Flemish origin, and went to England in the time of Queen Elizabeth.

Peter Folger, son of John Folger, was born in 1617, and came from Norwich, England, in 1635.

He went with his father to Martha's Vineyard, where he taught a school and surveyed land; he also assisted Thomas Mayhew, Jr., in his labors as a missionary among the Indians.

He was a Baptist, but it is believed that when an old man he embraced the views of Friends.

Although he was not one of the first proprietors of Nantucket, he may be regarded as a very early settler, having removed to the island in 1663.

"Nantucket, 4th July, 1663.

"These presents witnesseth that we whose names are underwritten do give and grant unto peter foulger, half a share of accommodations on the land above sayd, that is to say half so much as one of the twenty purchasers, both in respect of upland, meadow, wood, timber and other appurtenances belonging to him and his hiers forever on condition that he com to inhabit on Ifland aforesayd with his family within one year after the sale hereof. Likewise that the sayd peter shall atend the English in the way of an Interpreter between the Indians and them upon al necessary ocasions, his house lot to be layd at the place commonly called by the name of Rogers field so as may be most convenient.

" Witness our hands.

"John Smyth
"Thos Macy
"Edward Starbuck
"John Swayne
"Robert Barnard
"Richard Swayne
"John Rolfe
"Thos Mayhew

"Tristram Coffin Sr
   for myself and others being empowered by them.

"Peter Coffin
"Steven Greenleaf
"Tristram Coffin Jr
"William Pile for two shares
"Nathaniel Starbuck
"Thomas Coleman."

Cotton Mather describes Peter Folger as an "Able Godley Englishman who was employed in teaching the youth in Reading, Writing and the Principles of Religion by Catechism, being well-learned likewise in the Scriptures and Capable of Help in religious matters."

At Nantucket he was chosen clerk of the court and recorder July 21, 1673; he also surveyed lands for the settlers, and was regarded as the scholar of the community.

The varied employments of Peter Folger prove him to have been as versatile as industrious; to him, at least, "the knowing Folgers lazy" could not have been applied; and if there was ever any foundation in fact for the character which the little Nantucket rhyme has

Mrs. E. D. Gillespie.

fastened upon this family, it must have been earned by a later representative of the name.

His mantle fell upon some of his descendants, and he bequeathed to them decided ability.

"His son Eleazer, and Eleazer, Jr., were intelligent, literary and mathematical."

Peter Folger died in 1690; Mary, his widow, in 1704.

Abiah Folger, the youngest child of Peter Folger, and the only one born on Nantucket, married Josiah Franklin, of Boston.

Benjamin Franklin, son of Josiah and Abiah (Folger) Franklin, married Deborah Read, of Philadelphia.

Richard Bache, born in England, in 1737, immigrated to the United States, where he married, in 1767, Sarah, only daughter of Benjamin and Deborah (Read) Franklin. Richard Bache was Postmaster-General of the United States in 1776.

Richard Bache's marriage with Sarah, daughter of Benjamin Franklin, continues the Folger family line in Philadelphia, Mrs. E. D. Gillespie, of Philadelphia, being a granddaughter of Richard Bache.* This branch of Peter Folger's family has made its mark in many lines of work; there have been among the generations which have succeeded the great philosopher men who have reached distinction in the army and navy, as men of letters, at the bar, and in the service of the church, and women who in patriotic and educational work have proved the ability transmitted to them from their venerable ancestor.

---

* Other descendants in this line intermarried with Irwin, Hodge, Humphrey, Davis, Pepper, and Perry (of the family of Commodore Perry).

It is gratifying to note in the autobiography of Franklin that he was deeply interested in his ancestors, nor did he consider time lost when in England he made an effort to ascertain from records there the past history of his family.

That he did not lose sight of the fact that Nantucket contributed a very considerable factor to his ancestry is evidenced by his interest in the place and its people.

One of Franklin's biographers says:

"He took much pains to collect information about the Gulf Stream.

"This wonderful river in the ocean has been long known, but the first people to observe it closely were the Nantucket whalemen, who found that their game was numerous on the edges of it, but was never seen within its warm waters.

"In consequence of their more exact knowledge they were able to make faster voyages than other seamen. Franklin learned about it from them, and on his numerous voyages made many observations, which he carefully recorded.

"He obtained a map of it from one of the whalemen, which he caused to be engraved for the general benefit of navigation on the old London chart, then universally used by sailors."

This account is confirmed by Franklin's notes, in which he states that the Nantucket whalemen were extremely well acquainted with the "Gulph Stream" "from their island quite down to the Bahamas," and he further says that from Captain Folger he obtained a copy of the sketch or draft used by Nantucket whalemen, and caused it to be engraved on the London chart.

Alexander Starbuck, in his "History of the American Whalefishery," says, "it is substantially the same as is found on charts of the present day."

WALTER FOLGER, another descendant of Peter Folger, was the son of Walter and Elizabeth (Starbuck) Folger. Elizabeth was daughter of Thomas Starbuck.

Walter Folger first was son of Barzillai and Phebe (Coleman) Folger.

Barzillai was son of Nathan, who was son of Eleazer and Sarah (Gardner) Folger, and Eleazer was son of Peter Folger.

Walter Folger second practiced law for twenty years, and was for six years judge of the Court of Common Pleas, during which time no case decided by him was ever carried to a higher court; he was six years in the Massachusetts Senate, one year in the House of Representatives of Massachusetts, and four years in the Congress of the United States; in addition to this he was one of the best mathematicians and mechanics of his day. He has left as a record of his mechanical skill a remarkable clock, still in the possession of his family.

He commenced work upon this clock at the age of twenty-two, and, devoting to it his leisure hours only, completed it in the course of the second year.

It was put in motion July 4, 1790, and in 1901, though brown with age, is still a good time-keeper; the glass only which covered its face has been renewed. William C. Folger says, "He made not only the works but the case also, I am told."

"It is made of brass and steel. It keeps the date of the year and the day of the month; the sun and moon rise and set in accordance with those in the heavens; it also shows the earth's place on the ecliptic; it keeps the moon's nodes around the ecliptic; the wheel that keeps the date of the year revolves once in one hundred years, remaining still ten years, and at the expiration of each ten years it starts regularly one notch; the diurnal motion of the sun is represented by a circular metallic plate so adjusted that it is seen through a slit in the dial-plate at a greater or less meridian altitude, as the declination changes, rising and setting as in nature, and changing the time in conformity to the latitude, . . . giving also through the entire day the time of his rising and setting and place of the earth on the ecliptic; the moon is represented by a spherule exhibited to the eye in the same manner, but by having one hemisphere colored, and, by a process much more complicated, shows not only the rising, setting, and southing of the moon with the time of full sea at Nantucket, but also the chief phenomena dependent on the obliquity of the moon's path to the ecliptic, such as the hunter's and harvest moons.

"Some of these involve a motion of the works through a period of eighteen years and two hundred and twenty-five days, and the wheel by which the date of the year is advertised is so constructed that its revolution is only completed in one hundred years."

Walter Folger never learned a trade, never studied law with a lawyer, nor went to any institution of learning where anything above the alphabet, spelling, reading in the Bible, arithmetic, and surveying were taught.

Birthplace of Maria Mitchell,
Vestal Street, Nantucket.

MARIA MITCHELL, late Professor of Astronomy at Vassar College, whose mathematical ability needs no comment to the present generation, was a lineal descendant of Peter Folger. Maria Mitchell was daughter of William and Lydia (Coleman) Mitchell. Lydia Coleman was daughter of Andrew Coleman, who was son of Enoch, who was son of Jeremiah, who was son of John, who married Joanna Folger, daughter of Peter Folger. On the paternal side as well she was descended from Peter Folger, and from many of the early settlers on the island. (See page 141.)

William Mitchell filled many positions which brought him into touch with men of letters. He was at one time chairman of the Harvard Observatory Committee, and for a long time one of the Overseers of Harvard College; a member, also, of the Massachusetts Senate, and one of Governor Briggs' Council; and his associations were with the brilliant minds that public life in Boston knew in the earlier half of the nineteenth century.

In their home the children were accustomed to cultivated society. Mr. and Mrs. Mitchell entertained many people of rare attainments, as well as the ministering Friends who visited the island.

Here, at the age of twelve, Miss Mitchell began her astronomical observations.

Her brother, Prof. Henry Mitchell, referring to the eclipse of 1831, says: "It was this annular eclipse described in the next year's American Almanac as a 'splendid spectacle'—'beautiful and sublime,' that first called in the services of Maria Mitchell, as appears from the accompanying fac-simile of her father's observations at Vestal Street.

"We conjecture that the note signed 'M. M.' was added after her father's death in 1869, at the time his papers were gathered up.

* * * * * * *

"These observations of the eclipse made in concurrence with those of Paine at Monomoy and Bond at Dorchester had for practical object the determination of the longitude of the house in Vestal Street where the chronometers of the whale-ships were carried to be rated and set to Greenwich time."

"Mr. Mitchell came in time to be the rater of all chronometers of a fleet of ninety-two whale-ships requiring observations on every fine day of the year. We mention this to indicate how accustomed his daughter must have been to the talk of astronomy, even as the source, in part, of her daily bread."

The connection of the Barker family with Nantucket and with the family of Peter Folger furnishes a link between Nantucket and Plymouth.

JACOB BARKER, financier and merchant, was son of
    Robert Barker and Sarah Gardner.
Robert Barker was son of
    Samuel Barker and Bethiah *Folger*.
Samuel Barker was son of
    Isaac Barker and Judith *Prence*.
Bethiah Folger was daughter of
    John, and granddaughter of PETER FOLGER.

JUDITH PRENCE was daughter of
  GOVERNOR THOMAS PRENCE and Mary Collier,
    and granddaughter of
  WILLIAM COLLIER.

WILLIAM COLLIER, whose daughter Mary was second wife of Governor Prence, was a wealthy merchant, who came early to Plymouth and soon removed to Duxbury.* It is not known whether he brought with him a wife, but Savage says " four daughters of excellent character came with him,"—Sarah, who married Love Brewster; Mary, who married Thomas Prence; Elizabeth, who married Constant Southworth; and Rebecca.

William Collier was assistant governor twenty-eight years,† member of Council of War four years,‡ member of Provincial Congress in 1643, and one of the committee of two appointed by Congress to sign the Articles of Confederation.§ He died in Duxbury in 1671.

THOMAS PRENCE was born at Lechdale, Gloucestershire, England, in 1600; he died in Plymouth, Massachusetts, in 1673. He was governor of the Plymouth Colony eighteen years, assistant thirteen years, treasurer one year, member of the Council of War five years, commissioner twelve years, alternate commissioner several years. The N. E. Hist. and Gen. Reg., vol. vi., p. 234, thus speaks of him:

---

* Savage, vol. i., p. 443.
† Plymouth Colonial Records, vol. i., pp. 32-36, etc.
‡ Ibid., vol. ii., pp. 47, 64.
§ See Winsor's History of Duxbury, p. 90, and Savage, vol. i., p. 433.

"He was a worthy gentleman and very able for his office, and faithful in the discharge thereof, studious of peace, a well willer to all that feared God and a terror to the wicked."

Doubtless, from various records, Thomas Prence was a zealot in his own belief and intolerant of all whose views did not accord with his; it must be remembered that in that day intolerance was the rule and charity the exception.

Governor Prence and his associates believed they were engaged in their Master's service in any persecutions they were party to, and the author of "The Pilgrim Republic" says, "A severe execution of the laws was exceptional with them and they often exercised leniency on slight pretexts."

He further says, "Thomas Prence had ever swayed the courts in religious matters. Let it stand as a redeeming trait to his character that he used this influence to emancipate his people from the bonds of a world-wide superstition.* Prence also honored himself by zealously promoting public education. . . . The stern Calvinism which he cherished had long been losing its hold on the public mind, and the signs of the times were ominous to those conservative principles which he considered essential to a good government . . . it is probable that the weary Governor was quite ready to go when death summoned him from the Government-house April 8, 1673, at the age of seventy-three.†

---

* Witchcraft.

† For dates and authorities concerning the services of Thomas Prence, see Justin Winsor's History of Duxbury; Plymouth Col-

Wm. Mitchell
Eclipse of 2 mo 1831

Time by clock } Beginning	11·58·14
Formation of ring	1·29·35
Rupture of ring	1·31·17
End of the Eclipse	2·55·42
Duration of ring	1·42
Duration	— — —

clock too fast - 3'·7"

Mean — Time corrected

Beginning —	11·55·07
Formation of ring	1·26·28
Rupture of ring	1·28·10
End of eclipse	2·52·35
Duration of ring —	1·42
Duration of Eclipse	2·57·28

```
   12
11·55·07
─────────
   04·53
 2·52·35
─────────
 2·57·28
```

This time was noted by me;
I was 12½ years old. M. M.

Professor Henry Mitchell.

"Ten days later, with all the ceremony due to his office, he was laid on Burial Hill, in a grave now unknown."

Dr. Edward T. Tucker, in an article written for "The American Friend," and published in its issue dated Sixth month 20th, 1901, gives many interesting facts concerning the attitude of the Plymouth Colony toward Quakers and the intolerance of Governor Prence toward the sect. Among his descendants are many representatives of the Society.

"Arthur Howland, brother of John Howland, was summoned to appear at the house of John Alden to answer for entertaining a Quaker. . . .

"At a Court held June 1st, 1658, before Thomas Prence, Governor, and his assistants, Robert Harper, Ralph Allen, Jr., John Allen, Thomas Greenfield, Edward Perry, Richard Kirby, Jr., William Allen, Thomas Ewer, William Gifford, George Allen, Jr., Matthew Allen, Daniel Wing, John Jenkins, Jr., and George Webb, of Sandwich, were summoned and gave a reason for refusing to take the oath of fidelity to the government and to the mother country, as they declared it unlawful to take oath. . . .

"William Newland, of Sandwich, and Henry Howland, of Duxbury, were disfranchised for being abettors of and entertainers of Quakers. . . .

"Arthur Howland, of Marshfield, and Henry Howland, of Duxbury, were numbered among the staunch advocates of the Society in their respective localities. John Howland, their brother, was one of the company

---

ony Records; Savage; N. E. Hist. and Gen. Reg.; and The Pilgrim Republic, by John A. Goodwin.

in the Mayflower, nearly forty years before, and had been an influential resident in the Colony."

John Howland was not a member of the Society of Friends.

Arthur Howland, Jr., son of Arthur, married Elizabeth Prence after many years of opposition on the part of her father, Governor Prence.

His prejudice against Quakers was so strong that Arthur was fined five dollars for presuming to pay attention to Elizabeth, and forbidden to see her.

When, after years, the young people, faithful to each other, and regardless of their duty to parental authority, renewed the engagement, Arthur was again fined five dollars, which fine was duly paid, but the ardent lover prevailed, and history says Elizabeth Prence became "Mistress Arthur Howland."

WILLIAM ALLEN BUTLER belongs to this branch of the family, his great-grandmother having been a half-sister of Jacob Barker and daughter of the aforesaid Robert Barker.

Another descendant of Peter Folger was the late CHARLES JAMES FOLGER, who was born at Nantucket in 1818; when he was thirteen years of age the family removed to Geneva, New York. He graduated at Hobart College in 1836, read law with Mark H. Sibley, and was admitted to the bar in 1839. He was judge, State senator, chief justice, sub-treasurer of the United States, in New York, and finally Secretary of the Treasury of the United States.

CHAPTER X.

THOMAS GARDINER, AND HIS SONS RICHARD AND JOHN GARDNER.

WILLIAM C. FOLGER, in his notes on the Gardner family, makes the following entry: "Farmer, in his Register, says, 'Thomas Gardner came from Scotland;' a Nantucket tradition says he came from Sherborne, in the northern part of the County of Dorset, and that the former name of Nantucket (Sherburne) was given through the influence of his family. There is no question of the fact that they exercised considerable influence over the affairs of the town."

There are few natives of Nantucket who do not claim descent from Thomas Gardner.

From New England History and Genealogical Register, vol. xxv., pp. 48, 49, we learn that "Thomas Gardiner, the first of the Salem stock, came over in 1624 from Dorsetshire, England, near which the name had flourished for more than three centuries, and settled under the auspices of the Dorchester Company and Rev. John White, with thirteen others at Gloucester, Cape Ann, upon the grant of Lord Sheffield to Robert Cushman and Edward Winslow, made in January of that year.

NOTE.—Mr. Folger, referring to the characteristic "silent" as applied to the Gardner family, says: "They certainly have been less noisy and have displayed more shrewdness than many other families, and in proportion to their numbers have had the largest share of offices."

"Mr. Gardner was overseer of the plantation, John Tilley of the fisheries, Roger Conant being soon after appointed Governor.

"Not realizing the success they anticipated in founding a colony they removed, in 1626, to Naumkeag, or Salem, which continued the home of Mr. Gardner and his descendants down to the present century. He died in 1635."

Henry Drinker Biddle, in his "History of the Drinker Family," on page six, says:

"Sarah Gardner, the wife of Benjamin Balch, was the daughter of Thomas Gardner, the first *Governor* of the Cape Ann Colony."

Savage, Vol. II., p. 230, gives the following in substance:

Thomas Gardner, Salem, was first at Cape Ann employed by the projectors of the settlement to oversee the fisheries; 1624 or 5 he removed with Roger Conant; was made freeman 17 May, 1637, and was representative same year. He was also a member of the Town Council of Salem for a number of years.

The weight of authority would indicate that Thomas Gardiner and John Tilley were the chief rulers of the Cape Ann Colony during the time which preceded the appointment of Roger Conant as Governor.

As during that time they were in the highest position, other authorities than Mr. Biddle have referred to Thomas Gardiner as Governor, and as such he has been quoted through many generations.

From the Historical Collections of Essex Institute of Salem, we learn that the name of Gardiner has been known and respected throughout the entire history of the city.

He married: first, Margaret Frier, who was the mother of his children; second, Damaris Shattuck, widow.

Thomas Gardiner had several sons, among whom, as early settlers of Nantucket, although not original proprietors, were Richard and John, who took an active part in affairs civil and military.

Austin says that Richard Gardner lived at Salem from 1643 to 1666; he and his wife (Sarah Shattuck) were persecuted for attending Quaker Meeting, and went to Nantucket, where they spent the remainder of their lives.

In 1673, Governor Lovelace commissioned Richard as chief magistrate of Nantucket, " he to hold his commission until the next election and return and approbation of a new one by Francis Lovelace." *

Copy of " A Letter from the Secretary to ye Inhab^{ts} of Nantuckett. [Deeds III. 89, Secretary's Office.]

"New Yorke, Apr. ye 24th, 1673.

" Gent:—By the Governo^{rs} Ord^r I am to acquaint you, That hee Received your Letter (bearing Date the 3d Day of Aprill) about three weeks fince, by the Hands of Mr. Richard Gardner, together with eight

---

*Authority for this commission may be found on pp. 87, 88, in a manuscript volume entitled, Deeds, vol. 3, in the office of the Secretary of State in Albany.

NOTE.—Some descendants of Lion Gardiner live now on Nantucket; whether there is any connection between Thomas Gardiner and Lion Gardiner is not known.

Barrels of ffifh for two Yeares, Acknowledgement, and a Token of fifty weight of ffeathers, for which your Care of the Former and Kindnefs in the Latter hee Returns you Thanks. There came to the Governo^r in the Winter a Letter from Mr Tristram Coffin about your Election, but no other from you; in anfwer to which you had heard from him fooner, but the Difficulty of Conveyance hindered. You will now underftand the Governors Choice, by the Bearers hereof Mr. Richard and Captain John Gardner;

"That is, Mr. Richard Gardner for Chiefe Magiftrate this Yeare, and Capt. John Gardner for Chiefe Military Officer, for which they have Commiffions. They have alfo with them fome Additional Inftructions and Directions to Communicate to you; moft of which were Propofed by thofe two ffriends you sent who have prudently Managed the Truft you Repofed in them. They have alfo with them a Booke of the Lawes of the Government, and three Conftables Staves;

"As to your Non-performance of the Acknowledgement according to the Strictnefs of the Time, his Hono^r being fenfible that Opportunityes doe not very frequently prefent between these Places, hee is very well Satisfyed with your Civill Excufe. If at any Time you have other Propofalls to make, for the Good of yor Inhabitants, you may reft affured of his Hono^{rs} ready Complyance therein. This is all I have in Charge to Deliver unto you from the Governour, foe take Leave and Subscribe

"Gent: Yo^r very humble Servant

"MATTHIAS NICOLLS."

JOHN GARDNER was magistrate at Nantucket in 1680, and judge of probate from 1699 until his death, which occurred in 1706, at the age of eighty-two. He is referred to by Cotton Mather as being " well acquainted with the Indians, having divers years assisted them in their government, by instructing them in the laws of England and deciding difficult cases among them."* In 1673, John Gardner was appointed " Captain and Chief Military Officer of the Ffoot Company."

Copy of " Commiffion for Capt John Gardner of the Ifland of Nantucket, to bee Capt. of the Foot Company there. [Deeds III. 88, Secretary's Office.]

" Francis Lovelace, Esqr., &c: Governo^r Gen^{all} under his Royall H^s James Duke of Yorke and Albany, &c; of all his Territoryes in America; To Capt. John Gardner of ye Island Nantuckett. Whereas, You are one of the two Persons returned unto mee by the Inhab^{ts} of your Ifland, to bee the Chiefe Military Officer there, having conceived a good opinion of your ffittnefs and Capacity; By Vertue of the Commiffion and Authority

---

* From no records do we read of serious difficulties *on Nantucket* between the Indians and the white men; they followed the example of the settlers in fishing for whales, which were plentiful on that shoal-bound coast, and " became the most expert of the original whalers of Nantucket."

NOTE.—John Gardner's daughter Rachel married John Brown, of Salem, son of Elder John Brown and Hannah (Hobart).

Hannah Hobart was daughter of Rev. Peter Hobart, who was born in Hingham, County of Norfolk, England, in 1604, and died in Hingham, Massachusetts, January 20, 1679. (Hobart Family Memorial, Part I., pp. 103, 104, No. 23, III. A.)

He was the first minister of the Gospel in Hingham, Massachu-

unto mee given by his Royall Highneſſe, James Duke of Yorke and Albany, I have Constituted and Appointed, and by these Presents doe hereby Constitute and Appoint you John Gardner to be Captaine and Chiefe Military Officer of the ffoot Company rifsen or to bee rifen within the Iſlands of Nantuckett and Tuckanuckett; you are to take the said Company into your Charge and Care as Captaine thereof, and them duly to Exercise in Armes; and all Officers and Souldyers belonging to the said Company are to Obey you as their Captaine.

"And you are to follow fuch Orders and Inſtructions, as you ſhall from Time to Time Receive from mee or other your Superiour Officers according to the discipline of Warr; for the doeing whereof this ſhall be your Comiſſion.

---

setts, was educated at Cambridge, England, and came to New England June 8, 1635; was admitted freeman same year, and settled at Hingham in September, 1635.

Savage, vol. ii., p. 435, says he took his A.B. in 1625, his A.M. in 1629, that he wrote his name Hubberd, was of the Magdalen College, and had preached at divers places, last at Haverhill, in Suffolk, before coming here.

Savage further says,—

" Peter brought with him a wife and four children certainly,— viz.:

" Joshua Hobart.

" Jeremiah Hobart.

" Josiah Hobart.

" Elizabeth Hobart, m. John Ripley.

" And after coming here thirteen were added to the number,— viz.:

" Icabod Hobart.

" Hannah Hobart, died soon.

" Hannah Hobart, m. John Brown, of Salem.

" Bathsheba Hobart, m. Joseph Turner, of Scituate, 1640.

"Given under my Hand and Seale at Fort James in New Yorke this 15th Day of Aprill in the 25th Yeare of his Maties Reigne, Annoq^e Domini, 1673.

"FRAN. LOVELACE."

"Israel Hobart, *m.* Sarah Wetherill, dau. of Rev. William Wetherill, 1668.

"Jael Hobart, *m.* Joseph Bradford, son of Governor Bradford.

"Gershon Hobart, *m.* Sarah ——.

"Japhet Hobart, *m.*

"Nehemiah Hobart, *m.* Sarah Jackson, 1678.

"David Hobart, *m.* 1st, Joanna Quincy, dau. Edmund Quincy second; 2d, Sarah Joyce.

"Rebecca Hobart, *m.* Daniel Mason, of Stonington (as second wife).

"Abigail Hobart, *unm.*

"Lydia Hobart, *m.* Captain Thomas Lincoln, 1690 (as second wife), and [Savage adds] 'the patriarch died 1679.'

"In Rev. Peter Hobart's will, made four days before his death, he names fourteen living children, and wife Rebecca (probably daughter of Richard Ibrook), who was mother of the last six children; no mention is made in Hingham records of the death of the first wife.

"Edmund Hobart, father of Rev. Peter Hobart, was a member of the General Court, 1639-40-42, from Hingham, Massachusetts. He brought a wife and several children with him from England in 1635, and died in 1646, leaving Edmund, Joshua, Rev. Peter, Thomas, and two daughters, Rebecca and Sarah."

CHAPTER XI.

SAMUEL SHATTUCK.

THE name of Shattuck is associated with Nantucket through the marriage of Sarah Shattuck * to Richard Gardner, son of Governor Thomas Gardiner.

There has appeared to be some difficulty in finding exact and clear record concerning Samuel Shattuck, but the most likely history of his family is that there were two of the name—that Damaris, who in her widowhood married Thomas Gardiner, was widow of *Samuel* and mother of *Samuel*.

Damaris Shattuck was without much doubt a widow when she came to Massachusetts; it is believed by the family that her husband died on the voyage to America, a not infrequent occurrence in the long voyages of early times.

Two sons of Thomas Gardiner married daughters of their step-mother.

Richard Gardner married Sarah Shattuck, and they have many descendants among Nantucket's sons and

---

* It has been the belief of many descendants of Sarah (Shattuck) Gardner that she was a daughter of Samuel Shattuck, concerning whom this chapter is written, and Savage (vol. ii., p. 229) says, "Richard Gardner married Sarah Shattuck, probably daughter of Samuel;" other authorities, and those having most weight in this connection, give Samuel with Sarah in a list of the children of Damaris Shattuck (widow who married Thomas Gardiner).

daughters. George Gardner married Hannah Shattuck.

SAMUEL SHATTUCK, who is the subject of this chapter, was by a careful investigation of dates doubtless *son* of Damaris Shattuck.

He is described as " an inhabitant of Salem of good repute," was born in England about 1620; on coming to this country he settled in Salem, Massachusetts.

A stone still standing over his grave in Salem bears the following inscription:

" Here lyeth buried ye body of Samuel Shattuck aged 69 years who departed this life in ye 6th day of June 1689." He was present at a Friends' Meeting when Christopher Holder attempted to speak, and he " endeavored to prevent their thrusting a handkerchief into Holder's mouth lest it should have choked him," for which attempt he was carried to Boston and imprisoned till he had " given bond to answer it at the next Court and not to come to any Quaker meeting."

The following extracts are taken from the edition of Besse's " Collection of The Sufferings of the People called Quakers," printed in London in 1753 (vol. ii., pp. 187, 188).

A Letter of the Prisoners to the Magistrates at the Court in Salem.

" Friends:

"Whereas it was your Pleasures to commit us, whose names are underwritten, to the House of Correction in Boston, although the Lord the righteous Judge of Heaven and Earth is our witness, that we had done nothing worthy of Stripes or of Bonds, and we being committed by your Court to be dealt withal as the Law provides for foreign Quakers, as ye please to term us; and having some of us suffered your Law and Pleasures, now that which we do expect is, now to be set free by the same Law, as your Manner is with Strangers and not to put us in upon the Account of one Law and execute another Law upon us, of which, according to your own Manner, we were never convicted as the Law expresses. If you had sent us upon the Account of your new Law, we should have expected the Gaoler's Order to have been on that Account, which that it was not, appears by the Warrant which we have, and the Punishment which we bare, as four of us were whipped, among whom was one that had formerly been whipt, so now also, according to your former Law. Friends, let it not be a small Thing in your Eyes, the exposing, as much as in you lies, our families to Ruin.

"It's not unknown to you, the Season, and the Time of the Year, for those that live of Husbandry, and what their Cattle and Families may be exposed unto; and also such as live on Trade.

"We know if the Spirit of Christ did dwell and rule in you, these Things would take Impression upon your Spirits.

"What our Lives and Conversations have been, in that place is well known, and what we now suffer for, is much for false Reports and ungrounded Jealousies of Heresy and Sedition. These Things lie upon us to lay before you. As for our Parts, we have true Peace and Rest in the Lord in all our Sufferings, and are made willing in the Power and Strength of God, freely to offer up our Lives in this Cause of God, for which we suffer; Yea, and we do find, through Grace, the Enlargements of God in our imprisoned Estate, to whom alone we commit ourselves and Families, for the disposing of us according to his infinite Wisdom and Pleasure, in whose Love is our Rest and Life.

"From the House of Bondage in Boston, wherein we are made captives, by the Wills of Men, although made free by the Son of God, John VIII—36. In which we quietly rest this 16th of the Fifth month 1658.

"LAURENCE
"CASSANDRA } SOUTHWICK.
"JOSIAH
"SAMUEL SHATTUCK.
"JOSHUA BUFFUM."

"On the 11th of the Third Month, 1659, the aforesaid Laurence and Cassandra Southwick, their son Josiah, Samuel Shattuck, and others were called before the Court, and as they continued steadfast in what the governor was pleased to call rebellion against the Authority of the country the Sentence of Banishment was pronounced against them, and but a Fortnight's Time allowed for them to depart, on pain of Death, nor would they grant them any longer Time, though desired: So the said Samuel Shattuck, Nicholas Phelps, and Josiah Southwick were obliged to take an Opportunity that presented four Days after to pass for England by Barbadoes. The aged couple Laurence and Cassandra went to Shelter Island where shortly after they died within three Days of each other; and Joshua Buffum departed to Rhode Island." (Vol. II., page 198.)

Copy of the King's Letter or Mandamus.

"Trusty and Wellbeloved, we greet you well. Having been informed that several of our Subjects among you, called Quakers, have been and are imprisoned by you, whereof some have been executed, and others (as hath been represented unto us) are in Danger to undergo the Like: We have thought fit to signify our Pleasure, in that Behalf for the future, and do require, that if there be any of those People called Quakers amongst you, now already condemned to suffer Death, or other Corporal Punishment, or that are imprisoned, or obnoxious to the like Condemnation, you are to forbear to proceed any farther, but that you forthwith send the said Persons (whether condemned or imprisoned) over to this our Kingdom of England, together with their respective Crimes or Offences laid to their Charge, to the End such Course may be taken with them here, as shall be agreeable to our Laws and their Demerits. And for so doing, these our Letters shall be your sufficient Warrant and Discharge. Given at our Court at Whitehall the 9th Day of September 1661 in the thirteenth year of our Reign."

"Subscribed, To our Trusty and Welbeloved John Endicot Esq. and to all and every other the Governour or Governours of our Plantation of New England, and of the Colonies thereunto belonging, that now are or hereafter shall be; And to all and every the Minister's and Officers of our said Plantation and Colonies whatever within the Continent of New England.

"By His Majesty's Command.

"WIL. MORRIS."

(Vol. II., Page 225.)

"In procuring the aforesaid Letter or Mandamus from the King, Edward Burroughs was a principle Instrument for when the News of W. Leddra's Death came to the Ears of the Friends at London, and of the Danger many others of their Persuason were in, they were much concerned, especially the said Edward Burroughs, who speedily repaired to the Court and having got Access to the King's Presence, told him, *There was a Vein of innocent Blood opened in his Dominions, which if it were not stopped might overrun all.* To which the King replied, *But I will stop that Vein.* Then Burroughs desired him to do it speedily, for there was Danger of many others being soon put to Death.

"The King answered, *As speedy as you will* and ordered the Secretary to be called, and the Mandamus to be forthwith granted.

"A few Days after Edward Burroughs went again to the King, desiring Dispatch of the Business. The King said, He had no present Occasion to send a Ship thither, but if they would send one, they might as soon as they would.

"The King also granted his Deputation to Samuel Shattock who had been banished thence, to carry his Mandamus to New England.

"Whereupon an Agreement was made with Ralph

Goldsmith, one of the said People called Quakers, and Master of a good Ship, for 300*l* to sail forthwith.

"He immediately prepared for his Voyage and in about six weeks arrived in Boston Harbor, on a First-day of the Week.

"The Townsmen seeing a Ship with English Colours soon came on board and asked for the Captain.

"Ralph Goldsmith told them he was the Commander. They asked, Whether he had any Letters? He answered, *Yes.* But withal told them, *He would not deliver them that Day.*

"So they returned on shore again, and reported, that There were many Quakers come, and that Samuel Shattuck (who they knew had been banished on pain of Death) was among them.

"But they knew nothing of his Errand or Authority.

"Thus all was kept close, and none of the Ship's Company suffered to go on shore that Day.

"Next morning Ralph Goldsmith the Commander, with Samuel Shattuck, the King's Deputy, went on shore, and sending the Boat back to the Ship, they two went directly through the Town to the Governour's House, and knockt at the Door: He sending a Man to know their Business, they sent Him Word, that their Message was from the King of England, and that they would deliver it to none but himself.

"Then they were admitted to go in, and the Governour came to them and commanded Samuel Shattuck's Hat to be taken off, and having received the Deputation and the Mandamus, he laid off his own Hat, and ordering Shattuck's Hat to be given him again, perused the Papers, and then went out to the Deputy-

Governour's, bidding the King's Deputy and the Master of the Ship to follow him: Being come to the Deputy-Governour's and having consulted him, he returned to the aforesaid two Persons, and said, We shall obey his Majesty's Command.

"After this the Master of the Ship gave Liberty to his Passengers to come on shore, which they did and had a religious Meeting with their Friends of the Town, where they returned Praises to God for his Mercy manifested in this wonderful Deliverance.

"Not long after the following order at Boston was issued:

"To WILLIAM SALTER Keeper of the Prison at Boston.

"You are required, by Authority and Order of the General-Court forthwith to release and discharge the Quakers who at present are in your Custody: See that you dont neglect this.

"By Order of the Court
"EDWARD RAWSON, *Secretary.*
"BOSTON the 9th of December, 1661."

To the instrumentality of Samuel Shattuck, aided by Edward Burroughs, is due the discontinuance, for a time at least, of one of the most iniquitous persecutions ever carried on, instigated by those who themselves had suffered for conscience' sake. Whipping and imprisonment were later resorted to, but never to the same extent.

With this mandate from the king, Samuel Shattuck was safe to live thereafter a peaceable life in Salem.

The usual character accorded to the early settlers of New England for extraordinary Christian names is exemplified by a son Retire and a daughter Return, mentioned in records of Samuel Shattuck. These were supposed to be commemorative of his banishment and return.

These two children probably died young, as in the division of the property they are not mentioned; at all events the names have not descended.

Whittier, in characteristic manner, describes the interview between Governor Endicott and Samuel Shattuck.

. . . . . .

>The door swung open and Rawson the clerk
> Entered, and whispered under breath,
>"There waits below for the hangman's work
> A fellow banished on pain of death—
>Shattuck, of Salem, unhealed of the whip,
> Brought over in Master Goldsmith's ship
>At anchor here in a Christian port,
>With freight of the devil and all his sort!"
>
>Twice and thrice on the chamber floor
> Striding fiercely from wall to wall,
>"The Lord do so to me and more,"
> The Governor cried, "if 1 hang not all!

NOTE.—In Besse's History is an account of the death of William Robinson, Marmaduke Stephenson, William Leddra, and Mary Dyer, who suffered martyrdom by hanging in Boston in 1660 for their firm adherence to the principles of truth as professed by Friends. Wenlock Christisen was under sentence of death when Samuel Shattuck returned from England bearing the mandamus from King Charles Second requiring the release of all Friends from prison.

Bring hither the Quaker." Calm, sedate,
With the look of a man at ease with fate,
Into that presence, grim and dread
Came Samuel Shattuck, with hat on head.

"Off with the knave's hat!" An angry hand
  Smote down the offence; but the wearer said,
With a quiet smile, "By the king's command
  I bear his message, and stand in his stead."
In the Governor's hand a missive he laid,
With the royal arms on its seal displayed,
And the proud man spake as he gazed thereat,
Uncovering, "Give Mr. Shattuck his hat."

He turned to the Quaker, bowing low,—
  "The King commandeth your friends' release;
Doubt not he shall be obeyed, although
  To his subjects' sorrow and sin's increase.
What he here enjoineth, John Endicott,
His loyal servant, questioneth not.
You are free! God grant the spirit you own
May take you from us to parts unknown."

  .   .   .   .   .

With its gentler mission of peace and good will,
The thought of the Quaker is living still,
And the freedom of soul he prophesied
Is gospel and law where the martyrs died.

CHAPTER XII.

THOMAS MAYHEW AND THOMAS MAYHEW, JR.

That Thomas Mayhew was a proprietor of Nantucket has been previously shown. He selected "his sonne" Thomas Mayhew, Jr., as his associate.

It is probable that Thomas Mayhew, Sr., never had more than a business connection with Nantucket, but one of his descendants married a descendant of Peter Folger.

Thomas Mayhew was born early in 1592, and was a merchant of Southampton, England, but emigrated to America in 1633 or 1634, was admitted a freeman May 14, 1634, and early in 1635 settled at Watertown, Massachusetts, where he owned mills purchased of Mr. Cradock, and a farm; he was at one time proprietor of the Oldham farm. He was a selectman from 1637 to 1643, and a representative to the General Court from 1636 to 1644.

In 1641 he obtained a grant of Martha's Vineyard, and sent there his son Thomas and several other persons who settled at Edgartown. (History of Watertown.) He himself did not move to Martha's Vineyard until 1644 or 1645.

Note.—William C. Folger's MS. says, "The first Mayhew known in England was Simon, who went there in 1000 A.D. from Normandy, settled in County of Wiltshire, and from Wiltshire came Thomas Mayhew to America."

Whether he brought any other children from England has not been ascertained.

Cotton Mather says of him,—

"The worshipful Thomes Mayhew in the year 1641 obtained a grant of Martha's Vineyard, Nantucket and Elizabeth Isles to make a settlement.

"His son Mr Thomas Mayhew in the year 1642 settl'd at Martha's Vineyard with a few other Inhabitants where his Reputation for Piety, his Natural Gifts, besides the acquir'd by his Education (having attained no small knowledge in the Latin and Greek tongues; and being not wholly a stranger to the Hebrew) soon occasioned his Call to the Ministry among that handful.

"In 1647 he intended a short voyage for England, but alas, the ship wherein he took passage was never heard of."

Of Thomas Mayhew, the governor, he says,—

"I have already told my Reader that the Government of this People was the best (of all Governments) Monarchy; and it has been Judged not without Reason, that a main Obstruction in the Progress of the Gospel in the American Plantation, was, if not yet is, the Jealousie the Princes conceiv'd of the Invasion of their Government through the Pretences of Religion and the Eclipsing their Monarchical Dignity.

"Mr Thomas Mayhew therefore finding that the Princes of these Islands, who although they maintained their Absolute Power and Jurisdiction as Kings, were yet bound to do certain Homage to a Potent Prince on the Continent; and although they were no great People, yet had been wasted in Indian Wars, wherein the Great Princes on the Continent (not unlike European Princes for like Reasons of State) were not unassisting, whereby they were necessitated to make these Princes the Balance to decide their Controversies, and several Jurisdictions, by Presents annually sent, whereby obliging the Princes to give their several Assistance as Occasion requir'd.

"And seeing his son, as aforesaid, in a Zealous Endeavor for their Conversion he judged it meet that Moses and Aaron joyn Hands.

"He therefore prudently lets them know, that by Order from his Master the King of England, he was to govern the English which should inhabit these Islands;

"That his Master was in Power far above any of the Indian Monarchs; but that as he was Powerful so was he a great Lover of Justice:

"That therefore he would in no measure invade their Jurisdiction but on the Contrary assist them as Need required:

"That Religion and Government were distinct Things.

"Thus in no long time they conceiv'd no ill Opinion of the Christian Religion." (B VI., Magnalia Section III.)

In closing the history of Thomas Mayhew's Government he says,—

"I shall close the whole when I have told the Reader that their Children are generally taught to Read and Write.

"In one of their towns last winter viz: 1693, thirty Children were at school, twenty more of the same place, accidentally, being not supplied with books could not attend to it.

"Such who are too far distant from any school are often taught by some of their neighbors; in divers places there are lesser schools."

Thomas Mayhew, Jr., left three sons (who subsequently assumed a leading part in the affairs of these islands.) These sons were named Thomas, John, and Matthew.

To his grandchildren Thomas Mayhew alludes in a postscript of a letter to Governor Edmond Andros: *

"May it please yor Hono^r to image what I have on these Islands

Graund Sonnes	15
My sonnes sonnes sonnes	3
Daughters	3
Graund Daughters	11
	32

"I prayfe God two of my Grand-sons does preach to English and Indians, Matthew sometimes to the younge."

Thomas, the grandson, died in 1715, and John in 1689, aged thirty-seven years.

Experience Mayhew, a minister, author of "Indian Converts or Some Account of the Lives and Dyeing Speeches of Christianized Indians of Martha's Vineyard in New England," published in London, 1727, was a son of John Mayhew.

Jonathan Mayhew, who was born in Martha's Vineyard, October 8th, 1720, and died in Boston, July 9, 1766, was a clergyman and an advocate of liberalism; he was a son of Experience Mayhew.

---

* N. Y. Col. MSS., xxiv., Secretary's Office.

ALL THE WAY TO SHEARING PEN

CHAPTER XIII.

CUSTOMS, DOCUMENTS AND INCIDENTS OF NANTUCKET.

By early custom, all land on Nantucket, not set aside for homesteads, was held in common by proprietors, numbering twenty-seven, when the custom was established.

As time went on the number of proprietors increased, and by sale or inheritance the holdings of individuals were divided, and varied according to circumstances.

An acre and a half of land appears to have been originally the equivalent of a " sheep's common "; the area of a " cow's common " was eight times that of a sheep, and a " horse common " contained twice the area of a " cow's common."

After nearly a century and a half, and early in the nineteenth century, some individuals, wishing to hold their lands in severalty, petitioned to the organization of proprietors, but the end was not accomplished in this way. The case was carried to the Courts, and after

"Shearing Day."

several years of litigation was decided in favor of the petitioners, and by application to the judicial Court an owner could have his boundaries defined by commissioners appointed to set off his portion; in this way many titles have been secured.

The undivided lands continued to be held in common. On these commons the flocks and herds grazed throughout the year, until "Shearing Day," when, by their marks, the sheep were sorted and taken by their several owners to that portion of the island set apart for the gala occasion, which always attended the annual clipping.

Here were "washing ponds" and "sheep pens," and as the time for "shearing" approached booths were put up and stored with things to eat, which usually characterize a festivity of this kind.

There were at times from seven to ten thousand sheep on the commons, and the wool which the annual shearing afforded, furnished the homespun blankets and materials for clothing, which satisfied the simple demands of early days in Nantucket, as in other Colonial towns.

The following unique contract is from New York State Records, Deed I., 74, Secretary's Office, Albany, and bears date of "March 22, $16\frac{66}{67}$."

Richard Gardner had "granted to him halfe accommodacons, according to the Grants made to seamen and Tradesmen, upon condition that hee exercise himselfe as a Sea-man, and that he come to Inhabitt here with his ffamily before the End of May—68— And after that his Entrance here, not to depart the Island in

Point of dwelling for the space of three Years upon the Forfeiture of the Grant aforesaid."

In memoranda of William C. Folger, published in Nantucket *Inquirer and Mirror*, in 1862, is the following:

"Joseph Gardner the eldest son of Mr Richard Gardner had half a share of land on Nantucket Granted him 15th of February 1667. In consideration of which he was to supply the occasions of the Island in the way of a Shoe Maker and not leave the island for the space of four years."

The same account says: "Richard Gardner's Will gave to Joseph, eldest son, twice as much as to his other children who were left share and share alike."

Among old wills and deeds one often finds very amusing clauses, and generally the care of the unmarried women of the family was assured by the will of a parent.

The following extract from the will of Francis Macy is one of many instances; it was expected that other members of the family would supplement the provision for shelter by caring for daily needs:

"I give unto my Daughter Deborah Macy the south west chamber of my Dwelling houfe, so long as she Remains single; But if she should marry my will is that it Return to my sun francis."

Inventories were very exact, in some instances going so carefully into detail as to cover the amount of gingerbread in the closet.

No provision closet was well ordered unless stocked

with gingerbread, and for grand occasions doughnuts, and later "wonders," as the richer "cruller" was called. "Wonder" was a local term, and it is easy to fancy how such a name might originate if some goodwife produced an especially good article.

Recipes were known by the names of those who first prepared the viands they described, and manuscript copies of them were handed down from generation to generation.

The following are among the earliest recorded wills:

PROBATE RECORDS
FOR THE COUNTY OF NANTUCKET.

Book A, No. 1, p. 4.

The Probate of the Will of Edward Cartwrite deceased and administration granted thereon vnto his Widow Elizabeth Cartwrite Sole Executrix in the Same Will named Second day of october in the year of our Lord one thoufand Seven hundred and Six Before me at Sherbourn in Nantucket

PETER FOLGER   JAMES COFFIN.

WILL OF EDWARD CARTWRIGHT.
pp. 4 and 6.

In the Name of God Amen: the 28 day of August 1705 I Edward Cartright of Nantucket in the Province of Massachusetts Bay in New England being very Sick and weak in body, but of perfect mind and memory thanks be to God: therefore calling unto mind the mortallity of my body and knowing it is apointed for all men once to die, do make and ordain this my last will and testament that is to say first of all I give and recomend my Soul into the hands of God that gave it and my body I recomend to the earth to be buried in decent maner at the discretion of my Executrix and as touching such worldly Estate wherewith it hath pleased God to blefs me in this life I give demise and dispose of the same in the following maner and form

Imprimis I give and bequeath unto my Son Nicholas Cartright one third part of my lands on pocomook that end where his houfe now stands with one third part of my Meadow Item I give to my Son Sampson Cartright one third part of my land on pocomok that end whereon his house now stands with one third part of my Meadow Item I give to my Son Edward Cartright one half part of the remaining third of my land and Meadow with the one half of my dwelling houfe after my deceafe and after the death of his Mother the other Sixth part of my land and Meadow with the other half of my houfe

Item I give to my daughter Sufanna Cartright forty shillings at the day that She is married Item I give to my daughter Mary Cartright forty shillings at the day that she is married

Item I give and bequeath to My beloved Wife Elizabeth the one half of my dwelling houfe with the other Sixth part of my land and Meadow during her natural life I like wife confstitute Make and ordain Elizabeth my beloved wife my Sole Executrix of this my last will and testament ratifying and confirming this and no other to be my laft will and teftament In witnefs whereof I have hereunto Set my hand and Seal the day and year above written

     EDWARD CARTRIGHT [Seal]

Signed Sealed Published
pronounced and declared
by the S^d Edward Cartright
as his laſt Will & Testament
in the preſence of us
   the Subscribers
   WILLIAM GAYER
   RICHARD GARDNER
   ANNE BUNKER

PROBATE RECORDS
FOR THE COUNTY OF NANTUCKET.

Book A, No. 1, p. 25.

The probate of the will of William Gayer deceased and administration granted thereon unto his Daughters Damaris Coffin and Dorcas Starbuck Joynt Executrices in the same will named, twenty fourth day of October 1710.
          JAMES COFFIN
ELEAZER FOLGER Reg^r Jug of probats

WILL OF WILLIAM GAYER.

p. 26.

I William Gayer of the Island of Nantucket in the province of the Maſsachusets Bay in New England being Sick and weak in body but of Sound mind and memory do make & ordain this my last will and testament in manner and form following

First I give and bequeath unto my son Wiliam Gayer one whole share of land on the Island of Nantucket with all the priviledges and appurtenances belonging to sd whole share of land (if my sd son shall ever come hither again) to have and Injoy the sd land to him & his heirs forever Item I give to my Daughter Damaris Coffin one Eighth part of a share of land on the Island of Nantucket of that land I had of my father in law Edward Starbuck with all the priviledges and appurtenances belonging thereunto to have and to hold to her and her heirs forever

Item I give my Daughter Dorcas Starbuck one Eighth part of a Share of land on the Island of Nantucket of that land I had of my father in law Edward Starbuck with all the priviledges and appurtenances belonging thereunto to have and to hold to her and her heirs forever I do also give my part of the Island of Miskeget to my sd Davghters Damaris Coffin and Dorcas Starbuck Equally to be divided between them.

Item I give to my housekeeper Patience Foot one cow & fourty sheep with Commonages for them as also half the barn & tryhouse with half the garden with the half of the land and fence about my dwelling house and half the lot and fence that is towards Monomoy the horse pasture Excepted as also the west Chamber and Garret and half the leanto of my now dwelling house to hold and pofsefs the sd lands and other the premises to her the sd patience foot during her naturall life

Item I give to Africa a negro once my Servant twenty Sheep and Commonage for them and for one horse as also the East Chamber of my now dwelling house and half the leanto and all the other half of my barn and tryhouse with the half of all the lands and fence about my house and the half of the lot towards Monomoy to hold all the sd lands and other the premises to him the sd Africa during his naturall life and I will that my Daughter Damaris Coffin Shall have the use of the rest of my Dwelling house if she should come hither to live

Lastly I make and ordain my two Daughters Damaris Coffin and Dorcas Starbuck Joynt Executrices of this my last will and testament In witneſs whereof I have hereunto set my hand and Seall this twenty first day of September in the year of our Lord one thousand seven hundred & ten

WILLIAM GAYER [Seal]

Signed Sealed pronounced &
declared by the sd William
Gayer as his last will and testament
in the presence of us the subscribers

    RICHARD GARDNER
    ELEAZER FOLGER Junʳ   EUNICE GARDNER
    JABEZ BUNKER   JUDITH GARDNER

Thackeray says, referring to the age of King James, "Spelling was not an article of general commodity in the world then."

It is not positive evidence of illiteracy that at that early date spelling was inaccurate. The transition from Old English was not made in a hurry; and many years were to pass before the excellent rules and methods of to-day were perfected.

Persecution, which drove many to America, left them little with which to begin a new life; and the hardships experienced offered no opportunity for mental improvement.

The men of those early Colonial days were shrewd

enough in selecting localities for settling towns, and the women were helpmeets in doing what their hands found to do. What time had they to read beyond the Bible which they brought with them, which few appear to have neglected? The documents of those times often have considerable merit in their directness.

Considering the general improvement in English in the present day, it is a striking fact that deeds and other legal documents are not less verbose, and are quite as full of needless repetition as they were in Colonial days.

One anecdote of the Civil War suggests itself. The strong good sense of the Quaker element which pervaded Nantucket is here evident, as it has been on many other occasions in the history of the island.

The defenceless position of Nantucket has always been cause of alarm to its inhabitants in times of war, and ways and means of defence have been suggested from time to time.

Any one who is familiar with its geographical position, however, will appreciate how impossible it would have been to have made a complete and efficient stronghold, even at that time, when the long range of modern ordnance had not been arrived at.

During the Civil War a town meeting was called to consider the wisdom of placing two brass cannon on the North Cliff shore, looking toward the harbor.

It was the custom of the Quakers of Nantucket to let town meetings alone. They often could not approve their action, and, as they felt, removed their responsibility by non-attendance.

The particular town meeting in question was, however, a challenge to the non-combatant members of the Society of Friends.

One of them told the writer of the discomfiture of the keen advocates of defence, when the body of Friends appeared.

The narrator was a staunch " Quaker of the olden time, calm and firm and true."

As he approached the old Town Hall (which lives in history only) he was met by a warlike nephew, who said: " Why, Uncle ——, I thought you never attended the Town Meetings," to which the Friend replied: " I have reserved the privilege, and," he added, " the movement to place the cannon on Cliff Shore was voted down, a movement which would have been ridiculous, if our principles had nothing to do with it, and would have been no defence at all."

At all times, after the earliest settlement, notwithstanding the inaccessibility of the island, intercourse was frequent between the citizens of Sherburne and those of the " main-land "; however, many lived to a good old age without leaving the island.

A notable instance was in the life of one of Nantucket's respected citizens, who died in 1886, at the age of eighty-four, and once only left his native island.

He was sixty-seven years of age when he finally yielded to the entreaties of his friends, and went with a party to New Bedford, and from there to Fall River.

While at Fall River he noticed one of the Sound steamers, the Bay State, at the wharf. It was a larger steamer than he had seen, and he was greatly impressed with its magnificence. Captain Brown was very anxious to take him to New York and show him that great metropolis; he tendered him the finest state room on the boat, but all persuasions were unavailing. Our aged friend said he had already seen "more than he could realize" (a local use of the word), that he was a long way from home, and declared, "that if he ever lived to get back to Nantucket he would never leave the island again."

This is one of many anecdotes that might be told illustrating the contentment of the quiet folk who inhabited Nantucket in earlier days; they generally lived long and were useful, satisfied with the sphere in which circumstances had placed them, emphasizing by their lives their belief that

> God gives to every man,
> The virtue, temper, understanding, taste,
> That lifts him into life and lets him fall
> Just in the niche he was ordained to fill.

If, with the broader experience of to-day, we do not accept in full this creed of our ancestors, we may not be happier than they.

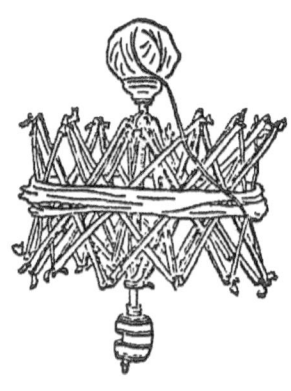

Watching for Whaleships.

CHAPTER XIV.

AN EXPLANATION OF THE NEUTRAL POSITION OF NANTUCKET DURING THE REVOLUTIONARY WAR.

THE wisdom of neutrality in Nantucket during the Revolutionary War was probably never questioned by a native of the island, but among their descendants it has been far different; they have doubted the patriotism of a people who could refrain from taking decided ground when so much was at stake.

To make the position of Nantucket at that time perfectly plain, one must go back to the latter part of the Seventeenth Century and follow closely the history of its fishing interests, and consider the toil of building up a business which would have been absolutely ruined had the islanders boldly taken sides with the Colonists.

Very early in its history the people of the island had undertaken whale fishing. Whales were plentiful along the coasts, small boats only were used in the capture of them, the fishermen venturing short distances from the shore and returning to their homes each night; by degrees they grew bolder, and undertook longer voyages; the number of vessels and of seamen increased

> Until to every wind of heaven
> Nantucket's sails were spread.

The following statistics, found in a report made to Congress by Thomas Jefferson in 1775, show how large a proportion of the Massachusetts income from "whaling" may be credited to Nantucket:

For Massachusetts there were employed
- 304 vessels,
- 27,840 tonnage,
- 4,059 seamen,

returning about 47,040 barrels of oil.

In which Nantucket was accredited with
- 150 vessels,
- 15,070 tonnage,
- 2,025 seamen,
- 30,000 barrels of oil.

About the year 1771 the gathering clouds on the political horizon made the more timid question seriously the wisdom of continuing their business.

French privateers were often encountered. Ship owners lost heavily in consequence, and in view of these depredations many heads of families began to cast about for means of livelihood attended with less risk than that of following the seas.

At first Nantucket had sent oil to England through other ports. At the time preceding the Revolution trade was carried on to a considerable extent directly with London, and if the threatened storm were to break, it may readily be imagined to what peril would be subjected the only industry which had brought gain and comparative wealth to Nantucket.

After deliberate weighing of the matter, a large number of citizens removed to North Carolina, thence to Indiana and Ohio; also to Maine, and New Bedford, Massachusetts; and quite a company united with Providence and Martha's Vineyard, in locating and settling the city of Hudson.

Articles of agreement were there drawn up by the Proprietors, and the settlement was inaugurated on much the same plan as that which more than a century before had been adopted in the settlement of Nantucket.

Thomas Jenkins, a native of Nantucket, was a pioneer in the Hudson movement, and to him largely is due the credit of what proved a successful venture.

The names of Nantucket proprietors of the Hudson settlement were as follows:

Thomas Jenkins.
Joseph Barnard
Stephen Paddack.
Charles Jenkins.
Gideon Gardner.
Reuben Folger.
Alexander Coffin.
Benjamin Hussey.
Shubael Worth.
Paul Hussey.
Benjamin Folger.
Benjamin Starbuck.
John Cartwright.

In spite of the exodus from Nantucket to the points above named, a considerable number remained and took chances, which, on the breaking out of the war, resulted disastrously. Many of their ships were seized by English men-of-war, and the problem by which they were confronted was a serious one; they could not readily turn their attention to agriculture, the soil was sterile, and money not at hand to make it otherwise; manufactures were out of the question, as the raw materials would have to be brought from the mainland across the Vineyard Sound,* and would be subject to danger from the Royal Navy.

To meet the extremity a committee composed of Benjamin Tupper, Timothy Folger,† William Rotch and Samuel Starbuck was sent to Newport and New York to interview the British Commanders, and the following agreement was arrived at: "That depredations should cease provided the town of Nantucket would observe strict neutrality."

A powerful factor in their non-partisanship or neutrality was the spirit of non-resistance fostered by Quakerism, which was a very widely prevailing religion on the island at that time.

---

* Vineyard Sound was that portion of the Atlantic Ocean which lies north of Martha's Vineyard and Nantucket, between them and the mainland, and was a great highway for vessels plying between England and America.

† Timothy Folger, son of Abishai, son of Nathan, son of Eleazer, son of Peter Folger, was a merchant and magistrate at Nantucket prior to and during the Revolution. After peace was established he removed to Dartmouth, Nova Scotia; afterwards to Milford Haven, Wales, where he was merchant and American Consul.

Timothy Folger.

Photographed from a Painting by George Fish, after Copley.

After arrangements with the English were completed, the American Colonists, believing that persistency in fitting out whaling vessels, and the protection which was given them, indicated loyalty to the Crown, themselves opened warfare upon the Nantucket ships.

"A town meeting was convened on the 25th of September, 1782, and a memorial prepared and adopted which was sent to the General Court of Massachusetts."

Referring to this, Mr. Alexander Starbuck says: "They urged that people in continental towns, where the broad country opened to them a place for retreat, could have but faint ideas of the suffering of those who were constantly liable to hostile invasion and whose insular position precluded all thought of escape."

They scorned the imputation that they had sought neutrality because of sympathy with England.

Doubtless tories were in about the same proportion upon the island as in other places throughout the country, but there were many citizens loyal to the interests of the American Colonies.

That portion of the petition which referred to the prosecution of their business reads as follows:

"We now beg leave to throw a few hints before you respecting the Whalefishery, as a matter of great importance to this Commonwealth. This place before the War, was the First in that branch of business, & employed more than One Hundred Sail of good Vessels therein which furnish'd a support not only for Five Thousand Inhabitants here, but for Thousands elsewhere, no place so well adapted for the good of the Community at large as Nantucket, it being destitute of every material necessary in the Business, and the Inhabitants might be called Factors for the Continent rather than Principals; as the war encreased the Fishery ceased, until necessity obliged us to make trial the last Year, with about seventeen sail of Vessels, Two of which were captured & carried to New York,* and one was burnt the others made saving voyages. The present Year we employed about Twenty Four sail in the same business, which have mostly Compleated their Voyages, but with little success; & a great loss will ensue; this we apprehend is greatly owing to the circumscribed situation of the Fishery; we are now fully sensible that it can no longer be pursued by us unless we have free liberty both from Great Britain & America to fish without interruption.

"As we now find One of our Vessels is captured & carried to New York, but without any oil on board, and Two others have lately been taken & carried into Boston & Salem, under pretense of having double papers on board, (Nevertheless we presume the Captors will not say that any of our Whalemen have gone into New York during the season as such a charge would have no foundation in Truth.)

"And if due attention is not paid to this valuable branch, which if it was viewed in all its parts, perhaps would appear the most advantageous, of any possess'd by this Government, it will be intirely lost, if the War continues: We view it with regret & mention it with Concern, & from the gloomy prospect now before us, we apprehend many of the Inhabitants must quit the Island, not being able even to provide Necessaries for

---

* Then in possession of the English.

the approaching Winter: some will retreat to the Continent & set down in the Western Governments; and the Most Active in the Fishery will most probably go to distant Countries, where they can have every encouragement, by Nations who are eagerly wishing to embrace so favorable an opportunity to accomplish their desires; which will be a great loss to the Continent in general, but more to this Government in particular.

"We beg leave to impress the consideration of this important subject, not as the judgment of an insignificant few, but of a Town which a few Years since stood the Third in Rank (if we mistake not) in bearing the Burthens of Government; It was then populous and abounded with plenty, it is yet populous, but is covered with poverty.

"Your Memorialists have made choice of Samuel Starbuck, Josiah Barker, William Rotch, Stephen Hussey and Timothy Folger, as their Committee who can speak more fully to the several matters Contain'd in this Memorial, or any other thing that may concern this County, to whom we desire to refer you.

"Signed in behalf of the Town by

"FREDERICK FOLGER,
"Town Clerk."

This memorial was referred to a committee made up of representatives from the Massachusetts Senate and House, who in their turn referred it to Congress.

Mr. Starbuck says that "in addition to the action of the General Court, the town also sent William

Rotch and Samuel Starbuck to Philadelphia to intercede personally in the matter."

Finally permits were granted and duly delivered. So much diplomacy and time were required to accomplish this, that when the permits were received the fleet was spent, and little profit was to be had from carrying on the business. The agreement of neutrality, however, was conscientiously carried out, and Nantucket struggled through the war, and experienced considerable prosperity after the proclamation of peace, which followed very closely on the negotiations with the General Court.

The whaling interests were renewed, but New Bedford had made great advance in her effort to secure control of the business. Gradually the number of vessels owned on the island grew less, and ultimately the inhabitants of Nantucket abandoned whale fishing altogether, and turned their attention to other pursuits.

The bustle and activity of the early times, the quiet calm about the place to-day, the decaying wharves and condition of business on the island are fittingly described in Mr. Arthur Ketchum's beautiful sonnet:

> Adrift in taintless seas she dreaming lies,
>   The island city, timeworn now and grey,
>   Her dark wharves ruinous, where once there lay
> Tall ships at rest from far sea industries.
> The busy hand of trade no longer plies
>   Within her streets. In quiet court and way
>   The grass has crept—and sun and shadows play
> Beneath her elms, in changing traceries;

NOTE.—One hundred and thirty-four whaling vessels belonging to Nantucket fell a prey to the English, and it is estimated that twelve hundred Nantucket men, mostly whalemen, were captured or perished during the Revolution.

The years have claimed her theirs, and the still peace
  Of wind and sun and mist, blown thick and white
Has folded her. The voices of the seas
  Through many a soft, bright day and brooding night
Have wrought her silence, wide as they and deep;
And dreaming of the past, she waits—asleep.

CHAPTER XV.

EXTRACTS FROM JOURNALS OF THOMAS CHALKLEY, JOHN RICHARDSON AND THOMAS STORY, GIVING SOME ACCOUNT OF THE RISE OF FRIENDS ON NANTUCKET.

Thomas Chalkley, after alluding to visits in "the eastern part of New-England," says:

"From thence I returned in order to get a passage to the isle of Nantucket; and from a place called Cushnet, we sailed over to the said island in about ten hours, where we tarried several days and had five meetings. The people did generally acknowledge to the truth, and many of them were tender-hearted. Some of the ancient people said, That it was never known that so many people were together on the island at once. After the first meeting was over, one asked the minister (so called) whether we might have a meeting at his house? He said with a good will, we might. This minister had some discourse with me and asked, What induced me to come hither, being such a young man?

John Richardson's Meeting.

I told him that I had no other view in coming there, than the good of fouls; and that I could fay with the apoftle that a neceffity was laid upon me, and wo would be to me if I did not preach the gofpel. Then, faid he, I wifh you would preach at my houfe in God's name. So next day we had a meeting at his houfe; and on the firft day we had the largeft meeting that we had on the ifland. It was thought there were above two hundred people. The Lord in his power did make his truth known to the praife of his name. Oh! how was my foul concerned for that people! The Lord Jefus did open my heart to them, and theirs to him. They were alfo loving and kind to us. The chief magiftrat of the ifland defired that I would have a meeting at his houfe; there being no fettled meeting of Friends before I came; and after meeting he difputed about religion with me. I thought we were both but poor difputants; and I cannot remember all that paffed between us, but that in the clofe of our difpute, he faid, I difputed with your friends in Barbadoes and they told me, that we muft eat the fpiritual flefh, and drink the fpiritual blood of Chrift;

"And, faid the Governor, did ever any one hear of such flefh and blood; for is it not a contradiction in nature that flefh and blood should be fpiritual?

"O furely, said I, the Governor has forgot himfelf; for what flefh and blood was that which Chrift faid, except ye eat my flefh and drink my blood ye have no life in you. . . .

"And from that time forward they have continued a meeting, and there is now a meeting-houfe, and a yearly meeting for worfhip; it is a growing meeting to this day, and several public friends are raised up amongst them who preach the gospel of Christ freely.

"At this time a friend was convinced, whose name was Starbuck, who became very serviceable, and lived and died an eminent minister of Christ on that island. Several scores of them came and accompanied us to the water-side; and when we embarked on board our sloop, they desired that I would come and visit them again."

John Richardson says, "It was much with me, when on Rhode Island to visit Nantucket, where there were but very few * Friends. . . .

"We landed safe, and as we went up an Ascent we saw a great many people looking towards the Sea, for great Fear had possess'd them, that our Sloop was a French Sloop loaded with Men and Arms, who were coming to invade the Island; I held out my Arms and told them, I knew not of any worse Arms than these on board.

"They said, they were glad it was no worse, for they had intended to have alarmed the Island, it being a time of war. I told the good-like People, for so they appear'd to me, That Peleg Slocum near Rhode Island, was Master of the Sloop, and that we came to visit them in the Love of God, if they would be willing

---

* The facts that Richard Gardner and his wife were persecuted for "attending Quaker meeting" in Salem, that they removed to Nantucket to escape that persecution, and that in 1673 he was commissioned Chief Magistrate there, indicate that his family was among the "few" and we find recorded also that Stephen Hussey and John Swain were Friends, before there was any organization of Friends on the island.

to let us have some Meetings, amongst them. They behaved themselves very courteously towards us and said, They thought we might.

"We then enquired for Nathaniel Starbuck, who we understood was in some degree convinced of the Truth, and having Directions to his House, we went thither and I told him, We made bold to come to his House, and if he was free to receive us we would stay a little with him, but if not, we would go elsewhere; for we heard he was a seeking religious Man and such chiefly we were come to visit;

"He said, We were very welcome. And by this Time came in his Mother Mary Starbuck who the Islanders esteemed as a Judge among them for little of Moment was done there without her, as I understood.

"At the first Sight of her it sprang in my Heart, To this Woman is the everlasting Love of God. I looked upon her as a Woman that bore some Sway in the Island, and so I said and that truly, We are come in the Love of God to visit you, if you are willing to let us have some Meetings among you: She said, She thought we might. . . .

"The next Consideration was Where shall this meeting be? She paused awhile and then said, I think at our House.

"I from thence gathered she had an Husband, for I thought the Word *our* carried in it some Power besides her own, and I presently found he was with us:

"I then made my Observation on him, and he appeared not a Man of mean Parts, but she so far exceeded him in Soundness of Judgment, Clearness of

Understanding and an elegant Way of expressing herself, and that not in an affected Strain, but very natural to her, that it tended to lessen the Qualifications of her Husband.

"The Meeting being agreed on and Care taken as to the Appointment of it, we parted, and I lay down to try if I could get any Sleep, . . . but Sleep vanished away from me, and I got up and walked to and fro in the Woods until the Meeting was mostly gathered. I was under a very great Load in my Spirit, but the Occasion of it was hid from me, but I saw it my Place to go to Meeting, the Order of which was such, in all the Parts thereof, I had not seen the like before; the large and bright rubbed Room was set with suitable Seats or Chairs, the Glass Windows taken out of the Frames and many Chairs placed without very conveniently, so, that I did not see anything awanting, according to the Place, but something to stand on, for I was not free to set my Feet upon the fine Cane Chair, lest I should break it.

"I am the more particular in this exact and exemplary Order than in some other things, for the Seats both within and without Doors, were so placed that the Faces of the People were towards the Seats where the publick Friends sat, and when so set, they did not look or gaze in our Faces, as some I think are too apt to do, which in my Thoughts bespeaks an unconcerned Mind. The Meeting being thus gathered and Set down in this orderly and ample manner (although there were but very few bearing our Name in it) it was not long before the Mighty Power of the Lord began to work, and in it my Companion * especially did appear in Testimony in the fore Part thereof. . . . I sat a considerable Time in the Meeting before I could see my Way clear to say anything, until the Lord's heavenly Power raised me and set me upon my Feet as if one had lifted me up, and what I had first in Commission to speak was in the words of Christ to Nicodemus, viz: Except a Man be born again, he cannot see the Kingdom of God: . . .

"As I was thus opened, and delivering these Things with much more than I can remember, the great Woman I felt for most of an Hour together, fought and strove against the Testimony, sometimes looking up in my Face with a pale and then with a more ruddy Complexion; but the Strength of the Truth increased, and the Lord's mighty Power began to shake the People within and without Doors; but she who was looked upon as a Deborah by these People, was loth to lose her outside Religion, or the Appearance thereof; When she could no longer contain, she submitted to the Power of Truth, and the Doctrines thereof, and lifted up her Voyce and wept.

"Oh! then the universal Cry and Brokenness of Heart and Tears was wonderful! From this Time I do not remember one Word that I spoke in Testimony, it was enough that I could keep upon the true Bottom, and not be carried away with the Stream above my Measure. . . . I remember Peleg Slocum (before mentioned) said after this Meeting, that the like he was never at, for he thought the Inhabitants of the

---

* James Bates, who was born in Virginia.

Island were shaken, and most of the People convinced of the Truth. However a great Convincement there was that Day, Mary Starbuck was one of the Number, and in a short Time after received a publick Testimony, as did also her son Nathaniel."

It would appear from a journal of Thomas Story, who was at Nantucket three years later, in 1704, that there was no settled meeting of Friends until sometime after his visit, wherein he felt it required of him to lay his concern before Mary Starbuck as the "instrument to bring it about."

Thomas Story says, "Before I proceed I think proper just to give a general Relation of the State of the People on the Island of Nantucket with respect to Religion at this Time. This small Island lies about 20 Leagues from the main Land of New England, inhabited by a mixed People of Various Nations and some among them called christianized Indians, but no settled Teachers of any Kind. . . .

"There was in this Island one Nathaniel Starbuck, whose Wife was a wise discreet Woman, well read in the Scriptures, and not attached unto any Sect, but in great Reputation throughout the Island for her Knowledge in Matters of Religion, and an Oracle among them on that Account, insomuch that they would not do any Thing without her Advice and Content therein;"

It would appear that several ministers of other religious denominations had visited the island from time to time, and had desired a settled maintenance there.

This was opposed by Mary Starbuck as "being contrary to the practice of the Apostles and Primitives and the Nature of the Maintenance of a Gospel Ministry, but she would consent so far, as that when any Preacher came among them, that they liked and staid some Time, and took Pains among them, every Family might give unto such what they pleased for the Help of themselves and their Families, if they had any, as Indian Corn (Maze) or other grain, Meal, Flesh, Fish or such other Provisions as they happened to have at the Time to spare, and Wool &c for Cloathing, but nothing certain or settled: For Ministers of Christ ought to travel abroad in the World in that Calling, and not to sit down in one place, unless they have Families to take care of and cannot leave them.

"And Some Time before this John Kinsey, one of our Ministers from Philadelphia, had been to visit them with good Acceptance and had good Service for Truth among them, and had been instrumental in the Hand of the Lord to beget a good liking in them to the Way of Truth, but received nothing from any of them, (for that is not our Way) on account of His Ministry; And I finding a like Concern at this Time and accompanied by Several Friends of both Sexes, we on the 13th Day of the Fifth month,* about the tenth Hour in the Morning, set Sail for the said Island in a Shallop belonging to our Friend Peleg Slocum, before mentioned, which under divine Providence, he himself chiefly conducted, and landed there the next Morning about six.

---

* 1704.

"At our landing we went up to the House of the Widow Mary Gardner where, after some Refreshment had, came to us Nathaniel Starbuck (Husband of Mary Starbuck before mentioned) and his son of the same name, and we proposed to them to have a Meeting that Day, but there being a court to sit then by Special Commission, . . . we found it improper at that Time, and some of our Company went Home with Nathaniel Starbuck, the elder, and others with his Son, where we were kindly entertained, tho' Strangers, and they at that Time, not in the Profession of Truth with us.

"On the 15th we had a Meeting at the House of Nathaniel Starbuck, the elder, which was pretty large and open, several of the People being tendered and generally satisfied with what they heard and felt of the Goodness and Mercy of God.

"On the 16th being the First Day of the Week, we had another Meeting there, which was not so large as was expected, by reason of two Priests, an elderly Man and a young one, the first from the Isle of Showles, and the other from Martha's Vineyard, who had a Meeting near us, the former being come to try if he could obtain a settled Maintenance among that People.

"And several being curious to hear this new Preacher in the Presbyterian Way, it made our Meeting something less than otherwise it might have been, yet it was considerably large, very open and encouraging, for the good Presence of the Lord was with us."

"Many of the Inhabitants of this Island are convinced of the Truth of some Points of the Doctrine of Truth, and some of them have been reached by the divine Virtue and Power of it, but some other Things they do not yet see, and, if there were no Cross, would, in all Appearance, come generally under our Profession; some few are for a Priest and to allow him some Maintenance (for they walk not by Faith but Sight), but the Majority is against it. So that one of these not being able to effect his Purpose went Home in a few Days, but the other staid a little longer. . . .

"This evening we ascended toward the upper Part of the Island to John Swains (one who came to our Meetings and there was only one more, that is Stephen Hussie, in all that Island under our name)."

. . . .

"But one night before we returned from this Island my sleep was taken from me under a concern of mind for the Settlement of a Meeting there; (And though there were two Men under the Profession of Truth among them . . . the chief Instrument pointed to in my Thoughts, by the Truth, for this Service, when we should be gone was Mary Starbuck, before mentioned, to whom I made it known, and in the Opening and Mind of Truth laid a Charge upon her to endeavor to have a Meeting established in their Family once a week at least, to wait upon the Lord with all who were convinced of Truth in the Neighborhood, and in the Island as they had Conveniency.

"This she received with Christian Gravity and it affected her much and became her Concern.

"Having first mentioned it to the Friends who were with me I proposed it likewise to her Children (her Husband being freely passive only in such Things, and naturally good temper'd) who were all discreet young

Men and Women, most of them married and hopeful; being all convinced of Truth, they were ready to embrace the Proposal.

"Then I advised them to wait sincerely upon the Lord in such Meetings (for they had no instrumental Teachers) and assured them that I had a firm Confidence in the Lord that he would visit them by his Holy Spirit in them, in his own Time, if they were faithful, held on and did not faint or look back.

"And accordingly, some time after we departed the Island, they did meet, and the Lord did visit them and gathered many unto himself, and they became a large and living Meeting in Him and several living and able Ministers were raised by the Lord in that Family, and of others, to the Honour of His own Arm, who is worthy forever."

The fact that each of the three ministers—Thomas Chalkley, John Richardson and Thomas Story—in turn felt satisfied that his visit brought about the awakening which led to the large meetings of Friends on Nantucket, is most natural.

The account of each in his journal is the best record we have, and indicates that in 1698, in 1701 and in 1704 there was a considerable revival among many of those people, and the encouragement given to each missionary was sufficient excuse for the satisfaction expressed.*

---

*As early as 1664, "Jane Stoakes," an Englishwoman, visited the island, and in a written record, accompanied by dates and believed to be authentic, Jane Stoakes is referred to as the first visiting Friend; again, in 1688, a Friend, who is not named, visited the settlement.

From such detail we conclude that the tendencies were strong towards Quakerism before the beginning of the eighteenth century, during which the principles of the Society of Friends were embraced by a large majority of the people.

Friends' Records of Nantucket Monthly Meeting state that it was established in 1708.

The following is a copy of the "minute of petition" of the Nantucket Friends, sent to Rhode Island Yearly Meeting:

"To Friends at ye yearly Meeting to be held on Rhoad Island

"Pursuant to ye good order of Truth as we have been informed by our friends Ebenezer Rocomb & Patrick Henderson & by whose advice also We do think it Would be for ye good of friends here to have a monthly meeting of bufiness among ourselves uppon this island of Nantucket hoping it Will tend to our Comfort & Preservation. We do Propose to friends at ye yearly meeting to be held on Rhoad Island ye 11-12 & 13 Days of ye 4 month nex yt if they see good it should be so they may make an Entry thereof, but if they see cause otherwise then Leave without making any Entry: & if friends alow us to have one, then to advise us what Quarterly meeting may be thought most convenient for us to be Joyned unto yt there we may apply ourselves in any necessary matter as we may have ocafion. and farther we do think it would be of Good service & acceptable to us if friends think Good yt we should have a General meeting for worship once in ye year & if fuiting With friends convenience to be in ye same month which ye yearly meeting on Rhoad Island is held on, as soon as possible after ye said yearly meeting is ended. So with the salutation of our Love to you We conclude your friends.

" Signed With advice of friends here by

Mary Starbuck	Nathl Starbuck Jr
Ann Trott	Stephen Hussey
Dorcas Starbuck	Jethro Starbuck
Priscilla Coleman	Barnabas Starbuck
	John Coleman Jr

" Nantucket y^e 26 day of y^e 3 $\frac{o}{m}$ 1708."

For many years the Society prospered, and its large meeting-houses were well filled.

The experience of Nantucket has been a repetition of the history of the Society of Friends in many localities; other religious denominations have attracted the younger people, and the older members, one by one, have passed from works to rewards, until at present no member of the Society of Friends resides on Nantucket.

In 1894 one meeting-house on the island was sold, and is at present the property of the Historical Society. Since that date the last meeting-house belonging to Friends has been sold to another denomination.

A Nantucket Street.

CHAPTER XVI.

AN IMPARTIAL JUDGMENT.

A PENNSYLVANIAN writing of Nantucket one hundred years after the settlement, having visited the island for the purpose of studying its manners and customs, says,—

". . . Here we have none but those which administer to the useful, to the necessary and to the indispensable comforts of life . . . The inhabitants abhor the very idea of expending in useless waste and vain luxuries the fruits of prosperous labor. . . . At home the tender minds of the children must be early struck with the gravity, the serious, though cheerful deportment of their parents; they are inured to a principle of subordination arising neither from sudden passions nor inconsistent pleasure. They are corrected with tenderness, nursed with most affectionate care, clad with that decent plainness from which they observe their parents never to depart; in short by the force of example, more than by precept, they learn to follow the steps of their parents and to despise ostentatiousness as being sinful. They acquire a taste for that neatness for which their fathers are so conspicuous; they learn to be prudent and saving; the very tone of voice in which they are addressed establishes them in that softness of diction which ever after becomes habitual. If they are left with fortunes, they know how to save them, and how to enjoy them with moderation and decency; if they have none they know how to venture; how to work and toil as their parents have done before them. . . . As the sea excursions are often very long, the wives are necessarily obliged to transact business, to settle accounts, and, in short, to rule and provide for their families. These circumstances being oft repeated give women the ability, as well as the taste for that kind of superintendency to which, by their prudence and good management, they seem to be in general very equal. This ripens their judgment and justly entitles them to a rank superior to other wives. To this dexterity in managing their husband's business whilst he is absent, the Nantucket women unite a great deal of industry. They spin or cause to be spun, abundance of wool and flax, and would be forever disgraced and looked upon as idlers, if all the family were not clad in good, neat and sufficient homespun cloth. First days are the only seasons when it is lawful for both sexes to exhibit garments of English manufacture, and even these are of the most moderate price and of the gravest colors."

This being the judgment of an outsider surely was impartial, and all of Nantucket descent will be willing to accept the views of a writer so flattering, especially as we have no means of judging of those times excepting by tradition.

Nearly one hundred and fifty added years have wrought many changes, and still we find a justifiable pride in all who claim descent from Mary Starbuck and her contemporaries.

If " the evil that men do lives after them," the lives of the early settlers must have been exceptionally ex-

A Nantucket Garden.

emplary; there seems to be little recorded discreditable to any of them.

Necessity made them what they were; there could be no idle hands among them; they must work or they must starve; and, at a very early date, the peace of a Quaker influence spread over them proportionate to that of Colonial Philadelphia, and to-day may be heard even among those who belong to the so-called " world's people " " the Thee and the Thou of the Quaker."

DETAIL OF DESCENT
FROM PROPRIETORS AND SETTLERS.

KEY TO REFERENCES.

In the following genealogical pages the small letters in the margin refer to the authorities in the code given below.

The *volume* and *page* are printed with the date in the marginal note.

Names in italics indicate that the ancestor so designated descends from one or more of the early settlers or their associates and that the detail of her ascent to said settler will in its turn be given.

CODE.

- a—Nantucket Town Records.
- b—Nantucket Probate Court Records.
- c—Nantucket Friends' Marriages.
    - c S—Sandwich Friends' Marriages.
    - c L—Lynn Friends' Marriages.
    - c N B—New Bedford Friends' Marriages.
    - c N C—North Carolina Friends' Marriages.
- d—Nantucket Friends' List of Members (births and deaths).
    - d S—Sandwich Friends' Births and Deaths.
    - d L—Lynn Friends' Births and Deaths.
    - d N B—New Bedford Friends' Births and Deaths.
    - d N C—North Carolina Friends' Births and Deaths.
- e—Published Genealogies.
    - e C—Coffin Family, by Allen Coffin.
    - e Cl—Coleman Family, by Silas B. Coleman.
    - e N C—Clarke Family (Descendants of Nathaniel Clarke).
    - e H—Hazard Family.
    - e K—Kimball Family.
    - e S—Swain Family.
    - e Sr—Sears Family.
    - e W—Wing Family, edition of 1881.
- f—Savage's New England Families.
- g—New England Historical and Genealogical Register.
- h—Macy Genealogy.
- i—One Hundred and Sixty Allied Families (Austin's).
- j—Rhode Island Genealogical Dictionary (Austin's).
- k—Wyman's Charlestown Estates.
- l—Otis's Barnstable Families.
- m—Barker Family, by Barker Newhall.
- m—(without figures) Barker Chart, by Barker Newhall.
- n—MSS. of Wm. C. Folger, of Nantucket.
- o—Arnold's Vital Statistics of Rhode Island.
- p—Boyd's History of Watertown (Mass.).
- q—American Ancestry.

r—History of Hingham, Mass.
s—Dow's History of Hampton, N. H.
t—Hoyt's Old Families of Salisbury and Amesbury.
u—Family MSS.
    u M—Mitchell Family MSS., by Rebecca G. Mitchell.
    u St—Stanton Family MSS.
    u Cr—Cornell Family MSS.
v—Hobart Memorial.
x—Shattuck Memorial.
y—Nantucket Inquirer, 1862, Gardner Family, by W. C. Folger.
z—Freeman's Cape Cod.
+ After.
— Before.
± About.

NOTE.—One who has no knowledge of Nantucket will find what will appear a needless repetition in the family lines given, but the Mary Coffins, Mary Starbucks, etc., were almost legion in different generations, therefore, for absolute clearness, "daughter of," etc., will be repeated in each instance.

CHAPTER XVII.

THE MITCHELL FAMILY.

There is a theory entertained by this family that its early history was located in Scotland, but Richard Mitchell, the first of the name of whom we have any record, lived at Brixton or Bricktown, Isle of Wight, and married Mary Wood.

The absence of records of this family on the beautiful island, which was the home of our ancestor, indicates that he immigrated there; his son Richard, born 1686, came to Rhode Island in 1708, and in the same year married Elizabeth Tripp; he died in 1722.

He was educated in the doctrines of the Church of England, and spent some time in the Royal Navy, but after coming to America became convinced of the principles of the Society of Friends.

One of his descendants says of him: "The firmness with which Richard Mitchell adhered to the religious faith he early adopted, the honesty and integrity that were maintained in all his transactions, the tender, thoughtful care for the welfare of his wife and young family, are striking traits which are inherited by many of his descendants.

" . . . He was blessed with a good understanding and sound judgment, and was capable of assisting and advising in matters of difficulty."

b. 2. 9, 1759 m. 12. 30, 1779 d. 11. 2, 1831	d 153 c ii. 280 d 153	Peleg Mitchell, Sr., married Lydia Cartwright.	b. 1. 10, 1762 (d 49) d. 2. 11, 1833 (d 158)
b. 7. 4, 1710 m. 12. 26, 1730-1 d. 10. 5, 1787	uM c l. 54 d 153	Peleg Mitchell, Sr., was son of Richard [3] Mitchell and Mary *Starbuck*.	b. 7. 8, 1715 (d 196) d. 10. 21, 1780 (d 153)
b. ± 1686 m. 1708 d. 1722	uM uM o 4	Richard [3] Mitchell was son of Richard [2] Mitchell and Elizabeth *Tripp*.	b. ± 1685 d. Feb. 13, 1740 (o)

m.	} uM	Richard [2] Mitchell was son of RICHARD [1] MITCHELL and Mary Wood.	
b. 1671 m. 10. 6, 1694 d. 8. 12, 1770	} a i. 5 d 196	Mary Starbuck was daughter of Jethro Starbuck and Dorcas *Gayer*.	{ b. 8. 29, 1675 (a i. 2) d. 10. 11, 1747 (d 196)
b. ± 1635 m. 1662 d. 6. 6, 1719	} a i. 11	Jethro Starbuck was son of Nathaniel Starbuck, Sr., and Mary *Coffin*.	{ b. Feb. 20, 1745 d. Sept. 13, 1717 (g xxiv. 150; a i. 11)
b. ± 1604 d. 12. 4, 1690	} a i. 4	Nathaniel Starbuck, Sr., was son of EDWARD STARBUCK and Katharine Reynolds.	
b. ± 1656 m. Jan.19,1681-2 d. May 3, 1730	} o iv. 45	Elizabeth Tripp was daughter of JAMES TRIPP and Mercy *Lawton*.	{ d. 1685 (eH)
b. 1628 d. 1678	} j 208 j 208; o	James Tripp was son of JOHN TRIPP and Mary *Paine*.	{ d. Feb. 12, 1687 (j 208)
d. Sep. 23, 1710 Will proved Oct. 24, 1710	} b A i. 26	Dorcas Gayer was daughter of WILLIAM GAYER and Dorcas *Starbuck*.	{ d. 1696 (11)
b. ± 1605 m. ± 1630 d. Oct. 2, 1681	} g xxiv.150 a i. 3	Mary Coffin was daughter of TRISTRAM COFFIN and Dionis Stevens.	{ d. + 1682 (eC)
	} eH	Mercy Lawton was daughter of GEORGE LAWTON and Elizabeth *Hazzard*.	
d. 1650	} j 208	Mary Paine was daughter of ANTHONY PAINE and Susanna ——.	
		Dorcas Starbuck was daughter of EDWARD STARBUCK and Katharine Reynolds.	
b. 1610 d. 1680	} eH	Elizabeth Hazard was daughter of THOMAS HAZARD and Martha ——.	{ d. 1669 (eH)
b. July 8, 1735 m. 2nd mo. 8, 1759 d. 10. 29, 1822	} h 94 d 49	Lydia Cartwright was daughter of James Cartwright and Love *Macy*.	{ b. June, 1740 d. Jan. 7, 1808 (h 93)

The Mitchell Family.

b. 1. 11, 1707 m. Mar.7, 1731-2 d. 5. 15, 1791 } a l. 28	James Cartwright was son of Hezediah Cartwright and Abigail Brown.	{ b. d. 9. 21, 1797 (n)
b. Jun. 26, 1677 } a i. 3	Hezediah Cartwright was son of Sampson Cartwright and Bethiah *Pratt*.	{ b. Feb. 11, 1679-80 d. 10. 19, 1741 (k l. 193)
d. 7. 2, 1705 } u l. 5	Sampson Cartwright was son of EDWARD CARTWRIGHT and Elizabeth Trott.	{ d. Aug. 11, 1729 (2d wife) (n)
b. June 2, 1715 m. May 30, 1738 d. May 21, 1793 } h 78, 94 e i. 90 h	Love Macy was daughter of Francis Macy and Judith *Coffin*.	{ b. Sept. 19, 1719 d. May 15, 1799 (h 94)
b. ± 1687 m. June 18, 1718 d. Mar. 16, 1759 } h 68 a h 68	Francis Macy was son of Thomas Macy and Deborah *Coffin*.	{ b. d. Sept. 23, 1760 (h 79)
b. July 14, 1655 m. d. Oct. 14, 1691 } h 67 h 67	Thomas Macy was son of John Macy and Deborah *Gardner*.	{ b. Feb. 12, 1658 d. 1712 (h 68)
b. 1608 d. 4. 19, 1682 } a l. 4	John Macy was son of THOMAS MACY and Sarah Hopcot.	{ b. 1612 d. 1706 (h 67)
b. Feb. 12, 1674-5 m. d. Dec. 24, 1712 } g xvi. 270 k ii. 771	Bethiah Pratt was daughter of Joseph Pratt and Dorcas *Folger*.	
b. ± 1590 d. April 19,1680 } k ii. 778 k ii. 771	Joseph Pratt was son of PHINEAS PRATT and Mary Priest.	{ d. + 1681-2 (k ii. 771)
b. June 12, 1694 m. d. Mar. 4, 1768 } g xxiv. 306 g xxiv. 306	Judith Coffin was daughter of Richard Coffin and Ruth *Bunker*.	
b. m. d. July1,1747 } g xxiv. 306	Richard Coffin was son of JOHN COFFIN, ESQ., and Hope *Gardner*.	{ b. 1669 d. Oct. 12, 1750 (g xxiv. 306.)
b. Aug. 12, 1640 m. Nov.or Dec. 3, 1663. d. July 23, 1720 } g xxiv. 151 eK 32 g xxiv. 151	John Coffin, Esq., was son of JAMES COFFIN and Mary Severance.	{ b. Aug. 5, 1645 (eK 32)
b. ± 1605 m. ± 1630 d. Oct. 2, 1681 } g xxiv. ib. (150 ib.; a l.3	James Coffin was son of TRISTRAM COFFIN and Dionis Stevens.	{ d. + 1682 (eC)

b. Oct. 30, 1647
m.
d. Sept. 5, 1711 } g xxiv. 151
g xxiv. 151
	Deborah Coffin was daughter of
	    LIEUTENANT JOHN COFFIN and Deborah *Austin*.
	Lieutenant John Coffin was son of
	    TRISTRAM COFFIN and Dionis Stevens.
		{ b.
		d. Feb. 4, 1718
		(g xxiv. 152)

b. 1626 m. 1652 d. Jan. 23, 1688 } x 361 x 361; i 101 a i. 4	Deborah Gardner was daughter of RICHARD GARDNER and Sarah *Shattuck*.	{ b. 1632 d. 1724

Richard Gardner was son of
    THOMAS GARDINER and Margaret Frier.

Dorcas Folger was daughter of
    PETER FOLGER and Mary Morrell.

Mary Priest was daughter of
    DEGORY PRIEST and Sarah (Allerton) (Vincent) Priest.

Ruth Bunker was daughter of
    Jonathan Bunker and Elizabeth *Coffin*.
Jonathan Bunker was son of
    William Bunker and Mary *Macy*.
William Bunker was son of
    George Bunker and Jane Godfrey.
George Bunker was son of
    WILLIAM BUNKER (Bon Cœur).

Hope Gardner was daughter of
    RICHARD GARDNER and Sarah *Shattuck*.
Richard Gardner was son of
    THOMAS GARDINER and Margaret Frier.

Deborah Austin was daughter of
    JOSEPH AUSTIN and Sarah *Starbuck*.

Elizabeth Coffin was daughter of
    JAMES COFFIN and Mary Severance.
James Coffin was son of
    TRISTRAM COFFIN and Dionis Stevens.

Mary Macy was daughter of
    THOMAS MACY and Sarah Hopcot.

Sarah Shattuck was daughter of
—— SHATTUCK and Damaris ——.   { (x 361)

Sarah Starbuck was daughter of
EDWARD STARBUCK and Katharine Reynolds.

Descendants of Peleg Mitchell, Sr., and Lydia Cartwright, descend also from:
Richard Mitchell,
Edward Starbuck (three times),
Tristram Coffin (four times),
James Coffin (twice),
John Coffin, Esq.,
Lieutenant John Coffin,
Thomas Gardiner (twice),
Richard Gardner (twice),
Joseph Austin,
John Tripp,
James Tripp,
William Gayer,
George Lawton,
Thomas Hazard,
Anthony Paine,
Thomas Macy (twice),
Phineas Pratt,
Degory Priest (Mayflower signer, 29th),
Edward Cartwright,
William Bunker (French Huguenot),
Peter Folger.

Mrs. Mary A. Woodbridge, daughter of Judge Brayton and Love (Mitchell) Brayton, and grand-daughter of Peleg Mitchell, Sr., and Lydia (Cartwright) Mitchell, was a lineal descendant (on the maternal side) of all the above-named settlers of Nantucket, and on the paternal side of Christopher Hussey.

She was the first president of the Woman's Christian Temperance Union of Ohio, and later, recording secretary of the National and World's Temperance Unions, and gave her time and life (dying while in the service of the Union) to the cause which she had espoused. While she was an enthusiast, she was in no sense a fanatic, being governed always by strong common sense, and a dignity which was nature's gift. She traveled extensively, and often addressed large audiences, in addition to her close and conscientious work with the pen in the discharge of her duties as secretary.

Professor Maria Mitchell (see chapter on Peter Folger) was another granddaughter of Peleg Mitchell, Sr., and Lydia (Cartwright) Mitchell.

From the "History of the Hazard Family" we learn that Thomas Hazard, progenitor of the Hazard family in America, was born in 1610, and died in 1680. He married first, Martha ———, who died in 1669; second, Martha, widow of Thomas Sheriff. She died in 1691.

On March 25th, 1638, he was admitted freeman in Boston; two years later freeman in Portsmouth, Rhode Island.

In 1639, he with eight others, signed a compact for the settlement of Newport, Rhode Island. September 2d, 1639, he was admitted freeman of Newport. In 1640, March 12th, he was appointed a member of the General Court of Elections.

His will, proved 1680, leaves Martha, whom he calls "his beloved yoke-fellow," as his sole executor.

George Lawton, of Portsmouth, Rhode Island, was admitted inhabitant of Aquidneck in 1638; he married Elizabeth, daughter of Thomas Hazard.

In 1648 he was a member of the Court of Trials.

In 1665, '72, '75, '76, '79, '80, Deputy.

His daughter, Mercy Lawton, married, January 19th, 1682, James Tripp, son of John Tripp and Susanna Paine. Mercy (Lawton) Tripp died in 1685.

John Tripp, born 1610, of Providence and Portsmouth, died 1678. He was one of the Court of Commissioners for 1654, '55, '61, '62, '63. (Rhode Island Colonial Records, Vol. I., pages 281-309, etc.)

Assistant, 1648, '70, '71, '73, '74, '75. (Ibid., Vol. I., page 210; Vol. II., pages 302-373, etc.)

Deputy to General Assembly, 1664, '66, '67, '68, '69, '70, '72. (Ibid., Vol. II., pages 22-150.)

James Tripp, son of John Tripp, was commissioned Ensign on December 25th, 1689, Dartmouth, Mass. (Plymouth Colonial Records, Vol. VI., page 223.)

William Gayer, Esq., spelled also Geare, came from Devonshire, England, was a citizen of Nantucket, and died there on the 23d of September, 1710. He was Judge of Court of Common Pleas, appointed October 16th, 1696; September 7th, 1699; June 29th, 1702, and June 6th, 1706. He was also one of five Judges appointed by the Governor of Massachusetts, in 1704, in the trial of the Indian " Sabo " for the crime of murder. (Mass. Civil List, page 112; New England His. and Gen. Reg., Vol. XXXI., page 237.)

William Gayer, of the firm of Gayer & Bunker, was especially able as a surveyor and " laid out plots."

Edward Cartwright, the first of the Nantucket family of that name, came from the Isles of Shoals, near Portsmouth, New Hampshire. He settled at Pocomo on Nantucket.

He had two wives. By his will, dated 1705, he gives Pocomo, then owned by him, to his sons Nicholas, Sampson, Edward, and wife Elizabeth. Sampson sold out in 1712 all but the house.

Edward Cartwright, Sr., died September 2d, 1705. Elizabeth Cartwright, his widow, born Trott, sister of John Trott, died August 11th, 1729. (Town Records.)

Degory Priest was the 29th signer of the Mayflower compact.

Prince says: " The year begins with the death of Degory Priest." " Priest is set down in the Leyden records as from London, and had been many years a member of the Leyden Company." " It is on record that he married, November, 1611, Sarah (Allerton) Vincent, widow of John Vincent; November, 1615, he was admitted a citizen of Leyden, and in April, 1619, he deposes that he is forty years of age and knows one Nicholas Claverly." (Leyden MS. Records.) " His widow married Cuthbert Cuthbertson, a Dutchman, who also was one of the Leyden Company, and Winslow calls him Godbert Godbertson, probably the name he owned in early life, and it met with changes which seemed to come to the Pilgrims, and those in marriage connected with them." (Mayflower Signers, Mail and Express, Part II., page 24.)

CHAPTER XVIII.

THE RUSSELL FAMILY.

b. 11. 20, 1754 m. 10, 30, 1777 d. 7. 3, 1825	} d 188 } c ii. 248 } d 190	John Russell, Jr., married Hepzibah *Coleman*.	{ b. 10. 15, 1759 { (d 44) { d. 6. 14, 1834 { (d 190)
b. 12. 3,1731-2 O.S. d. 10. 16, 1789	} c i. 60 } d 188	John Russell, Jr., was son of John Russell, Sr., and Ruth *Starbuck*.	{ b. 12. 24, 1714-5 { (d 17) { d. 10. 5, 1772 { (d 188)
b. 1680 m. Nov. 6, 1705 d. 1763	} n } u iii. 12 } h 68	John Russell, Sr., was son of DANIEL RUSSELL and Deborah *Macy*.	{ b. Mar. 3, 1679 { d. Aug. 16, 1742 { (h 67)

b. Aug., 1668
m. Nov. 20, 1690
d. Jan. 29, 1753
	} a i. 7;
	} g xxiv.
	  151
		Ruth Starbuck was daughter of
		    Nathaniel Starbuck, Jr., and Dinah *Coffin*.
			{ b.
			{ d. Aug. 1, 1750
			{ (g xxiv. 151)

b. ± 1635 m. 1662 d. 6. 6, 1719	} g i. 11 } eC 56 } u i. 11	Nathaniel Starbuck, Jr., was son of Nathaniel Starbuck, Sr., and Mary *Coffin*.	{ b. Feb. 20, 1645 { (g xxiv. 150) { d. 9. 13, 1717 { (u i. 11)
b. ± 1604 d. 12. 4, 1690	} u i. 1	Nathaniel Starbuck, Sr., was son of EDWARD STARBUCK and Katharine Reynolds.	
b. July 14, 1655 d. Oct. 14, 1691	} h 67	Deborah Macy was daughter of John Macy and Deborah *Gardner*.	{ b. Feb. 12, 1658 { d. 1712 { (h 68)
b. 1608 m. 9. 6, 1639 d. 4. 19, 1682	} i 169 ; a	John Macy was son of Thomas Macy and Sarah Hopcot.	{ b. 1612 { d. 1706 { (h 67)

b. Aug. 12, 1640
m. Nov. or
  Dec. 3, 1663
d. July 28, 1720
	} g xxiv.
	  151;
	} eK 32
	} ib.
		Dinah Coffin was daughter of
		    JAMES COFFIN and Mary Severance.
			{ b. Aug. 5, 1645
			{ (eK 32; g xxiv.
			{ 151)

b. ± 1605
m. ± 1630
d. Oct. 2, 1681
	} g xxiv.
	  ib. (150
	} u i. 3
		James Coffin was son of
		    TRISTRAM COFFIN and Dionis Stevens.
			{ b.
			{ d. + 1682

		Mary Coffin was daughter of TRISTRAM COFFIN and Dionis Stevens.	{ d. + 1682 { (eC)
b. ± 1626 m. 1652 d. Jan. 23, 1688	} x 361; } i 101 } a i. 4	Deborah Gardner was daughter of RICHARD GARDNER and Sarah *Shattuck*.	{ b. 1632 { d. 1724

} f ii. 230	Richard Gardner was son of THOMAS GARDINER and Margaret Frier.

	Sarah Shattuck was daughter of —— Shattuck and Damaris ——.	{ (x 361 ; 1 100)

b. 9. 14, 1708 m. 9. 8, 1733 O S d. 6. 23, 1781	} d 42 } c i. 62 } d 42	Hepzibah Coleman was daughter of Barnabas Coleman and Rachel *Hussey*.	{ b. d. 11. 9, 1796 (d 5; 1 144)
b. 8. 2, 1677 m. d. 1. 19, 1762	} i 220 ; } eCl 8 } d 42	Barnabas Coleman was son of John Coleman, Jr., and Priscilla *Starbuck*.	{ d. 3, 14, 1762 (d 42)
b. 1644 Estate settled Mar. 2, 1715-16	} eCl 7 } b i. 36	John Coleman, Jr., was son of John Coleman, Sr., and Joanna *Folger*.	{ d. 5. 18, 1719 (a i. 12)
b. 1602 d. 1685	} f 1. 431	John Coleman, Sr., was son of THOMAS COLEMAN and Susanna ——.	{ d. Nov. 16, 1650 (eCl 6)

b. 5. 13, 1682 m. 12. 7, 1711-2 d. 2. 10, 1767	} a 3 } a i. 19 } i 144	Rachel Hussey was daughter of Sylvanus Hussey and Abial *Brown*.	
b. 1632 m. 10. 8, 1676 d. 4. 2, 1718	} s ii. 761	Sylvanus Hussey was son of STEPHEN HUSSEY and Martha *Bunker*.	{ b. ± 1656 (s ii. 761)
b. 1599 d. 3. 6, 1686	} Eng. Parish Records ; s	Stephen Hussey was son of CHRISTOPHER HUSSEY and Theodate *Batchelder*.	{ b. d. 10., 1649 (s ii. 589)

	Priscilla Starbuck was daughter of Nathaniel Starbuck and Mary *Coffin*.	
d.	} a i. 4	Nathaniel Starbuck was son of EDWARD STARBUCK and Katharine Reynolds.	

d. 1690	} g xvi. 270	Joanna Folger was daughter of PETER FOLGER and Mary Morrell.	{ d. 1704 (g xvi. 270)

		Abial Brown was daughter of John Brown and Rachel *Gardner*.	{ b. 8. 3, 1662 (f ii. 228)
bapt. Sep. 1638	} f 1. 270	John Brown was son of JOHN BROWN and Hannah *Hobart*.	{ b. May 15, 1638 d. Sept. 11, 1691 (f ii. 335)

b.		Martha Bunker was daughter of
d. May 28, 1658 } f l. 299		George Bunker and Jane (Godfrey).

George Bunker was son of
WILLIAM BUNKER.

{ d. 10, 31, 1662 (a l. 1)

Theodate Batchelder was daughter of
REV. STEPHEN BATCHELDER.

b. 1601
d. 1660 } s ii. 589

Mary Coffin was daughter of
TRISTRAM COFFIN and Dionis Stevens.

Rachel Gardner was daughter of
CAPTAIN JOHN GARDNER and Priscilla Grafton.

b.
m. Feb. 20, 1654 } f ii. 228;
d. May, 1706* } 1 101

{ d. — 1717 (b A l. 39)

John Gardner was son of
THOMAS GARDINER and Margaret Frier.

Hannah Hobart was daughter of
Rev. PETER HOBART, who was son of
EDMUND HOBART.

b. 1604
m. 1627
d. Jan. 20, 1679 } v 22
b. ± 1570
m. ± 1597 } f ii. 433
d. Mar. 8, 1646 } v 100

Descendants of John Russell and Hepzibah (Coleman) Russell descend also from:
    Edward Starbuck (twice),
    Thomas Macy,
    James Coffin,
    Tristram Coffin (three times),
    Richard Gardner,
    John Gardner,
    Thomas Gardiner (twice),
    Thomas Coleman,
    Christopher Hussey,
    Peter Folger,
    Rev. Stephen Batchelder,
    Rev. Peter Hobart,
    Edmund Hobart.

---

* Will dated Dec. 2, 1705. First probated Oct. 2, 1706, b A i. 10, 12, 13. Final probate 24 April, 1717, widow Priscilla, being deceased (b A i. 39).

CHAPTER XIX.

THE SWAIN FAMILY.

b. 11. 10, 1745 m. 1. 29, 1767 d. 7. 26, 1814	d 197 c ii. 146 d 200	Francis Swain, Jr., married Lydia *Barker*.	b. 9. 27, 1749 (a l. 77) d. 9. 8, 1833 (d 200)
b. m. 11.31, 1736-7 OS	c l. 80	Francis Swain, Jr., was son of Francis Swain, Sr., and Mary *Paddack*.	d. 4. 26, 1775 (d 170)
b. m. 1. 6, 1711-2 d. 2. 28, 1744 O S	a l. 9 u	Francis Swain, Sr., was son of John Swain, 3d, and Mary *Swett*.	b. Feb. 2, 1689 d. ± 1764 (g vi. 57)
b. Sept. 1, 1664 d. 11. 29, 1730 O S	g xvi.	John Swain, 3d, was son of John Swain, Jr., and Experience *Folger*.	d. 6. 4, 1739 (g xvi.)
m. d. 1717 Will signed Feb. 9, 1714-5	l. 227 b A l. 32	John Swain, Jr., was son of JOHN SWAIN and Mary *Wier*.	d. — 1714 (l 227)
b. 1600 d. Apr. 14, 1682	e S 5 a l. 3	John Swain was son of RICHARD SWAIN and —— ——.	
b. 7. 22, 1677 m. 10. 15, 1706 d. 8., 1756	l 188 b A l. 27, 28	Mary Paddack was daughter of Nathaniel Paddack and Ann *Bunker*.	b. 9. 3, 1686 d. 1. 18, 1767 (l 188)
b. 1636 m. 1659 d. May 1, 1727	l 187 f iii. 328 f iii. 328	Nathaniel Paddack was son of ZECHARIAH PADDACK and Deborah *Sears*.	b. Sept., 1639 (e S r) d. Aug. 17, 1732 (l 187)
d. July 25, 1650	f iii. 328	Zechariah Paddack was son of ROBERT PADDACK and Mary ——.	d. + 1650 (l 187)
b. Sept. 16, 1661 m. May 12, 1687 Will proved Jan. 19, 1731	g vi. 57 s 988 s 988	Mary Swett was daughter of MOSES SWETT and Mary *Hussey*.	b. 11. 8, 1665 (s ii. 761)
b. ± 1626 m. Nov. 1, 1647 d. Jan. 29, 1677	g vi. 50 g vi. 54, 55; s 988	Moses Swett was son of BENJAMIN SWETT and Hester *Weare*.*	b. ± 1629 d. Jan. 16, 1718 (s 988)
d. 1690	g xvi. 270	Experience Folger was daughter of PETER FOLGER and Mary Morrell.	d. 1704 (g xvi. 270)

---

* Hester (Weare) Swett, daughter of Nathaniel Weare, and widow of Benjamin Swett, married Stephen Greenleaf, as second wife. Hester Weare's brother, Nathaniel, married Elizabeth Swain, daughter of Richard Swain.

The Swain Family.

d. Mar. 1680 } a l. 3	Mary Wier was daughter of NATHANIEL WIER or WEARE.	
b. 1648 m. Apr. 11, 1669 } h 67 d. June 6, 1712	Ann Bunker was daughter of William Bunker and Mary *Macy*.	b. Dec. 4, 1648 d. 1729 (h 67)
b. m. d. May 26, 1658 } f l. 299	William Bunker was son of George Bunker and Jane Godfrey.	d. 10. 31, 1662 (a l. 1)
	George Bunker was son of WILLIAM BUNKER.	
b. 1590 m. 1632 } eSr 32 d. Aug. 26, 1676	Deborah Sears was daughter of RICHARD SEARS and Dorothy Thatcher.	d. March 19, 1678-9 (eSr 32)
baptized Feb. 29, 1636 m. 9. 2, 1659 } s ll.760 d. 1711 s ll.761	Mary Hussey was daughter of JOHN HUSSEY and Rebecca Perkins.	b. m. d.
b. 1599 m. d. 3. 6, 1686 } s ll. 759, 760	John Hussey was son of CHRISTOPHER HUSSEY and Theodate *Batchelder*.	b. d. 1649 (s ll. 589)
b. d. Mar. 1, 1680 } a l. 3	Hester Weare was daughter of NATHANIEL WEARE and Sarah ———.	
d. 4. 19, 1682 } a	Mary Macy was daughter of THOMAS MACY and Sarah Hopcot.	b. 1612 d. 1706 (h 67)
b. ± 1561 d. 1660 } s ll. 589	Theodate Batchelder was daughter of REV. STEPHEN BATCHELDER.	

Descendants of Francis Swain and Lydia (Barker) Swain descend also on the paternal side from:
Richard Swain,
John Swain,
Zechariah Paddack,
Benjamin Swett,
Moses Swett,
Peter Folger,
Nathaniel Wier, Wyer, or Weare (twice),

William Bunker,
John Hussey,
Christopher Hussey,
Rev. Stephen Batchelder,
Thomas Macy.

Benjamin Swett, soldier in King Philip's War, Ensign, Lieutenant and Captain (Mass. Col. Records, pages 183, 254 and 338).

N. E. His. and Gen. Reg., Vol. VI., page 54, says: "Mr. Swett acquired great celebrity for his skill and daring in hunting and fighting the Indians, by whom he eventually lost his life while in command of the Massachusetts forces of the East. Swett won for himself a high rank among the heroes of the Colonial wars. He was always in that post which most required sagacity and courage."

Moses Swett, son of Benjamin, was a commissioner on the boundaries between New Hampshire and Massachusetts, 1695. (Provincial papers of New Hampshire, Vol. II., page 168.)

Richard Sears came to America in 1630 with the last of the Scrooby congregation of Leyden, and landed at Plymouth on May 8th.

The tax rates at Plymouth indicate that he was possessed of a large property. He was born in 1590, married Dorothy Thatcher in 1632, was a member of Plymouth Colonial Court in 1662, and died in 1676. Dorothy Sears died in 1680. Their later years were spent in Yarmouth, Mass.

Rev. Barnes Sears, the fifth president of Brown University, Providence, R. I., who succeeded Dr. Wayland in 1855, and held the office until 1867, was a descendant of Richard Sears.

NOTE.—For descent of Lydia Barker see Barker Family, page 155.

CHAPTER XX.

THE BARKER FAMILY.

b. Feb. 23, 1723 } a [. 77
m. Feb. 16, 1744 } d. L. 49

Robert Barker married
First, Jedidah Chase;
Second, Sarah Gardner,* widow of Hezekiah Gardner, and daughter of Abishai Folger and Dinah (Starbuck).

{ b. 2, 15, 1723
(a l. 77)

Children of the first wife were:
Judith Barker,
Margaret Barker,
Lydia Barker,
Mary Barker,
Robert Barker,
James Barker,
Francis Barker.

Children of the second wife were:
Jedidah Barker,
Mary Barker,
Abraham Barker,
Sarah Barker,
Isaac Barker,
Jacob Barker,

b.
m. Jan. 21, 1718 } g xvi.;
d. 2, 1739 } m 18

Robert Barker was son of
Samuel Barker and Bethiah *Folger*.
Samuel Barker was son of
Isaac Barker and Judith *Prence*.

{ b. Nov. 24, 1692
{ d. Jan. 29, 1774
(m 18)

b.
m. Dec. 28, 1665 } m 14
d. ± 1710

---

* Sarah Gardner, widow Hezekiah, had one son, Gideon Gardner.

b. " prob." 1616 d. 1681 } m 12	Isaac Barker was son of ROBERT BARKER and Lucy Williams.		d. bet. Mar. 7, 1681-2, and Feb. 18, 1689 (m 12)
b. 1659 d. 8. 23, 1732, OS } g xvi.	Bethiah Folger was daughter of John Folger and Mary *Barnard*.		b. ± 1667 d. 8. 6, 1737 (g xvi.)
d. 1690 } g xvi. 270	John Folger was son of PETER FOLGER and Mary Morrell.		d. 1704 (g xvi. 270)
b. ± 1601 m. Apr. 1, 1635 d. Mar. 29, 1673 } f iii. 477	Judith Prence was daughter of THOMAS PRENCE and Mary *Collier*.		
b. Jan. 15, 1642-3 } t 49 d. 4. 3, 1718 } a l. 12 Will proved June 11, 1718 } b A L 43	Mary Barnard was daughter of Nathaniel Barnard and Mary *Barnard*.		b. d. 1. 17, 1718 (a l. 12)
b. m. d. ± 1677 } t 49	Nathaniel Barnard was son of THOMAS BARNARD and Eleanor ———.		b. d. Nov. 27, 1694 (t 49)
d. 1671 }	Mary Collier was daughter of WILLIAM COLLIER.		
b. m. d. — 1682 } t 52	Mary Barnard was daughter of ROBERT BARNARD and Joanna Harvey.		d. Mar. 31, 1705 (a l. 38)
b. 1688 m. Oct. 2, 1707 } s 909 a iii. 12	Jedidah Chase, first wife of Robert Barker, was daughter of James Chase and Rachel *Brown*.		
b. April 1, 1650 m. Oct. 5, 1675 d. May 9, 1727 } s 909	James Chase was son of LIEUTENANT ISAAC CHASE and Mary Tilton.		
b. m. d. 1652 } p 404	Isaac Chase was son of THOMAS CHASE and Elizabeth *Philbrick*.		b. d. Feb. 11, 1677 (p 404)
m. } f ii. 288	Rachel Brown was daughter of John Brown and Rachel *Gardner*.		

m. 1658	} f L 271	John Brown was son of JOHN BROWN and Hannah *Hobart*.
b. m. d. ± 1667	} p 404	Elizabeth Philbrick was daughter of THOMAS PHILBRICK and Ann *Knapp*.
b. m. d. May, 1706	} f II. 229 } f II. 230	Rachel Gardner was daughter of CAPTAIN JOHN GARDNER and Priscilla Grafton. John Gardner was son of THOMAS GARDINER and Margaret Frier.
	} v L 103, 104	Hannah Hobart was daughter of REV. PETER HOBART and ———— ————.
d. 1646	} r	Rev. Peter Hobart was son of EDMUND HOBART and Margaret Dewey.
b. ± 1578 d. Aug. 30, 1658	} p 327	Ann Knapp was daughter of WILLIAM KNAPP.

Descendants from Robert Barker [4] and Jedidah (Chase) Barker descend also from:
    Robert Barker,[1]
    Peter Folger,
    Thomas Prence,
    Thomas Barnard,
    Robert Barnard,
    William Collier,
    Isaac Chase,
    Thomas Chase,
    John Brown,
    John Gardner,
    Thomas Gardiner,
    Thomas Philbrick,
    Rev. Peter Hobart,
    Edmund Hobart,
    William Knapp.

b. 10, 27, 1739 }n	Sarah Gardner, second wife of Robert Barker and widow of Hezekiah Gardner, was daughter of	
b. Sept. 27, 1700 } g xvi. m. 2 7m., 1735 } g xvi. d. 1, 22, 1788 } g xvi.	Abishai Folger and Dinah *Starbuck*.	{ b. 5, 23, 1713 (a l. 7) d. Sept. 1, 1798 (g xvi.)
	Abishai Folger was son of	
b. 1678 m. Dec. 29, 1699 } a l. 3 d. 7, 2, 1747 O S } g xvi.	Nathan Folger and Sarah Church.	
	Nathan Folger was son of	
b. 1648 m. 1671 } g xvi. d. 1716	Eleazer Folger and Sarah *Gardner*.	{ d. Dec. 19, 1729 (g xvi.)
	Eleazer Folger was son of	
d. 1690 } g xvi. 270	Peter Folger and Mary Morrell.	{ d. 1704 (g xvi. 270)
b. Feb. 20, 1676 } g xxiv. 152	Dinah Starbuck, widow of Benjamin Starbuck, was daughter of	
m. 9, 21, 1693 } g xxiv. 307	Stephen Coffin, Jr., and Experience *Look*.	{ b. Nov. 22, 1672 (a l. 2) d. 4, 17, 1759 (u)
d. 1725 } g xxiv. 152		
Will proved Aug. 10, 1728 } b l. 123	Stephen Coffin, Jr., was son of	
b. May 11, 1652 d. May 18, 1734 } g xxiv. 150	Stephen Coffin, Sr., and Mary *Bunker*.	{ b. 1652 (f i. 299) d. 1724 (g xxiv. 152)
b. ± 1605 m. ± 1630 d. Oct. 2, 1681 } g xxiv. a L [150	Stephen Coffin, Sr., was son of Tristram Coffin and Dionis Stevens.	
m. 1652 } f ii. 229	Sarah Gardner was daughter of Richard Gardner and Sarah *Shattuck*.	{ b. 1682 d. 1724
	Richard Gardner was son of Thomas Gardiner and Margaret Frier.	
b. 1646 }	Experience Look was daughter of Thomas Look and Elizabeth ——.	
d. May 26, 1658 } f i. 299	Mary Bunker was daughter of George Bunker and Jane Godfrey.	{ d. 10, 31, 1662 (a L 1)
	George Bunker was son of William Bunker.	
	Sarah Shattuck was daughter of —— Shattuck and Damaris ——.	

Descendants of Robert Barker [4] and Sarah (Gardner) Barker descend also from:
  Robert Barker,[1]
  Peter Folger (twice),
  Thomas Prence,
  William Collier,
  Thomas Barnard,
  Robert Barnard,
  Tristram Coffin,
  Stephen Coffin,
  Thomas Gardiner,
  Richard Gardner,
  Thomas Look,
  William Bunker.

CHAPTER XXI.

FAMILY OF LUCRETIA MOTT.

Lucretia Mott was born at Nantucket, January 3d, 1793, and died at her residence on Old York Road, near Philadelphia, November 11th, 1880.

She seems to have possessed many of the characteristics of Mary Starbuck. She was truly womanly, but firm and fearless in her convictions; living during a great crisis, she gave her strength, mentally and physically, to the philanthropic work of righting every wrong which she believed lay in her path of duty.

She was much beloved in the Religious Society of Friends, of which she was a member, and among whom she labored in the ministry for many years.

Her association with Nantucket was not abandoned because at an early age it ceased to be her residence. She visited it frequently, and continued in correspondence through many years with the earnest men and women who, like herself, battled in the cause of freedom for the African race.

A number of her letters to Nathaniel and Eliza Barney, of Nantucket, are published by Mrs. Anna Davis Hallowell in the "Life and Letters of James and Lucretia Mott." Throughout these letters much interest is shown in every cause she loved, much energy displayed in her desire for action, and much charity expressed for those whose early influences had dwarfed or rendered extinct the spirit of philanthropy.

b. 9. 5, 1766 m. 1. 28, 1790	d 43 c ii. 338	Thomas Coffin married Anna Folger.	b. 3. 25, 1771 (d 94)
b. Apr. 3, 1705 m. 4. 29, 1762 d. 11. 3, 1780	g xxiv. 306 c ii. 89 d 43	Thomas Coffin was son of Benjamin Coffin and Deborah *Macy.*	b. Apr. 17, 1726 (b 79) d. 11. 22, 1803 (d 43)

Family of Lucretia Mott.   161

b. 1671 m. Oct. 17, 1692 d. Oct. 29, 1721 } g xxiv. 151	Benjamin Coffin was son of Nathaniel Coffin and Damaris *Gayer*.	b. Oct. 24, 1673 d. Sept. 6, 1764 (g xxiv. 305)

b. Aug. 12, 1640 } g xxiv.
m. Dec. or   151
   Nov., 1720 } eK 32
d. July 28, 1720
	Nathaniel Coffin was son of
	   JAMES COFFIN and Mary Severance.
		b. Aug. 5, 1645
		  (eK 32)
		d.

b. ± 1605 m. ± 1630 } g xxiv. d. Oct. 2, 1681 } a i. (150	James Coffin was son of TRISTRAM COFFIN and Dionis Stevens.	
b. ± 1687 } g xxiv. m. 6. 18, 1718 } a [152 d. Mar. 16, 1759 } g xxiv. 152; h 78	Deborah Macy was daughter of Thomas Macy and Deborah *Coffin*.	b. d. Sept. 23, 1760 (h 79; g xxiv. 152)
b. July 14, 1655 } h 67 m. d. Oct. 14, 1691 } h 67	Thomas Macy was son of John Macy and Deborah *Gardner*.	b. Feb. 12, 1658 d. 1712 (h 68)
d. 4. 19, 1682 } a L 4	John Macy was son of THOMAS MACY and Sarah Hopcot.	b. 1612 d. 1706 (h 67)

b.
Will proved
  Oct. 24, 1710 } b A L 26
	Damaris Gayer was daughter of
	   WILLIAM GAYER and Dorcas *Starbuck*.	

b. ± 1604 m. d. 12. 4, 1690 } a L 4	Dorcas Starbuck was daughter of EDWARD STARBUCK and Katharine Reynolds.	
b. Oct. 30, 1647 d. Sept. 5, 1711 } g xxiv. 151	Deborah Coffin was daughter of LIEUTENANT JOHN COFFIN and Deborah *Austin*.	d. Feb. 4, 1718 (g xxiv. 152)
	Lieutenant John Coffin was son of TRISTRAM COFFIN and Dionis Stevens.	
b. 1626 } x 361 m. 1652 d. Jan. 23, 1668 } a L 4	Deborah Gardner was daughter of RICHARD GARDNER and Sarah *Shattuck*.	
} f II. 230	Richard Gardner was son of THOMAS GARDINER and Margaret Frier.	
b. m. 1659 d. 1683 } f L	Deborah Austin was daughter of Joseph Austin and Sarah *Starbuck*.	
	Sarah Starbuck was daughter of EDWARD STARBUCK and Katharine Reynolds.	
b. 7. 24, 1723 } n m. 10. 7, 1749 O S } c l. 170 d. 1815 } d 94	Anna Folger was daughter of William Folger and Ruth *Coffin*.	b. ± 1733 (n) d. 3. 11, 1814 (d 94)
b. Sept. 27, 1700 } g xvi. m. Nov. 6, 1727 } ib. d. 1. 22, 1778 } d 91	William Folger was son of Abishai Folger and first wife, Sarah *Mayhew*.	d. July 11, 1734 (g xvi.)

b. m. Dec. 29, 1699 d. 7. 2, 1747 O. S. } g xvi.	Abishai Folger was son of Nathan Folger and Sarah Church. Nathan Folger was son of	
b. 1648 m. 1677 } g xvi.	Eleazer Folger and Sarah *Gardner*. Eleazer Folger was son of	{ d. 12. 19, 1729 (n)
d. 1690 } g xvi. 270	PETER FOLGER and Mary Morrell.	{ d. 1704 (g xvi. 270)
	Ruth Coffin was daughter of	
b. June 12, 1694 m. d. Mar. 4, 1768 } g xxiv. 306 ib.	Richard Coffin and Ruth *Bunker*. Richard Coffin was son of	
b. d. July 1, 1747 } g xxiv. 306	JOHN COFFIN, ESQ., and Hope *Gardner*. John Coffin, Esq., was son of	{ b. 1669 d. Oct. 12, 1750 (g xxiv. 306)
b. Aug. 12, 1640 m. Nov. or Dec. 1663 d. July 28, 1728 } eK 32 g xxiv.	JAMES COFFIN and Mary Severance. James Coffin was son of	{ b. Aug. 5, 1645 (eK 32)
b. ± 1605 m. ± 1630 d. Oct. 2, 1681 } g xxiv. 150 a L3	TRISTRAM COFFIN and Dionis Stevens.	{ b. d. + 1682
	Sarah Mayhew was daughter of	
b. m. Dec. 8, 1699 d. 1710 } q x. 106 f iii. 185	Paine Mayhew and Mary Rankin. Paine Mayhew was son of	{ b. Oct. 13, 1677 d. May 8, 1761 (q x. 106)
	Matthew Mayhew and Mary Skiffe. Matthew Mayhew was son of	
	THOMAS MAYHEW, JR., and Jane Paine. Thomas Mayhew, Jr., was son of	{ b. 1621 d. 1657
b. 1591 d. 1681 } f iii. 185	THOMAS MAYHEW, SR.	
	Sarah Gardner was daughter of	
	RICHARD GARDNER and Sarah *Shattuck*. Richard Gardner was son of	
	THOMAS GARDINER and Margaret Frier.	
	Ruth Bunker was daughter of	
Will proved Sept. 13, 1721 } b A l. 89	Jonathan Bunker and Elizabeth *Coffin*. Jonathan Bunker was son of	{ b. d. Mar. 30, 1769 (g xxiv. 151.)
b. m. 4. 11, 1669 d. 6. 26, 1712 } a l. 1	William Bunker and Mary *Macy*. William Bunker was son of	{ b. Dec. 4, 1648 d. 1729 (h 67)
	George Bunker and Jane Godfrey. George Bunker was son of	
	WILLIAM BUNKER.	

Hope Gardner was daughter of
  RICHARD GARDNER and Sarah *Shattuck.*
Richard Gardner was son of
  THOMAS GARDINER and Margaret Frier.

Elizabeth Coffin was daughter of
  JAMES COFFIN and Mary Severance.
James Coffin was son of
  TRISTRAM COFFIN and Dionis Stevens.

Mary Macy was daughter of
  THOMAS MACY and Sarah Hopcot.

Descendants from Thomas Coffin and Anna Folger descend also from:
  Tristram Coffin (four times),
  James Coffin (three times),
  John Coffin, Esq.,
  Peter Folger,
  Richard Gardner (three times),
  Thomas Gardiner (three times),
  Thomas Mayhew, Sr.,
  Thomas Mayhew, Jr.,
  Edward Starbuck (twice),
  Thomas Macy (twice),
  Lieutenant John Coffin,
  William Gayer,
  William Bunker.

The children of Thomas and Anna (Folger) Coffin were:
  Sally Coffin, unmarried.
  Lucretia Coffin, married James Mott.
  Eliza Coffin, married Benjamin H. Yarnall, of Philadelphia.
  Mary Coffin, married Solomon Temple.
  Martha Coffin, married Peter Pelham, of Kentucky, a captain in the United States Army.
  Thomas M. Coffin, unmarried (the only son).

Descendants of Thomas Gardiner may be found in another branch of the Yarnall family.
Edward Yarnall married Caroline R. Cope.

Caroline R. Cope was daughter of
  Thomas Pim Cope and Mary Drinker.
Mary Drinker was daughter of
  John Drinker and Rachel Reynear.
John Drinker was son of
  Henry Drinker and Mary Gottier.
Henry Drinker was son of
  Joseph Drinker and Mary Janney.
Joseph Drinker was son of
  John Drinker, of Beverly, Massachusetts, and Ruth Balch.
Ruth Balch was daughter of
  Benjamin Balch, the first child born in the Massachusetts Bay Colony.
Benjamin Balch married Sarah Gardiner, daughter of Thomas Gardiner. Benjamin Balch, of Salem, was son of John and Anice Balch, a Somersetshire family, which dated from the Conquest. Benjamin Balch was living in 1706.

FAMILY OF JAMES MOTT AND LUCRETIA (COFFIN) MOTT.
Children.
Anna Mott, married Edward Hopper.
Thomas Mott, unmarried.
Maria Mott, married Edward Morris Davis.
Thomas Mott, married Marianna Pelham.
Elizabeth Mott, married Thomas S. Cavender.
Martha Mott, married George W. Lord.

Grandchildren.
CHILDREN OF EDWARD HOPPER AND ANNA (MOTT) HOPPER.
James Hopper,
Lucretia Hopper,

Maria Hopper,
George Hopper,
Isaac Hopper.

CHILDREN OF EDWARD MORRIS DAVIS AND MARIA (MOTT) DAVIS.

Anna Davis, married Richard Price Hallowell.
Henry Corbit Davis, married { 1st, Martha Mellor. 2d, Naomi Lawton.
Charles Davis.
Charles Davis.
William Morris Davis, married Ellen Bliss Warner.

CHILDREN OF THOMAS MOTT AND MARIANNA (PELHAM) MOTT.

Isabel Mott, married Joseph Parrish.
Emily Mott, married George R. Shaw.
Maria Mott.

CHILDREN OF THOMAS S. CAVENDER AND ELIZABETH (MOTT) CAVENDER.

Fanny Cavender, married Thomas Parrish.
Henry Cavender.
Charles Cavender.
Mary Cavender, married William J. Wilcox.

CHILDREN OF GEORGE W. LORD AND MARTHA (MOTT) LORD.

Ellen Lord, married Bernard De Schweinitz.
Bessie Lord.
Mary Mott Lord, married Julian Rumsey Linkham.
Anna Lord, married Herbert M. Lloyd.
Lucretia Lord, married Albert Strauss.

CHAPTER XXII.

FAMILIES OF THOMAS EARLE AND JOHN MILTON EARLE.

b. 10. 9, 1766 m. 10. 1, 1789 d. 1802	} d 133 } c ii. 332 } n	Uriel Hussey married Phebe Folger.	
b. 2. 6, 1753 m. 11. 6, 1777 d. 10. 10, 1822	} d 133 } c ii. 249 } n	Tristram Hussey married Sarah Folger.	
		Uriel Hussey was son of George Hussey.	
		Tristram Hussey was son of Batchelder or Bachiler Hussey.	

b. 7. 12, 1738
m. 2. 3, 1757
d. 9. 23, 1804
	} c ii. 25
	} n
		George Hussey and Batchelder Hussey
		   were brothers and sons of
			{ b. 11. 29, 1728-9
			{ (d 132)
			{ m. 10. 29, 1744
			  (c L 157)

b. May 13, 1682 m. 9. 8, 1723 d. 2. 10, 1767	} a l. 3 } c ii. 25 } d 132	Sylvanus Hussey, Sr., and Hepzibah *Starbuck*. Sylvanus Hussey was son of	{ b. 9. 8, 1700 O S { (d 196) { d. 12. 31, 1764 (d. 132)
b. 1632 m. 10. 8, 1676 d.	} s ii. 761	Stephen Hussey and Martha *Bunker*.	{ b. ± 1656 { d. (s ii. 761)

b. 1599
m.
d. 3. 6, 1686
	} Eng.
	} Parish
	} Records; s
		Stephen Hussey was son of
		   Christopher Hussey and Theodate *Batchelder*.
			{ d. 10, 1649
			  (s ii. 589)

b. Aug., 1668
m. Nov. 20, 1690
d. Jan. 29, 1753
	} g xxiv.
	} 151
	} ib.; d 196
		Hepzibah Starbuck was daughter of
		   Nathaniel Starbuck, Jr., and Dinah *Coffin*.
		Nathaniel Starbuck, Jr., was son of
			{ b.
			{ d. Aug. 1, 1750
			  (g xxiv. 151;
			  d 196)

b. ± 1634
m. 1662
d. 6. 6, 1719
	} a l. 11
	} eC 56
	} a l. 11
		Nathaniel Starbuck, Sr., and Mary *Coffin*.
		Nathaniel Starbuck, Sr., was son of
			{ b. Feb. 20, 1645
			{ d. Sept. 13, 1717
			  (g xxiv. 150;
			  a l. 11)

b. ± 1604 m. d. 12. 4, 1690	} a l. 4	Edward Starbuck and Katharine Reynolds.	

		Martha Bunker was daughter of
		   George Bunker and Jane Godfrey.
			{ d. 10. 31, 1662
			  (a l. 1)

d. May 26, 1658	} f l. 299	George Bunker was son of William Bunker.	

NOTE.—George Hussey's wife was Deborah Paddack, a descendant of Zechariah Paddack, who married Deborah Sears, of Yarmouth, a daughter of Richard Sears.

{ b. 1. 30, 1739
{ d. 12. 12, 1815
  (c ii. 25)

b. 1561 d. 1660	} s ii. 589	Theodate Batchelder was daughter of REV. STEPHEN BATCHELDER.	
b. Aug. 12, 1640 m. Nov. or Dec. 3, 1663 d. July 28, 1720	g xxiv. 151 ib.; eK ib. [32	Dinah Coffin was daughter of JAMES COFFIN and Mary Severance.	b. Aug. 5, 1645 (eK 32) d.
b. ± 1605 m. ± 1630 d. Oct. 2, 1681	g xxiv. 150 a l. 3	James Coffin was son of TRISTRAM COFFIN and Dionis Stevens.	b. d. + 1682 (eC)
		Mary Coffin was daughter of TRISTRAM COFFIN and Dionis Stevens.	
b. 9. 21, 1768 b. 3. 24, 1757	} d 94 } d 94	Phebe Folger } were sisters of Anna Folger Sarah Folger (the mother of Lucretia Mott) and their descent from early settlers of Nantucket, being identical with that of Anna Folger, will be found on a previous page, under "Family of Lucretia Mott."	b. 3. 25, 1771 (d 94)
m. 7. 13, 1820 m. 6. 6, 1821	} c iii. 7 } c iv. 74	Uriel Hussey's daughter Mary married Thomas Earle. Tristram Hussey's daughter Sarah married John Milton Earle.	

Descendants from them descend also from:
Edward Starbuck,
Christopher Hussey,
Stephen Hussey,
Rev. Stephen Batchelder,
Peter Folger,
James Coffin (three times),
Tristram Coffin (four times),
Thomas Mayhew, Sr.,
Thomas Mayhew, Jr.,
Richard Gardner (twice),
Thomas Gardiner (twice),
Thomas Macy,
William Bunker (twice).

Children of Thomas and Mary Earle have intermarried with the families of Van Leer, of Chester County; Earle, of Massachusetts; Gibbons, of Pennsylvania; and White, of Londonderry, Ireland.

CHAPTER XXIII.

SWIFT FAMILY.

m. 9. 5, 1821 } c iv. 75	Dr. Paul Swift married Dorcas Gardner, daughter of	b. 4. 2, 1798 (d 39) / d. 1877
b. 2. 11, 1769 } d 114 m. 9. 30, 1790 } c ii. 342 d. 1848	Zenas Gardner and Susanna Hussey.	b. 4. 24, 1771 (d 133) / d. 2. 7, 1842 (d 39)
	Zenas Gardner was son of	
b. 1730 m. 2. 7, 1754 O S } c l. 223 d. 3. 17, 1813 } d 114	Paul Gardner and Rachel *Starbuck*.	b. 4. 20, 1735 (a l. 54) / d. 8. 29, 1775 (d 114)
b. July 1, 1680 } a l. 3 d. June 17, 1760 } g xxiv. 152	Paul Gardner was son of Solomon Gardner and Anna *Coffin*.	b. — / d. 22 Apr. 1740 (g xxiv. 152)
b. Oct. 23, 1653 m. May 17, 1674 } y Will signed 20 Jan. 1727-8; proved July 17, 1728 (b A l. 135)	Solomon Gardner was son of Richard Gardner and Mary *Austin*.	d. June 1, 1721 O S (y)
b. ± 1626 } x 361 m. — 1652 } c l. 223 d. Jan. 23, 1688 } a l. 4	Richard Gardner was son of RICHARD GARDNER and Sarah *Shattuck*.	b. 1632 / d. 1724
} f ii. 230	Richard Gardner was son of THOMAS GARDINER and Margaret Frier.	
b. 10. 12, 1706 } a l. 8 m. 10. 2, 1728 OS } c i. 36 d. 1777 } d 196	Rachel Starbuck was daughter of Thomas Starbuck and Rachel *Allen*.	b. 12. 31, 1709 (a l. 7) / d. 5. 31, 1789 (d 196)
b. 1671 } uM m. 10, 1694 } a l. 7 d. 8. 12, 1770 } d 196	Thomas Starbuck was son of Jethro Starbuck and Dorcas *Gayer*.	b. 8. 29, 1675 (a l. 2) / d. 10. 11, 1747 (d 196)
b. ± 1635 } a l. 11 m. 1662 } eC 56 d. 6. 6, 1719 } a l. 11 ; g xxiv. 150	Jethro Starbuck was son of Nathaniel Starbuck, Sr., and Mary *Coffin*.	b. Feb. 20, 1643 / d. 9. 13, 1717 (g xxiv. 150; a l. 11)
b. ± 1604 } a l. 4 d. 12. 4, 1690	Nathaniel Starbuck, Sr., was son of EDWARD STARBUCK and Katharine Reynolds.	
b. May 11, 1652 } g xxiv. 150 d. May 18, 1734	Anna Coffin was daughter of Stephen Coffin and Mary *Bunker*.	b. ± 1652 (f l. 299) / d. 1724 (g xxiv. 152)
b. ± 1605 } g xxiv. 150 m. ± 1630 } ib. d. Oct.2, 1681 } ib. ; a l. 3	Stephen Coffin was son of TRISTRAM COFFIN and Dionis Stevens.	d + 1682 (eC)
b. — m. — 1659 } f l d. 1663	Mary Austin was daughter of JOSEPH AUSTIN and Sarah *Starbuck*.	

		Sarah Shattuck was daughter of —— Shattuck and Damaris ——.	
d. 1741	}	Rachel Allen was daughter of Edward Allen and Ann *Coleman*.	{ b. Nov. 10, 1675 (eCl 7) d. 1739
Will signed 21 Sept. 1710; proved Oct. 24, 1710	} b A l. 26	Dorcas Gayer was daughter of WILLIAM GAYER and Dorcas *Starbuck*.	{ b. d. 1696 (n)
		Mary Coffin was daughter of TRISTRAM COFFIN and Dionis Stevens.	
d. May 26, 1658	} f l. 299	Mary Bunker was daughter of George Bunker and Jane Godfrey. George Bunker was son of WILLIAM BUNKER.	{ d. Oct. 31, 1662 (a L 1)
b. ± 1604 d. 12. 4, 1690	} a L 4	Sarah Starbuck was daughter of EDWARD STARBUCK and Katharine Reynolds.	
b. Dec. 2, 1642 d. 1690	} eCl	Ann Coleman was daughter of Joseph Coleman and Ann *Bunker*.	{ b. ± 1654 (f l. 299)
b. 1602 d. 1685	} f l. 481	Joseph Coleman was son of THOMAS COLEMAN and Susanna ——.	{ d. Nov. 10, 1650 (eCl 6)
		Dorcas Starbuck was daughter of EDWARD STARBUCK and Katharine Reynolds.	
		Ann Bunker was daughter of George Bunker and Jane Godfrey. George Bunker was son of WILLIAM BUNKER.	
b. 5. 12, 1738 m. 2. 3, 1757 d. 1805	} d 132 c ii. 25	Susanna Hussey was daughter of George Hussey and Deborah *Paddack*.	{ b. 1. 30, 1739 (d 179) d.

Swift Family. 171

b. May 13, 1682 m. 9. 8, 1723 d. 2. 10, 1707 } a l. 3 c l. 25 d 132	George Hussey was son of Sylvanus Hussey and Hepzibah *Starbuck*.	b. Nov. 8, 1700 (a l. 7) d. 12. 31, 1764 (d 132)
b. 1630 m. 10. 8, 1676 d. 4. 2, 1718 } s ll. 761	Sylvanus Hussey was son of STEPHEN HUSSEY and Martha *Bunker*.	b. ± 1656 (f l. 299) d. 9. 21, 1743 (s ll. 761)
b. 1599 m. d. 3. 6, 1686 } Eng. Parish Records; s	Stephen Hussey was son of CHRISTOPHER HUSSEY and Theodate *Batchelder*.	d. 10, 1649 (s ll. 589)
d. Lost at sea 1743 } d 179	Deborah Paddack was daughter of Daniel Paddack and Susanna *Gorham*.	d. 7. 13, 1777 (d 179)
b. 9. 22, 1677 d. 1756 } b A l. 27, 28	Daniel Paddack was son of Nathaniel Paddack and Ann *Bunker*.	b. 9. 3, 1686 d. 1. 18, 1767 (1 188)
m. 1659 } f lll. 328	Nathaniel Paddack was son of ZECHARIAH PADDACK and Deborah *Sears*.	b. 1639 (eSr)
d. July 25, 1650 } f lll. 328	Zechariah Paddack was son of ROBERT PADDACK and Mary ———.	d. + 1650 (l 187)
b. Aug 9, 1668 m. Nov. 20, 1690 d. Jan. 29, 1753 } a l. 1 g xxiv. 151	Hepzibah Starbuck was daughter of Nathaniel Starbuck, Jr., and Dinah *Coffin*.	d. Aug. 1, 1750 (g xxiv. 151)
b. ± 1634-5 m. 1662 d. 6. 6, 1719 } a l. 11 eC a l. 11	Nathaniel Starbuck, Jr., was son of Nathaniel Starbuck, Sr., and Mary *Coffin*.	b. Feb. 20, 1645 d. 9. 13, 1717 (g xxiv. 150; a l. 11)
	Nathaniel Starbuck, Sr., was son of EDWARD STARBUCK and Katharine Reynolds.	
d. May 26, 1658 } f l. 299	Martha Bunker was daughter of George Bunker and Jane Godfrey.	d. Oct. 31, 1662 (a l. 1)
	George Bunker was son of WILLIAM BUNKER.	
b. 1561 d. 1660 } s ll. 589	Theodate Batchelder was daughter of REV. STEPHEN BATCHELDER.	
b. 23 June 1683 m. Dec. 25, 1703 d. 1743 } l 420	Susanna Gorham was daughter of Stephen Gorham and Elizabeth *Gardner*.	d. 1763
b. m. 2. 24, 1675 d. 1715 } l 183	Stephen Gorham was son of John Gorham and Mary *Otis*.	b. 3. 14, 1654 (l 183) d. 4. 1, 1732
bapt. 28 Jan. 1621 m. 1643 d. Feb. 5, 1676 } f ll. 281	John Gorham was son of JOHN GORHAM and Desire *Howland*.	b. ± 1623 d. 1683 (l 106)

b. 1648
m. April 11, 1669
d. June 6, 1712 } h 67
	Ann Bunker was daughter of
	   William Bunker and Mary *Macy*.
	William Bunker was son of
		{ b. Dec. 4, 1648
		  d. 1729
		    (h 67)

d. May 26, 1658 } f l. 299	George Bunker and Jane Godfrey.
	George Bunker was son of
	   WILLIAM BUNKER.
		{ d. Oct. 31, 1662
		    (a L 1)

b. 1590
m. 1632
B'd Aug. 26, 1676 } eSr 32
	Deborah Sears was daughter of
	   RICHARD SEARS and Dorothy Thatcher.
		{ Buried Mar.
		  19, 1678-9
		   (eSr 32)

b. Aug. 12, 1640
m. Nov. or
  Dec. 3, 1663
d. July 28, 1720 } g xxiv.
151
Ib. ;
eK 32
Ib.
	Dinah Coffin was daughter of
	   JAMES COFFIN and Mary Severance.
	James Coffin was son of
	   TRISTRAM COFFIN and Dionis Stevens.
		{ b. Aug. 5, 1645
		    (eK 32)

	Mary Coffin was daughter of TRISTRAM COFFIN and Dionis Stevens.	

b. May 19, 1664
d. 1723 } y
	Elizabeth Gardner was daughter of
	   James Gardner and Mary *Starbuck*.
	James Gardner was son of
	   RICHARD GARDNER and Sarah *Shattuck*.
	Richard Gardner was son of
	   THOMAS GARDINER and Margaret Frier.
		{ b. Mar. 30, 1663
		    (f lv. 57)

b. 1621
m. 1652
d. 1. 16, 1684 } i 183
	Mary Otis was daughter of
	   JOHN OTIS and Mary Jacob.
		{ d. + 1683
		    (i 183)

b. ± 1593
m. ± 1622
d. Feb. 23, 1672 }
	Desire Howland was daughter of
	   JOHN HOWLAND and Elizabeth *Tilley*.
		{ b. ± 1607
		  d. Dec. 21, 1687

b. 1608
m.
d. 4. 19, 1682 } h 67
a L 4
	Mary Macy was daughter of
	   THOMAS MACY and Sarah Hopcot.
		{ b. 1612
		  d. 1706
		    (h 67)

	Mary Starbuck was daughter of Nathaniel Starbuck, Sr., and Mary *Coffin*.	

Nathaniel Starbuck, Sr., was son of
EDWARD STARBUCK and Katharine Reynolds.

Sarah Shattuck was daughter of
—— Shattuck and Damaris ——.

Elizabeth Tilley was daughter of
JOHN TILLEY and ——.

Mary Coffin was daughter of
TRISTRAM COFFIN and Dionis Stevens.

Descendants of Dr. Paul Swift and Dorcas (Gardner) Swift descend also from:
Thomas Gardner (twice),
Richard Gardner (twice),
Tristram Coffin (five times),
James Coffin,
Edward Starbuck (four times)
Christopher Hussey,
Rev. Stephen Batchelder,
Joseph Austin,
Thomas Coleman,
Thomas Macy,
Robert Paddack,
Zechariah Paddack,
William Bunker (four times),
John Gorham,
John Howland,
John Tilley,
Richard Sears,
John Otis.

Paul Swift was born in Sandwich, Massachusetts, 1794. He was for some time a physician at Nantucket, where he is still remembered and respected.

In 1841 he moved to Philadelphia, where he practiced medicine until 1853, when he was appointed a teacher at Haverford School (soon after made a college); he remained there until 1865, when he resigned on account of ill health. He died in Philadelphia in 1866.

Daughters of Dr. Paul Swift and Dorcas (Gardner) Swift were:
Mary, married, 1846, Mr. Edwin Lamson, of Boston.
Katharine, married, first, Dr. Marcus A. Moore, of Boston; second, Mr. Robert Wharton.
Susan, married Mr. Albert H. Franciscus, of Philadelphia.
Elizabeth, married Mr. John E. Phillips, of Baltimore.

As an explanation of the theory entertained by many descendants that Elizabeth Tilley was daughter of John Tilley and Bridget Van der Velde, we quote the following from the exceedingly interesting "Register," recently published by "order of The General Congress" of The Society of Mayflower Descendants.

"John Tilley, the sixteenth signer of the Compact, came with his wife, whose name is unknown, and 'Elizabeth, their daughter.' He was one of the '10 of their principall men' who, with the boat's crew, made up the third and final party of exploration sent out from the Mayflower while at Provincetown Harbor. It is probable that he was a brother of Edward Tilley. Both he and his wife 'dyed a little after they came ashore.' Dr. Henry M. Dexter in a note to his edition of Mourts Relation 1865, quotes from the Leyden MS Records, '13-23 February 1615 John Telley, silk worker of Leyden married Bridget Van der Velde.' She could not have been the mother of Elizabeth Tilley who was born in 1607 and who married John Howland, and the explicitness of Bradford's record of this daughter would indicate that the silk worker 'John Telley' of Leyden was not identical with the Mayflower Pilgrim.

"Dr. Dexter wrote in 1888 that he was convinced that the Leyden record referred to another person. Until 1855 it was supposed through family tradition, that John Howland's wife was a daughter of Governor Carver, which gives some foundation for the belief that a relationship existed, and that Elizabeth Tilley may have been a granddaughter of the first Governor."

CHAPTER XXIV.

FAMILY OF WILLIAM ROTCH.

Joseph Rotch was born in Salisbury, England, May 6th, 1704, and went to Nantucket, subsequently to New Bedford, where he died, November 24th, 1784.

He was interested in whale fishery so successfully carried on by his son, William Rotch.

When the Revolutionary War broke out and the whaling business was practically ruined, William Rotch went to England, hoping to pursue the business there, but, meeting with little encouragement, finally went to Dunkirk, France, where special privileges from the French government were granted him.

He carried on the business there until 1794, when he returned to Nantucket, and after a year's residence on the island, went to New Bedford and resided there until his death in 1828. His great-grandson, now living in New Bedford, says: "He was a consistent Friend and had the courage of his convictions. I have heard my great-aunt, Mary Rotch, tell the following story:

"He was at Dunkirk at the time of the Napoleonic Wars; one day there came news of the great victory of Austerlitz.

"Municipal orders were issued commanding every one to illuminate in honor of the event. My great-grandfather was true to his principles and refused to obey the order, though every house in the street was a blaze of light.

"The good mayor of the city was very friendly with my grandfather and called to expostulate and if possible persuade him—fearing danger from the mob in those excited times, but Mr. Rotch refused.

"'Well,' said the mayor, finally, 'the street belongs

to the city, and I will do what I can,' so he sent and procured two large lanterns and had them placed directly in front of the house and detailed some gendarmes to walk up and down in front and explain to the people that those who lived there were not enemies, but good friendly people, who did not believe in war.

"His daughter, Elizabeth Rotch, was a remarkable woman, living to the advanced age of ninety-nine, and when over ninety had never used the back of a chair, but sat erect without support."

William Rotch is thus described by this grandson, who saw him when he himself was only four years of age: "He was a tall, venerable man with white hair and beard, and came into the room leaning on the back of a large arm chair on castors, attended by his black servant."

The appended extracts from an account of William Rotch, recently published in "The American Friend," and written by Augustine Jones, Superintendent of Friends School, at Providence, Rhode Island, form a fitting supplement to the account given above:

"William Rotch, a distinguished member of the Society of Friends, was born in 1734, in the island of Nantucket, Mass. His father, Joseph Rotch, his brother Francis, both Friends, were, like himself, largely interested in the whale fishery and shipping, early in Nantucket and later in New Bedford. This family did much to make Nantucket for a time the greatest center of this fishery in the world.

. . . .

"William Rotch says: 'From the year 1775 to the end of the war we were in continual embarrassments. Our vessels were captured by the English, and our small vessels and boats, sent to the continent for provisions, denied and sent back empty under pretence that we supplied the British, which was without the least foundation. Prohibitory laws were often made in consequence of these reports, unfounded as they were. By this inhuman conduct we were sometimes in danger of being starved.'

"He has given to us in his own language an interesting incident of his experience. . . .He had a lot of muskets taken for debt, with bayonets on them. He readily sold the muskets to whalers, who used them on their voyages to kill wild fowl. But he always reserved the bayonets, for their only use was to kill men.

"The bayonets were neglected and forgotten, until an application was made for them from the continent for use in war.

"He says: 'The time had now come to support our testimony against war or forever abandon it. As this very instrument was a severe test, I would not hesitate, and therefore promptly denied the applicant. My reasons for not furnishing the bayonets were demanded, to which I readily answered: " As this instrument is purposely made and used for the destruction of mankind, and I cannot put into one man's hand to destroy another that which I cannot use myself in the same way, I refuse to comply with thy demand.' " The person left me much dissatisfied. Others came and received the same denial. It made a great noise in the country, and my life was threatened. I would gladly have beaten them into pruning hooks. As it was, I took an early opportunity of throwing them into the sea.'

"The Committee of the General Court soon took him to Watertown for investigation. He says: 'I gave a full account of my proceedings and closed it by saying: " I sank them in the bottom of the sea, and I did it from principle. I have ever been glad that I had done it. If I have done wrong I am to be pitied." The chairman of the committee, one Major Hawley (a worthy character), then addressed the committee, and said: " I believe Mr. Rotch has given us a candid account of the affair, and every man has a right to act consistently with his religious principles. But I am sorry we cannot have the bayonets, for we want them very much." The major was desirous of knowing more of our Friend's principles, on which I informed him as far as he inquired.

. . . .

" 'In the year 1779, seven British armed vessels and transports, with troops from Newport, came to us. . . . They plundered us of much property—some from me.' Soon after, the town appointed a committee, consisting of William Rotch and two others, to represent its case to the commander of the army and navy. This committee went at once to Newport, where Captain Dawson commanded the navy and General Prescott the army. They succeeded, through great peril and extraordinary energy, in landing, against the protest of Captain Dawson. William Rotch says: 'I got on shore in the afternoon and found that I must wait on General Prescott. Knowing his brittle temper, and being in the afternoon, I almost dreaded to appear in his presence. However, let my treatment be what it would, I desired the meeting over.

" 'I was introduced by one of his aids. He received me very cordially, gave me his hand and said, "Mr. Rotch, will you have some dinner? I can give you good bread, though the rebels say we have none." I thanked him, saying I had dined. "Well," said he, "will you have a glass of wine?" ' He did not object to the wine —it was then in common use—but objected to the ceremonies. He said he meant no disrespect. 'General Prescott answered: "Oh, no; if a Quaker will be a Quaker, it is all I want of him." After some conversation, I mentioned that I did not wish to intrude further on his time, and rose to retire. "Oh, no," says he, "you must take some coffee." I accepted his kindness and gladly retired.'

" The committee could effect nothing, however, without going to New York, where they were well received and accomplished very much. He says: 'We applied to Sir Henry Clinton, through one of his aids, Major André, that fine young man who lost his life as a spy.'

. . . .

"William Rotch was the owner of the famous ship Bedford, of Nantucket, which had the honor of first displaying the American flag in British waters. There is a certain rich and racy relish to the following narration of an English historian of the period, who seemed to chronicle with some disdain:

"'The ship "Bedford," Captain Mooers, belonging to the Massachusetts, arrived in the Downes on the 3d of February, 1783, and was reported at the custom house on the 6th instant. She was not allowed regular entry until some consultation had taken place between the commissioners of the customs and the Lords of Council, on account of the many acts of Parliament in force against the rebels of America. She was loaded with four hundred and eighty-seven butts of whale oil, is American-built, manned wholly by American seamen, and belongs to the island of Nantucket, in Massachusetts. This is the first vessel which has displayed the thirteen rebellious stripes of America in any British port.'—Barnard's 'History of England,' 'Cyclopœdia of United States History,' Vol. I., p. 493."

"His brother Francis owned the ship Dartmouth, from which the tea was thrown into Boston harbor Twelfth month 16th, 1773. She was the first vessel built in New Bedford."

William Rotch "was prominent, in 1784, in New England Yearly Meeting, being on the Executive Committee which directed its business, and also on the committee to consider the state of the Society and devise measures for improvement. This was the first year of the Providence Friends School, which began at Portsmouth, R. I. He was a strong patron of it."

b. 10. 4, 1734 m. 10. 31, 1754 d.	d 188 c l. 229	William Rotch married Elizabeth Barney, of Nantucket. He was son of	b. 12, 3, 1735 (d 8)
b. May 6, 1704 m. 12. 21, 1733 O S d. Nov. 24, 1784	c l. 67	Joseph Rotch and Love *Macy*. Joseph Rotch was son of William Rotch and Hannah ——.	b. Feb. 9, 1713 (h 79) d. 11. 14, 1767 (d 188)

Family of William Rotch.

b. ± 1687 d. Mar. 16, 1759 } h 68 h 68	Love Macy was daughter of Thomas Macy [3] and Deborah *Coffin*.	{ b. d. Sept. 23, 1760 (h 79)
b. July 14, 1655 d. Oct. 14, 1691 } h 67	Thomas Macy was son of John Macy and Deborah *Gardner*.	{ b. Feb. 12, 1658 d. 1712 (h 68)
b. 1608 d. 4. 19, 1682 } i 169 h 67 a l. 4	John Macy was son of THOMAS MACY and Sarah Hopcot.	{ b. 1612 d. 1706 (h 67)
b. Oct. 30, 1647 d. Sept. 5, 1711 } g xxiv. 151 ib.	Deborah Coffin was daughter of LIEUTENANT JOHN COFFIN and Deborah *Austin*.	{ b. d. Feb. 4, 1718 (g xxiv. 152)
b. ± 1605 m. ± 1630 d. Oct. 2, 1681 } g xxiv. 150; a l. 8	Lieutenant John Coffin was son of TRISTRAM COFFIN and Dionis Stevens.	{ d. + 1682 (eC)
b. 1626 m. 1652 d. Jan. 23, 1668 } x 361; a l. 4 ib.	Deborah Gardner was daughter of RICHARD GARDNER and Sarah *Shattuck*.	{ b. 1632 d. 1724
	Richard Gardner was son of	
} f ll. 230	THOMAS GARDINER and Margaret Frier.	
b. m. 1659 d. 1663 } f L	Deborah Austin was daughter of Joseph Austin and Sarah *Starbuck*.	
b. ± 1604 d. 12. 4, 1690 } a l. 4	Sarah Starbuck was daughter of EDWARD STARBUCK and Katharine Reynolds.	
b. 4. 13, 1699 m. 1. 31, 1722 OS d. 4. 14, 1783 } n c i. 23 d 8	Elizabeth Barney was daughter of Benjamin Barney and Lydia *Starbuck*.	{ b. Sept. 15, 1704 (a l. 8) d. 4. 2, 1751 (d 8)
b. 12. 14, 1671 m. 12. 6, 1694 d. 8. 12, 1770 } uM a l. 7 d 196	Lydia Starbuck was daughter of Jethro Starbuck and Dorcas *Gayer*.	{ b. 8. 29, 1675 (a l. 2) d. 11. 12, 1747 (d 196)
b. ± 1638 m. 1662 d. 6. 6, 1719 } eC 56 a l. 11	Jethro Starbuck was son of Nathaniel Starbuck and Mary *Coffin*.	{ b. Feb. 20, 1645 (g xxiv. 150) d. 9. 13, 1717 (a l. 11)
	Nathaniel Starbuck was son of EDWARD STARBUCK and Katharine Reynolds.	
d. 7. 23, 1710 Will probated Oct. 24, 1710 } g xxxi. 298 b A L 26	Dorcas Gayer was daughter of WILLIAM GAYER and Dorcas *Starbuck*.	
	Dorcas Starbuck was daughter of EDWARD STARBUCK and Katharine Reynolds.	
	Mary Coffin was daughter of TRISTRAM COFFIN and Dionis Stevens.	{ d. 1696 (n)

Descendants from William and Elizabeth (Barney) Rotch descend also from:
> Thomas Macy,
> Lieutenant John Coffin,
> Tristram Coffin (twice),
> Richard Gardner,
> Thomas Gardiner,
> Edward Starbuck (three times),
> William Gayer.

CHAPTER XXV.

WING AND HATHAWAY CONNECTION WITH NANTUCKET FAMILIES.

b. 11. 29, 1734-5 } d 132
m. 1st, 12. 2, 1756 } c ii. 17
d. 7. 26, 1795

Sylvanus Hussey, Jr., of Lynn, Mass., married, first, Alice Gray; second, Lydia Wing.

b. 5. 28, 1737 } e W 59
m.
d.

Paul Wing, married Abigail Wing, sister of Lydia Wing.

b. 5. 13, 1682 } s ii. 761
m. 9. 8, 1723 } c i. 25
d. 2. 10, 1767 } d 132

Sylvanus Hussey, Jr., was son of
    Sylvanus Hussey, Sr., and Hepzibah *Starbuck*.

{ b. 11. 8, 1700 (a i. 7)
{ d. 12. 31, 1764 (d 132)

b. 1632
m. 10. 8, 1676
d. 1718
Will proved May 13, 1718 } s ii. 761 } b A i. 41

Sylvanus Hussey, Sr., was son of
    Stephen Hussey and Martha *Bunker*.

{ b. 11. 1, 1656
{ d. Sept. 21, 1744
{ (s ii. 761)

b. 1599 } Eng. Parish Rec.
d. 3. 6. 1686 } s ii. 760

Stephen Hussey was son of
    CHRISTOPHER HUSSEY and Theodate *Batchelder*.

{ d. 10, 1649
{ (s ii. 589)

b. Aug. 9, 1668 } a i. 1
m. Nov. 20, 1690 } g xxiv. 151
d. 9. 2, 1753 } d 196

Hepzibah Starbuck was daughter of
    Nathaniel Starbuck, Jr., and Dinah *Coffin*.

{ d. 8. 1, 1750
{ (d 196)

b. ± 1634 } a i. 11
m. 1662 } e C 56
d. 6. 6, 1719 } a i. 11

Nathaniel Starbuck, Jr., was son of
    Nathaniel Starbuck, Sr., and Mary *Coffin*.

{ b. Feb. 20, 1645
{ (g xxiv. 150)
{ d. Sept. 13, 1717
{ (a i. 11)

b. ± 1604
m.
d. 12. 4, 1690 } a i. 4

Nathaniel Starbuck, Sr., was son of
    EDWARD STARBUCK and Katharine Reynolds.

d. May 26, 1658 } f i. 299

Martha Bunker was daughter of
    George Bunker and Jane Godfrey.
George Bunker was son of
    WILLIAM BUNKER.

{ d. Oct. 31, 1662
{ (a i. 1)

b. ± 1561
d. 1660 } s ii. 589

Theodate Batchelder was daughter of
    REV. STEPHEN BATCHELDER.

{ d. 1649
{ (f l. 89)

b. Aug. 12, 1640
m. Nov. or
  Dec. 3, 1663
d. July 28, 1720
	eK
	g xxiv.
	151
		Dinah Coffin was daughter of
		  JAMES COFFIN and Mary Severance.*

b. ± 1605 m. ± 1630 d. Oct. 2, 1681	g xxiv. 150 ii l. 3	James Coffin was son of TRISTRAM COFFIN and Dionis Stevens.

Mary Coffin was daughter of
  TRISTRAM COFFIN and Dionis Stevens.

b. 4. 3, 1703 m. 3. 15, 1731-2 d. 4. 25, 1730	eW 53 eW 59	Paul Wing was son of Zaccheus Wing and Content Swift.
b. 1. 28, 1664 m. 1686 d. 3, 1740	eW 40 eW 52 ib.	Zaccheus Wing was son of Daniel Wing, Jr., and Deborah Dillingham.
b. 9. 5, 1641 m. Nov. 5, 1642	eW 39 f iv. 593	Daniel Wing, Jr., was son of Daniel Wing, Sr., and Hannah Swift.
		Daniel Wing was son of JOHN WING and Deborah *Batchelder*.

Deborah Batchelder was daughter of
  REV. STEPHEN BATCHELDER.

b. 1. 17, 1743 b. 1. 22, 1752 d. 8. 1, 1807 m. 1739	eW eW n	Abigail Wing } Lydia Wing } sisters, were daughters of Samuel Wing and Hepzibah *Hathaway*.
b. 8. 12, 1690 m. d. 2. 12, 1732	eW 52 eW 59	Samuel Wing was son of Samuel Wing and Dorothy ——.
		Samuel Wing was son of Daniel Wing, Jr., and Deborah Dillingham.
b. 9. 5, 1641 m. 1664	eW	Daniel Wing, Jr., was son of Daniel Wing, Sr., and Hannah Swift.
		Daniel Wing, Sr., was son of JOHN WING and Deborah *Batchelder*.
b. 1644 m. d. 1748	n	Hepzibah Hathaway was daughter of Thomas Hathaway and Hepzibah *Starbuck*.

---

* Mary Severance was the daughter of John Severance and Abigail Kimball. Abigail Kimball was daughter of Richard Kimball and Ursula Scott, who was daughter of Henry and Martha Scott, of Rattlesden, Suffolk County, England.

b. ± 1635 m. 1662 d. d. d, 1719	a l. 11 eC 56 a l. 11	Hepzibah Starbuck was daughter of Nathaniel Starbuck, Sr., and Mary *Coffin*.
b. ± 1604 d. 12. 4, 1690	a l. 4	Nathaniel Starbuck, Sr., was son of EDWARD STARBUCK and Katharine Reynolds.

b. Feb. 20, 1645
(g xxiv. 150)
d. 9. 13, 1717
(Ib.; a l. 11)

b. ± 1561 d. 1660	s ii. 589	Deborah Batchelder was daughter of REV. STEPHEN BATCHELDER.

Mary Coffin was daughter of
TRISTRAM COFFIN and Dionis Stevens.

Descendants of Sylvanus Hussey, Jr., and Lydia Wing descend also on the paternal side from:
Christopher Hussey,
Edward Starbuck,
William Bunker (French Huguenot),
Rev. Stephen Batchelder,
James Coffin,
Tristram Coffin (twice).

On the maternal side from:
John Wing,
Rev. Stephen Batchelder,
Edward Starbuck,
Tristram Coffin.

Descendants of Paul Wing and Abigail Wing descend also on the paternal side from:
John Wing,
Rev. Stephen Batchelder.

On the maternal side from:
John Wing,
Rev. Stephen Batchelder,
Edward Starbuck,
Tristram Coffin.

Hepzibah Wing, daughter of Samuel Wing and Hepzibah (Hathaway) and sister of Abigail and Lydia, above named, married William Coleman, of Nantucket, a direct descendant of Thomas Coleman. There were two children, William and Lydia Wing Coleman, neither of whom married.

The story is told of Lydia Wing Coleman, that on being invited to a party, she felt such a feminine reluctance to appear in a white dress which had seen service on too many similar occasions, that she embroidered figures in red over the entire surface, and was enabled to attend the festivity apparently in a new gown. She was a woman of considerable ingenuity, a teacher, and left behind her a reputation that to the younger generations was an example.

Samuel Wing, son of Paul and Abigail Wing, married, 5th mo. 8, 1799, Anna Rogers, of Marshfield, Plymouth County, Mass. The children of Samuel and Anna (Rogers) Wing were:

Mary R. Wing, unmarried.
Abraham R. Wing, married Mary S. Gardner, daughter of Prince Gardner and Mary Gorham.
Beulah R. Wing, married 12. 10. 1827 (cL), Moses Folger Rogers, of Lynn.
Lindley Moore Wing, married Elizabeth Holway.
Joseph R. Wing, married Mary Ann Wing, daughter of
Sands Wing and Ann Howland, of Long Plain.
Hepzibah Wing, unmarried.
Stephen R. Wing, married Elizabeth Collins Shove, daughter of David and Mary Sherman Shove.

Children of Abraham R. Wing and Mary S. (Gardner) Wing:
Mary Anna Wing,
Samuel Wing.

Children of Joseph R. Wing and Mary Ann (Wing) Wing:
Mary H. Wing, unmarried.
Elizabeth Wing, married Fred. Pond and John S. Perry, of New Bedford.

Child of Lindley Moore Wing and Elizabeth (Holway) Wing:
Charles Wing.

Children of Beulah (Wing) Rogers and Moses Folger Rogers:
Stephen Wing,
Alice Wing.

Children of Stephen R. Wing and Elizabeth Collins (Shove) Wing:
Alice Rogers Wing, married Daniel C. Maxfield, of Amesbury, Mass.
Anna Wing, married Elwood Paige, of Lynn, Mass.
David Shove Wing, died young.
Asa Shove Wing, died young.
Asa Shove Wing, married, 4th mo. 30, 1873, Sophia Rhoads, daughter of Samuel and Anna Rhoads, of Philadelphia.
Stephen Rogers Wing, married Lydia Remington.
Joseph Rogers Wing, died young.

Another connection between the Wing family and Nantucket was in the first marriage of Samuel Barker.

Samuel Barker, married, first, Deborah *Wing*, and, in 1718, second, Bethiah *Folger*.*

> Deborah Wing was daughter of
> > John Wing and Mary Perry.
>
> John Wing was son of
> > Stephen Wing and Sarah Briggs.
>
> Stephen Wing was son of
> > JOHN WING and Deborah *Batchelder*.
>
> Deborah Batchelder was daughter of
> > REV. STEPHEN BATCHELDER.

The only child of Samuel Barker and first wife, Deborah Wing, was Deborah Barker, who married Aug. 15, 1738 (a I. 39), Jonathan Burnell, of Boston, from whom descended the family of that name in Nantucket.

Descendants of Samuel Barker and first wife, Deborah Wing, descend also on the maternal side from:
> John Wing,
> Rev. Stephen Batchelder.

The lines of ascent on the paternal side will be found complete in the Barker Family (page 155).

---

* See Barker Family (page 155) supra.

CHAPTER XXVI.

NEWHALL CONNECTION WITH NANTUCKET FAMILIES.

Thomas [1] Newhall came from England in 1630.
Thomas [2] married Elizabeth Potter.
Joseph [3] married Susanna Farrar.
Samuel [4] married Keziah Breed.
Daniel [5] married Hannah Estes.

b. Sept. 9, 1770 } His. of Lynn, 485
d. 1857

Estes [6] Newhall, married, first, Hepzibah Wing; second, Miriam Philbrick.

{ m. 1815 (m)

Hepzibah Wing was daughter of Paul Wing and Abigail Wing. (See Wing and Hathaway Family, p. 183).

Children of Estes Newhall and Hepzibah Wing:
Paul Wing Newhall, who married Hannah Johnson, and Abby W. Newhall, who married Micajah Pratt.

Children of Estes Newhall and Miriam *Philbrick:*
Three daughters, who died young, and Joseph Philbrick Newhall, who married Elizabeth Huntington Barker.

Children of Paul Wing Newhall and Hannah Johnson:
Catharine Johnson Newhall, died unmarried.
Sarah Johnson Newhall, died unmarried.
William Estes Newhall, married October 8th, 1857, Philena Marshall Peterson.
George Newhall, died unmarried.
Abby Newhall.

Maria Newhall, died unmarried.
Elizabeth Newhall, died unmarried.
Mary Newhall.

Child of Joseph Philbrick Newhall and Elizabeth Huntington Barker.
Barker Newhall.

Hannah Johnson, wife of Paul Wing Newhall, was daughter of Samuel Johnson and Sarah Challis, of Amesbury, Mass., a descendant of Philip Challis, who was associated with Thomas Barnard, John Severance and Thomas Macy, in the early days of Amesbury. The name of Philip Challis appears in many civil and military lists of Amesbury.

Descendants of Paul Wing Newhall and Hannah Johnson descend also from:
John Wing (twice),
Rev. Stephen Batchelder (twice),
Edward Starbuck,
Tristram Coffin.

b. July 15, 1823
m. —Jan. 4, 1866
d. Sept. 2, 1869 } m 65
	Joseph Philbrick Newhall, married,
	   Elizabeth Huntington Barker,
	     daughter of
		{ b. Aug. 11, 1826
		{ d. May 8, 1880

b. Nov. 16, 1786 } m 41
m. Jan. 7th, 1819 } m 53
d. Feb. 24, 1855 } m 41
	Abraham Barker, who married
	   Margaret *Buffum*.
		{ b. Aug. 27, 1789
		{ d. Nov. 4, 1839
		  (m 53)

b. Nov. 30th, 1750 } m 29 m. Jan. 27, 1785 } m 40 d. June 19, 1837 } m 29	Abraham Barker was son of Benjamin Barker and Ann *Barker*.	{ b. Aug. 29, 1750 { d. Aug. 16, 1789

b. Feb., 1716 } m 19
m. Nov. 6, 1746 } m 28
d. Jan. 27, 1784 } m 19
	Benjamin Barker was son of
	   Prince Barker and Abigail *Keen*.
		{ b. Feb. 6, 1721
		{ d. Sept. 2, 1790
		  (m 28)

b. 1666
m. Oct. 23, 1707 } m 19
d. May 7, 1754 } m 14
	Prince Barker was son of
	   Isaac Barker and Elizabeth *Slocum*.
		{ b. Feb. 12, 1660
		{ d. Aug. 18, 1774
		  (m 19)

b. m. Dec. 28, 1665 } m 14 d. 1710	Isaac Barker was son of Isaac Barker and Judith *Prence*.	{ d. + 1710

b. ± 1616
m.
d. 1689
Will Feb. 18, } m 12
1689
	Isaac Barker was son of
	   ROBERT BARKER and Lucy Williams.
		{ b.
		{ d. bet. 1682 and
		  1689
		  (m 12)

b. Mar. 25, 1718 m. Feb. 20, 1745 } m d. Feb. 20, 1775	Ann Barker was daughter of Abraham Barker and Susanna Anthony.	b. Dec. 10, 1723 d. Aug. 10, 1801
b. Jan. 26, 1698 m. Dec. 1, 1715 } m d. 1750	Abraham Barker was son of James Barker and Elizabeth *Tucker*.	b. Aug 24, 1691 d. Apr. 2, 1768
b. 1662 m. d. Nov. 3, 1741 } m	James Barker was son of William Barker and Elizabeth *Easton*.	b. Feb. 18, 1666 d. Mar. 24, 1715
b. 1623 m. 1644 } m d. 1702	William Barker was son of James Barker and Barbara Dungan.	b. + 1628

	James Barker was son of
	  James Barker, who was son of
	JAMES BARKER,* of Portsmouth, and formerly of
	  Harwich, England.	

b. July 26, 1682 m. + 1713 } m d. 1736 (Duxbury) Will	Abigail Keen was daughter of BENJAMIN KEEN and Deborah *Barker*.	b. Nov. 7, 1686 d. — 1730 (Wid. Prince Howland)
b. Aug. 17, 1654 m. ± 1680 } m d. 1733 (Dartmouth)	Elizabeth Slocum was daughter of PELEG SLOCUM and Mary *Holder*.	b. Sept. 16, 1661 d. Sept. 20, 1737
b. 1606 m. Apr 1st, 1635 } d. Apr 8 1673	Judith Prence was daughter of THOMAS PRENCE and Mary *Collier*.	
b. Aug. 13, 1653 m. Nov. 28, 1690 } m d. Jan. 16, 1725	Elizabeth Tucker was daughter of ABRAHAM TUCKER and Hannah *Mott*.	b. Nov., 1663 d. Dec. 11, 1730
b. 1622 m. 1643 } m d. 1694	Elizabeth Easton was daughter of Peter Easton and Ann *Coggeshall*.	b. 1626 d. 1687
b. 1593 m. d. 1675 } m	Peter Easton was son of NICHOLAS EASTON, of Portsmouth, and Lymington, Herts County, England.	
b. Feb. 27, 1650 m. d. Sept. 25, 1729 }	Deborah Barker was daughter of Robert Barker and Alice ———.	
b. 1616 m. }	Robert Barker was son of ROBERT BARKER and Lucy Williams.	d. bet. 1681 and 1689

---

* It would appear that James Barker was not a relative of Robert, or if a relative, the connection antedates immigration to America.

Early Settlers of Nantucket.

b. 1631
m. 1660
d. June 13, 1688 } m
(Newport,1656)

Mary Holder was daughter of
CHRISTOPHER HOLDER * and Mary Scott.

{ d. Oct. 17, 1665

d. 1671
Plymouth, 1633 }
From London

Mary Collier was daughter of
WILLIAM COLLIER and Jane ———.

b. 1633
m.
d. 1711 } m

Hannah Mott was daughter of
JACOB MOTT and Joanna Slocum.†

{ b. May 16, 1642
d. Jan. 6, 1727

b. 1591
m.
d. 1647 } m

Ann Coggeshall was daughter of
JOHN COGGESHALL and Mary ———.

{ b. 1604
d. 1684

b. Oct. 17, 1743
m. Oct. 24, 1784 } m
d. May 20, 1829

Margaret Buffum was daughter of
David Buffum and Hepzibah Mitchell.‡

{ b. Jan. 4, 1750
d. June 21, 1834

b. Feb. 20, 1715
m. Jan. 2, 1738 } c i. 86
d. May 10, 1799

Hepzibah Mitchell was daughter of
James Mitchell and Ann Folger.

{ b. 11. 6, 1729
(d 93)
d. Aug. 6, 1777

b. ± 1686
m. 1708 } uM
d. July 24, 1722 } uM

James Mitchell was son of
Richard Mitchell and Elizabeth Tripp.

{ b. Nov. 21,
1684 or 5
d. Dec. 13, 1750

England } uM

Richard Mitchell was son of
RICHARD MITCHELL and Mary Wood.

b. Oct. 17, 1689 O S } n
m. 12. 1,1710-11 O S } c i. 6
d. April 19, 1772 } d 196

Ann Folger was daughter of
Jethro Folger and Mary Starbuck.

{ b. Dec. 31, 1692
(d 196)
d. 10. 22, 1773
(d 93)

b. 1659
m
d. 8. 23, 1732 } n

Jethro Folger was son of
John Folger and Mary Barnard.

{ b. 1667
d. 8. 6, 1737
(n)

b. 1617
m. 1644
d. 1690 } n

John Folger was son of
PETER FOLGER and Mary Morrill.

{ d. 1704
(n)

b. ± 1656
m. 1. 9, 1681-2 } J 208; o
d. May 30, 1730 } eH

Elizabeth Tripp was daughter of
JAMES TRIPP and Mercy Lawton.

{ d. ± 1685
(J 208 ; eH)

b. 1610
m.
d. 1678 } J 246

James Tripp was son of
JOHN TRIPP and Mary Paine.

{ d. Feb. 12, 1687

---

* Quaker martyr.
† Joanna Slocum was sister of Peleg Slocum; they were children of Giles Slocum and Joan ———.
‡ Widow of Peter Chase.

b. Aug. 9, 1668
m. Nov. 20, 1690
d. 9. 2, 1752 } a L 7
} d 196
	Mary Starbuck was daughter of
	   Nathaniel Starbuck, Jr., and Dinah *Coffin*.
		{ d. 8. 1, 1750
		  (d 196)

b. ± 1634
m. 1662
d.6. 6, 1719 } a l. 11
} eC
} a l. 11
	Nathaniel Starbuck, Jr., was son of
	   Nathaniel Starbuck, Sr., and Mary *Coffin*.
		{ b. 1645
		  d. Sept. 13, 1717
		  (a l. 11)

b. ± 1604 d. 12. 4, 1690 } a L 4	Nathaniel Starbuck, Sr., was son of EDWARD STARBUCK and Katharine Reynolds.	
b. Jan. 15, 1642-3 m. ± 1666 d. } t 49 } t 53	Mary Barnard was daughter of Nathaniel Barnard and Mary *Barnard*. Nathaniel Barnard was son of	
d. ± 1677 } t 49	THOMAS BARNARD and Eleanor ———.	{ d. Nov. 27, 1694 (t 49)
	And his wife, Mary Barnard, was daughter of	
d. 1682 } t 52	ROBERT BARNARD and Joanna Harvey.	{ d. Mar. 31, 1705 (a l. 38)
	Mercy Lawton was daughter of GEORGE LAWTON and Elizabeth *Hazard*. Elizabeth Hazard was daughter of	
b. 1610 d. 1690 } eH	THOMAS HAZARD and Martha ———.	

b. Aug. 12, 1640
m. Nov. or
Dec. 3, 1663
d. July 28, 1720 } g xxiv.
151
Ib.; eK
Ib. [32
	Dinah Coffin was daughter of
	   JAMES COFFIN and Mary Severance.
	James Coffin was son of
		{ b. Aug. 5, 1645
		  (eK 32)

b. ± 1605 m. ± 1630 d. Oct. 2, 1681 } g xxiv. 150 } a l. 3	TRISTRAM COFFIN and Dionis Stevens.	{ d. + 1682 (eC)
	Mary Coffin was daughter of TRISTRAM COFFIN and Dionis Stevens.	

Children of Joseph Philbrick Newhall and Elizabeth Huntington Barker descend on the paternal side from Samuel, son of Thomas Philbrick* and Ann (Knapp).

   * Thomas Philbrick was son of Thomas and Elizabeth Philbrick, who, with six children, came from Lincolnshire, England, in 1630, in the Arabella, reaching Salem June 12th. In July they went to Watertown; in 1645 to Hampton, now Seabrook. His house, built in 1651, has been in the family without interruption to the present time. Elizabeth, another child of Thomas Philbrick and Ann (Knapp) married Thomas Chase; they were the parents of Lieutenant Isaac Chase, whose granddaughter, Jedidah Chase, married Robert Barker.

On the maternal side from:
Robert Barker, of Duxbury, Mass. (twice),
James Barker, of Portsmouth,
Peleg Slocum,
Thomas Prence,
Nicholas Easton,
Christopher Holder,
William Collier,
John Coggeshall,
Richard Mitchell,
Peter Folger,
John Tripp,
James Tripp,
Edward Starbuck,
Thomas Barnard,
Robert Barnard,
George Lawton,
Thomas Hazard,
James Coffin,
Tristram Coffin (twice),
Abraham Tucker,
Jacob Mott,
Benjamin Keen.

CHAPTER XXVII.

FAMILY OF ABRAHAM MACY.

b. Feb. 4, 1808 } h 239	Catharine C. Macy, daughter of Abraham Macy and Elizabeth Coleman, married, October 6th, 1833, at Ghent, New York, Townsend Powell, son of James Powell and Martha Townsend	{ d. Apr. 18, 1856 (h 239)
b. Dec., 25, 1779 } h 150 m. Dec., 1800 } h 239 d. Aug. 29, 1844		
b. Aug. 23, 1807 m. Oct. 6, 1833 } h 239		

b. Aug. 7, 1739 } h 109
m. 12. 3, 1761 } c ii. 73
d. June 30, 1820 } h 107
	Abraham Macy was son of
	   Abraham Macy and Priscilla *Bunker*.
	Abraham Macy was son of
	   Abraham Macy and Anna *Worth*.
	Abraham Macy was son of
	   Richard Macy and Deborah *Pinkham*.
	Richard Macy was son of
	   John Macy and Deborah *Gardner*.
	John Macy was son of
	   THOMAS MACY and Sarah Hopcot.
		{ b. June 14, 1745
		  d. July 27, 1819
		  (h 150).

b. 7. 9, 1715 } d 152
m. 4. 8, 1738 } c i. 89
d. 7. 4, 1746 } d 152
		{ b. May 23, 1721
		  d. Oct. 31, 1795
		  (h 109)

b. Sept. 22, 1689 }
m. Sept. 8, 1711 } h 68
d. Dec. 25, 1779 } h 80
		{ b. Dec. 28, 1694
		  d. Dec. 13, 1767
		  (h 80)

b. July 14, 1655 }
m. } h 67
d. Oct. 14, 1691
		{ b. Feb. 12, 1658
		  d. 1712
		  (h 68)

b. 1608 }
d. 4. 19, 1682 } a l. 4
		{ b. 1612
		  d. 1706
		  (h 67)

b. 9. 5, 1711 } d 8
m. 11. 7, 1731-2 } c l. 59
d. 9. 3, 1786 } d. 9
	Priscilla Bunker was daughter of
	   Samuel Bunker and Priscilla *Coleman*.
	Samuel Bunker was son of
	   Jabez Bunker and Hannah *Gardner*.
	Jabez Bunker was son of
	   William Bunker and Mary *Macy*.
	William Bunker was son of
	   George Bunker and Jane Godfrey.
	George Bunker was son of
	   WILLIAM BUNKER.
		{ b. 9. 26, 1713
		  d. 7. 11, 1797
		  (d l. 42)

b. Nov. 7, 1678 } a L. 3
m. Nov. 19, 1706 } a iii. 12
d. 5. 6, 1750 } d. 8
		{ b. 5. 6, 1686
		  (a l. 7)
		  d. 3. 25, 1773
		  (d 8)

b. — 1648
m. Apr. 11, 1669 } h 67
d. June 6, 1712
		{ h. Dec. 4, 1648
		  d. 1729
		  (h 67)

b.
m.
d. 5. 26, 1658 }
		{ d. Jane Swain
		  Oct. 31, 1662
		  (a l. 1)

b.
m. Sept. 8, 1720 } l 426
d. 7. 14, 1790 } d l. 218
	Anna Worth was daughter of
	   Joseph Worth and Lydia *Gorham*.
		{ b. May 14, 1710
		  (f ii. 282)
		  d. 3. 1, 1763
		  (d l. 218)

b. May 19, 1666 m. Sept. 22, 1684	a l. 1 a l. 4	Joseph Worth was son of John Worth and Miriam *Gardner*.	b. July 14, 1685 d. 1702
b. m. Apr. 11, 1665 d. 1724	h 67	John Worth was son of William Worth and Sarah *Macy*.	b. Aug. 1, 1646 d. 1701 (h 67)
d. — 1718	g xxiv.	Deborah Pinkham was daughter of RICHARD PINKHAM and Mary *Coffin*.	b. 1665 (g xxiv. 151)
b. 1626 m. 1652 d. Jan. 23, 1668	x 361 a l. 4	Deborah Gardner was daughter of RICHARD GARDNER and Sarah *Shattuck*.	b. 1632 d. 1724
b. m.	f ll. 230	Richard Gardner was son of THOMAS GARDINER and Margaret Frier.	
b. Aug. 2, 1667 m. Nov. 1731 d. Jan. 19, 1762	g xvi. g xvi.	Priscilla Coleman was daughter of John Coleman and Priscilla *Starbuck*.	b. Oct. 25, 1696 (a l. 7) d. Mar. 14, 1762 (g xvi. 270; d 42)

b. 1644
m.
d. 1715
Estate settled
  Mar. 2, 1715-6
	f l. 431
	g xvi.
	b A l. 36
		John Coleman was son of
		   John Coleman and Joanna *Folger*.
			d. 5. 18, 1719
			(g xvi.;
			a l. 12)

b. ± 1599 d. 1682	f l. 431 f l. 431	John Coleman was son of THOMAS COLEMAN and Susanna ———.	d. Nov. 17, 1650 (f l. 431)

d. 1713	d 3;
	g xxiv.
	151
		Hannah Gardner was daughter of
		   Nathaniel Gardner and Abigail *Coffin*.
		Nathaniel Gardner was son of
		   RICHARD GARDNER and Sarah *Shattuck*.
		Richard Gardner was son of
		   THOMAS GARDINER and Margaret Frier.
			b.
			d. 3. 15, 1709
			(a l. 7;
			g xxiv. 151)

		Mary Macy was daughter of THOMAS MACY and Sarah Hopcot.	
b. Oct. 21, 1667 m. May, 1695 d. 1750	f ll. 282 f ll. 282	Lydia Gorham was daughter of Shubael Gorham and Puella *Hussey*.	b. Oct. 10, 1677 (a l. 3)
b. 1. 16, 1621 Bapt. Jan., 1621 m. 1643 d. 2. 5, 1676	f ll. 281 f ll. 281	Shubael Gorham was son of JOHN GORHAM and Desire *Howland*.	b. ± 1623 (l 106) d. 10. 13, 1683
b. 1575 m. d. ± 1643	l 407	John Gorham was son of RALPH GORHAM.	

Family of Abraham Macy. 197

b. 1550
m. 1572
d. 1576 }

Ralph Gorham was son of
    James Gorham and Agnes Bennington.

{ (1 407)

Miriam Gardner was daughter of
    RICHARD GARDNER and Sarah *Shattuck*.
Richard Gardner was son of
    THOMAS GARDINER and Margaret Frier.

Sarah Macy was daughter of
    THOMAS MACY and Sarah Hopcot.

b. Aug. 12, 1640 g xxiv.
m. Nov. or   151
  Dec. 3, 1683 { ib.;eK32
d. July 28, 1720 } ib.

b. ± 1605
m. ± 1630 } g xxiv.
d. Oct. 2, 1681   150

Mary Coffin [3] was daughter of
    JAMES COFFIN [3] and Mary Severance.
James Coffin was son of
    TRISTRAM COFFIN and Dionis Stevens.

{ b. Aug. 5, 1645
  (eK 32)

{ d. + 1682
  (eC)

Sarah Shattuck was daughter of
    —— Shattuck and Damaris ——.

b. ± 1634
m. 1662 } a l. 11
d. 6. 6, 1719   eC 56
          a L 11

b. ± 1604
d. 12. 4, 1690 } a l. 4

Priscilla Starbuck was daughter of
    Nathaniel Starbuck and Mary *Coffin*.
Nathaniel Starbuck was son of
    EDWARD STARBUCK and Katharine Reynolds.

{ b. Feb. 20, 1745
  (g xxiv. 15u)
  d. Sept. 13, 1717
  (a l. 11)

b.
m. 1644 } g xvi.
d. 1690   ib. [269

Joanna Folger was daughter of
    PETER FOLGER and Mary Morrell.

{ d. 1704
  (g xvi. 270)

Abigail Coffin was daughter of
    JAMES COFFIN and Mary Severance.
James Coffin was son of
    TRISTRAM COFFIN and Dionis Stevens.

b. 1632
m. 10. 8, 1676 } s ll. 761
d. 4. 2, 1718

b. 1599   Eng. Parish
m. ± 1630 } Records
d. 3. 6, 1686   s ii. 760

Puella Hussey was daughter of
    Stephen Hussey and Martha *Bunker*.
Stephen Hussey was son of
    CHRISTOPHER HUSSEY and Theodate *Bachelder*.

{ b. ± 1656
  d. 9. 21, 1744
  (s ii. 761)

{ d. 1649
  (s ii. 589)

b. ± 1593 m. ± 1622 d. Feb. 22, 1672	Desire Howland was daughter of JOHN HOWLAND and Elizabeth *Tilley*.	b. ± 1607 d. Dec. 21, 1687
	Mary Coffin [2] was daughter of TRISTRAM COFFIN and Dionis Stevens.	
	Martha Bunker was daughter of George Bunker and Jane Godfrey. George Bunker was son of WILLIAM BUNKER.	
b. 1561 m. d. ± 1660 } s ii. 589	Theodate Bachelder was daughter of REV. STEPHEN BACHELDER.	
	Elizabeth Tilley was daughter of JOHN TILLEY.	
b. 1737 m. 1762 d. Jan. 11, 1817 } h 86	Elizabeth (Coleman), wife of Abraham Macy, was daughter of Elihu Coleman and Elizabeth *Macy*.	b. Apr. 18, 1745 (h 85)
b. 7. 8, 1706 m. 11. 6, 1731 O S } d l. 42 d. 2. 16, 1785 } c l. 53	Elihu Coleman was son of Jethro Coleman and Lydia *Paddack*.	b. 2. 18, 1713 (l 188) d. 1. 21, 1747 (d l. 44)
d. 1. 19, 1762 } d 42	Jethro Coleman was son of John Coleman and Priscilla *Starbuck*.	b. Oct. 25, 1696 (a l. 7) d. 3. 14, 1762 (d 42)
b. Aug. 2, 1667 } a l. 1; d. 1715 } g xvi. Estate settled Mar. 2, 1715-6 } b A l. 36	John Coleman was son of John Coleman and Joanna *Folger*.	
b. 1602 d. 1685 } f l. 431	John Coleman was son of THOMAS COLEMAN and Susanna ——.	
b. April 8, 1725 } h 69 m. July, 1744 } h 86 d. June 17, 1798 } h 69	Elizabeth Macy was daughter of Jonathan Macy and Lois *Gorham*.	b. Nov. 5, 1727 d. Mar. 10, 1804 (h 86)
b. ± 1675 m. Apr. 25,1707 } h 67 d. Nov. 28, 1751 } h 67	Jonathan Macy was son of John Macy and Judith *Worth*.	b. Dec. 22, 1689 d. Nov. 8, 1767 (h 69)
b. July 14, 1655 } h 67 m. d. Oct. 14, 1691 } h 67	John Macy was son of John Macy and Deborah *Gardner*.	b. Feb. 12, 1658 d. 1712 (h 68)
	John Macy was son of THOMAS MACY and Sarah Hopcot.	

Family of Abraham Macy.

b. 9, 22, 1677 } i 188
m. 10. 15, 1706
d. 1756

Lydia Paddack was daughter of
    Nathaniel Paddack and Ann *Bunker*.

{ b. 9. 3, 1686
d. 1. 18, 1787
(i 188)

b. 1636 } eS 32
m. 1659
d. 5. 1, 1727

Nathaniel Paddack was son of
    ZECHARIAH PADDACK and Deborah *Sears*.

{ b. Sept., 1639
d. Aug. 17, 1732
(eSr 32)

d. 25 July, 1650 } f iii. 3:28

Zechariah Paddack was son of
    Robert Paddack and Mary ——.

{ d. + 1650
(i 187)

Priscilla Starbuck was daughter of
    Nathaniel Starbuck and Mary *Coffin*.
Nathaniel Starbuck was son of
    EDWARD STARBUCK and Katharine Reynolds.

Joanna Folger was daughter of
    PETER FOLGER and Mary Morrell.

b. 6. 23, 1683 } i 108
m. Dec. 25, 1703 } a i. 8
d. — 1743 } i 108

Lois Gorham was daughter of
    Stephen Gorham and Elizabeth *Gardner*.

{ b.
d. 7. 22, 1763
(i 108)

b. 2. 20, 1652 } i 107
m. 2. 24, 1675
d. 11. 11, 1716 } g

Stephen Gorham was son of
    John Gorham and Mary *Otis*.
John Gorham was son of
    JOHN GORHAM and Desire *Howland*.
John Gorham was son of
    RALPH GORHAM, son of James and Agnes Bennington.

{ b. 3. 14, 1654
d. 4. 1, 1732
(i 107; g)

Judith Worth was daughter of
    John Worth and Miriam *Gardner*.
John Worth was son of
    William Worth and Sarah *Macy*.

Deborah Gardner was daughter of
    RICHARD GARDNER and Sarah *Shattuck*.
Richard Gardner was son of
    THOMAS GARDINER and Margaret Frier.

b. — 1648 } h 67
m. Apr. 11, 1669
d. June 6, 1712

Ann Bunker was daughter of
    William Bunker and Mary *Macy*.

{ b. Dec. 4, 1648
d. 1729
(h 67)

d. 26 May, 1658 } f l. 299

William Bunker was son of
   George Bunker and Jane Godfrey.
George Bunker was son of
   WILLIAM BUNKER.

{ d. Jane Swain
Oct. 31, 1662
(a l. 1) }

b. Sept., 1639
m. 1659 } eSr 32
Buried Aug. 26, 1676 } eSr 32

Deborah Sears was daughter of
   RICHARD SEARS and Dorothy Thatcher.*

{ Buried Mar. 19, 1678-9
(eSr 32) }

Mary Coffin was daughter of
   TRISTRAM COFFIN and Dionis Stevens.

b. May 19, 1664
m.
d. 6. 1, 1723 }

Elizabeth Gardner was daughter of
   James Gardner and Mary *Starbuck*.
James Gardner was son of
   RICHARD GARDNER and Sarah *Shattuck*.
Richard Gardner was son of
   THOMAS GARDINER and Margaret Frier.

{ b. 3. 30, 1663
(a l. 1) }

b. 1621
m. ± 1652
d. 1. 16, 1684 } l 183

Mary Otis was daughter of
   JOHN OTIS and Mary Jacob.

{ d. + 1683
(l l83) }

Desire Howland was daughter of
   JOHN HOWLAND and Elizabeth *Tilley*.

Miriam Gardner was daughter of
   RICHARD GARDNER and Sarah *Shattuck*.
Richard Gardner was son of
   THOMAS GARDINER and Margaret Frier.

Sarah Macy was daughter of
   THOMAS MACY and Sarah Hopcot.

---

* It is not certain that she was his only wife or the mother of all, if any, of his children.—Sears Fam., p. 32.

P. 37, Will of Richard Sears—"I do beseech my brother Thacher, with his two sons as friends, in trust, to see this my last will performed." See "Descendants of Richard Sears," by Samuel P. May, for doubts as to wife Dorothy and her parentage. (Edition of 1890.)

Sarah Shattuck was daughter of
—— SHATTUCK and Damaris ——.

Mary Macy was daughter of
THOMAS MACY and Sarah Hopcot.

Mary Starbuck was daughter of
Nathaniel Starbuck and Mary *Coffin*.
Nathaniel Starbuck was son of
EDWARD STARBUCK and Katharine Reynolds.

Elizabeth Tilley was daughter of
JOHN TILLEY and —— ——.

Mary Coffin was daughter of
TRISTRAM COFFIN and Dionis Stevens.

Children of Abraham Macy and Elizabeth Coleman descend also on the paternal side from:
Thomas Macy (three times),
William Bunker (twice),
Richard Pinkham,
Thomas Gardiner (three times),
Richard Gardner (three times),
Thomas Coleman,
John Gorham,
Ralph Gorham,
Tristram Coffin (three times),
James Coffin (twice),
Edward Starbuck,
Peter Folger,
Christopher Hussey,
John Howland,
John Tilley,
Rev. Stephen Batchelder.

On the maternal side from:
Thomas Coleman,
Thomas Macy (three times),
Zachariah Paddack,
Edward Starbuck (twice),
Peter Folger,
John Gorham,
Ralph Gorham,
Thomas Gardiner (three times),
Richard Gardner (three times),
William Bunker,
Richard Sears,
Tristram Coffin (twice),
John Otis,
John Howland,
John Tilley.

Children of Townsend Powell and Catharine (Macy) were:
Aaron Macy Powell married Judith Anna Rice.
George T. Powell married Marcia Chace.
Elizabeth Powell married Henry Herrick Bond.

Aaron Macy Powell was a minister among Friends, and conspicuous in anti-slavery work; in his "Reminiscences," published by his widow, he refers to his interest having been awakened in the anti-slavery cause by John Woolman, Elihu Coleman, Anthony Benezet, Benjamin Lundy and others, chiefly members of the Society of Friends.

George T. Powell is director of the School of Practical Agriculture and Horticulture at Briarcliff Manor, New York.

Elizabeth *Powell* Bond has been Dean of Swarthmore College, Pennsylvania, since 1886.

CHAPTER XXVIII.

FAMILY OF JOSIAH MACY, OF NEW YORK.

b. Feb. 25, 1785 m. Feb. 6, 1805 d. } h 114, 170	Josiah Macy married Lydia Hussey.	b. Nov. 6, 1786 d. Sept. 25, 1861 (h 170)
b. Jan. 15, 1750 m. Dec. 3, 1778 d. June 18, 1816 } h 85, 115	Josiah Macy was son of Jonathan Macy and Rose *Pinkham*.	b. Feb. 22, 1758 d. Nov. 7, 1853 (h 115)
b. April 8, 1725 m. July, 1744 d. June 17, 1798 } h 69, 86	Jonathan Macy was son of Jonathan Macy and Lois *Gorham*.	b. Nov. 5, 1727 d. Mar. 10, 1804 (h 86)
b. ± 1675 m. Apr. 25, 1707 d. Nov. 28, 1751 } a lii. 12; h 67, 69	Jonathan Macy was son of John Macy and Judith *Worth*.	b. Dec. 22, 1689 d. Nov. 8, 1767 (h 69)
b. July 14, 1655 m. d. Oct. 14, 1691 } h 67	John Macy was son of John Macy and Deborah *Gardner*.	b. Feb. 12, 1653 d. 1712 (h 68)
b. 1608 d. 4. 19, 1682 } a l. 4	John Macy was son of THOMAS MACY and Sarah Hopcot.	b. 1612 d. 1706 (h 67)
b. 6. 6, 1730 } d 178	Rose Pinkham was daughter of Reuben Pinkham and Ann *Starbuck*.	b. 7. 22, 1736 (d 196)
b. 1. 14, 1705 m. 10. 4, 1728 OS d. 3. 2, 1782 } a 6 c l. 43 d 1781	Reuben Pinkham was son of Theophilus Pinkham and Deborah *Paddack*.	b. d. 9. 23, 1758 (d 178)
b. m. d. 1718 }	Theophilus Pinkham was son of RICHARD PINKHAM and Mary *Coffin*.	b. 1665 d. Feb. 1, 1741 (g xxiv. 151)
b. June 23, 1683 m. Dec. 25, 1703 d. } l 420 a l. 8; a iii. 12	Lois Gorham was daughter of Stephen Gorham and Elizabeth *Gardner*.	
b. Feb. 20, 1651 m. Feb. 20, 1674-5 d. } g lii. 358 l 107	Stephen Gorham was son of John Gorham and Mary *Otis*.	Bapt. May 1, 1653 (g ii. 282)
Bapt. Jan. 28, 1620-21 m. 1643 B'd Feb. 5, 1676 } l 408 f ii. 281	John Gorham was son of JOHN GORHAM and Desire *Howland*.	d. Oct. 13, 1683 (g iii. 358)
b. 1575 m. d. 1643 } l 407; g lii., 357 l 407; g lii., 357	John Gorham was son of RALPH GORHAM and ———— ————.	
b. 1550 m. 1572 d. 1576 } l 407	Ralph Gorham was son of James Gorham and Agnes Bennington.	

b. May 19, 1666 m. Sept. 22, 1684 d.	} a l. 1 a l. 4	Judith Worth was daughter of JOHN WORTH and Miriam *Gardner*.

Deborah Gardner was daughter of
   RICHARD GARDNER and Sarah *Shattuck*.
Richard Gardner was son of
   THOMAS GARDINER and Margaret Frier.

b. 1626 } x 361   { b. 1632
m. 1652   { d. 1724
d. Jan. 23, 1688 } a 4

d. Dec. 29, 1674 } x 361

Ann Starbuck was daughter of
   Paul Starbuck and Ann *Tibbetts*.
Paul Starbuck was son of
   Nathaniel Starbuck, Jr., and Dinah *Coffin*.
Nathaniel Starbuck, Jr., was son of
   Nathaniel Starbuck, Sr., and Mary *Coffin*.
Nathaniel Starbuck, Sr., was son of
   EDWARD STARBUCK and Katharine Reynolds.

b. Oct. 29, 1694   a l. 7;
m. 1. 26, 1718 O S   d 196
d. 5. 29, 1759   c l. 13 / d 196

b. Aug., 1668   g xxiv. 151
m. Nov. 20, 1690   ib.
d. 2. 9, 1753   ib.;d196

b. ± 1635   a l. 11
m. 1662   eC 56
d. 6. 6, 1719   a l. 11

b. ± 1604
d. 12. 4, 1690 } a 4

{ b. 7. 29, 1736 (d 196)
{ d. 8. 1, 1750 (d 196; g xxiv. 151)
{ b. Feb. 20, 1645 (g xxiv. 150)
{ d. 9. 13, 1717 (ib.; a l. 11)

Deborah Paddack was daughter of
   Nathaniel Paddack and Ann *Bunker*.
Nathaniel Paddack was son of
   ZACHARIAH PADDACK and Deborah *Sears*.
Zachariah Paddack was son of
   Robert Paddack and Mary ——.

b. 9. 22, 1677
m. 10. 15, 1706 } i 188
d. 8, 1756

b. Mar. 20, 1656
m. 1659 } e / f iii. 328
d. 1727

d. July 25, 1650 } f iii. 328

{ b. 9. 3, 1686 d. 1. 18, 1767 (i 188)
{ b. Sept., 1639 (eSr)

Mary Coffin was daughter of
   JAMES COFFIN and Mary Severance.
James Coffin was son of
   TRISTRAM COFFIN and Dionis Stevens.

b. Aug. 12, 1640
m. Nov. or Dec. 3, 1663 } g xxiv. 151 / ib.; eK / ib. [32
d. July 28, 1720

b. ± 1605
m. ± 1630 } g xxiv. / ib. [150 / ib.; a l.3
d. Oct. 2, 1681

{ b. Aug. 5, 1645 (eK 32)
{ d. + 1682 (eC)

Elizabeth Gardner was daughter of
   James Gardner and Mary *Starbuck*.
James Gardner was son of
   RICHARD GARDNER and Sarah *Shattuck*.
Richard Gardner was son of
   THOMAS GARDINER and Margaret Frier.

b. May 19, 1664 } y

b. 1626
m. 1652 } x 361 / a 4
d. Jan. 23, 1668

d. Dec. 29, 1674 } f ii. 230

{ b. Mar. 30, 1663 d. 1690 (f.57)
{ b. 1632 d. 1724

Mary Otis was daughter of
   JOHN OTIS and Mary Jacob.

b. 1621
m. ± 1652 } i 183
d. 1. 16, 1684

{ d. + 1683 (i 183)

Family of Josiah Macy.

b. 1592 m. ± 1622 d. 2. 22, 1673	Desire Howland was daughter of JOHN HOWLAND and Elizabeth *Tilley*.	b. 1607 d. 12, 21, 1687
	Miriam Gardner was daughter of RICHARD GARDNER and Sarah *Shattuck*. Richard Gardner was son of THOMAS GARDINER and Margaret Frier.	
	Sarah Shattuck was daughter of —— Shattuck and Damaris ——.	d. 11, 28, 1674 (x 361)
	Ann Tibbetts was daughter of Ephraim Tibbetts and Rose *Austin*.	b. 1678 (f L 81)
	Dinah Coffin was daughter of JAMES COFFIN and Mary Severance. James Coffin was son of TRISTRAM COFFIN and Dionis Stevens.	
	Mary Coffin was daughter of TRISTRAM COFFIN and Dionis Stevens.	
b. 1648 m. Apr. 11, 1669 d. June 6, 1712 } f l. 299 h 67	Ann Bunker was daughter of William Bunker and Mary *Macy*. William Bunker was son of	b. Dec. 4, 1648 d. 1720 (h 67)
d. May 26, 1658 } f l. 299	George Bunker and Jane Godfrey. George Bunker was son of WILLIAM BUNKER.	d. (Swain) Oct. 31, 1662 (a L 1)
Buried Aug. 26, 1676 } eS 32	Deborah Sears was daughter of RICHARD SEARS and Dorothy Thatcher.	Buried March 19, 1678-9 (eS 32)
b. ± 1634 m. 1662 d. 6. 6, 1719 } a l. 4 eC 56 a l. 11	Mary Starbuck was daughter of Nathaniel Starbuck, Sr., and Mary *Coffin*.	b. Feb. 20, 1645 (g xxiv. 150) d. Sept. 13, 1717 (a l. 11)

Early Settlers of Nantucket.

b. ± 1604
m.
d. 12. 4, 1690 } a l. 4

Nathaniel Starbuck, Sr., was son of
  EDWARD STARBUCK and Katharine Reynolds.

Elizabeth Tilley was daughter of
  JOHN TILLEY and —— ——.

Rose Austin was daughter of
  Thomas Austin and Ann ——.
Thomas Austin was son of
  JOSEPH AUSTIN and Sarah *Starbuck*.

b.
m. 1659
d. 1663 } f l. 81

d. 4. 19, 1682 } a l. 4

Mary Macy was daughter of
  THOMAS MACY and Sarah Hopcot.

{ b. 1612
  d. 1706
  (h 67) }

Mary Coffin was daughter of
  TRISTRAM COFFIN and Dionis Stevens.

Sarah Starbuck was daughter of
  EDWARD STARBUCK and Katharine Reynolds.

b. 5. 18, 1760
d. 6. 2, 1839 } n

Lydia Hussey was daughter of
  Zaccheus Hussey and Lydia *Folger*.
Zaccheus Hussey was son of
  Batchelder Hussey and Ann *Coffin*.
Batchelder Hussey was son of
  Sylvanus Hussey and Hepzibah *Starbuck*.
Sylvanus Hussey was son of
  STEPHEN HUSSEY and Martha *Bunker*.
Stephen Hussey was son of
  CHRISTOPHER HUSSEY and Theodate *Batchelder*.

{ b. 4. 20, 1739
  (d 94)
  d. 4. 28, 1842
  (n) }

b. 11. 20, 1728-9
m. 10. 29, 1748 O S
d. 4. 12, 1805 } n c l.157

{ h. July 12, 1729
  d. 1. 2, 1807
  (n) }

b. 1682
m. 9. 8, 1723
d. 2. 10, 1767 } a c l. 25

{ b. 11. 8, 1700
  (a 7)
  d. 12. 31, 1764
  (d) }

b. 1642
m. 10. 8, 1676
d. 4. 2, 1718 } s ll. 761

{ b. 1656
  (f l. 299)
  d. 9. 21, 1744
  (s ll. 761) }

b. 1599
m.
d. 3. 6, 1686 } Eng. Parish Records s

{ d. 1619
  (s ll. 580) }

Lydia Folger was daughter of
  William Folger and Ruth *Coffin*.
William Folger was son of
  Abishai Folger and Sarah *Mayhew*.

b.
m. 10. 7, 1749 O S
d. 6. 5, 1815 } c l. 170 d 94

{ b.
  d. 3. 11, 1814
  (d 94) }

d. 1. 22, 1778 } d 93

… *Family of Josiah Macy.* 207

b. 1678 } g xvi.
m. Dec. 29, 1699 } a i. 8
d. 7. 2, 1747 O S } g xvi.

Abishai Folger was son of
  Nathan Folger and Sarah Church.

{ d. 2. 13, 1745 O S (a) }

b. 1648
m. 1671
d. Dec. 19, 1716 } g xvi.

Nathan Folger was son of
  Eleazer Folger and Sarah *Gardner*.

{ d. Dec. 19, 1729 (g xvi.) }

d. 1690 } g xvi. 270

Eleazer Folger was son of
  PETER FOLGER and Mary Morrell.

{ d. 1704 (g xvi. 270) }

b.
m. Dec. 28, 1737 } a l. 36
d. Dec. 19, 1741 } g xxiv. 308

Ann Coffin was daughter of
  Daniel Coffin and Elizabeth Stratton.

b. Nov. 14, 1673 } g xxiv. 152

Daniel Coffin was son of
  Peter Coffin * and ——— ———.

b. May 11, 1652 } g xxiv. 150
d. May 18, 1734 } g xxiv. 150

Peter Coffin was son of
  Stephen Coffin and Mary *Bunker*.

{ b. 1652 (f l. 299) d. 1724 (g xxiv. 152) }

Stephen Coffin was son of
  TRISTRAM COFFIN and Dionis Stevens.

Hepzibah Starbuck was daughter of
  Nathaniel Starbuck, Jr., and Dinah *Coffin*.

Nathaniel Starbuck, Jr., was son of
  Nathaniel Starbuck, Sr., and Mary *Coffin*.

Nathaniel Starbuck, Sr., was son of
  EDWARD STARBUCK and Katharine Reynolds.

d. May 26, 1658 } f l. 299

Martha Bunker was daughter of
  George Bunker and Jane Godfrey.

{ d. Swain, Oct. 31, 1662 (a i. 1) }

George Bunker was son of
  WILLIAM BUNKER.

b. 1561
d. 1660 } s ii. 589

Theodate Batchelder was daughter of
  REV. STEPHEN BATCHELDER.

b. June 12, 1694 } g xxiv. 305
m.
d. Mar. 4, 1768 } g xxiv. 305

Ruth Coffin was daughter of
  Richard Coffin and Ruth *Bunker*.

d. July 1, 1747 } g xxiv. 151

Richard Coffin was son of
  JOHN COFFIN, Esq., and Hope *Gardner*.

{ b. 1669 d. Oct. 12, 1750 (g xxiv. 305) }

---

* Peter Coffin is said to have married in Boston, but there appears no further record of him.

John Coffin, Esq., was son of
  JAMES COFFIN and Mary Severance.
James Coffin was son of
  TRISTRAM COFFIN and Dionis Stevens.

b.
m. Dec. 8, 1699
d.

Sarah Mayhew was daughter of
  Paine Mayhew and Mary Rankin.
Paine Mayhew was son of
  Matthew Mayhew and Mary Skiffe.
Matthew Mayhew was son of
  THOMAS MAYHEW, JR., and Jane Paine.
Thomas Mayhew, Jr., was son of
  THOMAS MAYHEW, SR.

b. Oct. 3, 1677
d. May 8, 1761
(q x. 106)

b. 1621
d. 1657

b. 1591
d. 1681   f iii. 185

Sarah Gardner was daughter of
  RICHARD GARDNER and Sarah *Shattuck*.
Richard Gardner was son of
  THOMAS GARDINER and Margaret Frier.

Mary Bunker was daughter of
  George Bunker and Jane Godfrey.
George Bunker was son of
  WILLIAM BUNKER.

Dinah Coffin was daughter of
  JAMES COFFIN and Mary Severance.
James Coffin was son of
  TRISTRAM COFFIN and Dionis Stevens.

Mary Coffin was daughter of
  TRISTRAM COFFIN and Dionis Stevens.

Ruth Bunker was daughter of
  Jonathan Bunker and Elizabeth *Coffin*.
Jonathan Bunker was son of
  William Bunker and Mary *Macy*.

b. Feb. 25, 1675   g xxiv. 151

d. Mar. 30, 1769
(g xxiv. 151)

William Bunker was son of
  George Bunker and Jane Godfrey.
George Bunker was son of
  WILLIAM BUNKER.

Hope Gardner was daughter of
  RICHARD GARDNER and Sarah *Shattuck*.
Richard Gardner was son of
  THOMAS GARDINER and Margaret Frier.

Elizabeth Coffin was daughter of
  JAMES COFFIN and Mary Severance.
James Coffin was son of
  TRISTRAM COFFIN and Dionis Stevens.

Mary Macy was daughter of
  THOMAS MACY and Sarah Hopcot.

Sarah Shattuck was daughter of
  —— SHATTUCK and Damaris ——.

Descendants of Josiah Macy and Lydia Hussey descend also from:
  Thomas Macy (three times),
  Richard Pinkham,
  Ralph Gorham,
  John Gorham,
  Thomas Gardiner (five times),
  Richard Gardner (five times),
  Edward Starbuck (four times),
  Zachariah Paddack,
  Tristram Coffin (nine times),
  John Otis,
  John Howland,
  John Tilley,
  William Bunker, French Huguenot (four times),
  Richard Sears (Yarmouth),

Joseph Austin,
Christopher Hussey,
Stephen Hussey,
Peter Folger,
Rev. Stephen Batchelder,
James Coffin (five times),
John Coffin, Esq.
Thomas Mayhew, Sr.,
Thomas Mayhew, Jr.

A daughter of Josiah Macy, Ann Eliza Macy, married Isaac Macy, of Nantucket, son of Thomas Macy.

Another daughter, Lydia Hussey Macy, married, first, Jonathan Hasbrouck Stanton, Esq.; second, William R. Austin, of Boston.

Josiah H. *Macy*, son of Jonathan Hasbrouck *Stanton*, Esq., and Lydia Hussey (Macy), bore his name through act of legislature, his grandfather, Josiah Macy, making application for the change.

CHAPTER XXIX.

CORNELL CONNECTION WITH NANTUCKET.

Hon. Alonzo B. Cornell, twenty-fifth Governor of the State of New York, was inaugurated January 1st, 1880. He was son of

m. 1831 }uCr — Ezra Cornell and Mary Ann Wood.

Ezra Cornell was son of

m. July 4, 1805 }uCr — Elijah Cornell and Eunice *Barnard*.

Eunice Barnard was daughter of

b. 1. 24, 1743 }l 10
m. Dec. 4, 1767,
by Caleb
Bunker J. P.
Nantucket
Court }a l. 81 — Reuben Barnard of Nantucket, who married Phebe Coleman, also of Nantucket.

Reuben Barnard was son of

b. 6. 8, 1718 }d 8
m. 11, 14, 1741 }c i 107
d. 4. 20, 1800 }d 8 — Francis Barnard and Elizabeth *Macy*. { b. June 9, 1722 / d. June 1, 1765 / (h 78)

Francis Barnard was son of

b.
m. 11. 3, 1711 }c l. 5
d. 8 m, 1739 }d 8 — Benjamin Barnard and Judith *Gardner*. { d. 9, 17, 1765 / (d 8)

Benjamin Barnard was son of

b. Nov. 24, 1672 }a l. 2
d. 2. 29, 1718 }a l. 17 — Nathaniel Barnard, Jr., and Elizabeth *Coffin*. { b. Sept. 9, 1665 / (g xxiv. 152)

Nathaniel Barnard, Jr., was son of

b. Jan. 15, 1643 }t 49
d. 4. 3, 1718 }a l. 12 — Nathaniel Barnard, Sr., and Mary *Barnard*.

Nathaniel Barnard, Sr., was son of

d. ± 1677 }t 49 — THOMAS BARNARD and Eleanor ——. { d. (Little) / Nov. 27, 1694 / (t 49)

Elizabeth Macy was daughter of

b. ± 1687 }g xxiv. 152
d. Mar. 16, 1759 — Thomas Macy and Deborah *Coffin*. { d. Sept. 23, 1760 / (g xxiv. 152)

Thomas Macy was son of

b. July 14, 1655 }h 67
m.
d. Oct. 14, 1691 }h 67 — John Macy and Deborah *Gardner*. { b. Feb. 12, 1653 / (h 68) / d. 1712 / (h 68) }

John Macy was son of

d. 4. 19, 1682 }a l. 4 — THOMAS MACY and Sarah Hopcot. { b. 1612 / d. 1706 / (h 67) }

Judith Gardner was daughter of

b.
d. 1713 }g xxiv. 151 — Nathaniel Gardner and Abigail *Coffin*. { b. / d. Mar. 15, 1709 / (g xxiv. 151)

Nathaniel Gardner was son of

b. 1626 }x 361
m. 1652 }f ll. 229
d. Jan. 23, 1668 }a l. 4 — RICHARD GARDNER and Sarah *Shattuck*. { b. 1632 / d. 1724 }

Richard Gardner was son of
 THOMAS GARDINER and Margaret Frier.

Elizabeth Coffin (wife of Nathaniel Barnard, Jr.,)
 was widow of Peter Coffin, Jr., and
 daughter of
 Nathaniel Starbuck and Mary *Coffin*.
Nathaniel Starbuck was son of
 EDWARD STARBUCK and Katharine Reynolds.

Mary Barnard was daughter of
 ROBERT BARNARD and Joanna Harvey.

Deborah Coffin was daughter of
 JOHN COFFIN and Deborah *Austin*.
John Coffin was son of
 TRISTRAM COFFIN and Dionis Stevens.

Deborah Gardner was daughter of
 RICHARD GARDNER and Sarah *Shattuck*.
Richard Gardner was son of
 THOMAS GARDINER and Margaret Frier.

Abigail Coffin was daughter of
 JAMES COFFIN and Mary Severance.
James Coffin was son of
 TRISTRAM COFFIN and Dionis Stevens.

Sarah Shattuck, Sr., was daughter of
 —— SHATTUCK and Damaris ——.

Mary Coffin was daughter of
 TRISTRAM COFFIN and Dionis Stevens.

Deborah Austin was daughter of
 JOSEPH AUSTIN and Sarah *Starbuck*.

Cornell Connection.

b. 7. 12, 1719 m. d.	} d 42 n	Sarah Starbuck was daughter of EDWARD STARBUCK and Katharine Reynolds.	
		Phebe Coleman, wife of Reuben Barnard, was daughter of	
		Daniel Coleman and Elizabeth *Mooers*.	{ b. July 27, 1723 (n)
b. m. 8. 20, 1718 d. 1. 12, 1772	} c l. 12 d	Daniel Coleman was son of Solomon Coleman and Deliverance *Swett*.*	{ b. (s 987) d. 8. 2, 1783 (d 40)
b. 1644 m. d. 1715 Est. settled Mar. 2, 1715-6	} e Cl 7 n } b A l. 36	Solomon Coleman was son of John Coleman and Joanna *Folger*.	{ d. 5. 18, 1719 (a l. 12)
b. 1602 m. d. 1685	} f L 431	John Coleman was son of THOMAS COLEMAN and Susanna ———.	{ d. Nov. 16, 1650 (e Cl 6)
b. Oct. 11, 1722 d. April 8, 1740	} a l. 16 n	Elizabeth Mooers was daughter of Jonathan Mooers † and Elizabeth *Odar*.	{ b. Sept. 16, 1703 d. Apr. 22, 1784 (n)
b. Sept. 16, 1661 m. May 12, 1687	} s 987 s 988	Deliverance Swett was daughter of MOSES SWETT and Mary *Hussey*.	
b. as early as 1626 m. Nov. 1, 1647 d. June 29, 1677	} s 988	Moses Swett was son of BENJAMIN SWETT and Hester *Weare*.	{ b. ± 1629 d. Jan. 16, 1718 (s 988)
d. 1690	} g xvi. 270	Joanna Folger was daughter of PETER FOLGER and Mary Morrell.	{ d. 1704 (g xvi. 270)
m. May 6, 1701-2	} a iii. 12	Elizabeth Odar was daughter of ANTHONY ODAR and Sarah *Folger*.	{ d. Mar. 23, 1732 (g xvi. 270)
		Mary Hussey was daughter of JOHN HUSSEY and Rebecca *Perkins*.	
b. 1599 m. d. Mar. 6, 1686	} Eng. Parish Records s	John Hussey was son of CHRISTOPHER HUSSEY and Theodate *Bachelor*.	{ d. Oct., 1649 (s ii. 589)

---

 * Will of Moses Swett, 15th April, 1719, proved 19th January, 1731, mentions daughter Deliverance Coleman (N. E. His. & Gen. Reg., Vol. VI., p. 57.)

 † W. C. Folger says: Nantucket "Inquirer" of 4. 23. 1862.—Jonathan Mooer was a very probable son of Jonathan, who was son of Jonathan, who was son of Edward, who died in 1640, aged 26 years.

Hester Weare was daughter of
    NATHANIEL WEARE.

b. ± 1648
m. 1671
d. 1716 } g xvi.

Sarah Folger was daughter of
    Eleazer Folger and Sarah *Gardner*.

{ d. Dec. 19, 1729 (g xvi.)

Eleazer Folger was son of
    PETER FOLGER and Mary Morrell.

Rebecca Perkins was daughter of
    ISAAC PERKINS and Susanna ———.

b. 1561
d. 1660 } s ii. 589

Theodate Bachelor was daughter of
    REV. STEPHEN BACHELOR.

Sarah Gardner was daughter of
    RICHARD GARDNER and Sarah *Shattuck*.
Richard Gardner was son of
    THOMAS GARDINER and Margaret Frier.

Descendants from Reuben Barnard and Phebe Coleman descend also from:
    Thomas Barnard,
    Robert Barnard,
    Thomas Macy,
    Richard Gardner (three times),
    Thomas Gardiner (three times),
    Edward Starbuck (twice),
    Tristram Coffin (three times),
    James Coffin,
    Lieutenant John Coffin,
    John Hussey,
    Christopher Hussey,
    Isaac Perkins,
    Rev. Stephen Bachelor,
    Thomas Coleman,
    Moses Swett,
    Benjamin Swett,
    Peter Folger (twice),
    Anthony Odar (Isle of Wight).

Phebe (Coleman) Barnard's family removed to Nine Partners, N. Y., 10. 26. 1778. She and her children were received as members of Friends' Meeting at Nantucket, 8. 31. 1778 (Friends' Records of Nantucket).

Two of the Cornell family married into the Thorne family, of Flushing, L. I., viz.:

Richard and Joshua, sons of John Cornell, and Mary (Russell), of Rhode Island, removed to Cowneck, in 1676, and married respectively Hannah and Sarah Thorne.

CHAPTER XXX.

THE COGGESHALL FAMILY.

b. 6. 2, 1802 m. 11. 21, 1833 } uM d. 2. 21, 1885	Giles H. Coggeshall married Marianna Walters.	d. 5. 9, 1891 (uM)
b. 8. 28, 1758 m. 3. 10, 1793 } n uM d.	Giles H. Coggeshall was son of Caleb Coggeshall and Elizabeth *Hosier*.	b. 3. 14, 1770 d. 6. 20, 1851 (uM)
m. 1. 19, 1738 } n	Caleb Coggeshall was son of Job Coggeshall and Deborah *Starbuck*.*	b. 1. 19, 1739 d. 10. 13, 1781 (n)
b. Dec. 17, 1672 } j 49	Job Coggeshall was son of Caleb Coggeshall and Mercy Mitchell.	
b. 1623 m. Dec. 22, 1652 } j 49 d. May 1, 1688	Caleb Coggeshall was son of JOSHUA COGGESHALL and Joan West.	b. 1631 d. Apr. 24, 1676 (j 49)
b. 1591 d. Nov. 27, 1647 } j 49	Joshua Coggeshall was son of JOHN COGGESHALL and Mary Stanton.	b. 1604 d.—Nov. 8, 1684 (j 49)
b. England m. 6. 3, 1768 } a uM d. 1. 10, 1805	Elizabeth Hosier was daughter of Giles Hosier and Elizabeth *Mitchell*.	b. 5. 9, 1746 (uM) d. 1826 or 27 (uM)
b. June 18, 1709 m. Oct., 1729 } g xxiv. d. Nov. 27, 1780 } 308	Deborah Starbuck was daughter of Tristram Starbuck and Deborah *Coffin*.	b. 1708 d. 1789 (g xxiv. 308)
b. Aug. 9, 1668 } g xxiv. m. Nov. 20, 1690 } 151; a l.1 d. Jan. 29, 1753 } ib.	Tristram Starbuck was son of Nathaniel Starbuck, Jr., and Dinah *Coffin*.	d. Aug. 1, 1750 (g xxiv. 151)
b. ± 1634 } a l. 11 m. 1662 } cC 56 d. 6. 6, 1719 } a l. 11	Nathaniel Starbuck, Jr., was son of Nathaniel Starbuck, Sr., and Mary *Coffin*.	b. Feb. 20, 1645 (g xxiv. 150) d. 9. 13, 1717 (a l. 11)
b. ± 1604 } a L 4 d. 12. 4, 1690	Nathaniel Starbuck Sr., was son of EDWARD STARBUCK and Katharine Reynolds.	

* Deborah Coggeshall, daughter of Job and Deborah (Starbuck) Coggeshall, married, as second wife, Paul Macy, a descendant of Thomas Macy.

NOTE.—Mary Stanton, born 6. 4, 1668, was daughter of John Stanton, who was son of Robert Stanton, Robert being the progenitor, also, of the Edwin M. Stanton family.

The Coggeshall Family. 217

b. 4. 20, 1715 m. 1. 2, 1738 d. 10. 5, 1799 } uM c L 86 uM	Elizabeth Mitchell was daughter of James Mitchell and Ann *Folger*. James Mitchell was son of	b. 11. 6, 1720 (d l. 93) d. 8. 6, 1777 (uM)
b. ± 1686 m. ± 1708 d. 1722 }	RICHARD MITCHELL and Elizabeth *Tripp*. Richard Mitchell was son of RICHARD MITCHELL and Mary Wood.	b. ± 1685 d. 1740 (o iv.)
b. 12. 12, 1680 m. 1705 at Nan. d. Feb. 22, 1764 } n a ill. 12 g xxiv. 308	Deborah Coffin was daughter of Samuel Coffin and Miriam *Gardner*. Samuel Coffin was son of	b. July 14, 1685 d. Sept. 17, 1750 (g xxiv. 308)
b. Oct. 30, 1647 m. d. Sept. 5, 1711 } g xxiv. 151 g xxiv. 151	LIEUTENANT JOHN COFFIN and Deborah *Austin*. Lieutenant John Coffin was son of	d. Feb. 4, 1718 (g xxiv. 152)
b. ± 1605 m. ± 1630 d. Oct. 2, 1681 } g xxiv. 150 a L 3	TRISTRAM COFFIN and Dionis Stevens.	d. + 1682 (eC)

b. Aug. 12, 1640
m. Nov. or
Dec. 3, 1663
d. July 28, 1720 } g xxiv.
151
Ib.;eK32
g xxiv.
151
	Dinah Coffin was daughter of
	    JAMES COFFIN and Mary Severance.
	James Coffin was son of
	    TRISTRAM COFFIN and Dionis Stevens.
		b. Aug. 5, 1645
		(eK 32)

	Mary Coffin was daughter of TRISTRAM COFFIN and Dionis Stevens.	
b. 8. 17, 1689 m. 12. 1, 1710-11 d. 4. 19, 1772 O S } a l. 15 c L 6 d l. 93	Ann Folger was daughter of Jethro Folger and Mary *Starbuck*. Jethro Folger was son of	b. Dec. 31, 1692 (a L 7) d. 7. 22, 1773 (d l. 93)
b. 1659 m. d. 8. 23, 1732 O S } n n	John Folger and Mary *Barnard*. John Folger was son of	b. Feb. 24, 1667 (a l. 1) d. 8. 6, 1737 O S
d. 1690 } g xvi.	PETER FOLGER and Mary Morrell.	d. 1704 (g xvi.)

b. ± 1656
m. Jan. 19, 1681-2
d. May 30, 1730 }
	Elizabeth Tripp was daughter of
	    JAMES TRIPP and Mercy *Lawton*.
	James Tripp was son of
	    JOHN TRIPP and Mary Paine.
		d. ± 1685

b. Oct. 23, 1653 m. May 17, 1674 Will proved July 17, 1728 } y b A l. 135	Miriam Gardner was daughter of Richard Gardner [2] and Mary *Austin*.	d. June 1, 1721 (y) [O S

Richard Gardner ² was son of
  RICHARD GARDNER ¹ and Sarah *Shattuck*.
Richard Gardner ¹ was son of
  THOMAS GARDINER and Margaret Frier.

b. 1626 } x 361;
m. 1652
d. Jan. 23, 1668 } a L 4

d. Dec. 29, 1674 } x

{ b. 1632
{ d. 1724

Deborah Austin was daughter of
  JOSEPH AUSTIN and Sarah *Starbuck*.

b.
m. 1659 } f L
d. 1663

Mary Starbuck was daughter of
  Nathaniel Starbuck, Jr., and Dinah *Coffin*.
Nathaniel Starbuck, Jr., was son of
  Nathaniel Starbuck, Sr., and Mary *Coffin*.
Nathaniel Starbuck Sr., was son of
  EDWARD STARBUCK and Katharine Reynolds.

Mary Barnard was daughter of
  Nathaniel Barnard and Mary *Barnard*.
Nathaniel Barnard was son of
  THOMAS BARNARD and Eleanor ——.

b. Jan. 15, 1642-3 } t 49
d. 4. 3, 1718 } b A l.
              } a l. 12

d. ± 1677 } t 49

{ d. 1. 17, 1717-18
{ (a L 12)

{ d. (Little)
{ Nov. 27, 1694
{ (t 49)

Mercy Lawton was daughter of
  GEORGE LAWTON and Elizabeth *Hazard*.

} eH

Mary Austin was daughter of
  JOSEPH AUSTIN and Sarah *Starbuck*.

b.
m. 1659 } f L
d. 1663

Sarah Shattuck was daughter of
  —— SHATTUCK, SR., and Damaris ——.

{ (x 361)

Dinah Coffin was daughter of
  JAMES COFFIN and Mary Severance.
James Coffin was son of
  TRISTRAM COFFIN and Dionis Stevens.

Mary Coffin was daughter of
   TRISTRAM COFFIN and Dionis Stevens.

d. 1682   } t 52

Mary Barnard was daughter of
   ROBERT BARNARD and Joanna Harvey.

} eH

Elizabeth Hazard was daughter of
   Thomas Hazard and Martha ——.

Sarah Starbuck was daughter of
   EDWARD STARBUCK and Katharine Reynolds.

Descendants from Giles H. Coggeshall and Marianna Walters descend also from:
   John Coggeshall,
   Joshua Coggeshall,
   Edward Starbuck (four times),
   George Lawton,
   Thomas Hazard,
   Joseph Austin (twice),
   Tristram Coffin (five times),
   James Coffin (twice),
   Lieutenant John Coffin,
   Richard Mitchell [2] (Rhode Island),
   Richard Mitchell,[1]
   Peter Folger,
   John Tripp,
   James Tripp,
   Thomas Gardiner,
   Richard Gardner,
   Thomas Barnard,
   Robert Barnard.

John Coggeshall was Deputy to Massachusetts Court, 1634-37. (Mass. Col. Rec. Vol. I., pp. 116, 135, etc.) Assistant Newport, R. I., 1640-44 (R. I. Col. Rec. Vol. I., pp. 101, 110, etc.) President of R. I. Colony, 1647.

(R. I. Col. Rec. Vol I., p. 148.) Treasurer, 1664-1672. (Pierce's Lists, p. 121.)

Elizabeth Coggeshall, daughter of Giles Hozier and Elizabeth (Mitchell) Hozier, was born at Newport, Rhode Island, on the " 14th of Third month, 1770."

In 1793 she married Caleb Coggeshall, and in 1802 they removed to New York.

She was a minister of the Society of Friends, active in the old world, and in our own country, visiting meetings and families, wherever there was a settlement of Friends.

During a period of thirteen years she visited all the meetings of Friends in America. Her second pilgrimage to England was made in 1813, when the war between England and America was in progress, and transportation was difficult; application was made to the Government, and Elizabeth Coggeshall was permitted to take passage in company with prisoners of war.

CHAPTER XXXI.

STANTON CONNECTION WITH NANTUCKET.

b. Dec. 19, 1814 d. Dec. 24, 1869 b. 5. 1, 1788 m. Feb. 24, 1814 d. Nov. 5, 1873 } uSt	Edwin McMasters Stanton was son of David Stanton and Lucy Latham Norman.	b. Nov. 27, 1793 d. Nov. 5, 1873 (uSt)
b. 1746 m. 1774 d. 1799 } h 83	David Stanton was son of Benjamin Stanton and Abigail *Macy*.	b. 1753 d. 1824 (h 82)
b. 6. 25, 1688 m. ± 1745 d. 1751 } uSt	Benjamin Stanton was son of Henry Stanton and Lydia Albertson.	
b. 1645 d. Oct. 3, 1713 } uSt	Henry Stanton was son of John Stanton and Mary (Clarke) Cranston.	b. 1641 d. April 7, 1711 (uSt)
b. 1598-9 d. Aug. 29, 1672 } uSt	John Stanton was son of Robert Stanton and Avis ——.	
b. Sept. 12, 1714 m. Nov., 1739 d. 10. 13, 1778 } h 68, 82 dNC	Abigail Macy was daughter of David Macy and Dinah *Gardner*.	b. d. 6. 13, 1796 (dNC)
b. ± 1675 m. April 25, 1707 d. Nov. 28, 1751 } h 67, 69	David Macy was son of John Macy, Jr., and Judith *Worth*.	b. Dec. 22, 1689 d. Nov. 8, 1767 (h 69)
b. July 14, 1655 m. d. Oct. 14, 1691 } h 67	John Macy, Jr., was son of John Macy, Sr., and Deborah *Gardner*.	b. Feb. 12, 1658 d. 1712 (h 68)
d. 4. 19, 1682 } a l. 4	John Macy, Sr., was son of THOMAS MACY and Sarah Hopcot.	b. 1612 d. 1706 (h 67)
b. July 1, 1680 m. d. June 17, 1760 } g xxiv. 152; a L 3 g xxiv. 152	Dinah Gardner was daughter of Solomon Gardner and Anna *Coffin*.	b. d. Apr. 22, 1740 (g xxiv. 152)
b. Oct. 23, 1653 m. May 17, 1674 d. May 3, 1728 O S } n	Solomon Gardner was son of Richard Gardner, Jr., and Mary *Austin*.	d. June 1, 1721 (y) [OS
b. 1626 m. 1652 d. Jan. 23, 1668 } x 361; a L 4	Richard Gardner, Jr., was son of RICHARD GARDNER, SR., and Sarah *Shattuck*.	b. 1632 d. 1724

NOTE.—Other members of this family of the name, who have located on or lived in and near Nantucket, appear to have descended from John, a half-brother of Henry Stanton.

Early Settlers of Nantucket.

{ f ii. 230

Richard Gardner, Sr., was son of
   THOMAS GARDINER and Margaret Frier.

b. May 19, 1666 } a l. 1
m. 1684
d.

Judith Worth was daughter of
   John Worth and Miriam *Gardner*.
John Worth was son of
   WILLIAM WORTH and Sarah *Macy*.

{ b. July 14, 1665
(a l. 4)

b.
m. April 11, 1665 } h 67
d. Oct., 1724

{ b. Aug. 1, 1646
d. 1701
(h 67)

Deborah Gardner was daughter of
   RICHARD GARDNER, SR., and Sarah *Shattuck*.
Richard Gardner, Sr., was son of
   THOMAS GARDINER and Margaret Frier.

b. May 11, 1652 } g xxiv.
m.   152
d. May 18, 1734 } ib.

Anna Coffin was daughter of
   Stephen Coffin and Mary *Bunker*.
Stephen Coffin was son of
   TRISTRAM COFFIN and Dionis Stevens.

{ b. ± 1652
(f l. 299)
d. 1724
(g xxiv. 152)

b. ± 1605
m. ± 1630 } g xxiv.
d. Oct. 2, 1681 } a l. 3 [150

{ d. + 1682
(eC)

b. 1659
d. 1663 } f L

Mary Austin was daughter of
   Joseph Austin and Sarah *Starbuck*.

{ Quint's Old
Dover,
pp. 180-131

Sarah Shattuck was daughter of
   ——Shattuck and Damaris ——.

Miriam Gardner was daughter of
   RICHARD GARDNER, SR., and Sarah *Shattuck*.
Richard Gardner, Sr., was son of
   THOMAS GARDINER and Margaret Frier.

Sarah Macy was daughter of
   THOMAS MACY and Sarah Hopcot.

d. May 26, 1658 } f l. 299

Mary Bunker was daughter of
   George Bunker and Jane Godfrey.
George Bunker was son of
   WILLIAM BUNKER.

{ d. Oct. 31, 1662
(a l. 1)

b. ± 1604
m.
d. 4. 12, 1690 } a l. 4

Sarah Starbuck was daughter of
   EDWARD STARBUCK and Katharine Reynolds.

Descendants of Benjamin Stanton and Abigail Macy descend also from:
    Thomas Macy (twice),
    Richard Gardner (three times),
    Thomas Gardner (three times),
    Tristram Coffin,
    Edward Starbuck,
    William Bunker.

CHAPTER XXXII.

CONNECTION OF THE WATERMAN FAMILY WITH NANTUCKET.

Alexander McKenzie, Pastor of the First Church (Congregational), Cambridge, Mass., descends from Nantucket settlers through the marriage of his grandfather

m. Aug. 26, 1794 } a L 134

Martin McKenzie and Hepzibeth Waterman.

b. March 5, 1745
m. Feb. 22, 1769 } a L 83
d. Jan. 22, 1824

Hepzibeth Waterman was daughter of
Thaddeus * Waterman and Hepzibah *Coffin*.

{ b. Jan. 9, 1754
{ d. Oct. 16, 1841

b. Mar. 24, 1723 } g xxiv. 307
d. Mar. 14, 1789 } lb.

Hepzibah Coffin was daughter of
Jonathan Coffin and Priscilla Coffin.
Jonathan Coffin was son of

{ b. Oct. 19, 1723
{ (g xxiv. 309)
{ d. Mar. 27, 1796

b. Aug. 28, 1692 } g xxiv.
m. Nov. 24, 1711 } lb. [306
d. Feb. 5, 1773 } lb.

Jonathan Coffin and Hepzibah *Harker*.
Jonathan Coffin was son of

{ b. 1694
{ d. Dec. 31, 1773
{ (g xxiv. 307)

b. Aug. 12, 1640 } g xxiv. 151
m. Nov. or
Dec. 3, 1663 } lb.;eK32
d. July 28, 1720 } lb.

JAMES COFFIN and Mary Severance.
James Coffin was son of

{ b. Aug. 5, 1645
{ (eK 32)

b. ± 1605 } eC 18;
m. ± 1630 } g xxiv.
d. Oct. 2, 1681 } 150;
a L 3

TRISTRAM COFFIN and Dionis Stevens.

{ d. + 1682
{ (eC)

b. July 28, 1698 } g xxiv. 309
d. Jan. 15, 1780 } lb.

Priscilla Coffin was daughter of
Josiah Coffin and Elizabeth *Coffin*.
Josiah Coffin was son of

{ b. Oct. 27, 1703
{ d. 1774
{ (g xxiv. 154)

b. Sept. 16, 1663 } g xxiv. 152
m.
d. 1726 } lb.

Jethro Coffin and Mary *Gardner*.
Jethro Coffin was son of

{ b. May, 1670
{ d. Oct. 27, 1767
{ (g xxiv. 153)

b. 1631
m.
d. Mar. 21, 1715 } g xxiv. 150 } lb.

PETER COFFIN and Abigail *Starbuck*.

---

* The Town Records give the name Thaddeus; family tradition says Jedidiah; it is not impossible that a Recorder's mind may lapse for a moment and a Christian name may be handed down incorrectly, since all human agencies fail sometimes. The records, however, will continue to be accepted, as there is no higher authority.

Peter Coffin was son of
   TRISTRAM COFFIN and Dionis Stevens.

Hepzibah Harker was daughter of
   Ebenezer Harker * and Patience *Folger*.

b.
m. May 19, 1692 } g xxiv.
d. Aug. 2, 1741 } ib. [154

Elizabeth Coffin was daughter of
   James Coffin and Ruth *Gardner*.
James Coffin was son of
   JAMES COFFIN and Mary Severance.
James Coffin was son of
   TRISTRAM COFFIN and Dionis Stevens.

{ b. Jan. 26, 1676-7
d. Oct. 4, 1748
(g xxiv. 154)

b.
m.
d. May 6, 1706 } n
} f ii. 230
} †

Mary Gardner was daughter of
   JOHN GARDNER and Priscilla Grafton.
John Gardner was son of
   THOMAS GARDINER and Margaret Frier.

b. — 1604
m.
d. 12. 4, 1696 } a L. 4

Abigail Starbuck was daughter of
   EDWARD STARBUCK and Katharine Reynolds.

d. 1690 } g xvi.
270

Patience Folger was daughter of
   PETER FOLGER and Mary Morrell.

{ d. 1705
(g xvi. 270)

Ruth Gardner was daughter of
   JOHN GARDNER and Priscilla Grafton.
John Gardner was son of
   THOMAS GARDINER and Margaret Frier.

---

* William C. Folger expresses doubt of given name of Mr. Harker.

† Also, Essex County Probate Records at Salem. Will dated July 10th, 1668, mentions sons Thomas, John, George, Samuel, Richard and Joseph; daughters Sarah Balch, Ruth Grafton and Miriam Hills.

Descendants from Thaddeus Waterman and Hepzibeth (Coffin) descend also from:
  Tristram Coffin (three times),
  Peter Coffin,
  James Coffin (twice),
  Thomas Gardiner (twice),
  John Gardner (twice),
  Edward Starbuck,
  Peter Folger.

Avis Waterman, sister of Hepzibah, and daughter of Thaddeus Waterman and Hepzibah (Coffin), married John Sherman, Jr., whose daughter, Lydia Spooner Sherman, married Simeon Smith Bicknell, Preceptor in Marblehead Academy, afterwards pastor and instructor in Vermont, New York and Wisconsin.

The daughter of Simeon Smith Bicknell, Lydia Matilda Bicknell, married Norman Fox Hopkins.

New England History and Genealogical Register, Vol. XIV., p. 373, gives the following account of Captain Robert Waterman, of New Orleans, brother of Avis and Hepzibeth Waterman. He was born in 1785 and died April 29th, 1860:

"He was a native of Nantucket, and, like most of those hardy islanders, followed the sea from boyhood, commencing at the age of eleven years.

"For some time he commanded one of the packet ships between New York and Liverpool. He was a fine specimen of the American shipmaster of the old school, courageous, courteous and inflexibly honest."

CHAPTER XXXIII.

THE WADLEY, OR WADLEIGH, FAMILY.

The family of Dole Wadley includes many names of Nantucket settlers, or of those closely associated with them.

DOLE WADLEY married, September, 1860, Elizabeth Carrol Pierce.

Their daughter, Sarah Wadleigh, married Edward Everett Capehart.

b. Oct. 19, 1782
m. Feb. 2, 1812 } q viii. 73
d. June 6, 1826

Dole Wadleigh, or Wadley, was son of
  Dole Wadley and Sarah *Colcord*.

b. Nov. 3, 1743
m. } ib.
d. April 5, 1821

Dole Wadley was son of
  Joseph Wadley and Elizabeth *Dole*.   { b. Mar. 2, 1744 (q viii. 73)

b. Sept. 7, 1711
m. Jan. 5, 1737 } ib.
d. Jan. 23, 1792

Joseph Wadley was son of
  Joseph Wadleigh and Anne *Swaine*.   { b. 1710 (s 986)

Sarah Colcord was daughter of
  John Colcord and Lydia *Morrill*.

b. 1725
m. } f l. 425
d. 1824

John Colcord was son of
  Ebenezer Colcord and Patience Stevens.

Ebenezer Colcord was son of

b. May 20, 1695 } s 644

  Ebenezer Colcord and Hannah *Fellows*.   { b. July 20, 1697 (t 156)

b. ± 1655 } s 643
d. Oct. 5, 1736

Ebenezer Colcord was son of
  Samuel Colcord and Mary Ayer.   { b. March 22, 1660-1

b. 1615 or 16
m. } s 643
d. Feb. 10, 1682

Samuel Colcord was son of
  Edward Colcord and Ann ———.

b. July 2, 1702
m. Dec. 21, 1731 } eNC 30
d. Jan. 4, 1776

Elizabeth Dole was daughter of
  Benjamin Dole and Sarah *Clark*.*

b. July 29, 1689 } ib. 27
m. Mar. 7, 1709 } ib. 29
d. May 3, 1753 } ib. 27

Sarah Clark was daughter of
  Nathaniel Clark and Sarah *Greenleaf*.   { b. Nov. 3, 1692 (eNC 27) d.

---

* N. E. Reg., 1884, p. 78, says: *Supposed* to have married Sarah Clark.

b. Mar. 13, 1666 m. Dec. 15, 1685 d. Oct., 1690	eNC 21 ib. 24 ib. 21	Nathaniel Clark was son of Nathaniel Clark and Elizabeth Toppan.		b. Oct. 16, 1665 (eNC 24)
b. 1644. m. Nov. 23, 1663 d. Aug. 25, 1690	w 1, 384 eNC 20 ib. 16	Nathaniel Clark was son of Nathaniel Clark and Elizabeth *Somerby*.		b. Nov. 1, 1646 d. Mar. 15, 1716 (ib. 20; f iv. 140)

Ann Swaine was daughter of
   Caleb Swaine and Hannah ———.

b. m. Oct. 20, 1676 d.	s 986	Caleb Swain was son of William Swain and Mary Webster.		b. Dec. 19, 1658 (s 1033)
b. ± 1619 m. d. Oct. 20, 1657	s 986; n	William Swain was son of William Swain and Prudence Marston.		
b. 1600 d. Apr. 14, 1682	eS 5 a L 3	William Swain was son of RICHARD SWAIN and ——— ———.		

Lydia Morrill was daughter of
   William Morrill and Lydia Trask.

b. Dec. 22, 1703 Pub. † Feb. 19, 1728-9 d. 1757	t 255	William Morrill was son of Abraham Morrill and Eleanor *True*.		b. Nov. 4, 1705 (t 326) d. — 1734-5 (t 335)
b. Jan. 13, 1646 m. Jun. 2, 1681	t 156	Hannah Fellows was daughter of Samuel Fellows and Abigail *Barnard*.		b. Jan. 20, 1656 (t 50)
b. ± 1612 m. d. ± 1677	t 49	Abigail Barnard was daughter of THOMAS BARNARD and Eleanor ———.		d. Little, Nov. 27, 1694 (t 49)
b. Oct. 30, 1665 m. Mar. 1, 1685-6 d. Aug. 6, 1694	t 184 t 186	Sarah Greenleaf was daughter of Samuel Greenleaf and Sarah Kent.		
Bapt. Aug. 10, 1628 m. Nov. 13, 1651	t 183	Samuel Greenleaf was son of STEPHEN GREENLEAF and Elizabeth *Coffin*.		d. Nov. 19, 1678 (t 184)
b. ± 1590 m. d. Mar. 24, 1670-71	t 183	Stephen Greenleaf was son of EDMUND GREENLEAF and Sarah Dole.		d. Jan. 18, 1663 (t 183)

Bapt. Mar. 17, 1612
m.
d. Oct. 2, 1652
	f iv.
	140
		Elizabeth Somerby was daughter of
		   Henry Somerby and Judith *Greenleaf*.
		Judith Greenleaf * was daughter of
		   EDMUND GREENLEAF and Sarah Dole.
				b. Sept. 2, 1625
				d. Dec. 15, 1705
				(t 183)

---

* Judith (Greenleaf), widow of Henry Somerby, married Tristram Coffin, Jr.

† Banns published.

Eleanor True was daughter of
  William True and Eleanor *Stevens*.
Eleanor Stevens was daughter of
  Sergeant Benj. Stevens and Hannah *Barnard*.
Hannah Barnard was daughter of
  THOMAS BARNARD and Eleanor ——.

b. 1670 } p 334
m. 1692
d. Mar. 8, 1733-4

b. 1650 } t 50
m. Oct. 28, 1673   t 326
d. Mar. 13, 1689-90

b. ± 1612 } t 49
m.
d. ± 1677

{ b. Jan. 2, 1674-5
  d. April 29, 1768
  (p 326)

{ b. Nov. 24, 1649
  (t 50)
  d. Feb. 27, 1711-
  [12

{ d. Little,
  Nov. 27, 1694
  (p 49)

Elizabeth Coffin was daughter of
  TRISTRAM COFFIN and Diones Stevens.

b. ± 1605 } g xxiv.
m. ± 1630   150
d. Oct. 2, 1681

{ d. + 1682
  (eC)

Elizabeth Carroll Pierce was daughter of
  Elbridge Gerry Pierce and Sarah Jane *Gorham*.
Sarah Jane Gorham was daughter of
  Barney Gorham and Jane Johnson.
Barney Gorham was son of
  Stephen Gorham and Sarah *Freeman*.
Stephen Gorham was son of
  Josiah Gorham and Priscilla *Sears*.
Josiah Gorham was son of
  Joseph Gorham and Sarah Sturgis.
Joseph Gorham was son of
  JOHN GORHAM and Desire *Howland*.
John Gorham was son of
  RALPH GORHAM * and —— ——.

b. July 22, 1710 } eS 67
m. Mar. 16, 1758   eF 91
d.

b. Sept. 7, 1692 } eB 425
m. Mar. 11, 1721-2
d. April 3, 1775

b. Feb. 16, 1653-4 } eB 413
m. 1678
d. July 9, 1726   eB 415

Bapt. Jan. 28, } eB 408
  1620-21
m. 1643
d. Feb. 5, 1676

b. 1575 } eB 407
m.   g iii. 257
d. ± 1643

{ b. Oct. 15, 1737
  (eF 91)

{ b. July 1, 1701
  (eS 67)

{ d. Oct. 13, 1683
  (g iii. 358)

Sarah Freeman was daughter of
  John Freeman and Joanna Picket.
John Freeman was son of
  John Freeman and Mercy Watson.
John Freeman was son of
  John Freeman and Sarah Merrick.
John Freeman was son of
  JOHN FREEMAN and Mercy *Prence*.

b. Aug. 3, 1709 } eF 51
m. Jan. 29, 1730-1

b. July, 1678 } eF 34
m. ± 1701

b. Dec. 1651 } eF 27
m. Dec. 18, 1672
d. July 27, 1721   eF 35

b.
m. Feb. 13, 1649-50 } eF 27
d. Oct. 28, 1719   eB 386
Aet. 98

{ b. 1685
  (eF 35)

{ b. Aug. 1, 1654
  d. Apr. 21, 1696
  (eF 35)

---

* N. E. Hist. and Gen'l Reg., X., 293, has: "Father of Ralph, who emigrated to New England, was James Gorham, of Benefield, born 1550, married Agnes Bennington 1572."

b. ± 1675
m. Sep. 19, 1700 } eS 67
d. May 7, 1750

b.
m.
d. Jan. 13, 1697-8 } eS 48

b.
m.
Buried Aug. 26, 1676 } eS 32

Priscilla Sears was daughter of
    Joseph Sears and Hannah Hall.
Joseph Sears was son of
    Silas Sears and Anna Bursell.
Silas Sears was son of
    RICHARD SEARS and Dorothy Thatcher.

{ b. ± 1680
(eS 67)
d July 28, 1753 }

{ d. Mar. 4, 1725-6
(eS 48) }

{ Buried March
19, 1678-79
eS 32) }

{ b. ± 1593
m. — 1624
d. 1687 }

Desire Howland was daughter of
    JOHN HOWLAND and Elizabeth *Tilley*.

{ b. ± 1607 }

m. 1624 }

Mercy Prence was daughter of
    GOVERNOR THOMAS PRENCE and Mary *Brewster*.

Elizabeth Tilley was daughter of
    JOHN TILLEY and ——— ———.

b. 1566-67 }

Mary Brewster was daughter of
    WILLIAM BREWSTER (Mayflower).

Descendants of Dole Wadley and Elizabeth Carroll Pierce descend also from
    William Brewster,
    John Tilley,
    Thomas Prence,
    John Howland,
    Richard Sears,
    John Freeman,
    Ralph Gorham,
    John Gorham,
    Thomas Barnard, twice;
    Edmund Greenleaf, twice;
    Stephen Greenleaf,
    Tristram Coffin,
    Richard Swain,
    Edward Colcord.

CHAPTER XXXIV.

FAMILY OF COFFIN COLKET.

Tristram Coffin Colcord was born in Epping, New Hampshire, October 15th, 1809, and died in Philadelphia, April 5th, 1883. He was the first of his name in Philadelphia, coming here about 1830. He was associated with many corporations during his life, and at the time of his death was President of the Philadelphia City Passenger Railway Company, the Philadelphia, Germantown and Norristown Railroad Company and the Chestnut Hill Railroad Company.

After coming to Philadelphia he dropped the name of Tristram and spelled his surname Colket, conforming to the usual pronunciation.

He was therefore known in Philadelphia business circles as Coffin Colket. He married, March 21, 1839, Mary Pennypacker Walker, b. in Chester County, Pa., Sept. 3, 1819. He left four sons and three daughters. His widow died November 15, 1889.

b. Mar. 7, 1758 d. Jan. 15, 1836	Coffin Colket was son of Peter Colcord and Phebe *Hamilton*.	b. 1760 d. July 8, 1857
b. Newmarket Will proved Jan. 16, 1797	Peter Colcord was son of Edward Colcord and Jane *Coffin*.	b. Dover, Mar. 11, 1721-2
b. Hampton, Mar. 4, 1683-4 Settled at Newmarket	Edward Colcord was son of Jonathan Colcord.	
b. ± 1655 at Hampton d. Oct. 5, 1736, Kingston s 643	Jonathan Colcord was son of Samuel Colcord and Mary Ayer.	d. Kingston, N. H., May 29, 1739
	Samuel Colcord was son of EDWARD COLCORD and Ann ———.	
d. — 1778	Phebe Hamilton was daughter of James Hamilton and Phœbe Broughton, of Portsmouth, New Hampshire.	

232   *Early Settlers of Nantucket.*

b. 1691
m. Nov. 18, 1719
d. Dover, June 21, 1761

b. Jan. 18, 1665
m. ± 1685
d. Jan. 23, 1717

b. 1631 in England
America, 1642 } g xxiv.
d. Exeter, N.H. March 21, 1715

b. 1605
America, 1642 } g xxiv. 150
d. Nantucket, Oct. 2, 1681 } a l. 3

Jane Coffin was daughter of
Tristram Coffin⁴ and Jane Heard.   { b. June 18, 1699

Tristram Coffin⁴ was son of
Tristram Coffin³ and Deborah *Colcord*.   { b. May 21, 1664

Tristram Coffin³ was son of
PETER COFFIN² and Abigail *Starbuck*.

Peter Coffin² was son of
TRISTRAM COFFIN¹ and Dionis Stevens.   { d. + 1682 (eC)

b. ± 1617
d. Feb. 10, 1681-2

Deborah Colcord was daughter of
EDWARD COLCORD and Ann ——.   { d. June 24, 1689

b. ± 1604
d. 12, 4, 1690 } a l. 4

Abigail Starbuck was daughter of
EDWARD STARBUCK and Katharine Reynolds.

Edward Colcord¹ from England arrived at Piscataquay River, 1631 (Prov. Papers, N. H., 1, 110); Exeter, 1638; Dover, 1640; Hampton, 1644; died at Hampton, February 10th, 1681-2.

Descendants from Coffin Colket descend also from:
Tristram Coffin,
Peter Coffin,
Edward Starbuck,
Edward Colcord (twice).

Samuel Colcord, son of Edward Colcord and Ann ——, was Representative, 1682 (Savage, I., 424); Grantee of Kingston (State Papers, New Hampshire, II., 131).

Mary Ayer (wife of Samuel Colcord, of Kingston, N. H.) was daughter of Thomas Ayer, of Haverhill. The authority given for this is "Essex Registry of Deeds," Book 51, leaf 204, in which Mary Colcord and her husband, Samuel Colcord, convey land of her father, Thomas Ayer, of Haverhill, in 1725.

The "Essex Antiquarian" (May number, 1900) gives wife of Samuel Colcord as Mary, daughter of Thomas and Elizabeth (Hutchins) Ayer.

Elizabeth Hutchins was a daughter of John and Frances Hutchins, of Newbury. (Family Papers.)

"History of Newbury" gives Elizabeth among children of John and Frances Hutchins.

Frances was once presented at court for wearing a silk hood, but was discharged "upon testimony of her being brought up above the ordinary ranke." ("History of Newbury," page 58.) The law permitted those only who were worth two hundred pounds to wear "a silk hood and scarfe." This was probably intended to accomplish the same end as the rule laid down by the Quakers that Friends shall "be careful to live within the bounds of their circumstances."

John Hutchins died February 6th, 1685-6; his widow, Frances, April 5th, 1694.

CHAPTER XXXV.

JOHN GREENLEAF WHITTIER.

The blood of more than one of the pioneers of Nantucket flowed in the veins of the poet Whittier.

The descent from Christopher Hussey, which was a tradition of the Whittier family, and was believed by the poet himself, appears upon late investigation to be without foundation.

His ancestry has been traced to Richard Hussey, who possibly was a descendant of Christopher, but this is not probable. Thomas Whittier, the progenitor of the Whittier family, came from Wiltshire, England, in 1638, settled at Newbury, afterwards removed to Salisbury, thence to Haverhill. He married Ruth Green, a relative of John Rolfe, who was associated with the proprietors of Nantucket, and with Thomas Whittier came to America in the ship Confidence.

Henry Rolfe, brother of John, in his will, dated "15th 12th 1642," gave his "kinsman Thomas Whittier a swarme of bees."

b. Dec. 17, 1807 d. Sept. 7, 1892	John Greenleaf Whittier was son of	
b. Nov. 22, 1760 m. Oct. 3, 1804 d. June 11, 1830	John Whittier and Abigail *Hussey*.	b. Sept. 3, 1779 d. Dec. 28, 1857
b. Mar. 31, 1716 m. July 12, 1739 d. Oct. 10, 1796	John Whittier was son of Joseph Whittier, 2d, and Sarah *Greenleaf*.	b. Mar. 5, 1721 d. Mar. 17, 1807
b. May 8, 1669 m. May 24, 1694 d. Dec. 25, 1739	Joseph Whittier, 2d, was son of Joseph Whittier and Mary Peaslee.	b. July 14, 1672
d. in Haverhill, Nov. 28, 1696	Joseph Whittier was son of THOMAS WHITTIER and Ruth Green.	d. July, 1710

NOTE.—The above facts concerning Mr. Whittier's ancestry are taken from a careful compilation of original records, verified by wills and deeds, the result of several years of extended research by Charles C. Whittier, Boston, Mass.

b. Dec. 12, 1742 m. May 3, 1769 d. April 17, 1814	Abigail Hussey was daughter of Samuel Hussey and Mercy *Evans*.	d. Jan. 25, 1828
b. June 23, 1699 m. ± 1737 d. Feb. 8, 1712	Samuel Hussey was son of Joseph Hussey and Elizabeth (Robinson) (Tibbetts *).	b. July 30, 1712 d. May 3, 1773

From Eng.,
  Dover, N. H.
d. ± 1733
	Joseph Hussey was son of
	  RICHARD HUSSEY and Jane ——.	

b. Jan. 25, 1691-2 m. June 7, 1714 d.	Sarah Greenleaf was daughter of Nathaniel Greenleaf and Judith *Coffin*.	b. Feb. 23, 1693 d. Dec. 17, 1769
b. Feb. 11, 1667-8 m. Nov. 12, 1689 d. Sept. 13, 1740	Nathaniel Greenleaf was son of Tristram Greenleaf and Margaret Piper.	b. June 16, 1668
b. ± 1628 m. Nov. 13, 1651 d. Oct. 31, 1690	Tristram Greenleaf was son of STEPHEN GREENLEAF and Elizabeth *Coffin*.	b. in Eng., 1634 d. Nov. 19, 1678

b. ± 1590
d. 1670-1
	Stephen Greenleaf was son of
	  EDMUND GREENLEAF and Sarah Dole.
		d. Jan. 18,
		  1662-63

b. March 28, 1708 m. ± 1740 d. Dec. 7, 1768	Mercy Evans was daughter of Joseph Evans and Elizabeth Hanson.	b. Sept. 12, 1707
b. June 4, 1682 m. April 6, 1704 d. ± Dec., 1750	Joseph Evans was son of Joseph Evans and Mercy Horne.	b. ± 1680

b.
m. ± 1681
d. Feb. 27, 1696-7
	Joseph Evans was son of
	  ROBERT EVANS † and Ann (Thompson) (Hodgdon) (as second wife).
		d. — May 30,
		  1727

b. Aug. 18, 1664 m. 1685 d. Aug. 31, 1725	Judith Coffin was daughter of Stephen Coffin and Sarah Atkinson.	
b. 1632 m. Mar. 2, 1653 d. Feb. 4, 1704	Stephen Coffin was son of TRISTRAM COFFIN, JR., and Judith (*Greenleaf*) (Somerby).	
m. 1630 d. 1681	Tristram Coffin, Jr., was son of TRISTRAM COFFIN and Dionis Stevens.	g xxiv. 150 a i. 3

---

* Widow of Henry Tibbetts and daughter of Timothy and Mary (Roberts) Robinson.

† Robert Evans's first wife was Elizabeth *Colcord*, daughter of Edward and Ann Colcord, of Hampton.

Elizabeth Coffin was daughter of
TRISTRAM COFFIN and Dionis Stevens.

b. 1590
d. Mar. 24, 1670-1

Judith (Greenleaf) (Somerby) was daughter of
EDMUND GREENLEAF and Sarah Dole.

d. Jan. 18, 1662-3

John Greenleaf Whittier descended from:
Thomas Whittier,
Richard Hussey,
Stephen Greenleaf,
Edmund Greenleaf (twice),
Tristram Coffin (twice),
Tristram Coffin, Jr.,
Robert Evans.

NOTE.—Mary Peaslee, who married Joseph Whittier, was born in Amesbury, July 14th, 1672. She was daughter of Joseph Peaslee and Ruth Barnard. Ruth Barnard, who was daughter of Thomas and Eleanor Barnard, was born October 16th, 1651, and married January 21st, 1671-2.

This connection gives Whittier another ancestor among the original proprietors of Nantucket.

CHAPTER XXXVI.

THE NATHAN BUNKER FAMILY.

This family was of Huguenot origin. The name formerly was Bon Cœur.

George Bunker, son of William, was drowned May 26th, 1658, at Topsfield, Mass., leaving a widow, Jane Godfrey Bunker, and several children. She married Richard Swain, and they removed to Nantucket, where have lived many Bunker descendants.

Nathan Bunker[2] of the prominent shipping firm of Lea & Bunker, who owned a large amount of shipping in Philadelphia at the beginning of the nineteenth century, was married, 1812, after the manner of Friends, to Elizabeth Thorne Clement, associating this branch with many families of Long Island, New Jersey and Pennsylvania.

The Nathan Bunker line here given is accepted by many of the family. A question was raised concerning Nathan Bunker's[2] father, Nathan Bunker, and a theory advanced that Nathan[2] was son of William, but search in the Bunker MS. at Nantucket has disproved this, as by it one son only is attributed to William Bunker, and he died unmarried.

The children of Nathan Bunker and Elizabeth Thorne Clement were:

Hannah C. Bunker, who married James W. Paul, of Philadelphia, and three sisters, who married respectively Rear-Admiral Dahlgren, Amos Taylor and Hon. S. Abbott Lawrence, of Boston.

238   *Early Settlers of Nantucket.*

Nathan Bunker ² married, 1812, Elizabeth Thorne Clement.

Nathan Bunker ² was son of
b. 11. 8, 1768 } d 11   Nathan Bunker ¹ and Hepzibeth Pinkham.
Nathan Bunker ¹ was son of
b. Oct. 9, 1731 O S } a l. 67
m. 12. 7, 1750 O S } c l. 191   Shubael Bunker and Lydia *Paddack*.   { b. 2. 18, 1732 (d 178)
Shubael Bunker was son of
d. 8. 14, 1757 }   Zecariah Bunker and Desire *Gorham*.   { b. 10. 9, 1726 (i 107)
Zecariah Bunker was son of
b. Feb. 25, 1675 } f l. 299   Jonathan Bunker and Elizabeth *Coffin*.   { d. Mar. 30, 1769 (g xxiv. 151)
Jonathan Bunker was son of
b. 1648
m. Apr. 11, 1669 } h 67
d. June 6, 1712   William Bunker and Mary *Macy*.   { b. Dec. 4, 1648 d. 1729 (h 67)
William Bunker was son of
d. May 26, 1658 } f l. 299   George Bunker and Jane Godfrey.   { d. June Swain, Oct. 31, 1662 (a l. 1)
George Bunker was son of
WILLIAM BUNKER.

Lydia Paddack was daughter of
b. 9. 12, 1707
m. 12. 1, 1726-7 O S } l 108; 168
d. 1743 } d 177   Daniel Paddack and Susanna *Gorham*.   { b. 10. 8, 1705 (l 108 ; 188) d. 7. 13, 1777 (d 177)
Daniel Paddack was son of
b. 9. 22, 1677
m. 10. 15, 1706
d. 8 mo. 1756 } b A l. 27, 28   Nathaniel Paddack and Ann *Bunker*.   { b. 9. 3, 1686 d. 1. 18, 1767 (l 188)
Nathaniel Paddack was son of
b. 3. 20, 1636
m. 1659
d. 5. 1, 1727 } l 187   ZACHARIAH PADDACK and Deborah *Sears*.   { d. 8. 17, 1732 (l 187)
Zachariah Paddack was son of
d. 7. 25, 1650 } l 187   ROBERT PADDACK and Mary ———.   { d. 1650 (l 187)

Desire Gorham was daughter of
b. Oct. 21, 1667
m. 1695-6
d. 1750 } f ll. 282
f ll. 282
l 107   Shubael Gorham and Puella *Hussey*.   { b. 10. 21, 1677 d. 1748 (a l. 3)
Shubael Gorham was son of
Baptized Jan. 28, 1621
m. 1643
d. Feb. 5, 1676
b. 1575 } g ll. 86;
f ll. 281
f ll. 281
l 407   JOHN GORHAM and Desire *Howland*.   { b. ± 1623 d. 10. 13, 1683 (l 137)
John Gorham was son of
d. ± 1643
b. 1550
m. 1572
d. 1576 } l 407   RALPH GORHAM, who was son of
James Gorham and Agnes Bennington.

b. Aug. 12, 1640
m. 1663, Nov. or Dec. 3
d. July 28, 1720 } g xxiv. 151;
eK 32   Elizabeth Coffin was daughter of
JAMES COFFIN and Mary Severance.   { b. Aug. 5, 1645 (eK 32)

b. ± 1605 m. ± 1630 d. Oct. 2, 1681	g xxiv. 150 Ib.; a. i. 3	James Coffin was son of TRISTRAM COFFIN and Dionis Stevens.	d. + 1682 (eC)
d. 4. 19, 1682	a i. 4	Mary Macy was daughter of THOMAS MACY and Sarah Hopcot.	b. 1612 d. 1706 (h 67)
b. 1683 m. Dec. 25, 1703 d. 1743	i 108 a iii. 12 i 108	Susanna Gorham was daughter of Stephen Gorham and Elizabeth *Gardner*.	
b. 2. 20, 1652 m. d. 11. 11, 1716	g	Stephen Gorham was son of John Gorham and Mary *Otis*.	b. 3. 14, 1654 d. 4. 1, 1732 (g)
b. 1. 16, 1621 m. 1643 d. 2. 5. 1676	f ii. 281	John Gorham was son of JOHN GORHAM and Desire *Howland*. John Gorham was son of RALPH GORHAM, who was son of James Gorham and Agnes Bennington.	
		Ann Bunker was daughter of William Bunker and Mary Macy. William Bunker was son of George Bunker and Jane Godfrey. George Bunker was son of WILLIAM BUNKER.	
b. 1590 m. 1632 d. 1676	eSr 32	Deborah Sears was daughter of RICHARD SEARS and Dorothy Thatcher.	d. 1680 (eSr 132)
b. 1632 m. 10. 8, 1676 d. 4. 2, 1718	s 761	Puella Hussey was daughter of STEPHEN HUSSEY and Martha Bunker. Stephen Hussey was son of	b. 1656 d. 9. 21, 1744 (s ii. 761)
b. 1599 m. d. 3. 6, 1686	Eng. Parish Records s	CHRISTOPHER HUSSEY and Theodate Bachelor.	d. 10 mo., 1649
b. 1621 m. 1652 d. 1. 16, 1684	i 183	Mary Otis was daughter of JOHN OTIS and Mary Jacobs.	d. + 1683
b. 1592 m. ± 1622 d. 2. 23, 1673		Desire Howland was daughter of JOHN HOWLAND and Elizabeth *Tilley*.	b. 1607 d. 12. 21, 1687

b. 5. 19, 1664	Elizabeth Gardner was daughter of
d. 6. 1, 1723	James Gardner and Mary *Starbuck*. {b. 3. 30, 1663 / d. 1696}
	James Gardner was son of
b. ± 1626 / m. 1652 / d. 1. 23, 1688 } a i.	Richard Gardner and Sarah *Shattuck*. {b. 1632 / d. 1724}
	Richard Gardner was son of
} f ii. 230	Thomas Gardiner and Margaret Frier.

Mary Macy was daughter of
Thomas Macy and Sarah Hopcot.

b. 1608 / m. 9. 6, 1639 / d. 4. 19, 1682 } a i. 4

{b. 1612 / d. 1706 (h 67)}

Martha Bunker was daughter of
George Bunker and Jane Godfrey.
George Bunker was son of
William Bunker.

Theodate Bachelor was daughter of
Rev. Stephen Bachelor.

} s ii. 589

Elizabeth Tilley was daughter of
John Tilley.

Mary Starbuck was daughter of
Nathaniel Starbuck and Mary *Coffin*.
Nathaniel Starbuck was son of
Edward Starbuck and Katharine Reynolds.

b. ± 1634 / m. 1662 / d. 6. 6, 1719 } eC 56 / a i. 11

{b. Feb. 20, 1645 / (g xxiv. 150) / d. 9. 13, 1717 (a i. 11)}

b. 1605 / d. 1690 } a i. 4

Sarah Shattuck was daughter of
—— Shattuck and Damaris ——.

{ Died Damaris Gardner }

Mary Coffin was daughter of
Tristram Coffin and Dionis Stevens.

b. ± 1605 / d. Oct. 2, 1661 } a i.3

Descendants of Nathan Bunker and Elizabeth Thorne Clement descend also on the paternal side from:
  William Bunker (three times),
  Robert Paddack,

Zachariah Paddack,
John Gorham (twice),
Ralph Gorham (twice),
Tristram Coffin (twice),
Thomas Macy (twice),
Richard Sears,
Christopher Hussey,
Stephen Hussey,
John Otis (twice),
John Howland (twice),
Thomas Gardiner,
Richard Gardner,
Rev. Stephen Bachelor,
John Tilley (twice),
Edward Starbuck.

b. 1757 m. 1778	Elizabeth Thorne Clement was daughter of James Clement and Mary *Thorne*.	b. 1757 d. 1818
b. 1720 m. 1740	James Clement was son of Jacob Clement and Elizabeth Tilly.	Widow dau. Nathl. Cooper
b. 1678 m. 1705	Jacob Clement * was son of Jacob Clement and Ann *Harrison*.	

b.
m. 1669
d. 1724
	Jacob Clement was son of
	    JAMES CLEMENT and Jane ———.
	James Clement was son of
	    Gregory Clement.	

b. 1733
m. 1754
d. 1823
	Mary Thorne was daughter of
	    Captain Joseph Thorne and Elizabeth Cheeseman.
	Captain Joseph Thorne was son of
	    Thomas Thorne and Letitia *Hinchman*.	

---

* Jacob Clement settled at Haddonfield, New Jersey, 1743. His father settled at Flushing, Long Island, in 1640. Gregory Clement, father of James, was M. P. for Camelsford and one of the Judges of Charles I. in 1648.

Thomas Thorne was son of
JOSEPH THORNE, of Flushing, Long Island.

Letitia Hinchman was daughter of
JOHN HINCHMAN and Sarah Harrison.

John Hinchman was among the early settlers of Flushing, L. I. The earliest mention of him is in the valuation of estates in 1675. Joseph Thorne also settled at Flushing. Two sons of Joseph Thorne, Thomas and John, married Letitia and Ann, daughters of John Hinchman.

John Hinchman and the Thorne family removed to New Jersey late in the seventeenth century.

APPENDIX I.

APPENDIX I.

Adams, Alexander, *m.* Mary Coffin.* (Savage, vol. i., p. 8, 1652.)

Barnard,[2] Nathaniel, Sr., son of Thomas Barnard and Eleanor (———), *m.* Mary Barnard, dau. Robert Barnard and Joanna (Harvey). (W. C. Folger MS.)

Barnard,[3] Nathaniel, Jr.,† *d.* Feb. 28, 1718, son of Nathaniel Barnard, Sr., *m.* 1st, in 1702, Elizabeth (Coffin), widow of Peter Coffin, Jr., and dau. Nathaniel Starbuck and Mary (Coffin) (Nantucket Probate Records); 2d, Dorcas Manning, dau. Dennis Manning (Nantucket Friends' Records), and 3d, "1st of 12th mo., called Feb.," 1709, Judith Folger, widow of Peter Folger, Jr., and daughter Stephen Coffin and Mary (Bunker) (Friends' Marriages, Book I., p. 2).

Barnard, Judith, widow of Nathaniel Barnard, Jr., *m.* 1722, Stephen Wilcox. (Friends' Records, Book I., p. 24.) Judith Barnard died Dec. 28, 1760.

CHILD OF NATHANIEL BARNARD, JR., AND DORCAS (MANNING).

Barnard,[4] Dorcas, *b.* Oct. 9, 1707, *m.* 1726, "8th day of 7th Mo., O. S.," Jacob Barney, *b.* Feb. 2, 1705. (Town Records, Book I., p. 34.)

CHILDREN OF NATHANIEL BARNARD, JR., AND JUDITH (COFFIN) (FOLGER) BARNARD.

Barnard,[4] Elizabeth, *d.* Nov. 15, 1729.
Barnard,[4] Peter, *d.* Apr. 27, 1775.
Barnard,[4] Eunice, *d.* Sept. 19, 1727.

---

* Mary (Coffin) Adams was a sister of Tristram Coffin, Sr. Benjamin Franklin Folger, genealogist, says she had four children, and from them descended the illustrious family of that name in Massachusetts.

† Nathaniel Barnard, Jr., *d.* Feb. 28, 1718. His estate was not settled until 1728-29.

Barnard,[4] Nathaniel, d. 1743, m. Hepzibah Hussey, dau. Sylvanus Hussey. (W. C. Folger MSS.)

Barney, Benjamin, son Jonathan and Sarah Barney, Rhode Island, m. 1st, Lydia Starbuck, dau. Jethro and Dorcas Starbuck. (Nantucket Friends' Records, Bk. I., p. 23, 1722); 2d, Huldah Bunker, widow Simeon and dau. Bachelor Hussey (Ibid., p. 221).

Barney, Benjamin, son Benjamin and Lydia Barney, m. Jemima Jenkins, dau. Peter and Abigail Jenkins. (Ibid., p. 217, 1753.)

Barney, Jonathan, m. Abial Coffin, dau. Barnabas Coffin. (W. C. Folger MSS.)

Barney, Jacob, of Newport, m. Dorcas Barnard, dau. Nathaniel and Dorcas Barnard. (Nantucket Town Records, Bk. I., p. 34, 1726.)

Barney, Phebe, dau. Benjamin and Huldah (Bunker) Barney, m. Joseph Swain. (W. C. Folger MSS., Barney Family.)

Barker, Isaac, m. Judith Prence, dau. Gov. Thomas Prence. (Winsor's History of Duxbury, 1665.)

Barker, Samuel, son Isaac and Judith Barker, m. 2d Bethiah Folger, dau. John and Mary (Barnard) Folger (Savage, vol. i., p. 115, Jan. 21, 1718).

Barker, Isaac, son Isaac and Judith (Prence) Barker, m. Elizabeth Slocum, dau. Peleg Slocum and Mary Holder. (Family Records, 1707.)

Barker Robert, son of Samuel and Bethiah (Folger) Barker, b. Feb. 23, 1722-3, d. April 26, 1780, m. February 16, 1744, 1st, Jedidah Chase, dau. James and Rachel (Brown) Chase, of Nantucket, b. Feb. 15, 1723, d. Sept. 14, 1762 (Nantucket Town Records, Bk. I., p. 49); 2d, April, 1763, Sarah Gardner, widow of Hezikiah Gardner and dau. of Abishai and Dinah (Starbuck) Folger, of Nantucket, b. Oct. 16, 1739, d. Mar. 24, 1833 (W. C. Folger MSS. and Barker Newhall).

CHILDREN OF ROBERT BARKER AND FIRST WIFE, JEDIDAH (CHASE.)

Barker, Judith, b. Jan., 1745, m. Feb. 4, 1762, Shubael Gardner, son of Reuben and Theodate (Coffin) Gardner. (W. C. Folger MSS.)

Barker, Margaret, b. May 29, 1747, m. 1st, Feb. 7, 1765, Paul, son of George and Elizabeth Hussey, of Nantucket (Ibid.);

2d, Thomas, son of Thomas and Judith Jenkins, of Hudson, N. Y., b. 1741. (Ibid., 1808.)

Barker, Lydia, b. Nov. 10, 1749, d. Sept. 8, 1833, m. Jan. 29, 1767, Francis Swain, son of Francis and Mary (Paddack) Swain (Nantucket Friends' Records).

Barker, Mary, unm. (W. C. Folger MSS.).

Barker, Robert, unm. (Ibid.)

Barker, James, m. 1st, Feb. 2, 1786, Sarah, dau. of William and Hepzibah Coffin, of Saratoga; 2d, April 9, 1807, Lydia, dau. of Prince and Deborah Gardner.

Barker, Francis, m. 1786, Deborah Russell (Nantucket Town Records, Bk. IV., p. 120), dau. of Sylvanus and Anna Russell (Barker Newhall).

CHILDREN OF ROBERT BARKER AND SECOND WIFE, SARAH GARDNER.

Barker, Jedidah, m. July 9, 1807, William Macy, son of William and Mary (Barney) Macy. (Macy Genealogy, p. 121.)

Barker, Mary, m., 1st, Apr. 8, 1813, Walter Allen, of Smithfield, R. I. (W. C. Folger MSS.); 2d, Dec. 30, 1847, Moses Farnum, of Waterford, Mass. (Ibid.)

Barker, Abraham, m. May 17, 1809, Priscilla Hopkins, dau. of Gerard and Rachel (Wilson) Hopkins, of Baltimore. (Ibid.) and (Barker Newhall.)

Barker, Sarah, m. Andrew Sigourney, of Boston. (Ibid.)

Barker, Isaac, unm.

Barker, Jacob, m. Aug. 27, 1801, Elizabeth Hazard, dau. of Thomas and Anna Rodman Hazard. (Genealogy of Rodman Family, No. 331, pp. 73, 74.)

CHILDREN OF JACOB BARKER AND ELIZABETH HAZARD.[*]

Barker, Robert, died in infancy.
Barker, Robert, unm.
Barker, Thomas, unm.
Barker, William Hazard, m. Nov. 14, 1832, Jeanette James, dau. of William and Catharine (Barber) James, of Albany, New York.
Barker, Andrew Sigourney, unm.

---

[*] Authority, Rodman Family and Barker Newhall.

Barker, Anna Hazard, *m.* Oct. 3, 1840, Samuel G., son of Thomas W. and Lydia (Gray) Ward, of Boston.

Barker, Elizabeth, *m.*, 1st, Baldwin Brower, or Brewer; 2d, William T. Van Zandt, son of Thomas and Mary (Underhill) Van Zandt, of New York; 3d, John Jacob, son of John and Ellen (Long) McCaulis.

Barker, Sarah, *m.*, 1st, John C. Harrison, of Baltimore; 2d, William G. Hunt, of New Orleans.[*]

Barker, Abraham, *m.*, 1st, June 3, 1842, Sarah Wharton, dau. of William and Deborah (Fisher) Wharton; 2d, June 28, 1871, Katharine, dau. of James and Phebe (Riggs) Crane.

Barker, Mary, died young.

Barker, John W., died young.

Brown, John (Elder), *m.* Hannah Hobart, dau. Peter Hobart. (Savage, vol i., p. 271, 1658.)

Brown, John, *m.* Rachel Gardner, dau. Capt. John Gardner, (Ibid., vol. ii., p. 288.)

Brock, John, *m.* Merib Mitchell. (Nantucket Town Records, Bk. I., p. 148, 1800.)

Buffum, David, Sr., *m.* Hepzibah Mitchell. (Family Records, 1784.)

Bunker, Elizabeth, *m.* Thomas Look, of Tisbury. (W. C. Folger, Bunker Family, p. 60, 1646.)

Bunker,[1] William (French Huguenot).

Bunker,[2] George, *m.* Jane Godfrey.

Bunker,[3] William, son George Bunker and Jane (Godfrey), *m.* Mary Macy, dau. Thomas Macy and Sarah Hopcot. (Nantucket Town Records, Bk. I., p. 1, 1669.)

Bunker,[4] Benjamin, *m.* Deborah Paddack, dau. Zachariah Paddack.

Bunker,[5] Thomas, *m.* Anna Swain, dau. Richard Swain.

Bunker,[6] Richard, *m.* Eunice Mitchell, *b.* October 7, 1749, dau. of Richard Mitchell and Mary Starbuck.

---

[*] Atty. Gen'l. of La., 1876; Secretary of Navy, 1881, and Minister to Russia, 1882.

Children of Richard Bunker and Eunice (Mitchell).

Bunker,⁷ Anna, b. 1769, d. 1769.
Bunker, Abraham, b. 1770, d. 1770.
Bunker, Lydia, b. 1771, d. 1847.
Bunker, Richard, b. 1773, d. 1799.
Bunker, Jethro, b. 1776, d. 1845.
Bunker, Laban, b. 1778, d. 1782.
Bunker, Isaiah, b. 1781, d. 1801.
Bunker, Laban, b. 1783, d. 1844, m. Deborah Macy.
Bunker, David, b. 1785, d. 1848, m. Derdanna Carpenter.
Bunker, Eunice M., b. 1788, d. 1834.

Bunker, Nathan, m. Elizabeth Thorne Clement. (Family Record, 1812.)
Bunker, Nathan, m. Hepsibeth Pinkham (Ibid., 1781.)
Bunker, Shubael, m. Lydia Paddack. (Ibid., 1751.)
Bunker, Zachariah, m. Desire Gorham (by John Coffin, justice of peace). (Nantucket Town Records, Bk. I., p. 23, 1728.)
Bunker, Jonathan, son William Bunker, m. Elizabeth Coffin. (Allen Coffin, LL.B., p. 56.)
Bunker, George, son William Bunker, m. Deborah Coffin. (Town Records.)
Bunker, Ann, dau. George Bunker and Jane (Godfrey), m. Joseph Coleman. (Family Papers.)

Butler, William, m. Eunice Coffin.* (Savage, vol. i., p. 8.)

Butler, William, m. Mary Jenkins (by Josiah Coffin, justice of peace). (Nantucket Town Records, Bk. I., p. 56, 1747.)

Cartwright,¹ Edward, Sr., m., 1st, —— ——; 2d, Elizabeth Trott. (W. C. Folger MSS.)

Child of Edward Cartwright and First Wife.

Cartwright,² Nicholas, d. 1706, m. Orange Rogers, dau. William Rogers and Martha Barnard, dau. Robert Barnard. (Ibid.)

---

* Eunice Coffin was sister of Tristram Coffin, Sr.

CHILDREN OF EDWARD CARTWRIGHT AND SECOND WIFE, ELIZABETH TROTT.

Cartwright,[2] Sampson, b. 1697, m. Bethia Pratt, dau. Joseph Pratt and Dorcas Folger (Ibid.).
Cartwright,[2] Susanna, b. 1680, m. William Stratton. (Ibid.)
Cartwright,[2] Edward, b. 1683, m. Ruth West, dau. Dr. Thomas West, of Martha's Vineyard. (Ibid.)
Cartwright,[2] Mary, unm., d. 1719. (Ibid.)

CHILDREN OF NICHOLAS CARTWRIGHT AND ORANGE ROGERS.

Cartwright,[3] Sarah, b. 1695, m. George Brown. (Ibid.)
Cartwright,[3] Eleanor, b. 1697, m. —— ——. (Ibid.)
Cartwright,[3] Hope, b. 1699, m. Thomas Crook. (Ibid.)
Cartwright,[3] Lydia, b. 1701, m. John Deskau. (Ibid.)
Cartwright,[3] Nicholas, Jr., b. 1705. (Ibid.)

CHILDREN OF SAMPSON CARTWRIGHT AND BETHIA PRATT.

Cartwright,[3] Alice, b. 1702, m. David Gwin, of Salem. (Ibid.)
Cartwright,[3] Hezidiah, b. 1707, m. March 7, 1731, Abigail Brown, dau. Dr. Joseph Brown and Tabitha Frost, widow of John Frost and dau. John Trott (by John Coffin, justice of peace). (Ibid.)
Cartwright,[3] Dorcas, died young. (Ibid.)
Cartwright,[3] Phineas, died young. (Ibid.)
Cartwright,[3] Thomas, died young. (Ibid.)
Cartwright,[3] Mary, died young. (Ibid.)

CHILDREN OF EDWARD CARTWRIGHT AND RUTH WEST.

Cartwright,[3] Bryant, m. Oct., 1732, Elizabeth Weeks. (Ibid.)
Cartwright,[3] Edward, m. Jan. 1, 1749, Jane Magee. (Ibid.)
Cartwright,[3] Silas. (Ibid.)
Cartwright,[3] Samuel, b. 1716, m. Anna Swain, dau. John (England). (Ibid.)

NOTE.—Orange Cartwright, widow of Nicholas, was married on the 18th of March, 1708, to Morris Farris, and some time after removed to Cape Cod. (Ibid.)

Appendix.

CHILDREN OF HEZIDIAH CARTWRIGHT AND ABIGAIL BROWN.

Cartwright,⁴ Priscilla, b. 1733, d. 1810, *unm*. (Ibid.)

Cartwright,⁴ James, b. 1735, d. 1822, *m*., 1st, Ruth Gardner, dau. Uriah Gardner (no children) (Ibid.); 2d, Love Macy, dau. Francis Macy and Judith Coffin (Records of Friends, Nantucket, 1759.)

Cartwright,⁴ Rachel, b. 1737, d. 1776, *m*. Jabez Macy, Jr., son of Jabez Macy and Sarah Starbuck. (W. C. Folger MSS.)

Cartwright,⁴ Mary, b. 1737, d. 1819, *m*. First month, 1759, Ebenezer Coffin, son Alexander. (Ibid.)

Cartwright,⁴ Abigail, b. 1741, d. 1826, *m*. Barnabas Gardner, son Jonathan Gardner and Patience. (Ibid.)

Cartwright,⁴ Joseph, b. 1743, *unm*. (Ibid.)

Cartwright,⁴ Jonathan, b. 1745, d. 1789, *m*. Deborah Macy, dau. Robert Macy and Abigail Barnard. (Ibid.)

Cartwright,⁴ Thomas, b. 1746, d. *unm*. at sea. (Ibid.)

Cartwright,⁴ Benjamin, b. 1748, d. 1812, *m*., 1st, Elizabeth Bunker, dau. David Bunker and ——; 2d, Abigail Paddack, dau. Jonathan Paddack and ——. (Ibid.)

Cartwright,⁴ Bethiah, b. 1750, d. 1793, *m*. Mar. 3, 1768, John Macy, son Robert Macy and Abigail Barnard. (Ibid.)

Cartwright,⁴ John, b. 1752, d. 1837, *m*. Nov. 16, 1776, Mary Starbuck, dau. Edward Starbuck and Damaris ——. (Ibid.)

Cartwright,⁴ Elihu, b. 1754. (Ibid.)

Cartwright,⁴ William, b. 1755, d. 1813 at sea, *unm*. (Ibid.)

Cartwright,⁴ Seth, b. 1760, d. 1811, *m*. in Virginia, Polly ——. (Ibid.)

Coffin, Tristram, Sr.,* *m*. Dionis Stevens. (N. E. Hist. and Gen. Reg., vol. xxiv., p. 150, 1630.)

CHILDREN OF TRISTRAM COFFIN, SR., AND DIONIS STEVENS.

Coffin, Peter, *m*. Abigail Starbuck, dau. of Edward Starbuck and Katharine Reynolds. (N. E. Hist. and Gen. Reg., vol. xxiv., p. 150.)

Coffin, Tristram, Jr., *m*. Judith Somerby (widow Henry), dau. Edmund Greenleaf. (Ibid., p. 151, 1652.)

---

* Benjamin Franklin Folger, genealogist, says, "It is worthy of note at that period, that neither Tristram Coffin nor any of his children married a second time."

Coffin, Elizabeth, m. Stephen Greenleaf. (Ibid., p. 150, 1651.)
Coffin, James, m. Mary Severance, dau. of John Severance, of Salisbury, Massachusetts. (Ibid., p. 151, 1663.)
Coffin, Mary, m. Nathaniel Starbuck. (Ibid., p. 150, 1662.)
Coffin, John (Lieutenant), m. Deborah Austin, dau. of Joseph Austin and Sarah Starbuck. (N. E. Hist. and Gen. Reg., vol. xxiv., pp. 151, 152, 1668.)
Coffin, Stephen, m. Mary Bunker, dau. of George Bunker and Jane Godfrey. (Ibid., p. 152.)

CHILDREN OF PETER COFFIN AND ABIGAIL STARBUCK.

Coffin, Abigail, m. Daniel Davidson, of Ipswich. (Ibid., p. 150, 1673.)
Coffin, Peter, m. Elizabeth Starbuck, dau. Nathaniel and Mary Starbuck. (Ibid., p. 152, 1682.)
Coffin, Jethro, m. Mary Gardner, dau. John Gardner. (Ibid., pp. 152, 153.)
Coffin, Tristram, m. Deborah Colcord. (Ibid., p. 152.)
Coffin, Robert, m. Joanna Dyer (widow), dau. Hon. John Gilman, of Exeter. (Ibid., p. 150.)
Coffin, Edward, m. Anna Gardner, dau. Capt. John and Priscilla Gardner. (Ibid., p. 150.)
Coffin, Elizabeth, m. Col. John Gilman, of Exeter. (Ibid., p. 151, 1698.)

CHILDREN OF TRISTRAM COFFIN, JR., AND JUDITH SOMERBY.

Coffin, Judith, m. John Sanborn, of Hampton, New Hampshire. (Ibid., p. 151, 1674.)
Coffin, Deborah, m. Joseph Knight. (Ibid., 1677.)
Coffin, Mary, m. Joseph Little, son of George Little and Alice (Poor). (Ibid., 1677.)
Coffin, James, m. Florence Hooke. (Ibid., p. 153, 1685.)
Coffin, John, unm. (Ibid., p. 151.)
Coffin, Lydia, m., 1st, Moses Little, son of George Little and Alice (Poor) (Ibid., p. 151); 2d, John Pike (Ibid., p. 151, 1695.)
Coffin, Enoch, unm. (Ibid.)
Coffin, Stephen, m. Sarah Atkinson. (Ibid., p. 153, 1685.)
Coffin, Peter, m. Apphia Dole, dau. Richard Dole. (Ibid., p. 154.)

Coffin, Hon. Nathaniel,* *m.* March 29, 1693, Sarah, widow of Henry Dole and dau. Captain Samuel Brocklebank and Hannah (——). (Ibid., p. 154.)

CHILDREN OF JAMES COFFIN AND MARY SEVERANCE.

Coffin, Mary, *m.* 1st, Richard Pinkham, of Portsmouth (came from Isle of Wight), (Ibid., p. 151); 2d, James Gardner, son Richard and Sarah Gardner (Ibid.).

Coffin, James, Jr., *m.* 1st, Love Gardner, dau. Richard and Sarah; 2d, Ruth Gardner, dau. John and Priscilla Gardner (Ibid., p. 154, 1692).

Coffin, Nathaniel, *m.* Damaris Gayer, dau. William and Dorcas Gayer. (Town Records of Nantucket, Bk. I., p. 5, 1692.)

Coffin, John, *m.* Hope Gardner, dau. Richard and Sarah Gardner. (N. E. Hist. and Gen. Reg., vol. xxiv., p. 306.)

Coffin, Dinah, *m.* Nathaniel Starbuck, Jr. (Ibid., p. 151, 1690.)

Coffin, Deborah, *m.* George Bunker, son William and Mary Bunker. (Ibid., p. 151, 1695.)

Coffin, Ebenezer, *m.* Eleanor Barnard, dau. Nathaniel Barnard. (Ibid., p. 306, 1700.)

Coffin, Joseph, *m.* Bethiah Macy, dau. John Macy. (Ibid., p. 306, 1719.)

Coffin, Benjamin, *unm.* (Ibid., p. 151.)

Coffin, Ruth, *m.* Joseph Gardner, son Richard Gardner.2 (Ibid., p. 151.)

Coffin, Abigail, *m.* Nathaniel Gardner. (Ibid.)

Coffin, Experience, *unm.* (Ibid.)

Coffin, Jonathan, *m.* Hepzibah Harker, dau. Ebenezer Harker. (Ibid., p. 307.)

Coffin, Elizabeth, *m.* 1st, Jonathan Bunker, son William and Mary Bunker (Ibid.); 2d, Thomas Clark (Ibid., p. 151.)

---

* In Joshua Coffin's History of Newbury, p. 337, is the following, copied from Hon. Nathaniel Coffin's note-book:

"1731. An account of some things my son Edmund had of me. Paid for his learning and his books and his medicine, £70."

Children of Lieutenant John Coffin and Deborah Austin.

Coffin, Lydia, *m.* 1st, John Logan; 2d, John Draper; 3d, Thomas Thaxter, of Hingham. (Ibid., p. 152.)

Coffin, Peter, *m.* 1st, Christian Condy (Ibid., p. 307); 2d, Hope, dau. Joseph and Bethiah (Macy) Gardner (Ibid.).

Coffin, Enoch, *m.* Beulah Eddy. (Ibid., p. 307, 1700.)

Coffin, Samuel, *m.* Miriam Gardner, dau. Richard Gardner, Jr. (Ibid., p. 308, 1705.)

Coffin, Hannah, *m.* Benjamin Gardner, son Richard Gardner, Jr. (Ibid., p. 152.)

Coffin, Tristram, *m.* Mary Bunker, dau. William Bunker. (Ibid., p. 308, 1714.)

Coffin, Deborah, *m.* Thomas Macy,[3] son John Macy. (Ibid., p. 152, 1708.)

Children of Stephen Coffin and Mary Bunker.

Coffin, Dinah, *m.* Jacob Norton. (Ibid., p. 152.)

Coffin, Peter, *m.* ——— ———, in Boston. (Ibid.)

Coffin, Stephen, Jr., *m.* Experience Look, dau. Thomas Look. (Nantucket Town Records, Bk. I., p. 8, 1693.)

Coffin, Judith, *m.* 1st, Peter Folger[3] (*d.* 1707), son Eleazer Folger (N. E. Hist. and Gen. Reg., vol. xxiv., p. 152); 2d, Nathaniel Barnard, son Nathaniel Barnard (Ibid., p. 152); 3d, Stephen Wilcox (Ibid., p. 152, 1722).

Coffin, Susanna, *m.* Peleg Bunker, son William Bunker. (Ibid., p. 152.)

Coffin, Mehitable, *m.* Armstrong Smith. (Ibid., p. 152.)

Coffin, Anna, *m.* Solomon Gardner, son Richard Gardner, Jr. (Ibid., p. 152.)

Coffin, Hepzibah, *m.* Samuel Gardner. (Ibid., p. 152.)

Coffin, Paul, *m.* Mary Allen, dau. Edward Allen, 1729. (Allen Coffin, LL.B., p. 58.)

Coffin, Richard, *m.* Ruth Bunker. (N. E. Hist. and Gen. Reg., vol. xxiv., p. 306.)

Coffin, Ebenezer, *m.* Eleanor Barnard. (Ibid., p. 306, 1700.)

Coffin, Thomas, *m.* Anna Folger. ("Life and Letters of James and Lucretia Mott," by Anna Davis Hallowell; also B. F. Folger, genealogist, 1779.)

CHILDREN OF THOMAS COFFIN AND ANNA FOLGER.

Coffin, Lucretia, *m.* James Mott, of Long Island. ("Life and Letters of James and Lucretia Mott," by Anna Davis Hallowell, 1811.)

Coffin, Eliza, *m.* Benjamin H. Yarnall, of Philadelphia. (Ibid., 1814.)

Coffin, Mary, *m.* Solomon Temple. (Ibid., 1824.)

Coffin, Martha, *m.* Peter Pelham, of Kentucky. (Ibid., 1824.)

Coffin, Thomas, *unm.*

Coffin, Nathaniel, *m.* Elizabeth Coleman. (Nantucket Friends' Records, 1757.)

Coggeshall, Joshua, *m.* 1st, Joan West (Savage, vol. i., p. 422); 2d, Rebecca Russell (1677).

Coggeshall, Job, *m.*, among Friends, Deborah Starbuck. (W. C. Folger MSS., Starbuck Family, p. 61.)

Coggeshall, Caleb, *m.* Elizabeth Hosier. (Family Records, 1793.)

Coggeshall, Giles Hosier, *m.* Marianna Walters. (Ibid., 1833.)

Coleman, Thomas, *m.* 1st, Susanna; 2d, Mary (widow Edmund Johnson); 3d, Margery (Joshua Coffin's "History of Newbury," Appendix, p. 298, 1648.)

Coleman, John, 1st, son Thomas Coleman, *m.* Joanna Folger. (William C. Folger MSS.)

Coleman, John, 2d, son John Coleman, 1st, *m.* Priscilla Starbuck. (Ibid.)

Coleman, Dorcas,* *m.* John Tillotson. (Joshua Coffin's "History of Newbury," Appendix, p. 298.)

Coleman, Jeremiah, *m.* Sarah Pratt (by William Worth, justice of peace). (Nantucket Town Records, Bk. I., p. 10, 1714-15.)

Coleman, Andrew, *m.* Lydia Folger. (W. C. Folger MSS., 1791.)

Coleman, Enoch, *m.* Mary Myrick. (Ibid., 1748.)

Coleman, Barnabas, son John Coleman, 2d, *m.* Rachel Hussey, as second wife. (Nantucket Friends' Records, Bk. I., p. 62, 1733.)

Coleman, Nathaniel, was son of Barnabas and his first wife.

---

* Dorcas Coleman was a sister of Thomas Coleman, the proprietor.

CHILDREN OF BARNABAS COLEMAN AND RACHEL HUSSEY.

Coleman, Sarah, *m.* George Folger. (W. C. Folger MSS., 1752.)
Coleman, Abial, *m.* Timothy Folger. (Ibid., 1753.)
Coleman, Rebecca, *m.* Nathaniel Coffin. (Ibid.)
Coleman, Judith, *m.* Andrew Worth. (Ibid.)
Coleman, Seth, *m.* Deborah Swain, dau. Reuben Swain. (Nantucket Friends' Records, 1768.)
Coleman, Sylvanus, *m.* 1st, Mary Swift (Ibid., 1768); 2d, Phebe Brown (1779).
Coleman, William, *m.* 1st, Abigail Barnard (Nantucket Friends' Records, Bk. II., p. 109, 1770); 2d, Hepzibah Wing (Sandwich Friends' Records, 1780).
Coleman, Barnabas, *m.* 1st, Abial Clark, by Caleb Bunker, justice of peace (Nantucket Town Records, Bk. I., p. 106, 1776); 2d, Sarah Morse (W. C. Folger MSS.).
Coleman, Hepzibah, *m.* John Russell. (Nantucket Friends' Records, 1777).
Coleman, Elizabeth, *m.* Abishai Folger, Jr. (W. C. Folger MSS., 1772.)
Coleman, Obed, *m.* Elizabeth Swain. (Nantucket Friends' Records, 1780.)

Cornell, William, *m.* Lydia Hussey. (Nantucket Town Records, Bk. I., p. 145, 1709.)

Dole,[1] Richard, *b.* England, 1624; Newbury, 1639; *m.* 1st, May 3, 1647, Hannah Rolfe; 2d, March 4, 1679, Hannah, widow of Captain Samuel Brocklebank, of Rowley; 3d, Patience Walker, of Haverhill. (Hist. of Newbury, 300, 301.) Richard Dole's will was proved July 30th, 1705.

Dole,[2] John, son of Richard,[1] *m.* Oct. 23, 1676, Mrs. Mary Gerrish. (Hist. of Newbury, p. 301.)
Dole,[2] Richard, son of Richard,[1] *m.* June 7, 1677, Sarah Greenleaf. (Ibid., p. 301.)
Dole,[2] Benjamin, son of Richard,[1] *m.* Dec. 11, 1700, Frances, dau. Captain Samuel Sherman. (Ibid., p. 301.)
Dole,[2] William, son of Richard,[1] *m.* Oct. 13, 1684, Mary Brocklebank, dau. of his father's second wife. (Ibid., p. 301.)
Dole,[2] Henry, son of Richard,[1] *m.* Sarah Brocklebank, dau. of his father's second wife. (Ibid., p. 301.)

Appendix.

Dole,[2] Apphia, dau. of Richard,[1] m. Peter Coffin, son of Tristram Coffin, Jr. (Ibid., p. 299.)

Dole,[2] Abner, son of Richard,[1] m. 1st, Nov. 1, 1694, Mary Jewett, who died 1695; 2d, Jan. 5, 1697, Sarah Belcher. (Ibid., p. 301.)

Earle, Thomas, m. Mary Hussey. (W. C. Folger, p. 184, 1820.)
Earle, John Milton, m. Sarah Hussey. (Ibid., 1821.)

Folger, John, m. Meribah Gibbs (probably second wife). (N. E. Hist. and Gen. Reg., vol. xvi., Folger Family.)
Folger, Peter, m. Mary Morrell. (Savage, vol. ii., pp. 177, 178.)

Children of Peter Folger and Mary Morrell.

Folger, Eleazer, m. Sarah Gardner, dau. Richard and Sarah (Shattuck) Gardner. (Savage, vol. ii., p. 177, 1671.)
Folger, Joanna, m. John Coleman. (Ibid.)
Folger, Bethiah, m. John Barnard, son Robert Barnard. (Ibid., 1669.)
Folger, Dorcas, m. Joseph Pratt. (Ibid., 1675.)
Folger, Patience, m. 1st, Ebenezer Harker. (Savage; vol. ii., p. 177); 2d, James Gardner, as second wife (Ibid., p. 228).
Folger, Bethsua, m. Joseph Pope, of Salem. (Savage, vol. ii., p. 177.)
Folger, John, m. Mary Barnard, dau. Nathaniel Barnard. (Ibid.)
Folger, Experience, m. John Swain, Jr., son of John Swain, the proprietor. (Ibid.)
Folger, Abiah, m. Josiah Franklin. (N. E. Hist. and Gen. Reg., vol. xvi., Folger Family.)

Children of Eleazer Folger and Sarah Gardner.

Folger, Eleazer, Jr., m. 1st, Bethia Gardner (Nantucket Town Records, Bk. I., p. 24); 2d, Mary Marshall (Ibid., p. 10; 1717).
Folger, Peter, m. Judith Coffin, dau. Stephen and Mary Coffin (N. E. Hist. and Gen. Reg., vol. xvi., pp. 271-274, Folger Family.)
Folger, Nathan, m. Sarah Church. (Nantucket Town Records, Bk. I., p. 8, 1699.)
Folger, Sarah, m. Anthony Oder. (Ibid., p. 6, 1702.)
Folger, Mary, m. John Arthur. (Nantucket Town Records, Bk. I., p. 9, 1704.)

CHILDREN OF NATHAN FOLGER AND SARAH CHURCH.

Folger, Abishai, m. 1st, Sarah Mayhew (W. C. Folger MSS., 1727); 2d, Dinah Starbuck, widow Benjamin, and dau. Stephen Coffin, Jr. (Ibid.)

Folger, Peter, m. Christian Swain. (Nantucket Town Records, Bk. I., p. 45, 1731.)

Folger, Barzillai, m. Phebe Coleman. (Nantucket Friends' Records, 1730.)

Folger, Timothy, m. Anna Chase. (Nantucket Town Records, Bk. I., p. 30, 1733.)

Folger, Leah, m. 1st, Richard Gardner, son of Richard, Jr. (Ibid., p. 16, 1724); 2d, Seth Paddack, son Joseph Paddack (W. C. Folger MSS., Gardner Family, p. 4).

Folger, Judith, m. Thomas Jenkins. (Nantucket Town Records, 1728-29.)

Folger, Esther, unm.

CHILDREN OF ABISHAI FOLGER AND FIRST WIFE, SARAH MAYHEW.

Folger, William, m. Ruth Coffin, dau. Barnabas Coffin. (Nantucket Friends' Records, Bk. I., p. 170, 1749.)

Folger, George, m. 1st, Sarah Coleman (Ibid., 1752); 2d, Sarah Shove, dau. of Barnabas.

Folger, Timothy, m. Abial Coleman. (Nantucket Friends' Records, 1753.)

CHILDREN OF ABISHAI FOLGER AND SECOND WIFE, DINAH STARBUCK.

Folger, Sarah, m. 1st, Hezekiah Gardner (Nantucket Friends' Records, 1758); 2d, Robert Barker (W. C. Folger MSS.).

Folger, Hepzibah, m. Daniel Hussey, Jr. (Nantucket Friends' Records, 1760.)

Folger, Dinah, m. Seth Jenkins. (George H. Folger MSS., p. 194.)

Folger, Abishai, m. Elizabeth Coleman. (Nantucket Friends' Records, 1773.)

Folger, Reuben, m. Phebe Folger. (Nantucket Town Records, Bk. I., p. 112, 1783.)

Folger, Robert, m. Elizabeth Folger, dau. Benjamin Folger. (W. C. Folger MSS., p. 9.)

Children of William Folger and Ruth Coffin.

Folger, Judith, m. Zaccheus Bunker, son of Zachery and Desire Bunker. (Nantucket Friends' Records, 1767.)

Folger, William, Jr., m. Susan Swain. (Nantucket Town Records, Bk. I., 1798.)

Folger, Sarah, Jr., m. Tristram Hussey. (Nantucket Friends' Records, 1777.)

Folger, Lydia, m. Zaccheus Hussey. (Nantucket Town Records, Bk. I., 1780.)

Folger, Richard, m. Sarah Pease (by George Bunker, justice of peace). (Ibid., p. 15, 1722.)

Folger, Francis, unm.

Folger, Elizabeth, m. as second wife Josiah Barker, son Josiah and Elizabeth Barker. (Nantucket Friends' Records, 1786.)

Folger, Phebe, m. Uriel Hussey. (Ibid., 1789.)

Folger, Anna, m. Thomas Coffin. (Ibid., 1790.)

Folger, Mayhew,* m. Mary Joy, dau. Francis and Phebe Joy. (Ibid., 1798.)

Folger, Walter, 1st, m. Elizabeth Starbuck, dau. Thomas and Rachel Starbuck. (W. C. Folger MSS., p. 18.)

Folger, Walter, 2d, m. Anna Ray, dau. Alexander and Elizabeth Ray. (Ibid., p. 19.)

Folger, Walter, 3d, m. Polly Folger, dau. Simeon and Phebe Folger. (Nantucket Town Records, Bk. I., p. 177, 1809.)

Folger, Dinah, m. Stephen Chase. (Ibid., p. 47, 1742.)

Folger, Judith, m. James Gardner. (Ibid., p. 52, 1746.)

Folger, Nathaniel, m. Priscilla Chase. (Ibid., 1718.)

Folger, George, Jr., son George and Sarah Folger, m. Rebecca Slocum. (W. C. Folger MSS.)

Folger, George Gill, son George, Jr., m. Anna Barker, dau. Francis Barker. (Ibid., 1807.)

Folger, Jethro, m. Mary Starbuck, dau. Nathaniel Starbuck, Jr., and Dinah (Coffin). (Nantucket Friends' Records, Bk. I., p. 6, 1710.)

Folger, Barzillai, m. Miriam Gardner. (Nantucket Town Records, Bk. I., p. 163, 1803.)

Folger, Uriah, m. Anna Gardner. (Ibid., p. 157, 1803.)

---

* Captain Mayhew Folger found the lost mutineers of the ship "Bounty" on Pitcairn Island in 1809.

Folger, Ann, *m.* James Mitchell. (See Mitchell Family Records, 1738.)

Gardiner, Thomas, *m.* 1st, Margaret Frier; 2d, Damaris Shattuck. (Savage, vol. ii.)

CHILDREN OF THOMAS GARDINER AND MARGARET FRIER.

Gardner, Seeth, *m.* Joseph Grafton, 2d. (Savage, vol. ii., p. 229.)
Gardner, Richard, *m.* Sarah Shattuck. (Ibid., 1652.)
Gardner, George, *m.* Hannah Shattuck. (Ibid., p. 228.)
Gardner, John, *m.* Priscilla Grafton. (Ibid.)
Gardner, Samuel, *m.* Mary White. (Ibid., p. 230.)
Gardner, Joseph, *m.* Ann Downing, dau. Emanuel Downing. (Ibid.)
Gardner, Sarah, *m.* Benjamin Balch. (Ibid.)
Gardner, Miriam, *m.* John Hill, or Hall. (Ibid.)

CHILDREN OF RICHARD GARDNER 1ST, AND SARAH SHATTUCK.

Gardner, Joseph, *m.* Bethia Macy, dau. Thomas and Sarah (Hopcot) Macy. (Savage, vol. ii., p. 229, 1670.)
Gardner, Sarah, *m.* Eleazer Folger, son Peter and Mary (Morrell) Folger. (Ibid., 1671.)
Gardner, Richard, Jr., *m.* Mary Austin. (Ibid., p. 230, 1674, and Nantucket Town Records, Bk. I., p. 2.)
Gardner, Deborah, *m.* 1st, John Macy, son Thomas Macy[1] (Savage, vol. ii., p. 229); 2d, Stephen Pease (Macy Genealogy, p. 67).
Gardner, Damaris.
Gardner, James,[*] *m.* 1st, Mary Starbuck, dau. Nathaniel Starbuck, Sr.; 2d, Patience Folger, dau. Peter Folger; 3d, Rachel Brown, widow John Brown, of Salem, and dau. Capt. John Gardner; 4th, Mary Pinkham, widow Richard Pinkham, and dau. James Coffin and Mary Severance. (Savage, vol. ii., p. 227.)

---

[*] Children of James Gardner and first wife, Mary Starbuck, were Samuel, Jethro, Barnabas, Jonathan, Elizabeth, Mehitable. Patience (Folger) Gardner had no children. Rachel (Brown) Gardner had one son, James Gardner. Fourth wife, Mary (Pinkham) Gardner, had no *Gardner* children.

Gardner, Miriam, *m.* John Worth. (Ibid., p. 229, 1684.)

Gardner, Nathaniel, *m.* Abigail Coffin, dau. James and Mary (Severance) Coffin. (Ibid.)

Gardner, Hope, *m.* John Coffin. ("Ye Coffin Family," by Allen Coffin, LL.B., p. 56, 1692.)

Gardner, Love.

CHILDREN OF JOHN GARDNER AND PRISCILLA GRAFTON.

Gardner, John, *m.* Susanna Green, of Salem. (W. C. Folger MSS., Gardner Family, p. 30.)

Gardner, Joseph. (Savage, vol. ii., p. 228.)

Gardner, Priscilla, *m.* John Arthur (second wife). (Ibid.)

Gardner, Benjamin, died young. (Ibid.)

Gardner, Rachel, *m.* 1st, John Brown; 2d, James Gardner (third wife). (Ibid.)

Gardner, Benjamin.

Gardner, George, *m.* Eunice Starbuck, dau. Nathaniel Starbuck, Sr. (W. C. Folger MSS., Gardner Family.)

Gardner, Ann, *m.* Edward Coffin.

Gardner, Nathaniel.

Gardner, Mary, *m.* Jethro Coffin. (W. C. Folger MSS., Gardner Family.)

Gardner, Mehitable, *m.* Ambrose Dawes, Jr. (Ibid.)

Gardner, Ruth, *m.* James Coffin, Jr. (Ibid.)

Gardner, Solomon, son Richard, Jr., *m.* Anna Coffin, dau. Stephen Coffin and Mary (Bunker). (W. C. Folger MSS., Gardner Family.)

Gardner, Paul, son Solomon, *m.* Rachel Starbuck, dau. Thomas and Rachel Starbuck. (Nantucket Friends' Records, vol. i., p. 223.)

Gardner, Paul, Jr., *m.* 1st, Sarah Mitchell, dau. Jethro Mitchell; 2d, Merab Spooner, dau. Seth and Dinah Spooner; 3d, Lydia Fitch. (W. C. Folger MSS., p. 154.)

Gardner, Zenas, son Paul and Rachel Gardner, *m.* Susanna Hussey. (Nantucket Friends' Records, vol. ii., p. 342.)

Gardner, Richard, son of Richard, Jr., *m.* Leah Folger. (Nantucket Town Records, Bk. I., p. 16, 1724.)

Gardner, Miriam, dau. Richard Gardner, Jr., *m.* Samuel Coffin, son Lieutenant John Coffin.

Gorham,[1] Ralph, *b.* 1575. First of the family in America, came from Benefield, England, to Duxbury, Mass.

Gorham,[2] John (Captain), son Ralph Gorham, *m.* 1643, Desire Howland, dau. John Howland and Elizabeth Tilley. (Plymouth Col. Records, vol. ii., p. 79.)

CHILDREN OF JOHN GORHAM (1621-1676) AND DESIRE HOWLAND.

Gorham,[3] Desire, *m.* July 10, 1661, John Hawes, son Edmund Hawes. ("One Hundred and Sixty Allied Families," pp. 106, 107.)

Gorham,[3] Temperance. (Ibid.)

Gorham,[3] Elizabeth. (Ibid.)

Gorham,[3] James, *m.* Hannah Huckins, dau. Thomas Huckins and Rose (———). (Ibid.)

Gorham,[3] John, *m.* Feb. 24, 1675, Mary Otis, dau. John Otis and Mary (Jacob). (Ibid.)

Gorham,[3] Joseph. (Ibid.)

Gorham,[3] Jabez, *m.* Hannah (———). (Ibid.)

Gorham,[3] Mercy, *m.* George Dennison, son George Dennison and Ann (Barrowdale). (Ibid.)

Gorham,[3] Lydia, *m.* Jan. 11, 1684, John Thatcher, son Anthony Thatcher and Elizabeth (Jones.) (Ibid.)

Gorham,[3] Hannah. (Ibid.)

Gorham,[3] Shubael, *m.* May, 1695, Puella Hussey, dau. Stephen Hussey and Martha (Bunker). (Ibid.)

CHILDREN OF JOHN GORHAM (1652-1716) AND MARY OTIS.

Gorham,[4] John, died young. (Ibid., pp. 107, 108.)

Gorham,[4] Temperance, *m.* 1696, Stephen Clapp, son Samuel Clapp and Hannah (Gill). (Ibid.)

Gorham,[4] Mary, *m.* 1699, Joseph Hinckley, son Samuel Hinckley and Mary (Fitzrandle). (Ibid.)

Gorham,[4] Stephen, *m.* Dec. 25, 1703, Elizabeth Gardner, dau. James Gardner and Mary (Starbuck). (Ibid.)

Gorham,[4] Shubael, *m.* Dec. 23, 1708, Mary Thatcher, dau. John Thatcher and Lydia (Gorham). (Ibid.)

Gorham, John, *m.* 1st, Feb. 14, 1705, Ann Brown; 2d, Feb. 10, 1712, Prudence Crocker, dau. Joseph Crocker and Anne (Howland). (Ibid.)

Gorham,⁴ Thankful, *m.* June 16, 1710, John Fuller, son John Fuller and Hannah (———). (Ibid.)

Gorham,⁴ Job. (Ibid.)

Gorham,⁴ Mercy, *m.* March 20, 1718, Sylvanus Bourn, son Melatiah Bourn and Desire (Chipman). (Ibid.)

CHILDREN OF STEPHEN GORHAM (1683-1743) AND ELIZABETH GARDNER. Ibid.

Gorham,⁵ Mary, *m.* March, 1721, Andrew Gardner, son Nathaniel Gardner and Abigail (Coffin).

Gorham,⁵ Susanna, *m.* 1st, Oct., 1726, Daniel Paddack, son Nathaniel Paddack and Ann (Bunker); 2d, Jan., 1752, Jonathan Folger, son John Folger and Mary (Barnard).

Gorham,⁵ Nathaniel, *m.* Jan. 6, 1736, Mary Soley, dau. John Soley and Dorcas (Coffin).

Gorham,⁵ Sarah, *m.* Feb. 18, 1734, Daniel Hussey, son Sylvanus Hussey and Abial (Brown).

Gorham,⁵ Barnabas, *unm.*

Gorham,⁵ Zaccheus, *unm.*

Gorham,⁵ Elizabeth, *m.* 1st, Aug., 1740, David Bunker, son Benjamin Bunker and Deborah (Paddack); 2d, William Russell, son Daniel Russell and Deborah (Macy).

Gorham,⁵ Eunice, *m.* Jan. 1, 1744, Peleg Gardner, son Jethro Gardner and Keziah Folger.

Gorham,⁵ Stephen.

Gorham,⁵ Josiah, *m.* Jan. 3, 1753, Deborah Lovell, dau. James Lovell.

Gorham,⁵ Lois, *m.* Sept., 1744, Jonathan Macy, son of John Macy and Judith (Worth).

Gorham,⁵ Lydia, *m.* Feb. 14, 1750, William Swain, son William Swain and Jemima (Coffin).

NOTE.—The Gorham family came to England soon after the Norman Conquest from Gorram, in Brittany; hence the name. ("One Hundred and Sixty Allied Families," p. 109.)

CHILDREN OF DESIRE GORHAM AND JOHN HAWES.
Fourth generation from John Howland. (Ibid., p. 106.)

Elizabeth Hawes.
Mercy Hawes.
Edmund Hawes.
John Hawes.
Joseph Hawes.
Jabez Hawes.
Isaac Hawes.
Benjamin Hawes.
Ebenezer Hawes.
Desire Hawes.
Experience Hawes.

CHILDREN OF JAMES GORHAM AND HANNAH HUCKINS.
Fourth generation from John Howland. (Ibid., p. 106.)

Desire Gorham.
James Gorham.
Experience Gorham.
John Gorham.
Mehitable Gorham.
Thomas Gorham.
Mercy Gorham.
Joseph Gorham.
Jabez Gorham.
Sylvanus Gorham.
Ebenezer Gorham.

CHILDREN OF JABEZ GORHAM AND HANNAH ———.
Fourth generation from John Howland. (Ibid., p. 107.)

Samuel Gorham.
Jabez Gorham.
Shubael Gorham.
Isaac Gorham.
John Gorham.
Joseph Gorham.
Hannah Gorham.
Benjamin Gorham.
Thomas Gorham.
Elizabeth Gorham.

CHILDREN OF MERCY (GORHAM) AND GEORGE DENNISON.

Fourth generation from John Howland. (Ibid., p. 107.)

Edward Dennison.
Joseph Dennison.
Mercy Dennison.
Samuel Dennison.
Elizabeth Dennison.
Desire Dennison.
Thankful Dennison.
George Dennison.

CHILDREN OF LYDIA (GORHAM) AND JOHN THATCHER.

Fourth generation from John Howland. (Ibid., p. 107.)

Lydia Thatcher.
Mary Thatcher.
Desire Thatcher.
Hannah Thatcher.
Mercy Thatcher.
Judah Thatcher.
Mercy Thatcher.
Ann Thatcher.
Joseph Thatcher.
Benjamin Thatcher.
Mercy Thatcher.

CHILDREN OF SHUBAEL GORHAM AND PUELLA HUSSEY.

Fourth generation from John Howland. (Ibid., p. 107.)

George Gorham.
Abigail Gorham.
Lydia Gorham.
Hannah Gorham.
Theodate Gorham.
Daniel Gorham.
Desire Gorham.
Ruth Gorham.
Deborah Gorham.
Sally Gorham.

CHILDREN OF TEMPERANCE (GORHAM) AND STEPHEN CLAPP.
Fifth generation from John Howland. (Ibid., p. 107.)

John Clapp.
Rachel Clapp.
Thomas Clapp.
Stephen Clapp.
Nathaniel Clapp.

CHILDREN OF MARY (GORHAM) AND JOSEPH HINCKLEY.
Fifth generation from John Howland. (Ibid., p. 107.)

John Hinckley.
Isaac Hinckley.
Mercy Hinckley.
Mary Hinckley.
Thankful Hinckley.

CHILD OF SHUBAEL GORHAM AND MARY THATCHER.
Fifth generation from John Howland. (Ibid., p. 107.)

John Gorham.

CHILDREN OF JOHN GORHAM AND FIRST WIFE, ANN BROWN.
Fifth generation from John Howland. (Ibid., p. 107.)

Benjamin Gorham.
Nathaniel Gorham.
Joseph Gorham.
Thankful Gorham.
Mary Gorham.
Abigail Gorham.
Rachel Gorham.
Prudence Gorham.

CHILDREN OF THANKFUL (GORHAM) AND JOHN FULLER.
Fifth generation from John Howland. (Ibid., p. 107.)

Hannah Fuller.
John Fuller.
Mary Fuller.
Bethiah Fuller.
Nathaniel Fuller.

CHILDREN OF MERCY (GORHAM) AND SYLVANUS BOURN.

Fifth generation from John Howland. (Ibid., p. 108.)

Desire Bourn.
Mary Bourn.
Melatiah Bourn.
William Bourn.
Hannah Bourn.
Mercy Bourn.
Abigail Bourn.
Sylvanus Bourn.
Eunice Bourn.
Richard Bourn.

CHILDREN OF MARY (GORHAM) AND ANDREW GARDNER.

Sixth generation from John Howland. (Ibid., p. 108.)

Christopher Gardner.
Nathaniel Gardner.
Stephen Gardner.
Thomas Gardner.
Andrew Gardner.
Solomon Gardner.
Josiah Gardner.
Zachariah Gardner.
Mary Gardner.
Abigail Gardner.
Elizabeth Gardner.

CHILDREN OF SUSANNA (GORHAM) AND DANIEL PADDACK.

Sixth generation from John Howland. (Ibid., p. 108.)

Elizabeth Paddack.
Stephen Paddack.
Lydia Paddack.
Susanna Paddack.
Eunice Paddack.
Deborah Paddack.
Barnabas Paddack.

CHILDREN OF SARAH (GORHAM) AND DANIEL HUSSEY.
Sixth generation from John Howland. (Ibid., p. 108.)

Stephen Hussey.
Elizabeth Hussey.
Daniel Hussey.
Rachel Hussey.

CHILDREN OF ELIZABETH (GORHAM) AND DAVID BUNKER.
Sixth generation from John Howland. (Ibid., p. 108.)

Lois Bunker.
Eunice Bunker.
David Bunker.
Solomon Bunker.
Alexander Bunker.
Elizabeth Bunker.

CHILDREN OF EUNICE (GORHAM) AND PELEG GARDNER.
Sixth generation from John Howland. (Ibid., p. 108.)

Kesiah Gardner.
Rachel Gardner.
Barzillai Gardner.
Sarah Gardner.
Elizabeth Gardner.

CHILDREN OF JOSIAH GORHAM AND DEBORAH LOVELL.
Sixth generation from John Howland. (Ibid., p. 108.)

James Gorham.
Abigail Gorham.
Stephen Gorham.
John Gorham.
Josiah Gorham.
Deborah Gorham.

CHILDREN OF LOIS (GORHAM) AND JONATHAN MACY.
Sixth generation from John Howland. (Ibid., p. 108.)
Elizabeth Macy.
Miriam Macy.
Jonathan Macy.
Barnabas Macy.
Solomon Macy.
Susanna Macy.
Samuel Macy.
Peleg Macy.
Judith Macy.
Samuel Macy.
Seth Macy.

CHILDREN OF LYDIA (GORHAM) AND WILLIAM SWAIN.
Sixth generation from John Howland. (Ibid., p. 108.)
John Swain.
Elizabeth Swain.
Hepzibeth Swain.
Lydia Swain.
Abner Swain.

Greenleaf, Stephen, Sr., m. 1st, Elizabeth Coffin (N. E. Hist. and Gen. Reg., vol. xxiv., p. 150); 2d, Esther,* widow Captain Benjamin Swett (Hist. of Newbury, p. 304).

CHILDREN OF STEPHEN GREENLEAF AND ELIZABETH COFFIN.
Greenleaf, Stephen, m. Elizabeth Gerrish, dau. William Gerrish. ("Ye Coffin Family," Allen Coffin, LL.B., p. 55, and Hist. of Newbury, 1676.)
Greenleaf, Sarah, m. Richard Dole, of Newberry, son Richard Dole. (Ibid., 1677.)
Greenleaf, Daniel, unm. (Ibid.)
Greenleaf, Elizabeth, m. Thomas Noyes, son James Noyes. (Hist. of Newbury, p. 312, 1677.)
Greenleaf, John, m. Elizabeth Hills. (Ibid., p. 304, 1685.)

---

* Esther Greenleaf, second wife of Stephen Greenleaf, Sr., died in 1718, aged eighty-nine.

Greenleaf, Samuel, m. Sarah Kent, dau. John Kent. (Ibid., p. 304, 1689.)

Greenleaf, Tristram, m. Margaret Piper. (Ibid., p. 304, 1689.)

Greenleaf, Edmund, m. Abigail Somerby, dau. Abiel Somerby. (Ibid., p. 304, 1691.)

Greenleaf, Judith, unm. (Ibid.)

Greenleaf, Mary, m. Joshua Moody, son Caleb Moody. (Allen Coffin, LL.B.)

Greenleaf, Sarah, dau. Nathaniel, and granddau. Tristram and Margaret (Piper) Greenleaf, m. Joseph Whittier, 2d. (Whittier Family Records.)

Hosier, Giles, m. Elizabeth Mitchell. (Family Papers, 1768.)

Hussey, John, m. Mary Wood. (Eng. Records, 1593; see page 50.)

Hussey, Christopher, son John Hussey, m. 1st, Theodate Batchelder (Ibid., 1632); 2d, Ann Mingay (Ibid., 1658).

CHILDREN OF CHRISTOPHER HUSSEY AND THEODATE BATCHELDER.

Hussey, Stephen, m. Martha Bunker, dau. George and Jane (Godfrey) Bunker. (W. C. Folger MSS., 1676.)

Hussey, John, m. Rebecca Perkins, dau. Isaac and Susanna Perkins, of Hampton. (Savage, vol. ii., p. 507, 1659.)

Hussey, Mary, m. 1st, Thomas Page, son Robert and Lucy Page (Dow's Hist. of Hampton, vol. ii., p. 890, 1664); 2d, Henry Green (Savage, vol. ii., p. 507, 1691; 3d, Henry Dow, son Henry and Joan Dow (Dow's Hist. of Hampton, vol. ii., p. 679).

Hussey, Theodate.

Hussey, Huldah, m. John Smith, son John Smith. (Savage, vol. ii., p. 507, 1667.)

NOTE.—Savage, vol. ii., pp. 507, 508, gives:

Robert Hussey, Duxbury, 1643-45; probably died 1667.

Robert Hussey, Dover, in tax-list 1659.

Robert Hussey, Boston, 1690.

Children of Stephen Hussey and Martha Bunker.

Hussey, Puella, m. Shubael Gorham, son John and Mary (Otis) Gorham. (Nantucket Probate Records, Book A I., p. 41, 1695.)

Hussey, Abigail, m. 1st, Thomas Hause (Nantucket Town Records, Bk. I., p. 5, 1700); 2d, Joseph Marshall, son James and Ruth (Hawkins) Marshall (W. C. Folger MSS.).

Hussey, Sylvanus, m. 1st, Abial Brown,* dau. John and Rachel (Gardner) Brown (Nantucket Town Records, Bk. I., p. 9, 1711-12); 2d, Hepzibah Starbuck, dau. Nathaniel Starbuck, Jr., and Dinah (Coffin) (Nantucket Friends' Records, Bk. I., p. 25, 1720).

Hussey, Batchelor, m. Abigail Hall. (Nantucket Town Records, Bk. I., p. 8, 1704.)

Hussey, Daniel, unm.

Hussey, Mary, m. 1st, Jonathan Worth, son John and Miriam (Gardner) Worth (Nantucket Town Records, Bk. I., p. 9, 1707); 2d, Ebenezer Barnard, son Nathaniel and Mary Barnard (W. C. Folger MSS.).

Hussey, George, m. Elizabeth Starbuck, dau. Nathaniel, Jr., and Dinah (Coffin) Starbuck. (Nantucket Friends' Records, Bk. I., p. 10, 1717.)

Hussey, Theodate, m. James Johnson. (Nantucket Town Records, Bk. I., p. 21, 1726.)

Children of Sylvanus Hussey, Sr., and Abial Brown.

Hussey, Obed, m. 1st, Margaret Wilson, dau. John and Margaret Wilson (Nantucket Town Records, Bk. I., p. 26, 1730); 2d, Mary Calef, dau. Ebenezer and Elizabeth (Fitch) Calef (Ibid., Bk. I., p. 56, 1748).

Hussey, Daniel, m. Sarah Gorham, dau. Stephen and Elizabeth (Gardner) Gorham. (Ibid., Bk. I., p. 29, 1734-35.)

Hussey, Rachel, m. 1st, Barnabas Coleman, son John and Priscilla (Starbuck) Coleman (Nantucket Friends' Records, Bk. I., p. 62, 1733); 2d, Paul Bunker, son Jabez and Hannah (Gardner) Bunker (Nantucket Friends' Records, vol. ii., p. 340).

---

* Abial Brown was great-granddaughter of Peter Hobart. See pp. 84, 85 supra, and Savage, vol. ii., p. 271, 435; also History of Hingham, Massachusetts, vol. iv., p. 335.

Hussey, Jonathan, *m.* Hepzibah Starbuck, dau. Paul and Ann (Tibbets) Starbuck. (Friends' Records, Bk. I., p. 93, 10th mo. 25th, 1738.)

Hussey, Seth, *m.* Sarah Jenkins, dau. Matthew and Mary (Gardner) Jenkins. (Nantucket Friends' Records, Bk. I., p. 110, 1742.)

CHILDREN OF SYLVANUS HUSSEY, SR., AND HEPZIBAH STARBUCK.

Hussey, Christopher, *m.* Mary Coffin, dau. Jonathan and Hepzibah (Harker) Coffin. (Nantucket Town Records, Bk. I., p. 48.)

Hussey, William, *m.* Abigail Starbuck, dau. Paul and Ann (Tibbets) Starbuck. (Nantucket Friends' Records, Bk. I., p. 52, 1746.)

Hussey, Batchelor, *m.* Anna Coffin, dau. Daniel and Mary (Blake) Coffin. (Ibid., p. 157, 1748.)

Hussey, Nathaniel, *m.* Judith Coffin, dau. Francis and Theodate (Gorham) Coffin. (Ibid., p. 185, 1750.)

Hussey, Hepzibah, *m.* Nathaniel Coleman, son Barnabas and Elizabeth (Barnard) Coleman. (Ibid., p. 172, 1749.)

Hussey, Sylvanus, Jr., *m.* 1st, Alice Gray, dau. Jeremiah and Theodate Gray (Friends' Records, vol. ii., p. 17, 1756); 2d, Lydia Wing, dau. Samuel and Hepzibah (Hathaway) Wing (Sandwich Friends' Records, p. 52).

Hussey, George, *m.* Deborah Paddack, dau. Daniel and Susanna (Gorham) Paddack. (Nantucket Friends' Records, Book II., p. 25, 1757.)

Hussey, Joseph, *m.* Mary Raymer. (Ibid., p. 137, 1766.)

CHILDREN OF GEORGE HUSSEY AND DEBORAH PADDACK.

Hussey, Rhoda, *m.* Tristram Folger, son Barzillai and Phebe (Coleman) Folger. (Nantucket Friends' Records, vol. ii., p. 234, 1776.)

Hussey, Eunice, *m.* Peleg Easton, son Peleg and Mary (Frye) Easton. (Ibid., p. 253, 1778.)

Hussey, George Gorham, *m.* Lydia Chase, dau. Francis and Naomi (Gardner) Chase. (Ibid., p. 292, 1784.)

Hussey, Uriel, *m.* Phebe Folger, dau. William and Ruth (Coffin) Folger. (Ibid., p. 332, 1789.)

Appendix.

Hussey, Sylvanus, *m.* Prudence Pease, dau. John and Jerusha (Norton) Pease. (Nantucket Town Records, Dec. 25, 1794.)

Hussey, Barnabas. (Nantucket Friends' Records.)

Hussey, Susanna, *m.* Zenas Gardner, son Paul and Rachel (Starbuck) Gardner. (Ibid., p. 342, 1790.)

Hussey, Deborah, *m.* Robert Brayton, son Israel and Elizabeth (Lawton) Brayton. (Ibid., vol. iv., p. 4, 1795.)

Hussey, Alice, *unm.* (Ibid.)

Hussey, Rachel, *m.* Joseph Austin, son Jeremiah and Patience (Fish) Austin. (Ibid., vol. iv., p. 44, 1808.)

Hussey, Mary, *m.* Peleg Swain. (Nantucket Town Records, Bk. I., p. 25, 1730.)

Hussey, Tristram, son Bachelor Hussey, *m.* Sarah Folger, dau. William and Ruth (Coffin) Folger. (W. C. Folger MSS., p. 171, 1777.)

Hussey, Sarah, *m.* John Milton Earle, son Pliny and Patience Earle. (Ibid., p. 180, 1821.)

Hussey, Daniel, *m.* Anna Starbuck. (Nantucket Town Records, Bk. I., p. 133, 1793.)

Hussey, Mary, *m.* Thomas Earle, son Pliny and Patience Earle. (W. C. Folger MSS., 1820.)

Hussey, Reuben, *m.* Elizabeth Woodbury. (Nantucket Town Records, Bk. I., p. 50, 1744.)

Hussey, Zaccheus, *m.* Lydia Folger. (Nantucket Court Records, Bk. I., p. 24.)

Hussey, Simeon, *m.* Abigail Bunker. (Ibid., Bk. II., p. 2, 1784.)

Hussey, Albert, *m.* Rebekah Shove. (Ibid., Bk. I., p. 28, 1785.)

Hussey, James, *m.* Eunice Swain. (Ibid., 1786.)

Hussey, Samuel, *m.* Charlotte Bartlett. (Ibid., Bk. II., p. 4, 1780.)

Hussey, Nathaniel, *m.* Elizabeth Swain. (Ibid., p. 6, 1790.)

Hussey, Ebenezer, *m.* Mehitable Smith. (Ibid., Bk. I., p. 4, 1770.)

Hussey, Reuben, *m.* Phebe Bunker. (Ibid., p. 5, 1772.)

Hussey, Jethro, *m.* Margaret Coffin. (Ibid., p. 12, 1766.)

Hussey, John, son Bachelor and Abigail, *m.* Jedidah Coffin, dau. Joseph and Bethiah Coffin. (Nantucket Friends' Records, Bk. I., p. 67, 1733-34.)

Hussey, Bethiah, *m.* Bachelor Bunker. (Nantucket Town Records, Bk. I., p. 73, 1759.)

Hussey, Abigail, m. Joseph Myrick. (Ibid., p. 76, 1763.)
Hussey, Hepzibah, m. Job Bunker. (Court Records, Bk. I., p. 29, 1767.)
Hussey, Sarah, m. John Darling. (Ibid., p. 1, 1767.)
Hussey, Mary, m. Ebenezer Perkins. (Ibid., p. 26, 1783.)
Hussey, Elizabeth, m. Thomas Delano. (Ibid., p. 25, 1781.)
Hussey, Lydia, m. Alexander Coffin. (Ibid., p. 28, 1784.)
Hussey, Susanna, m. Obed Barnard. (Ibid., 1786.)
Hussey, Abiel, m. Philip Pollard. (Ibid., p. 2, 1786.)
Hussey, Abigail, m. Bachelor Bunker. (Ibid., p. 14, 1773.)

DAUGHTERS OF GEORGE AND ELIZABETH (STARBUCK) HUSSEY.

Hussey, Ruth, m. Nathaniel Gardner, son Nathaniel and Mary Gardner. (Nantucket Friends' Records, Bk. I., p. 146, 1746.)

Hussey, Elizabeth, m. Peleg Coffin, son Francis and Theodate Coffin. (Ibid., p. 163, 1749.)

Hussey, Martha, m. Richard Swain, son Richard and Elizabeth Swain. (Ibid., p. 197, 1751.)

Hussey, Deborah, m. Peter Coffin, son Paul and Mary Coffin. (Ibid., p. 87, 1738.)

Hussey, Lydia, m. Clothier Pierce, son Clothier and Hannah Pierce, of Newport. (Ibid., p. 113, 1742.)

Hussey, Dinah, m. Reuben Folger, son Jonathan and Margaret Folger. (Ibid., p. 125, 1743-44.)

Hussey, Christopher, m. Lydia Manchester. (Nantucket Court Records, Bk. I., p. 2, 1769.)
Hussey, Sarah, m. John Waterman. (Ibid., Bk. II., p. 2, 1786.)
Hussey, Abigail, m. Perez Waterman. (Ibid., Bk. I., p. 12, 1765.)
Hussey, Abiel, m. Francis Pinkham. (Ibid., p. 29, 1787.)
Hussey, Mary, m. Thaddeus Gardner. (Ibid., Bk. II., p. 3, 1788.)
Hussey, Elizabeth, m. Peter Chace. (Ibid., p. 5, 1789.)
Hussey, Abiel, m. Nathaniel Coffin. (Ibid., Bk. I., p. 7, 1752.)
Hussey, Elizabeth, m. David Basitard or Basihard. (Ibid., p. 8, 1755.)
Hussey, Lydia, m. Simeon Bunker. (Ibid., p. 2, 1769.)
Hussey, Margaret, m. Thomas Snow. (Ibid., p. 15, 1768.)
Hussey, Huldah, dau. Bachelor and Abigail Hussey, m. Simeon

Bunker, son Jonathan and Elizabeth Bunker. (Nantucket Friends' Records, Bk. I., p. 71, 1734-35.)

Hussey, Jedidah, dau. Bachelor and Abigail Hussey, m. Benjamin Coffin, son Nathaniel and Damaris Coffin. (Ibid., p. 32, 1726.)

Hussey, Elizabeth, dau. Daniel and Sarah Hussey, m. Benjamin Coffin, son Benjamin and Jedidah Coffin. (Ibid., 1754.)

MACY FAMILY.

Macy,[1] Thomas, m. Sarah Hopcot.

CHILDREN OF THOMAS MACY AND SARAH HOPCOT.
Macy Family, p. 67.

Macy,[2] Sarah, *unm.*

Macy,[2] Sarah, *m.* April 11, 1665, William Worth, son of John Worth. (Ibid., p. 67.)

Macy,[2] Mary, *m.* April 11, 1669, William Bunker, son of George Bunker and Jane (Godfrey). (Ibid., p. 67.)

Macy,[2] Bethiah, *m.* March 30, 1670, Joseph Gardner, son of Richard Gardner and Sarah (Shattuck). (Ibid., p. 67.)

Macy,[2] Thomas, *unm.*

Macy,[2] John, *m.* Deborah Gardner, dau. of Richard Gardner and Sarah (Shattuck). (Ibid., p. 67.)

Macy,[2] Francis, *unm.*

CHILDREN OF JOHN MACY (1655-1691) AND DEBORAH GARDNER.
Ibid., pp. 67, 68.

Macy,[3] John,* *m.* April 25, 1707, Judith Worth, dau. John Worth and Miriam (Gardner). (Ibid., p. 68.)

Macy,[3] Sarah, *m.* John Barnard, son Nathaniel Barnard and Mary (Barnard). (Ibid., p. 68.)

Macy,[3] Deborah, *m.* Daniel Russell. (Ibid., p. 68.)

---

* John and Judith (Worth) Macy were the first of the name who joined the Society of Friends; they became members in 1711 (Macy Gen., p. 68), three years after the Society was established on the island.

NOTE.—Figure over surname in Macy family indicates generation from Thomas Macy, proprietor and settler.

Macy,[3] Bethiah, *m.* 1st, Joseph Coffin, son James Coffin and Mary Severance; 2d, John Renough. (Ibid., p. 68.)

Macy,[3] Jabez, *m.* Nov. 7, 1712, Sarah Starbuck, dau. Jethro Starbuck and Dorcas Gayer. (Ibid., p. 77.)

Macy,[3] Mary, *m.* July, 1711, Solomon Coleman, son John Coleman and Joanna (Folger). (Ibid., p. 68.)

Macy,[3] Thomas, *m.* Deborah Coffin, dau. Lieu. John Coffin and Deborah Austin, June 18, 1708. (Ibid., p. 78.)

Macy,[3] Richard,* *m.* 1st, Sept. 8, 1711, Deborah Pinkham, dau. Reuben Pinkham and Mary (Coffin); 2d, June 8, 1769, Alice Paddack, dau. Joseph Paddack and Sarah Gardner. (Ibid., p. 80.)

CHILDREN OF JOHN MACY (1675-1751) AND JUDITH WORTH.
Ibid., pp. 68, 69.

Macy,[4] Miriam, *m.* July, 1725, Zephaniah Coffin, son of Stephen Coffin and Experience (Look). (Ibid., p. 68.)

Macy,[4] Sylvanus, *unm.*

Macy,[4] Seth, *unm.*

Macy,[4] Eliab, *unm.*

Macy,[4] David, *m.* Nov., 1739, Dinah Gardner, dau. Solomon Gardner and Anna (Coffin). (Ibid., p. 82.)

Macy,[4] Anna, *m.* Oct., 1734, Joseph Jenkins, son of Matthew Jenkins and Mary (Gardner). (Ibid., p. 68.)

Macy,[4] Bethiah, *unm.*

Macy,[4] John, *m.* Aug. 13, 1743, Eunice Coleman, dau. Elihu Coleman and Jemima (Barnard). (Ibid., p. 83.)

Macy,[4] Judith, *m.* 1753, William Clasby, Jr., son William Clasby and Abial (Gardner). (Ibid., p. 69.)

Macy,[4] Jonathan, *m.* July, 1744, Lois Gorham, dau. Stephen Gorham and Elizabeth (Gardner). (Ibid., p. 85.)

Macy,[4] William, *m.* Nov. 13, 1746, Mary Barney, dau. Benjamin Barney and Lydia (Starbuck). (Ibid., p. 86.)

Macy,[4] Sarah, *m.* Oct., 1746, Richard Gardner, son Solomon Gardner and Anna (Coffin). (Ibid., p. 69.)

Macy,[4] Abigail, *unm.*

---

* Richard Macy built the first wharf on Nantucket, in 1723, also the first windmill. (Macy Gen., p. 81.)

NOTE.—John Worth, who married Miriam Gardner, was son of William Worth and Sarah Macy.

Appendix.

CHILDREN OF JABEZ MACY (1683-1776) AND SARAH STARBUCK.
Ibid., pp. 77, 78.

Macy,4 George, *unm.*

Macy,4 Eunice, *m.* July, 1742, Richard, son of John Beard. (Ibid., p. 78.)

Macy,4 Dorcas, *unm.*

Macy,4 Jethro, *m.* May, 1750, Hepzibah Worth, dau. William Worth and Mary (Butler). (Ibid., p. 87.)

Macy,4 Daniel, *m.* 1755, Abigail Swain, dau. Caleb Swain and Margaret (Paddack). (Ibid., p. 88.)

Macy,4 Matthew, *m.* 1755, 1st, Abigail Coffin, dau. Benjamin Coffin and Jedidah (Hussey); 2d, Abigail Gardner. (Ibid., p. 88.)

Macy,4 Lydia, *m.* 1775, Matthew Jenkins, son of Peter Jenkins and Abigail (Gardner). (Ibid., p. 78.)

Macy,4 —— *unm.*

Macy,4 Jabez, *m.* 1767, Rachel Cartwright, dau. Hezidiah Cartwright and Abigail (Brown). (Ibid., p. 89.)

CHILDREN OF THOMAS MACY* (1687-1759) AND DEBORAH COFFIN.
Ibid., pp. 78-79.

Macy,4 Joseph, *m.* 1728, Hannah Hobbs, dau. Benjamin Hobbs. (Ibid., p. 90.)

Macy,4 Robert, *m.* Jan. 3, 1731, Abigail Barnard, dau. Benjamin Barnard and Judith (Gardner). (Ibid., p. 97.)

Macy,4 Love, *m.* Feb. 21, 1733, Joseph Rotch, son William Rotch and Hannah (——). (Ibid., p. 79.)

Macy,4 Francis, *m.* March, 1738, Judith Coffin, dau. Richard Coffin and Ruth (Bunker). (Ibid., p. 93.)

Macy,4 Nathaniel, *m.* Jan., 1741, Abigail Pinkham, dau. Shubael Pinkham and Abigail (Bunker). (Ibid., p. 94.)

Macy,4 Lydia, *m.* Dec., 1747, Jethro Coleman, son John Coleman and Priscilla (Starbuck). (Ibid., p. 79.)

---

* "Thomas Macy 3 about 1720 assisted in capturing and killing a whale; he either took or sent his share of the whalebone to England, where he sold it, and purchased a bolt of Irish Linen, a clock, and a copy of Sewell's History." The clock has a place on a genealogical tree. It descended to Joseph, Paul, and Obed Macy, traveled to New Garden, N. C., to Ohio, and finally to Troy, N. Y.

Macy,⁴ Elizabeth, *m.* Oct., 1741, Francis Barnard, son Benjamin Barnard and Judith (Gardner). (Ibid., p. 79.)

Macy,⁴ Thomas, *unm.*

Macy,⁴ Deborah, *m.* Benjamin Coffin, son Nathaniel Coffin and Damaris (Gayer). (Ibid., p. 79.)

Macy,⁴ Anna, *m.* Nov., 1752, Richard Worth, son Richard Worth and Sarah (Hoag). (Ibid., p. 79.)

Macy,⁴ Hepzibah, *m.* Nov., 1752, Thomas Davis. (Ibid., p. 79.)

CHILDREN OF RICHARD MACY (1689-1779) AND FIRST WIFE, DEBORAH PINKHAM. Ibid., 80, 81.

Macy,⁴ Lydia, *unm.*

Macy,⁴ Zaccheus, *m.* Oct. 2, 1734, Hepzibah Gardner, dau. Samuel Gardner and Patience (Swain). (Ibid., p. 95.)

Macy,⁴ Abraham, *m.* April, 1738, Anna Worth, dau. Joseph Worth and Lydia (Gorham). (Ibid., p. 109.)

Macy,⁴ Mary, *m.* Feb., 1749, Benjamin Marshall, son Joseph Marshall and Mercy (Short). (Ibid., p. 81.)

Macy,⁴ Caleb, *m.* Dec. 8, 1749, Judith Gardner (widow James Gardner), dau. Daniel Folger and Abigail (Folger). (Ibid., p. 110.)

Macy,⁴ Judith, *m.* Sept., 1742, Jonathan Bunker, son Peleg Bunker and Susanna (Coffin). (Ibid., p. 81.)

Macy,⁴ Ruth, *m.* Aug., 1744, Joseph Starbuck, son Paul Starbuck and Ann (Tibbetts). (Ibid., p. 81.)

Macy,⁴ Hannah, *unm.*

Macy,⁴ Richard, *unm.*

Macy,⁴ Priscilla, *unm.*

Macy,⁴ Benjamin, *m.* Abigail Brown, dau. George Brown and Abigail Trott. (Ibid., p. 111.)

Macy,⁴ Sylvanus, *unm.*

CHILDREN OF DAVID MACY, b. 1714, d. in North Carolina, AND DINAH GARDNER. Ibid., p. 82.

Macy,⁵ Stephen, *m.* Oct., 1760, Mercy Allen, dau. Nathaniel Allen and Mercy (Skiff). (Ibid., p. 111.)

Macy,⁵ David, *m.* Hannah White, dau. Isaac White and Catharine (Stanton). (Ibid., p. 112.)

Macy,⁵ Miriam, *m.* Dec., 1761, Robert Gardner, son Robert Gardner and Jedidah (Folger). (Ibid., p. 82.)

Macy,[5] Anna, *m.* Oct., 1763, Enoch Macy, son Joseph Macy and Hannah Hobbs. (Ibid., p. 82.)

Macy,[5] Sarah, *m.* Oct., 1766, Timothy Russell, son William Russell and Ruth (Swain). (Ibid., p. 82.)

Macy,[5] Hepzibah, *unm.*

Macy,[5] Abigail,* *m.* 1774, Benjamin Stanton, son Henry Stanton and Lydia (Albertson). (Ibid., p. 83; N. C. Friends' Records.)

CHILDREN OF JOHN MACY, b. 1721, AND EUNICE COLEMAN.
Ibid., pp. 83, 84.

Macy,[5] Bethiah, *m.* Nov., 1761, Paul Macy, son of Joseph Macy and Hannah (Hobbs). (Ibid., p. 84.)

Macy,[5] Judith, *m.* Dec., 1767, Reuben Bunker, son Reuben Bunker and Mary (Chase). (Ibid., p. 84.)

Macy,[5] Eliab, *unm.*

Macy,[5] Jemima, *m.* Barzillai Gardner, son Stephen Gardner and Jemima (Worth). (Ibid., p. 84.)

Macy,[5] Eunice, *unm.*

Macy,[5] John, *m.* Rhoda Gardner, dau. Stephen Gardner and Jemima (Worth). (Ibid., p. 113.)

Macy,[5] Elihu, *unm.*

Macy,[5] Eunice, *unm.*

Macy,[5] Barachiah, *m.* March 20, 1783, Lucinda Barnard, dau. Benjamin Barnard and Eunice (Fitch). (Ibid., p. 113.)

Macy,[5] Merab, *m.* Jan. 8, 1783, Timothy Macy, son Jethro Macy and Hepzibah (Worth). (Ibid., p. 84.)

Macy,[5] Abigail, *unm.*

Macy,[5] Micajah, *unm.*

Macy,[5] Amy, *m.* Libni Barnard, son Benjamin Barnard and Eunice (Fitch). (Ibid., p. 84.)

Macy,[5] Clement.

---

* Grandmother of Edwin M. Stanton, who was appointed Atty. Genl., December 20, 1860, and remained in Mr. Buchanan's Cabinet until Lincoln's inauguration March 4, 1861. Mr. Lincoln appointed him Secretary of War January 11, 1862; after the death of Lincoln he continued in that position until suspended by Mr. Johnson Aug. 12, 1867.

CHILDREN OF JONATHAN MACY (1725-1798) AND LOIS GORHAM.
Ibid., pp. 85, 86.

Macy,[5] Elizabeth, m. 1762, Elihu Coleman, son of Jethro Coleman and Lydia (Paddack). (Ibid., p. 86.)

Macy,[5] Jonathan, m. Dec. 3, 1778, Rose Pinkham, dau. Reuben Pinkham and Ann (Starbuck). (Ibid., p. 114.)

Macy,[5] Barnabas, m. Feb., 1784, Abial Clasby, dau. Joseph Clasby and Lydia (Starbuck). (Ibid., p. 117.)

Macy,[5] Solomon, *unm.*

Macy,[5] Susanna, *unm.*

Macy,[5] Samuel, *unm.*

Macy,[5] Peleg, m. Oct. 28, 1784, Sarah Starbuck (widow of Zaccheus Starbuck), and daughter of John Hunt Wendall and Sarah (Tilden). (Ibid., p. 117.)

Macy,[5] Judith, *unm.*

Macy,[5] Samuel, m. 1st, June 29, 1786, Lydia Folger, dau. Walter Folger and Elizabeth (Starbuck); 2d, June, 1832, Mary Clasby, dau. William Clasby and Hepzibah (Coleman). (Ibid., p. 119.)

Macy,[5] Seth, *unm.*

CHILDREN OF WILLIAM MACY (1727-1753) AND MARY BARNEY.
Ibid., p. 86.

Macy,[5] Sarah, *unm.*

Macy,[5] Lydia, *unm.*

Macy,[5] William, Jr., m. 1st, Dec. 12, 1771, Anna Hussey, dau. Paul Hussey and Anne (Varney); 2d, May, 1807, Jedidah Barker, dau. Robert Barker and Sarah (Folger). (Ibid., p. 120.)

CHILDREN OF JETHRO MACY, b. 1728, died in North Carolina,
AND HEPZIBAH WORTH. Ibid., 87.

Macy,[5] Hepzibeth, m. Thomas Pierce. (Ibid., p. 87.)

Macy,[5] Mary, m. Samuel Coffin, son William Coffin and Priscilla Paddack. (Ibid., p. 87.)

Macy,[5] Jethro, m. 1777, Susanna Wilcox, dau. John Wilcox and Hannah (Coffin). (Ibid., p. 121.)

Macy,[5] Gayer, m. Anna Clasby, dau. Charles Clasby and Anna (———). (Ibid., p. 122.)

Macy,⁵ Jedidah, *m.* Joseph Swain, son Nathaniel Swain and Bethiah (Macy). (Ibid., p. 87.)

Macy,⁵ Timothy, *m.* Jan. 8, 1783, Merab Macy, dau. John Macy and Eunice (Coleman). (Ibid., p. 123.)

Macy,⁵ Elizabeth, *unm.*

Macy,⁵ Huldah, *m.* Nov. 15, 1792, Asa Barnard, son Tristram Barnard and Margaret (Folger). (Ibid., p. 87.)

CHILDREN OF DANIEL MACY (1731-1785) AND ABIGAIL SWAIN.
Ibid., p. 88.

Macy,⁵ Sylvanus, *m.* 1st, May 30, 1782, Dinah Bunker, dau. Paul Bunker and Hannah (Gardner); 2d, Oct. 3, 1798, Mary Foster (widow of John Foster), and dau. Francis Swain and Mary (Paddack). (Ibid., p. 124.)

Macy,⁵ Lydia, *unm.*

Macy,⁵ Margaret, *m.* 1787, Obed Paddack, son of Jonathan Paddack and Kesia (Gardner). (Ibid., p. 88.)

Macy,⁵ Uriah, *m.* 1787, Eunice Barney, dau. Benjamin Barney and Jemima (Jenkins). (Ibid., p. 124.)

Macy,⁵ Daniel, *unm.*

Macy,⁵ Abigail, *m.* 1791, Matthew Barney, son Benjamin Barney and Jemima (Jenkins). (Ibid., p. 88.)

CHILDREN OF MATTHEW MACY, d. 1792, FIRST WIFE, ABIGAIL COFFIN; SECOND WIFE, ABIGAIL GARDNER.
Ibid., pp. 88-89.

Macy,⁵ Matthew, *m.* Lydia Barnard, dau. Benjamin Barnard and Eunice (Fitch). (Ibid., p. 125.)

Macy,⁵ Sarah, *m.* Stephen Springer. (Ibid., p. 89.)

Macy,⁵ Abigail, *m.* Joseph Coffin, son Peter Coffin and Priscilla (Coleman). (Ibid., p. 89.)

Macy,⁵ Elizabeth, *m.* Libni Coffin, son Libni Coffin and Hepzibeth (Starbuck). (Ibid., p. 89.)

Macy,⁵ George,* *m.* 1785, Matilda Folger, dau. Reuben Folger and Dinah (Hussey). (Ibid., p. 126.)

---

* George Macy, certainly, was child of second wife.

DAUGHTER OF JABEZ MACY (1737-1767) AND RACHEL CARTWRIGHT. Ibid., p. 89.

Macy,[5] Lydia, *m.* Dec. 28, 1786, Uriah Starbuck, son of Sylvanus Starbuck and Mary (Howes). (Ibid., p. 89.)

CHILDREN OF JOSEPH MACY (1709-1772) AND HANNAH HOBBS. Ibid., p. 90.

Macy,[5] Mary, *m.* Sept., 1753, Paul Way, son John Way and Mary (Long). (Ibid., p. 90.)

Macy,[5] Thomas, *m.* Jan., 1755, Mary Starbuck, dau. Tristram Starbuck and Deborah (Coffin). (Ibid., p. 126.)

Macy,[5] Bethiah, *m.* Oct., 1755, Nathaniel Swain, son Caleb Swain and Margaret (Paddack). (Ibid., p. 90.)

Macy,[5] Joseph, *m.* Nov., 1757, Mary Starbuck, dau. William Starbuck and Anna (Folger). (Ibid., p. 127.)

Macy,[5] Henry, *m.* 1st, Jan. 31, 1760, Sarah Swain, dau. Caleb Swain and Margaret (Paddack); 2d, March 24, 1791, Elizabeth Coffin (widow of Benjamin), and dau. Daniel Hussey and Sarah (Gorham). (Ibid., p. 128.)

Macy,[5] Paul, *m.* 1st, Nov., 1761, Bethiah Macy, dau. John Macy and Eunice (Coleman); 2d, Jan. 26, 1817, Deborah Coggeshall, dau. Job Coggeshall and Deborah (Starbuck). (Ibid., p. 131.)

Macy,[5] Enoch, *m.* Oct., 1763, Anna Macy, dau. David Macy and Dinah (Gardner). (Ibid., p. 132.)

CHILDREN OF ROBERT MACY (1710-1771) AND ABIGAIL (BARNARD). Ibid., pp. 92, 93.

Macy,[5] Nathaniel, *m.* Jan., 1761, Hepzibeth Macy, dau. Zaccheus Macy and Hepzibeth (Gardner). (Ibid., p. 134.)

Macy,[5] Lydia, *m.* Dec., 1751, Abishai Gardner, son of Robert Gardner and Jedidah (Folger). (Ibid., p. 92.)

Macy,[5] Elizabeth, *m.* 1st, Dec., 1762, Alexander Mooers, son Thomas Mooers and Mary (Stratton); 2d, William Coffin, son Benjamin Coffin and Jedidah (Hussey) (William Coffin's third wife). (Ibid., p. 92.)

Macy,[5] Judith, *m.* Aug., 1758, Benjamin Stratton, son Caleb Stratton and Lois (Oder). (Ibid., p. 93.)

Macy,[5] Benjamin, *unm.*

Macy,[5] Robert, *m.* 1st, March 2, 1772, Anna Jones, dau. Silas Jones and Anna (Heath); 2d, Sept. 13, 1798, Phebe Jenkins, dau. Joseph Jenkins and Ruth (Clark). (Ibid., p. 135.)

Macy,[5] John,* *m.* 1st, March 3, 1768, Bethiah Cartwright, dau. Hezediah Cartwright and Abigail (Brown); 2d, March 5, 1794, Phebe Macy, dau. Abraham Macy and Priscilla (Bunker). (Ibid., p. 136.)

Macy,[5] Deborah, *m.* Dec., 1769, Jonathan Cartwright, son Hezidiah Cartwright and Abigail (Brown). (Ibid., p. 93.)

Macy,[5] Abigail, *m.* Thomas Butts. (Ibid., p. 93.)

Macy,[5] Mary, *unm.*

Macy,[5] Eunice, *m.* Francis Bunker, son Shubael Bunker and Lydia (Paddack). (Ibid., p. 93.)

Macy,[5] Benjamin, *unm.*

CHILDREN OF FRANCIS MACY (1715-1793) AND JUDITH COFFIN.
Ibid., pp. 93, 94.

Macy,[5] Love, *m.* Dec., 1758, James Cartwright, son Hezidiah Cartwright and Abigail (Brown). (Ibid., p. 94.)

Macy,[5] Reuben, *m.* 1st, April, 1767, Anna Barnard, dau. Robert Barnard and Hepzabeth (Coffin); 2d, Judith Myrick (widow of Jethro Myrick), dau. Thomas Jenkins· and Judith (Folger). (Ibid., p. 138.)

Macy,[5] Phebe, *m.* Jan., 1763, Benjamin Hussey, son John Hussey and Jedidah (Coffin). (Ibid., p. 94.)

Macy,[5] Seth, *unm.*

Macy,[5] Francis, *m.* 1st, Hannah Mackrell, from Pool, England (married in London); 2d, June, 1798, Elizabeth Brown, dau. Joseph Brown and Mary (Ellis). (Ibid., p. 142.)

Macy,[5] Judith, *m.* Dec., 1772, Benjamin Coffin, son Benjamin Coffin and Rebecca (Coffin). (Ibid., p. 94.)

Macy,[5] Anna, *m.* Oct., 1774, Tristram Jenkins, son Peter Jenkins and Abigail (Gardner). (Ibid., p. 94.)

---

*John Macy, son· of Robert Macy, of the fifth generation from Thomas Macy,[1] signed his last will when he was eighty-eight years old, and had nineteen children.

The Macy family was a close corporation for many years. Up to 1800 very few surnames appear, excepting such as may be classed among orthodox Nantucket names. Upon these many changes were rung. Since that date record of intermarriages with many other families may be found.

Macy,⁵ Ruth, *m.* Obediah Folger, son Barzillai Folger and Phebe (Coleman). (Ibid., p. 94.)

Macy,⁵ Deborah, *unm.*

Macy,⁵ Lydia, *unm.*

Macy,⁵ Lydia, *m.* July, 1784, Edward Starbuck, son Edward Starbuck and Damaris (Worth). (Ibid., p. 94.)

CHILDREN OF NATHANIEL MACY (1719-1783) AND ABIGAIL PINKHAM. Ibid., pp. 94, 95.

Macy,⁵ Shubael, *m.* Dec., 1761, Eunice Gardner, dau. Robert Gardner and Jedidah (Folger). (Ibid., p. 143.)

Macy,⁵ Tristram, *m.* 1765, Miriam Barnard, dau. William Barnard and Mary (Coffin). (Ibid., p. 144.)

Macy,⁵ George, *m.* Dec. 28, 1769, Margaret Paddack, dau. Paul Paddack and Anna (Coffin). (Ibid., p. 145.)

Macy,⁵ Deborah, *unm.*

Macy,⁵ Nathaniel, Jr., *m.* 1st, Elizabeth Broch, dau. William Broch and Elizabeth (———); 2d, Mercy Dunham, dau. Jethro Dunham and Mercy (———). (Ibid., p. 145.)

Macy,⁵ Eunice, *m.* Solomon Coffin, son Zephaniah Coffin and Abigail (Coleman). (Ibid., p. 95.)

Macy,⁵ Peter, *m.* Nov., 1781, Sarah Folger, dau. Timothy Folger and Abial (Coleman). (Ibid., p. 146.)

Macy,⁵ Phebe, *m.* 1st, 1778, Paul Barnard, son William Barnard and Mary (Coffin); 2d, Paul Worth, son John Worth and Mary (Gardner). (Ibid., p. 95.)

Macy,⁵ Elizabeth, *m.* 1787, Barzillai Macy, son Caleb Macy and Judith (Gardner). (Ibid., p. 95.)

Macy,⁵ Thomas, *unm.*

Macy,⁵ Abishai, *m.* July 19, 1794, Phebe Worth, dau. Andrew Worth and Judith (Coleman). (Ibid., p. 147.)

CHILDREN OF ZACCHEUS MACY (1713-1797) AND HEPZIBAH GARDNER. Ibid., pp. 95, 96.

Macy,⁵ Mary, *m.* Jan., 1753, John Ray, son Samuel Ray and Mary (Fullerton). (Ibid., p. 96.)

Macy,⁵ Hannah, *m.* July, 1756, Reuben Swain, son Stephen Swain and Eleanor (Ellis). (Ibid., p. 96.)

Macy,⁵ Phebe, *m.* 1756, William Stanton, son Samuel Stanton and Sarah (Coffin). (Ibid., p. 96.)

Macy,[5] Richard, *m.* Aug., 1759, Miriam Coffin, dau. Zephaniah Coffin and Abigail (Coleman). (Ibid., p. 148.)

Macy,[5] Hepzibeth, *m.* Nathaniel Macy, son Robert Macy and Abigail (Barnard). (Ibid., p. 96.)

Macy,[5] Priscilla, *m.* Enoch Ray, son Samuel Ray and Mary (Fullerton). (Ibid., p. 96.)

Macy,[5] David, *unm.*

Macy,[5] Ruth, *m.* Aug., 1768, Thomas Barnard, son Thomas Barnard and Sarah (Hoag). (Ibid., p. 96.)

Macy,[5] Abishai, *unm.*

Macy,[5] Deborah, *m.* Daniel Ray, son Samuel Ray and Elizabeth (Coleman). (Ibid., p. 96.)

Macy,[5] Lydia, *unm.*

Macy,[5] Latham, *m.* Oct. 2d, 1777, Lydia Russell, dau. John Russell and Ruth (Starbuck). (Ibid., p. 149.)

Macy,[5] Jemima, *unm.*

Macy,[5] Samuel, *unm.*

CHILDREN OF ABRAHAM MACY (1715-1746) AND ANNA WORTH.
Ibid., p. 109.

Macy,[5] Abraham, *m.* Dec. 3, 1761, Priscilla Bunker, dau. Samuel Bunker and Priscilla Coleman. (Ibid., p. 149.)

Macy,[5] ——, *unm.*

Macy,[5] Anna, *m.* Oct., 1761, Edward Allen, son Ebenezer Allen and Christiana (Heath). (Ibid., p. 109.)

Macy,[5] Reuben, *m.* 1st, Dec. 31, 1767, Elizabeth Bunker, dau. Samuel Bunker and Priscilla (Coleman); 2d, Sept. 21, 1774, Ruth Howard, dau. Edward Howard and Phebe (Hart). (Ibid., p. 153.)

CHILDREN OF CALEB MACY (1719-1798) AND JUDITH GARDNER.
Ibid., p. 110.

Macy,[5] Keziah, *unm.*

Macy,[5] Elisha, *m.* 1774, Phebe Gardner, dau. Jonathan Gardner and Miriam (Worth). (Ibid., p. 154.)

Macy,[5] Sylvanus, *m.* July 3, 1779, Anna Pinkham, dau. Daniel Pinkham and Eunice (Jenkins). (Ibid., p. 155.)

Macy,[5] Barzillai, *m.* Elizabeth Macy, dau. Nathaniel Macy and Abigail (Pinkham). (Ibid., p. 156.)

Macy,⁵ Obed, *m.* Feb. 2, 1786, Abigail Pinkham, dau. Daniel Pinkham and Eunice (Jenkins). (Ibid., p. 157.)
Macy,⁵ Caleb, *unm.*
Macy,⁵ Judith, *unm.*
Macy,⁵ Keziah, *unm.*
Macy,⁵ Ruth, *m.* Nov. 9, 1796, Job Chase, son Benjamin Chase and Martha (——). (Ibid., p. 110.)

CHILDREN OF STEPHEN MACY (1741-1822) AND MERCY ALLEN.
Ibid., pp. 111, 112.

Macy,⁶ Stephen, Jr., *m.* Jan., 1784, Phebe Swain, dau. David Swain and Martha (Hussey). (Ibid., p. 159.)
Macy,⁶ Edmund, *m.* Jan. 1, 1790, Susanna Coleman, dau. Seth Coleman and Deborah (Swain). (Ibid., p. 159.)
Macy,⁶ Solomon, *m.* Nov., 1790, Lydia Coleman, dau. Nathaniel Coleman and Hepzibeth (Hussey). (Ibid., p. 160.)
Macy,⁶ Job, *m.* Dec., 1795, Deborah Gardner, dau. Prince Gardner and Deborah (Barnard). (Ibid., p. 161.)
Macy,⁶ Hepzibah, *m.* Oct., 1794, Abraham Coleman, son Nathaniel Coleman and Hepzibeth (Hussey). (Ibid., p. 112.)
Macy,⁶ David, *m.* 1st, 1804, Susan Stubbs; 2d, May, 1808, Sally Stubbs, daughters James Stubbs and Rebecca Ellis. (Ibid., p. 162.)

NOTE.—Through five generations the marriages of this family are here given complete; after that time so many of the name went to Hudson, N. Y., North Carolina, and thence to Indiana and Ohio that only such as seem to have been closely associated with Nantucket are given, and no mention is made of unmarried children after the fifth generation.

NOTE.—Stephen was a favorite name in the Macy family, and leads to some confusion:
Macy,⁶ Stephen, son of Stephen,⁵ David,⁴ *m.* Jan. 1784, Phebe Swain, dau. David Swain and Martha Hussey. (Ibid., p. 159.)
Macy,⁶ Stephen, son John,⁵ John,⁴ John,³ John,² Thomas,¹ *m.* Mary Gardner. (Ibid., p. 165.)
Macy,⁶ Stephen, son David,⁵ David,⁴ John,³ John,² Thomas,¹ *m.* Sarah Baldwin. (Ibid., p. 163.)

CHILDREN OF JONATHAN MACY (1750-1816) AND ROSE PINKHAM.
Ibid, pp. 114, 115.

Macy,[6] Ann, m. Oct., 1801, Peleg Slocum Folger, son George Folger and Rebecca (Howland). (Ibid., p. 115.)

Macy,[6] Avis, m. Feb., 1812, Charles Barney, son Daniel Barney and Lydia (Coffin). (Ibid., p. 115.)

Macy,[6] Josiah, m. Feb. 6, 1805, Lydia Hussey, dau. Zaccheus Hussey and Lydia Folger). (Ibid., p. 170.)

Macy,[6] Robert, m. Dec. 16, 1821, Mary B. Coffin, dau. Shubael Coffin and Priscilla (Starbuck). (Ibid., p. 186.)

Macy,[6] Eliza, m. Joseph Havens, of Canada. (Ibid., p. 115.)

SON OF BARNABAS MACY (1752-1802) AND ABIAL CLASBY. Ibid, p. 117.

Macy,[6] George, m. May 10, 1815, Eunice Easton, dau. Peleg Easton and Eunice (Hussey). (Ibid., p. 187.)

CHILDREN OF PELEG MACY (1760-1838) AND SARAH STARBUCK.
Ibid, pp. 117, 118.

Macy,[6] Eunice, m. Simeon Brewer, son Daniel Brewer and Susanna Breed. (Ibid., p. 118.)

Macy,[6] Peleg, m. 1st, Feb. 8, 1809, Lucretia Folger, dau. Tristram Folger and Rhoda (Hussey); 2d, Nov. 3, 1833, Lydia Jenkins (widow Reuben Jenkins), and dau. Tristram Folger and Rhoda (Hussey). (Ibid., p. 188.)

Macy,[6] Sarah, m. March 8, 1810. George Easton, son Peleg and Eunice (Hussey). (Ibid., p. 118.)

Macy,[6] John W., m. Jan. 1, 1812, Sallie Swain, dau. Thomas Swain and Deborah (Cartwright). (Ibid., p. 188.)

Macy,[6] Rebecca, m. Jan. 1826, Benjamin Knowles, son William Knowles and Avis (———). (Ibid., p. 118.)

Macy,[6] Mary, m. May 4, 1820, William Watson, son Joel Watson and Elizabeth (Skinner). (Ibid., p. 118.)

Macy,[6] Charles, m. Jan. 29, 1826, Mary Jenkins, dau. William Jenkins and Deborah (Russell). (Ibid., p. 191.)

Macy,[6] Josiah, m. 1st, Sept., 1825, Eliza Swain, dau. Peleg Swain and Priscilla (Barrett); 2d, Oct. 7, 1866, Caroline Meader, dau. Thomas Meader and Deborah (Burnell). (Ibid., p. 192.)

Macy,⁶ Gorham, *m.* Dec. 9, 1813, Lucretia Clark, dau. Isaiah Clark and Love (Bunker). (Ibid., p. 189.)

Macy,⁶ Edward, *m.*, 1st, Nov. 1, 1815, Eliza Swain, dau. Thomas Swain and Deborah (Cartwright); 2d, Jan. 2, 1820, Eunice A. Hallett, dau. Thomas Hallett and Rachel (——). (Ibid., p. 190.)

CHILDREN OF SAMUEL MACY (1765-1838) AND FIRST WIFE, LYDIA FOLGER. Ibid., pp. 119, 120.

Macy,⁶ Rebecca, *m.* Henry Dingman. (Ibid., p. 119.)

Macy,⁶ Elizabeth, *m.* July, 1811, J. Franklin Coleman, son Obed Coleman and Elizabeth (Swain). (Ibid., p. 120.)

Macy,⁶ Judith, *m.* 1826, Stephen Swift, of Dartmouth. (Ibid., p. 120.)

Macy,⁶ Hannah, *m.* Giddeon Swain, son Jonathan Swain and Rachel (Fish). (Ibid., p. 120.)

CHILDREN OF WILLIAM MACY, JR. (1751-1814) AND FIRST WIFE, ANNA HUSSEY. Ibid., pp. 120, 121.

Macy,⁶ Anna, *m.* 1765, Moses Mitchell, son of Jethro Mitchell and Rachel (Hussey). (Ibid., p. 121.)

Macy,⁶ Mary, *m.* 1801, Hezikiah Barnard, son Nathaniel Barnard and Margaret (Swain). (Ibid., p. 121.)

Macy,⁶ Eliza, *m.*, 1st, 1803, Allen Howland, son Cornelius Howland and ——; 2d, Peter Barney, son Benjamin Barney and Jemima (Jenkins). (Ibid., p. 121.)

Macy,⁶ William W., *m.*, 1st, Jan., 1807, Phebe Starbuck, dau. Edward Starbuck and Lydia (Macy); 2d, 1834, Miriam P. H. Houghton, dau. Abel Houghton, of Lynn, Mass. (Ibid., p. 194.)

Macy,⁶ Thomas W., *m.* Sept. 28, 1815, Lydia B. Townsend, dau. Thomas Townsend and Phebe (Baxter). (Ibid., p. 195.)

Macy,⁶ James, *m.* Sept. 30, 1817, Eliza Inott, dau. Robert Inott and Judith Folger. (Ibid., p. 196.)

CHILDREN OF SYLVANUS MACY (1756-1813) AND FIRST WIFE, DINAH BUNKER. Ibid, p. 124.

Macy,⁶ Dinah, *m.* Jan. 30, 1805, Paul Macy, son Sylvanus Macy and Anna (Pinkham). (Ibid., p. 124.)

Macy,⁶ Daniel, *m.* Rebecca Smith, of Boston. (Ibid., p. 199.)

Macy,⁶ Jethro, *m.*, 1st, Aug. 30, 1812, Lydia Ray, dau. David Ray and Anna (Coggeshall); 2d, Dec., 1819, Deborah Gorham, dau. James Gorham and Parnal (Gardner). (Ibid., p. 200.)

Macy,⁶ William Gayer, *m.*, 1st, Feb., 1818, Phebe Clasby, dau. Lot Clasby and Elizabeth (Coffin); 2d, Emeline (widow of Thomas Clasby), and dau. William Chase and Merab (Gardner). (Ibid., p. 200.)

DAUGHTER OF HENRY MACY AND FIRST WIFE, SARAH SWAIN. Ibid., pp. 128, 129.

Macy,⁶ Susanna, *m.* 1785 Shubael Swain, son Reuben Swain and Hannah (Macy). (Ibid., p. 129.)

DAUGHTER OF FRANCIS MACY (1750-1817) AND HANNAH MACKRELL. Ibid, p. 142.

Macy,⁶ Hannah Mackrell, *m.* April 9, 1807, Oliver C. Gardner, son Latham Gardner and Priscilla (Gardner). (Ibid., p. 142.)

DAUGHTERS OF SHUBAEL MACY (1742-1812) AND EUNICE GARDNER. Ibid, pp. 143, 144.

Macy,⁶ Anna, *m.* Aug. 28, 1797, Thomas Ray, son Daniel Ray and Deborah (Macy). (Ibid., p. 143.)
Macy,⁶ Merab, *m.* Daniel Coffin, son Nathaniel Coffin and Priscilla (Gardner). (Ibid., p. 144.)
Macy,⁶ Peggy, *m.* Frederick Folger, son Charles Folger and Lydia (Coleman). (Ibid., p. 144.)

CHILDREN OF RICHARD MACY (1742-1814) AND MIRIAM COFFIN. Ibid., p. 148.

Macy,⁶ Priscilla, *m.* March 27, 1794, Paul Ray, son John Ray and Mary (Macy). (Ibid., p. 148.)
Macy,⁶ Miriam, *m.* July 17, 1804, George Prince, of Sweden. (Ibid., p. 148.)
Macy,⁶ Job. *m.* July 17, 1791, Anna Way, dau. Seth Way and Deborah (Chadwick). (Ibid., p. 235.)

CHILDREN OF LATHAM MACY (1759-1793) AND LYDIA RUSSELL. Ibid., p. 149.

Macy,⁶ Simeon, *m.* Oct. 31, 1799, Phebe Allen, dau. Daniel Allen and Phebe (Folger). (Ibid., p. 236.)
Macy,⁶ Deborah, *m.* Jan., 1800, Moses Joy, son David Joy and Phebe (Coffin). (Ibid., p. 149.)

CHILDREN OF SYLVANUS MACY (1756-1833) AND ANNA PINKHAM.
Ibid., pp. 155, 156.

Macy,⁶ Paul, m. Jan. 30, 1805, Dinah Macy, dau. Sylvanus Macy and Dinah (Bunker). (Ibid., p. 244.)
Macy,⁶ Eunice, m. Nov., 1804, Gideon Folger, son of Walter Folger and Elizabeth (Starbuck). (Ibid., p. 155.)
Macy,⁶ John, m. Aug. 7, 1808, Eliza Barnard (widow Thomas Barnard and dau. Andrew Myrick and Abiel (———). (Ibid., p. 245.)
Macy,⁶ Rachel, m. March, 1810, Roland Hussey, son John Hussey and Lydia (Barnard). (Ibid., p. 155.)
Macy,⁶ Barzillai, m. Mary Hussey, dau. John Hussey and Lydia (Barnard). (Ibid., p. 246.)
Macy,⁶ Lydia, m., 1st, March, 1819, Robert Bunker, son Barnabas Bunker and Lydia (Gardner); 2d, Jan., 1822, Frederick C. Macy, son Thomas Macy and Phebe (Bunker). (Ibid., p. 156.)

CHILDREN OF OBED MACY (1762-1844) AND ABIGAIL PINKHAM.
Ibid., p. 157.

Macy,⁶ Thomas,* m. 1st, April 7, 1808, Elizabeth Swain, dau. Tristram Swain and Rachel (Bunker); 2d, Sept. 9, 1824, Eunice Coffin, dau. Zenas Coffin and Abial (Gardner); 3d, Oct. 22, 1843, Christina Gale (widow of Edmund Gale), dau. Samuel Stubbs and Christina (Worth). (Ibid., p. 246.)
Macy,⁶ Reuben, m. March 3, 1816, Hannah Mitchell, dau. Peleg Mitchell, Sr., and Lydia (Cartwright). (Ibid., p. 248.)
Macy,⁶ Mary, unm.
Macy,⁶ Peter, m. 1st, March 31, 1817, Ann Swain, dau. Gilbert Swain and Margaret (Barnard); 2d, Nov. 6, 1828, Elizabeth Gardner, dau. Jared Gardner and Eunice (Coffin). (Ibid., p. 249.)
Macy,⁶ Elizabeth, unm.
Macy,⁶ Elizabeth, m. April 3, 1817, Edmund W. Macy, son Edmund Macy and Susanna (Coleman). (Ibid., p. 157.)
Macy,⁶ Mary, unm.

---

* Isaac Macy ⁷ (son of Thomas,⁶ Obed,⁵) married Nov. 6, 1839, Ann Eliza Macy,⁷ dau. of Josiah Macy ⁶ and Lydia (Hussey). Philip Macy, another son of Thomas Macy, married Feb. 23, 1843, Susan C. Wilson, dau. John Wilson and Lydia (Gibbs). (Ibid., pp. 373, 374.)

Macy,[6] Daniel P., *m.* Aug. 18, 1825, Alice Swain, dau. Hezekiah Swain and Lydia (Fish). (Ibid., p. 250.)

Macy,[6] Eunice, *m.* Nov. 4, 1824, David Mitchell, son James Mitchell and Elizabeth (Anthony). (Ibid., p. 157.)

Macy,[6] Judith, *unm.*

Son of Peter Macy and Sarah Folger. Ibid., pp. 146, 147.

Macy,[6] Charles, *m.* Oct. 7, 1813, Anna Bunker, dau. Barnabas Bunker and Lydia (Gardner). (Ibid., p. 233.)

Son of Abraham Macy and Priscilla Bunker. Ibid., p. 150.

Macy,[6] Abraham, *m.* 1800, Elizabeth Coleman, dau. Elihu Coleman and Elizabeth (Macy). (Ibid., p. 238.)

Children of Abraham Macy and Elizabeth Coleman.

Macy,[7] Aaron C.,* *m.* 1st, Oct. 2, 1823, Sarah Hull Clapp; 2d, April 17, 1840, Jane Williamson. (Ibid., p. 359.)

Macy,[7] Rebecca.

Macy,[7] George G.

Macy,[7] Catharine, *m.* Oct. 6, 1833, Townsend Powell. (Ibid., p. 230.)

Macy,[7] Rhoda.

Daughter of Charles Macy and Anna Bunker.

Macy,[7] Lucretia F., *m.* March 15, 1836, Robert F. Gardner, son Benjamin Gardner and Rachel (Folger). (Ibid., p. 233.)

Daughters of Stephen Macy, Jr. (1761-1825) and Phebe Swain. Ibid., p. 159.

Macy,[7] Lydia, *m.* Aug. 16, 1803, John Munroe. (Ibid., p. 159.)

Macy,[7] Susan, *m.* Thomas Starbuck. (Ibid., p. 159.)

---

* This family lived at Ghent, New York.

CHILDREN OF EDMUND MACY (1766, lost at sea about 1809) AND
    SUSANNA COLEMAN. Ibid., pp. 159, 160.

Macy,[7] Sarah, m. June 28, 1811, Philip H. Folger, son George Folger and Rebecca (Slocum). (Ibid., p. 160.)

Macy,[7] Edmund W., m. 1817 Elizabeth Macy, dau. Obed Macy and Abigail (Pinkham). (Ibid., p. 251.)

Macy,[7] Elizabeth, m. Dec. 4, 1817, Alexander G. Hussey, son Paul Hussey and Judith (Gardner). (Ibid., p. 160.)

Macy,[7] James E., m. July 4, 1833, Mary Ann L. Emery, dau. George Emery and Elizabeth (Pierce). (Ibid., p. 252.)

CHILDREN OF SOLOMON MACY (1768-1855) AND LYDIA COLEMAN.
    Ibid., p. 160.

Macy,[7] Eunice, m. March 6, 1811, Obed Marshall, son Obed Marshall and Susanna (Burnell). (Ibid., p. 160.)

Macy,[7] George, m. Aug. 1, 1830, Eliza Gifford, dau. Prince Gifford and Hannah (Chadwick). (Ibid., p. 252.)

Macy,[7] Lydia, m. 1817, William Bartlett, son Thomas Bartlett and Mehitable (Rhodes). (Ibid., p. 160.)

CHILDREN OF JOB MACY (1770-1852) (SON OF STEPHEN AND
    MERCY ALLEN) AND DEBORAH GARDNER. Ibid., p. 161.

Macy,[7] Lydia, m. Jan. 27, 1820, Gorham Hussey, son George Gorham Hussey and Lydia (Chase). (Ibid., p. 161.)

Macy,[7] Prince G., b. 1796, d. 1827. (Lost at sea.)

Macy,[7] Hepzibeth, m. July 14, 1825, Robert B. Chase, son Stephen Chase and Peggy (Barnard). (Ibid., p. 161.)

Macy,[7] Joseph, m. Aug. 18, 1825, Susan Hussey, dau. George Gorham Hussey and Lydia (Chase). (Ibid., p. 253.)

Macy,[7] Seth, m. Tirzah Gibbs (widow of Seth Gibbs), dau. Solomon Bearce and Hannah (Green). (Ibid., p. 253.)

Macy,[7] Susan, m. April 16, 1835, William C. Gifford, son Robert Gifford and Ruth (Starbuck). (Ibid., p. 161.)

Macy,[7] Charles G., m. Sept. 22, 1839, Margaret B. Swain, dau. Micajah Swain and Priscilla (Barrett). (Ibid., p. 254.)

Macy,[7] Edmund, m. Oct. 19, 1837, Elizabeth W. Chase, dau. Peter Chase and Lurania (———). (Ibid., p. 253.)

Macy,[7] Elizabeth, m. Oct. 11, 1840, Freeman Parker, son Joshua Parker and Deborah (Black). (Ibid., p. 161.)

Macy,[7] Mary, unm.

Appendix.

CHILDREN OF JOB MACY (1770-1850) (SON OF RICHARD MACY AND MIRIAM COFFIN) AND ANNA WAY.
Ibid., pp. 235, 236, and Family Papers.

Macy,[7] Alexander, *m.* July 3, 1817, Maria Pinkham, dau. Peter and Desire (Clark) Pinkham. (Ibid., pp. 353, 354.)

Macy,[7] Lydia W., *m.* Oct. 31, 1816, James B. Coleman, son Obed Coleman and Elizabeth (Swain). (Ibid., p. 235.)

Macy,[7] Deborah W., *m.* Oct. 14, 1819, John Sherman, son John Sherman and Margaret (Ellis). (Ibid., p. 235.)

Macy,[7] Mary, *m.* April 5, 1826, Caleb Folger, son Shubael Folger and Mary (Gardner). (Ibid., p. 236.)

Macy,[7] Elizabeth, *unm.*

Macy,[7] Seth W.,* *m.* June 5, 1831, Mehitable K. Potter, dau. Restcom Potter and Deborah (Doubleday). (Ibid., p. 355.)

Macy,[7] Anna W., *m.*, 1st, Oct. 4, 1836, Frederick Gardner, son Hezekiah Gardner and Rebecca (Barrett); 2d, March 9, 1851, Thomas G. Folger, son Shubael Folger and Mary (Gardner). (Family Papers.)

CHILDREN OF JOHN W. MACY (SON OF PELEG MACY AND SARAH (STARBUCK) AND SALLY SWAIN. Macy Gen., pp. 188, 189.

Macy,[7] George W., *m.* Aug. 20, 1835, Lydia Percival, dau. Benjamin Percival and Phebe (Swift). (Ibid., p. 282.)

Macy,[7] Lucy S., *m.* Nov. 17, 1834, Francis Mitchell, son Samuel Mitchell and Hepzibeth (Joy). (Ibid., p. 189.)

CHILDREN OF EDWARD MACY (SON OF PELEG MACY) AND ——.
Ibid., p. 190.

Macy,[7] Lydia S., *m.*, 1st, Aug. 5, 1835, Alexander C. Joy, and 2d, May 24, 1839, Reuben Joy (brothers). (Ibid., p. 191.)

Macy,[7] Lucretia F., *m.* Oct. 15, 1859, James M. Bunker, son Reuben Bunker and Rachel (Chase). (Ibid., p. 191.)

---

* Seth W. Macy, son of Job Macy and Anna (Way), was a man of great integrity and much respected in Newport public life. He filled many positions of trust, from the Town Council to the Senate of Rhode Island.

Macy,[7] Eunice A., m. May 8, 1859, Andrew W. Hussey, son Shubael Hussey and Eunice (Fitch). (Ibid., p. 381.)

Macy,[7] Alfred, son of Peter Macy and Elizabeth (Gardner), m. May 2, 1857, Anne Mitchell, dau. William Mitchell and Lydia (Coleman). (Ibid., p. 375.)

Macy,[8] George Nelson, son of George Wendall Macy and Lydia (Percival), m. Mary Macy Hayden, dau. George C. Hayden and Phebe (Swain). George Nelson Macy served during the Civil War and acquired the rank of General. (Ibid., pp. 282-381.)

Macy,[8] Alexander, Jr., son Alexander,[7] Job,[6] and Anna Way, m. Dec. 5, 1841, Lydia S. Gardner, dau. Oliver C. Gardner and Hannah M. (Macy[6]), dau. Francis.[5] (Ibid., p. 422.)

Oliver C. Gardner's house on Vestal Street may well be reckoned one of the termini of the underground railroad; every child of Nantucket fifty years ago was familiar with Arthur and Lucy Cooper, fugitive slaves, then bowed with age; their story never failed to awaken interest. To the home of Mr. Gardner they found their way, and were cleverly tracked by their pursuers; not less clever was the man who sheltered them, adroitly engaging in conversation at his front door those who sought the poor, aged colored man and wife, until the couple had been disguised and helped to escape by the back door.

When this was accomplished Mr. Gardner invited the pursuers to search the premises, but the slaves were well out of the way and were sheltered by other friends; they lived many years on Nantucket.

Miss Anna Gardner, daughter of Oliver C. Gardner and Hannah M. (Macy), has recently died at Nantucket at an advanced age.

The first Anti-Slavery Convention held on the island in the summer of 1841 was called together by her.

At this gathering were present William Lloyd Garrison, who, on the evening of October 16, 1830, had opened his warfare on slavery, and Rev. Samuel May, who, on the Sunday following Mr. Garrison's speech, in the Unitarian Church on Summer Street, Boston, preached the first sermon delivered under the "new crusade."

Frederick Douglass also was present at the meeting convened by Miss Gardner, and at that time made his first speech in a cause for which in later years he labored so earnestly.

Mitchell,[1] Richard, *m.* Mary Wood. (W. C. Folger MSS. and Mitchell Family Records.

Mitchell,[2] Richard, *m.* 1708 Elizabeth Tripp, dau. James Tripp. (Ibid.)

Mitchell,[3] Richard, *m.* Mary Starbuck, dau. Jethro Starbuck and Dorcas Gayer. (Nantucket Friends' Records, Book I., p. 54, 1731.)

CHILDREN * OF RICHARD MITCHELL[3] AND MARY STARBUCK.

Mitchell,[4] Elizabeth, *b.* 1732, *d.* young.
Mitchell,[4] Richard, *b.* Sept. 27, 1735, *d.* 1819, *m.* Hepzibeth Barnard, dau. Robert Barnard and Hepzibeth ———. (1755, Nantucket Friends' Records, Book I., p. 233.)
Mitchell,[4] Elizabeth, *b.* Aug. 2, 1737, *d.* 1761, *m.* Josiah Barker, son of Samuel Barker and Bethiah Folger. (Family Papers.)
Mitchell,[4] Jethro, *b.* March 18, 1739, *d.* 1817, *m.* Rachel Hussey, dau. Daniel Hussey and Sarah ———. (1759, Friends' Records, Bk. II., p. 53.)
Mitchell,[4] Joseph, *b.* April 7, 1741, *d.* 1826, *m.* 3, 2, 1763, 1st, Mary Swain, dau. Richard Swain (Friends' Records, Bk. II., p. 95); 2d, Mary Calender (Family Papers).
Mitchell,[4] Mary, *b.* May 10, 1743, *d.* 1782, *m.* Shubael Coffin, son of Zaccheus Coffin and Mary ———. (1763, Friends' Records, Bk. II., p. 93.)
Mitchell,[4] William, *b.* Oct. 1, 1745, *m.* Oct. 29, 1767, Hannah Rodman. (Rodman Family.)
Mitchell,[4] Eunice, *b.* Oct. 7, 1749, *m.* Richard Bunker, son of Thomas Bunker and Anna Swain. (1768, Friends' Records, Bk. II., p. 176.)
Mitchell,[4] Benjamin, *b.* Oct. 10, 1752, lost at sea 1771.
Mitchell,[4] James, *b.* Nov. 11, 1755, *m.* Elizabeth Barnard, dau. Abisha Barnard and Elizh ———. (Family Papers.)

---

* The following note is found with this family record: "There must have been three others not recorded."

Mitchell,[4] Peleg, *b.* Feb. 9, 1759, *d.* 1831, *m.* 12, 30, 1779, Lydia Cartwright (dau. James Cartwright and Love Macy), *b.* Jan. 10, 1762, *d.* Feb. 11, 1833. (Friends' Records, Nantucket.)

CHILDREN OF RICHARD MITCHELL[4] AND HEPZIBAH BARNARD.

Mitchell,[5] Elizabeth, *m.* Edward Tillett Emmet. (Friends' Records, Bk. II., p. 220.)

Mitchell,[5] Paul, *m.* Meraba Coffin, dau. Alexander Coffin and Eunice (Bunker). (Nantucket Friends' Records, Bk. II., p. 259.)

Mitchell,[5] Christopher, *m.* Jemima Folger. (Nantucket Town Records, Bk. I., p. 112.)

Mitchell,[5] Laban, *m.* Elizabeth Freeborn. (Nantucket Friends' Records, Bk. II., p. 336.)

Mitchell,[5] Benjamin.

Mitchell,[5] David, *m.* Eunice Gardner, dau. —— and Ruth Gardner. (Nantucket Friends' Records, Bk. II., p. 378.)

CHILDREN OF JETHRO MITCHELL AND RACHEL HUSSEY.

Mitchell,[5] Daniel, *b.* 1760, *d.* 1760. (Friends' Records.)

Mitchell,[5] Obed., *m.* Lydia Gardner, dau. Paul Gardner and Rachel (Starbuck). (Ibid.)

Mitchell,[5] Sarah, *b.* 1765, *d.* 1793. (Ibid.)
Mitchell,[5] Silvanus, *b.* 1768, *d.* 1773. (Ibid.
Mitchell,[5] Elihu, *b.* 1772, *d.* 1772. (Ibid.)
Mitchell,[5] David, *b.* 1773, *d.* 1773. (Ibid.)
Mitchell,[5] Moses. (Ibid.)
Mitchell,[5] Aaron. (Ibid.)

Mitchell,[5] Jethro, *m.* 1805, Mercy Green, Jr., dau. Thomas Green, of Nova Scotia. (Friends' Records, Bk. IV., p. 30.)

CHILDREN OF WILLIAM MITCHELL AND HANNAH RODMAN. (Friends' Records and Family Papers.)

Mitchell,[5] Joseph, *m.* 1779, Lydia Swain, widow Josiah Swain and dau. Abisha Pinkerton. Removed to New York State.

Mitchell,[5] Mary, *m.* —— Sutton. Removed to New York State.

Mitchell,[5] Thomas. Removed to New York State.

Mitchell,[5] William. Removed to New York State.
Mitchell,[5] Anna. Removed to New York State.
Mitchell,[5] Jethro. Must have been born after removal.
Mitchell,[5] Richard. Must have been born after removal.

CHILDREN OF PELEG MITCHELL AND LYDIA CARTWRIGHT.

Mitchell,[5] George, *b.* 1781, *d.* in infancy.
Mitchell,[5] Joseph, *b.* 1782, drowned at sea 1805.
Mitchell,[5] George, *b.* 1784, *m.*, 1st, Phebe Chase, dau. of Francis Chase and Naomi —— (Nantucket Friends' Records, Book II., p. 429, 1807); 2d, Susan Barnard, dau. Thomas Barnard and Alice Freeborn (Friends' Records, Book III., p. 33, 1834.)
Mitchell,[5] Mary, *b.* 1785, *d.* Oct. 9, 1857, *m.*, 1st, Edward Hussey; 2d, William Stubbs.
Mitchell,[5] Love, *b.* 1787, *d.* 1805, *unm.*
Mitchell,[5] Sally, *b.* 1789, *d.* 1805, *unm.*
Mitchell,[5] William, *b.* Dec. 20, 1791, *d.* April 1, 1869, *m.* 1812, Lydia Coleman, dau. Andrew Coleman. (Friends' Records, Nantucket, Book II., p. 452.)
Mitchell,[5] Hannah, *b.* 1794, *d.* April 2, 1859, *m.* Reuben Macy, son of Obed Macy and Abigail Pinkham. (Ibid., Bk. II., p. 459, 1816.)
Mitchell,[5] Lydia, *b.* 1798, *d.* Nov. 7, 1871, *m.* (her second cousin) Richard Mitchell, of Newport. (Ibid., Book III., p. 2, 1818.)
Mitchell,[5] Peleg, *b.* 1802, *d.* Aug. 1, 1882, *m.*, 1st, 1822, Mary Ann Whippey (no children); 2d, Aug. 3, 1837, Mary S. Russell, dau. Barnabas Russell and Mary Swain. (Friends' Records, Nantucket.)
Mitchell,[5] Love, *b.* 1806, *d.* March 23, 1869, *m.* Isaac Brayton. (Nantucket Friends' Records, Book III., p. 19, 1825.)

CHILDREN OF OBED MITCHELL [5] (WHO WAS SON OF JETHRO MITCHELL [4] AND RACHEL HUSSEY) AND LYDIA GARDNER.

Mitchell,[6] Rachel, *m.* 1st, Moses Dame; 2d, James Thornton.
Mitchell,[6] Sarah, *m.* 1st, George W. Coffin (Friends' Records, Bk. IV., p. 56); 2d, Smith Upton (Friends' Records, Bk. IV.).
Mitchell,[6] Samuel, *m.* 1807, 1st, Hepzibah Joy, dau. Francis and Jedidah Joy; 2d, Susan Alley. (Ibid., IV., p. 38.)

Mitchell,[6] James, *m.* 1820, Lydia G. Clasby, dau. John Clasby and Sarah ———. (Ibid., III., p. 98.)

Mitchell,[6] Thomas, *d.* young.

Mitchell,[6] Obed, *m.* Phebe Upton. (Mitchell Family MSS.)

Mitchell,[6] Thomas, *m.* Lucy Swain (1812), dau. Thomas Swain and Deborah (———). (Friends' Records, Bk. IV., p. 57.)

CHILDREN OF DAVID MITCHELL[5] AND EUNICE GARDNER.

Mitchell,[6] Albert.

Mitchell,[6] Lydia, *m.* Thomas A. Green.

Mitchell,[6] Mary, *m.* Walter Underhill. (Friends' Records, Bk. IV., p. 81.)

Mitchell,[6] John R., *m.* Eliza Brock.* (Mitchell Family Papers.)

CHILDREN OF LABAN MITCHELL AND ELIZABETH FREEBORN.

Mitchell,[6] Daniel, *m.* Eliza Hussey, dau. Tristram Hussey. (Friends' Records, Bk. IV., p. 48.)

Mitchell,[6] Matthew, *m.* 1st, Susan Swain, dau. Gilbert and Ann Swain; 2d, Margaret A. Johnes (Family Papers).

Mitchell,[6] Moses, *unm.*

Mitchell,[6] Edward, *unm.*

Mitchell,[6] Isaac, *m.*, 1st, Elizabeth Gardner (Friends' Records, Bk. III., p. 28); 2d, Mary Ann Anthony (Family Papers).

Mitchell,[6] Joseph, *m.*, 1st, Sarah Folger, dau. Uriah Folger; 2d, Judith Folger, dau. Thomas A. Folger. (Family Papers.)

Mitchell,[6] Alice, *unm.*

CHILDREN OF PAUL MITCHELL AND MERABA COFFIN.

Mitchell,[6] Merab, *m.* John Brock. (Family Papers.)

Mitchell,[6] Eunice, *m.*, 1st, Tristram Coffin; 2d, Barzillai Hussey; 3d, Benjamin Barnard.

Mitchell,[6] Frederick, *m.*, 1st, Eunice Russell (Friends' Records, Bk. II., p. 422); 2d, Annie Chase (widow) (Family Papers).

Mitchell,[6] George G., *m.* Mary Hussey, dau. Peter Hussey.

---

* Parents of Walter Mitchell, Episcopal clergyman, for a number of years rector of St. Mark's Church, Philadelphia, Pa.

Appendix.

Mitchell,⁶ Richard, *m.* Frances Lincoln.
Mitchell,⁶ Paul, *unm.*
Mitchell,⁶ Hepzibeth,* *m.* 1820, 1st, George Brayton, son of Robert Brayton; 2d, William Hussey, son of Sylvanus Hussey. (Mitchell Family Papers.)
Mitchell,⁶ Seth, *m.* sisters, 1st, Hannah Bunker; 2d, Lydia M. Gardner, widow of Samuel Gardner, daus. of Hezikiah Bunker. (Family Papers.)

Mitchell, James, *m.* Ann Folger, dau. Jethro Folger and Mary (Starbuck). (Nantucket Friends' Records, Book I., p. 86, 1738.)

Newhall, Estes, son Daniel Wing Newhall and Hannah (Swift) Newhall, *m.* 7th mo. 4, 1793, Hepzibah Wing, dau. Paul Wing and Abigail (Wing). (Sandwich Friends' Records.)
Newhall, Paul Wing, son of Estes Newhall and Hepzibah Wing, *m.* Hannah Johnson, dau. Samuel and Sarah Johnson. (Newhall Family Records, 1831.)

Paddack, Zechariah, *m.* Deborah Sears. (Swain Family, see page 152.)
Paddack, Nathaniel, *m.* Ann Bunker. (Probate Record, Bk. A i., pp. 27, 28.)

CHILDREN OF NATHANIEL PADDACK.

Paddack, Deborah, *m.* Theophilus Pinkham. (Friends' Records, Bk. I., p. 43, 1728.)
Paddack, Love, *m.* George Swain, son of John Swain and Experience Folger. (Ibid., p. 48, 1729.)

---

* Hepzibeth (Mitchell) (Brayton) Hussey died in California in 1896, aged 92 years. Elizabeth A. Brayton, dau. of Hepzibeth Mitchell, and her first husband, George Brayton, married John C. Mitchell, son of James Mitchell and Lydia (Clasby).
The daughter of John C. Mitchell and Elizabeth (Clasby) married Reuben M. Swain, son of Charles A. Swain, of Nantucket, and —— Hussey (sister of Hannah and Rachel Hussey, of Mill Street).
Rachel Hussey was a respected member of the Society of Friends, and earned her daily bread by spinning yarn long after the art was lost to others on the island.

Paddack, Lydia, m. Jethro Coleman. (Ibid., Bk. I., p. 58, 1731.)
Paddack, Paul, m. Ann Coffin. (Nantucket Town Records, Bk. I., p. 43, July 24, 1740.)
Paddack, Mary, m. Francis Swain. (Friends' Records, Bk. I., p. 80, 1736.)
Paddack, Dinah, m. Christopher Worth. (Ibid., 1738.)
Paddack, Priscilla, m. William Coffin. (Ibid., Bk. I., p. 101, 1740.)
Paddack, Daniel, m. Susanna Gorham. (Nantucket Friends' Records, Bk. I., p. 38.)
Paddack, Elizabeth, m. Joseph Swain, 11, 2, 1745, called January. (Ibid., Bk. I., p. 157.)
Paddack, Stephen, m. Eunice Coffin. (Ibid., Bk. I., p. 191, 1751.)

Paddack, Susanna, m. 1st, Matthew Gardner (Ibid., Bk. I., p. 204, 1752); 2d, George Freeborn (Ibid., Bk. II., p. 149, 1767.)
Paddack, Eunice, m. 1st, Joseph Coffin (Ibid., Bk. II., p. 10, 1775); 2d, Robert Clasby (Ibid., Bk. II., p. 345, 1790.)
Paddack, Deborah, m. George Hussey. (Ibid., Bk. II., p. 25, 1757.)
Paddack, Barnabas, m. Abigail Gardner. (Ibid., Bk. II., p. 113, 1764.)

Paddack, Nathaniel, m. Deborah Pinkham (by "Bezaleel Shaw, Minister of the Gospel"). (Nantucket Court Records, Book I., p. 25, 1782.)

Pinkham, Reuben, m. Anna Starbuck (by Jeremiah Gardner, justice of peace). (Nantucket Town Records, Book I., p. 68, 1755.)

Prence, Thomas, m. 1st, Patience Brewster, dau. Elder Brewster (1624); 2d, Mary Collier, dau. William Collier (Winsor's History of Duxbury, p. 248, 1635); 3d, —— Freeman, widow Samuel Freeman (Plymouth Colonial Records, vol. i., p. 34, 1662).

Rodman, Joseph, m. Mary Miller. (Gen. of Rodman Family, p. 27, 1745.)

Rodman, Hannah, dau. Joseph, *m.* William Mitchell, son Richard and Mary (Starbuck) Mitchell. (Ibid., 1767).
Rodman, Clark, son Joseph, *m.* Abigail Lawton. (Ibid., p. 39, 1775.)
Rodman, David, *m.* Joanna Mitchell. (Ibid.)
Rodman, Thomas, *m.* Mary Borden. (Ibid., p. 27, 1750.)
Rodman, Elizabeth, dau. Thomas, *m.* William Rotch, Jr. (Ibid., p. 41, 1782.)
Rodman, Samuel, son Thomas and Mary, *m.* Elizabeth Rotch. (Ibid., p. 39, 1780.)
Rodman, Anna, *m.* Thomas Hazard. (Ibid., p. 32, 1780.)

Rotch,[1] William and Hannah, from England, were at Salem, Mass., for a time.
Rotch,[2] Joseph, son William Rotch and Hannah (——), of Salem, Mass., *b.* in Salisbury, England, May 6, 1704, *m.* "21st day of 12th mo. called February," 1733-34, Love Macy, dau. Thomas Macy and Deborah (Coffin). (Friends' Records, Nantucket, Book I., p. 69.)
Rotch,[3] William, son Joseph Rotch and Love Macy, *m.* 31st day of 10th month, 1754, Elizabeth Barney, dau. Benjamin Barney and Lydia (Starbuck). (Ibid., Book I., p. 229.)

CHILDREN OF WILLIAM ROTCH AND ELIZABETH BARNEY.

"Rotch,[4] William, Jr., of 'Sherborn,'* son of William Rotch and Elizabeth Barney, *m.* 17th of 7th month, 1782, Elizabeth Rodman, of 'Lemister,'† in the County of Worcester, in the government of Massachusetts Bay, in New England," dau. Thomas Rodman, late of Newport, Rhode Island, and Mary (——). (Ibid., Book II., p. 285.)
Rotch,[4] Elizabeth, *m.* Samuel Rodman, of Newport.
Rotch,[4] Susanna, *d.* young.
Rotch,[4] Benjamin, *m.* Elizabeth Barker.
Rotch,[4] Thomas.
Rotch,[4] Lydia.
Rotch,[4] Mary.

---

* Nantucket.
† Leominster.

Rotch, Sarah, dau. of William Rotch, Jr., and Elizabeth Rodman, *m.* James Arnold, of Providence, R. I.; *d.* at New Bedford May 9, 1860. (Gen. of Rodman Family, p. 72, Oct. 29, 1807.)

Russell,[1] Daniel, *m.* Deborah Macy. (Macy Genealogy, pp. 67, 68.)

Russell,[2] John, 1st, *m.* Ruth Starbuck. (Nantucket Friends' Records, Book I., p. 60, 1731-32.)

Russell,[3] John, 2d, *m.* Hepzibah Coleman. (Ibid., 1777.)

Russell,[4] Barnabas, *m.* Mary Swain. (Ibid., 1811.)

Russell,[2] Jonathan, *m.* Patience Swain. (W. C. Folger MSS.)

Russell, Sylvanus, *m.* Anna Coffin. (Ibid.)

Russell, Uriah, *m.* Lydia Swain. (Ibid.)

Sears, Richard, *m.* Dorothy Thatcher. (Swain Family, see p. 153.)

Stanton, Samuel, son John and Elizabeth Stanton, *m.* Sarah Coffin, dau. Samuel and Miriam Coffin. (Nantucket Friends' Records, Book I., p. 68, 1733-34.)

Stanton, Giles E., *m.* Hannah Beebe. (Nantucket Town Records, Book I., p. 103, 1805.)

Stanton, Benjamin, *m.* Abigail Macy. (See Macy Family, p. 83, 1774.)

Starbuck, Edward, *m.* Katharine Reynolds. (N. E. Hist. and Gen. Reg., vol. viii., p. 68.)

CHILDREN OF EDWARD STARBUCK AND KATHARINE REYNOLDS.

Starbuck, Nathaniel, *m.* Mary Coffin. (See Coffin Family, p. 252.)

Starbuck, Jethro, *unm.*

Starbuck, Sarah, *m.* 1st, William Story, *d.* 1658 (N. E. Hist. and Gen. Reg., vol. viii., p. 129, 1658); 2d, Joseph Austin, *d.* 1663 (W. C. Folger MSS.); 3d, Humphrey Varney, as second wife (1664).

Starbuck, Dorcas, *m.* William Gayer. (W. C. Folger MSS.)

Starbuck, Abigail, *m.* Peter Coffin. (See Coffin Family, p. 252.)

Starbuck, Esther, *m.* Humphrey Varney. (W. C. Folger MSS.)

Children of Nathaniel Starbuck, Sr., and Mary Coffin.

Starbuck, Mary, *m.* James Gardner, son Richard Gardner. ("Ye Coffin Family," by Allen Coffin, LL.B., pp. 57, 58.)

Starbuck, Elizabeth, *m.* 1st, Peter Coffin, Jr. (N. E. Hist. and Gen. Reg., 1682); 2d, Nathaniel Barnard, Jr. (Nantucket Probate Records, Bk. A. I., pp. 22, 23.)

Starbuck, Nathaniel, Jr., *m.* Dinah Coffin. (See Coffin Family, p. 253, 1690.)

Starbuck, Jethro, *m.* Dorcas Gayer. (Nantucket Town Records, Bk. I., p. 7, 1694.)

Starbuck, Eunice, *m.* George Gardner, son of John Gardner. (W. C. Folger MSS.)

Starbuck, Priscilla, *m.* John Coleman, 2d, grandson Thomas Coleman.[1] (Ibid.)

Starbuck, Hepzibah, *m.* Thomas Hathaway, of Dartmouth, Massachuetts. (W. C. Folger MSS.)

Children of Nathaniel Starbuck, Jr., and Dinah Coffin.

Starbuck, Mary, *m.* Jethro Folger, 12. 1. called Feb. 1710-11. (Friends' Records, Bk. I., p. 6.)

Starbuck, Paul, *m.* 1st, Ann Tibbets (Ibid., Bk. I., p. 13, 1718); 2d, 1737, Keziah Gardner, widow Jethro (Ibid., Bk. I., p. 85); 3d, Elizabeth Coffin, widow Daniel (Ibid., Bk. I., p. 193, 1751).

Starbuck, Priscilla, *m.* Shubael Coffin. (Ibid., Bk. I., p. 11, 1717.)

Starbuck, Elizabeth, *m.* George Hussey. (Ibid., Bk. I., p. 10, 1717.)

Starbuck, Hepzibah, *m.* Sylvanus Hussey, Sr. (Ibid., Bk. I., p. 25.)

Starbuck, Abigail, *m.* 1st, Thomas Howe (Town Records, 1723); 2d, John Way (Friends' Records, Bk. I., p. 104, 1741).

Starbuck, Benjamin, *m.* Dinah Coffin, dau. Stephen Coffin, Jr. (Friends' Records, Bk. I., p. 53, 1730.)

Starbuck, Tristram, son Nathaniel, Jr., and Dinah (Coffin) Starbuck, *m.* Deborah Coffin, dau. Samuel and Miriam Coffin. (Nantucket Friends' Records, Bk. I., p. 49, 1729.)

Starbuck, Ruth, *m.* John Russell. (Ibid., p. 60, 1731-32.)

Starbuck, Anna, *m.* Peter Barnard. (Friends' Records, Bk. I., p. 66, 1733.)

Swain,¹ Richard,* m. 1st, ——; 2d, Sept. 15, 1658 (Hist. of Hampton, Bk. II., p. 986), Jane (Godfrey) Bunker, widow of George Bunker. Jane Bunker d. 1662. (Nantucket Town Records.)

CHILDREN OF RICHARD SWAIN AND FIRST WIFE.

Swain,² Francis, m. Martha ——. (W. C. Folger MSS., p. 61.)
Swain,² William, of Hampton, New Hampshire, m. Prudence Marston. (Ibid.)
Swain,² Dorothy, m. 1st, Thomas Abbott; 2d, Edward Chapman. 3d, Archelaus Woodman. (Ibid.)
Swain,² Elizabeth, m. 1656, Nathaniel Wier or Weare. (N. E. Hist. and Gen. Reg., vol. xxv., p. 246.)
Swain,² John, m. Mary Wier or Weare. (Dow's Hist. of Hampton.)
Swain,² Grace, m. Nathaniel Boulter.
Swain,² Nicholas, d. 1650.

CHILD OF RICHARD SWAIN AND JANE (GODFREY) (BUNKER) SWAIN.

Swain,² Richard, b. in Hampton Jan. 13, 1660.

Swain,³ John, Jr., son of John Swain and Mary Wier, m. Experience Folger, dau. Peter Folger and Mary (Morrell). (See Folger Family, p. 257.)
Swain,⁴ John, son of John Swain, Jr., and Experience Folger, m. Jan. 6, 1711-12, Mary Swett, dau. Moses Swett and Mary (Hussey). (Nantucket Town Records, Bk. I., p. 9.)
Swain,⁴ William, Sr., son John Swain, Jr., m. 1727 (Friends' Records, Bk. I., p. 40), Jemima Coffin. (Family Papers.)

---

* "One Hundred and Sixty Allied Families," p. 228, says Richard Swain's wife Elizabeth came to America in the "Planter" in the April previous to his arrival on the "True Love." His sons, Francis and William, came in the "Rebecca," and his daughter Elizabeth in the "Susan and Ellen," "in care of various friends."

NOTE.—Francis Swain went to Long Island; William remained at Hampton, N. H. Richard, the only child of Jane, removed to New Jersey, and has many descendants there.

Appendix. 305

Swain,[5] William, Jr., *m.* Feb. 14, 1750, 1st, Lydia Gorham, dau. Stephen Gorham and Elizabeth (Gardner); 2d, Mary Pollard. (Family Papers.)

Swain,[5] Francis, son of John Swain and Mary Swett, *m.* Nov. 1, 1736, O. S., Mary Paddack, dau. Nathaniel Paddack and Ann Bunker. (Nantucket Friends' Records, Bk. I., p. 80.)

Swain,[6] Francis, son Francis Swain and Mary Paddack, *m.* Jan. 29, 1767, Lydia Barker, dau. Robert Barker and Jedidah Chase. (Nantucket Friends' Records, Bk. II., p. 146.)

Swain,[7] Mary, dau. Francis Swain and Lydia Barker, *m.* Second month, 1811, Barnabas Russell, son John Russell and Hepzibah Coleman. (Friends' Records, Nantucket.)

Swain, Mary, dau. of William Swayne, Jr., and Mary Pollard,* *m.* Reuben Waite (as first wife). Reuben Waite's second wife was Nancy Wood, dau. James Wood and Lydia Swain, and great-granddaughter of Stephen Gorham and Elizabeth (Gardner).

Swain, Elizabeth, *m.* 1791, Benjamin Swift. (Nantucket Town Records, Bk. I., p. 129.)

Swain, Joseph, *m.* Phebe Barney, dau. Benjamin Barney and Huldah (Bunker). (1774, Friends' Records, Bk. II., p. 218.)

Swain, John (called England), *b.* in England, *d.* at Nantucket, 1749, *m.* Patience Skiff, dau. James Skiff, Jr., and Sarah (Barnard). (Probate Records, Bk. II., p. 137.)

Swift, Dr. Paul, *m.* Dorcas Gardner. (Friends' Records, Bk. IV., p. 75, 1827.)

Tripp, John, *m.* Mary Paine, dau. Anthony Paine. (Rhode Island His. Magazine.)

Wier, Hester, *m.* 1st, Benjamin Swett (Hist. of Newbury, p. 319); 2d, Stephen Greenleaf, Sr. (Hist. of Newbury, p. 304). (1679.)

Wing, Samuel, *m.* Hepzibah Hathaway. (See page 184.)

---

* Mary Pollard was daughter of Philip Pollard and Mehitable (Gardner), who was daughter of James Gardner and Mary (Starbuck).

Wing, John (Sandwich), *m.* Deborah Batchelder, dau. Rev. Stephen Batchelder. (See page 184.)

Wing, Stephen, son of John Wing and Deborah (Batchelder), *m.* Sarah Briggs.

Wing, John, son of Stephen Wing and Sarah (Briggs), *m.* July 22, 1685, Mary Perry, dau. Edward Perry. (Sandwich Friends' Record, Bk. I., 74.)

Wing, Paul, *m.* Abigail Wing. (Sandwich Friends' Records, 1763.)

Wing, Zaccheus, *m.* Content Swift. (Ibid., 1731.)

NOTE.—In recorded dates we often find two years given,—i.e., 1637-38. In what was known as old style, the year began March 25, and when the new or present style was adopted many were not pleased with the innovation; recorders therefore accommodated themselves to the caprice of the people, and gave the date in accordance with both methods. This will account for any discrepancy covering not more than three months.

NOTE.—William C. Folger, whose MSS. are here quoted, was Corresponding Member of the New England Genealogical Society, and prepared a number of Nantucket Genealogical notes for Savage.

APPENDIX II.

APPENDIX II.

The break in the records connecting the early Norman Coffins with Tristram Coffin's family has never been satisfactorily filled, and much time and money has already been expended in the effort to do this; it is not likely that it will be accomplished unless some new place of abode of this family is discovered which may present new records and information. The country in which they were known to have lived has been thoroughly looked over, and its records exhaustively examined. The genealogical table following is the earliest data in direct line of which there is absolute record.

The following extracts from The Exeter District Probate Registry are offered as evidence that Tristram Coffin had more education than many of his contemporaries:

"1628 April 3 The Will dated 4 January 1627-8 of John Coffin of Brixton Devon was proved in the court of the adn of Totnes.

The Testator gave to the Poor of Brixton 10/—

Joan, Deborah, Eunice, and Mary Coffin 20/— each at 12 years old.

Mathue Simnell 10/—

John Coffin £10 at 12 ·

Tristram Coffin all residue, and he apptd him Executor.

"The testator made his mark and the Will was sealed in the presence of

Hennery Tammas

*Maethal Simnell

*"Doubtful whether same person as in body of Will or not, the witness may be a Martha Simnell. By another paper it is 'Martha' and she is also the person to whom the 10s. is given in the will."

"The Inventory enclosed in the bundle is that of Peter Coffyn, taken 5 March 1627-8 by Richard Worth Clerk; Phillip Avent, and George Roper £236,5,7 and it included chattles on years and lifes £160.

"The legal proceedings were taken by Nicholas Coffin and Ann Winson or (Wynson) alias Coffin brother and sister of the testator, against the Executor and were apparently commenced at Plimpton on 17 January 1627-8.

"The answers of the two witnesses to the interrogatories administered on the part of the promoters of the suit go to show

"THAT the testator and Martha Simnell could read but not write, that Henry Thomas could neither read nor write and that Tristram Coffin could do both. THAT the Will was written by Tristram on a certain Friday evening in an upper chamber of the testators house where he (the testator) was lying sick. THAT the Will was read by testator himself and sealed by him with a key and that he and the witnesses made their marks and that all their names were written by Tristram, THAT the reason why the Will was written by Tristram was that there was no one else present who could write and that he could not get any other to write it, as the sickness was very infectious. THAT the allegation was that two or three days before New Years Day then last past John Coffin the testator instructed Tristram to make his Will and told him that Nicholas Coffin his (testator) brother's son should be Executor, and that instead of acting on these instructions Tristram put in his own name and that when the testator read the Will so drawn he tore the paper.*

"At the hearing however the promoters did not appear and sentance was pronounced for the will propounded by Tristram on 2 April 1628."

* The paper is NOT torn.

It would appear from the above that the effort to prove Tristram at fault was unavailing, and from the fact that the paper was not torn, we conclude Tristram was the executor his uncle John Coffin intended.

Genealogy Chart

NICHOLAS = **JOAN**
will proved Nov. 3, 1613 — d. after her husband

Children of Nicholas and Joan:

- **TRISTRAM** — will proved Oct. 16, 1602, unmarried
- **PHILLIP** = (wife) — living 1602, had *Tristram* living 1613
- **THOMAS** = **ALICE** — will proved Nov. 27, 1616, buried Nov. 19, 1616; Alice bur. Nov. 13, 1619
- **PETER** (oldest son) = **JOAN THEMBER** — will proved Mar. 13, 1627; b. ab. 1580; Joan d. Boston, Mass., May, 1661

Children of Thomas and Alice:

- **LIONEL** = **JOAN** — adm. Mar. 30, 1636, had I. Richard, II. Joan
- **NICHOLAS** — living in 1628, minor in 1602, had Nicholas

Children of Peter and Joan Thember:

- **JOAN** — living in 1602 but not mentioned in her father's will of 1613, but evidently married Phillip Avent. Peter mentions him as brother-in-law
- **ANN** = **WINSTON** — m. before 1628
- **JOHN** — will proved April 3, 1628, unmarried
- **TRISTRAM** = **DIONIS STEVENS**

Children of Tristram and Dionis Stevens:

- **JOHN** — not of age in 1627; did not come to America
- **JOAN** — not of age in 1627; did not come to America
- **DEBORAH**
- **EUNICE** = **WM. BUTLER** — Savage, vol. i., p. 8
- **MARY** = **ALEX. ADAMS** — 1652; Savage, vol. i., p. 8

Appendix. 311

The appended Will of John Stevens, father of Robert, who was father of Dionis (Stevens) Coffin, gives us a generation further back in this line.

All these papers have come into the hands of the writer since the main text of this book was completed. They have been acquired by a descendant of Tristram Coffin, and are careful abstracts or copies of the English records.

EXTRACTED FROM THE DISTRICT REGISTRY ATTACHED TO THE PROBATE DIVISION OF THE HIGH COURT OF JUSTICE AT EXETER.

In the Archdeaconry Court of Totnes.

In the name of God amen &c The IXth— day of Marche ano Dni 1608 I John Stephen of Brixton being sicke and weake in body but of pfect remembrance thankes be given to God doe make and ordayne this my last Will and Testamt in mannr and forme following:

Imprimis I give and commend my Soule into the hands of God my Creator and my body to the Earth whence it was taken.

Itm I give and bequeath towards the benefit of the Church IIs. Itm. I give unto the poore of the Pish of Brixton IIs. Itm I give unto Johan the Daughter of Robt Stephen my sonne my black heiffer. Itm I give unto Robt Algar my sonne-in lawe my best dublett my best coat my best hat my best breeches my best shirt my best stockins & my best shoes and my best shirt band. Itm. I give unto Robt Algar XXs. Itm. I give unto my Daughter Elizabeth Thorne the wife of James Thorne XXs Itm. I give unto Dunes the wife of Robt Stephen the sume of Fower pounds a yeare to be payed unto her yearly during her naturall life out of my living in fford. the tyme of payment to beginne imedyatly after my death or ye death of Robt Stephen my sonne. Itm. I give unto Johan Prowes Xs. Itm. I give unto Walter Bowman if he be serving in my house at the tyme of my death Vs. Itm I give unto Willm the sonne of Robt. Stephen XIId. Itm I give unto Tristra the sonne of Robt Stephen XIId. Itm I give unto John Stephen the sonne of Robt Stephen my standing bedstead my chest my coffer standing in my chamber to remayne in the house for his use after the death of my sonne Robt Stephen all the residew of my goods moveable and unmoveable my debts and legacyes payed I give and bequeath unto my sonne Robt Stephen whom I make Executor of this my last Will and Testamt. ———————

———————Signe Johis T. Stephens (seal)—
Presente me—Timotheo Hayte Clico.———

An Inventory of all the Goods and chattells of John Steven of Brixton deceased taken valued & prsd by Robt Algar, Tymothe Hayte and others the XVth daie of ffebruary ano Dni 1611

Imprimis on chest	Xs
Itm two bedsteads	XXs
Itm two little fether beds one fether pillow and one fether bolster and bedclothes	£III Xs
Itm his wearing apparrell	XLs
Itm certayne yron implemts and other household stuffe	IIIs IIIId
Suma total	£VII IIIs IIIId

This will, in its mention of "my sonne Robt Stephen" and "Dunes the wife of Robt Stephen", proves the name of Robert's father and gives one generation more upon which to build by further research.

Copied from the original Coffin School Medal.

Appendix.

The fact that this picture of "1642" has been supposed by some descendants of Tristram Coffin to be an authentic copy from an original representation of the first Chief Magistrate of Nantucket, led to a query concerning it.

The appended reply explains its existence, and gives interesting facts concerning the medals which Admiral Sir Isaac Coffin bestowed upon the trustees of the Coffin School.

The interest in education, which had already made considerable progress, was stimulated by him. This interest continued for many years, during which time the schools of Nantucket were second to none in that vicinity.

October 17th, 1901.

Dear Mrs. Hinchman:

The photo you name of Tristram Coffin is copied from one side of the Coflin School Medal, and is wholly ideal. The medal is about two inches in diameter, so the photograph is much enlarged. There were quite a number of medals struck in bronze, and one, I have seen, white metal.

Each of the original trustees of the school had one. The Admiral had them struck in England after the school was established, and forwarded to the island. In his letter accompanying them he said the *gilt* one is for the President of the Trustees. It was at that time supposed to be gold and for transmission to succeeding Presidents; while in the possession of one of the later Presidents it was stolen by one of his juvenile relatives, who also believed it to be gold and tried to melt it into an ingot. He could not get heat enough to melt the bronze, but succeeded only in burning off the gilt. I have a number of them in a good state of preservation.

One was recently found in San Francisco while excavating for a foundation. It was on a site where a Nantucket man had lived in the rugged days of California life and lost it.

I cannot now recall who the person was, but I published an article on it at the time in response to an inquiry in a San Francisco paper, which gave pictures of both sides of the medal.

I made a plaster cast of one many years ago, and succeeded in moulding a rough copy in base metal, which I subsequently deposited with the Nantucket Historical Society.

The little photos of some half dozen ancient paintings of members of the Coflin family were copied from painted portraits then adorning the walls of the Portledge Manor House, near Bideford, County Devon, England, and are true to life as the painter artist could make, but there is no portrait nor personal description of our ancestor, Tristram Coffin, that I have ever seen, and I know of but one genuine autograph extant in Nantucket in all the public records and documents I have examined.

The costume upon the medal was doubtless made up from a knowledge of what constituted the dress of the period of 1642, the year Tristram emigrated from England.

I have discussed that period in my life of T. C. to some extent, and I have fallen upon nothing historical since the Coffin Reunion that would change my estimate of Tristram prior to his emigration to America nor of his career in America.

Very respectfully,   ALLEN COFFIN.

Richard Coffin, Esq., of Portledge,

Sheriff of Devonshire in 1699.

NAMES OF MINISTERS OF THE SOCIETY OF
FRIENDS AND THEIR COMPANIONS WHO
VISITED NANTUCKET FROM
1664 TO 1847.

NAMES OF MINISTERS OF THE SOCIETY OF FRIENDS AND THEIR COMPANIONS WHO VISITED NANTUCKET FROM 1664 TO 1847.

DATE	NAME	RESIDENCE
1664—	Jane Stoaks,	Old England
	("tis thought was the first friend on this island from O. E.")	
1698—	Thomas Turner,	Old England
	Hugh Copperthwait,	Long Island
	Thomas Chalkly,	Old England
	John Easton,	Rhode Island
	Joanna Mott,	Rhode Island
1699—	Ebenezer Slocum,	Conanicut
	Jacob Mott and son,	R. I.
	Jacob Mott, Jr.,	Rhode Island
1701—	Walter Clark,	} R. I.
	Jacob Mott (2d time),	
	Jacob Mott, Jr. (2d time),	R. I.
	("this time he first appeared in Publick.")	
	Thomas Thompson,	Old England
	John Clarke,	Old England
	Susanna Freeborn,	} R. I.
	Ruth Fry, not publick,	
1702—	Jedidah Allen,	New Jersey
	Thomas Cornell,	Rhode Island
	John Richardson,	Old England
	James Bates,	Virginia
	Jacob Mott (3d time),	R. I.
	Susanna Freeborn (2d time),	R.I.
	Peleg Slocum,	Dartmouth
1703—	John Kinsey,	Woodbridge
	Richard Gove,	Old England
	John Hussey,	New Castle, Del. (then Penna.)
	Ephraim Hicks,	Rhode Island
	Peleg Slocum,	Dartmouth
1704—	Thomas Chalkly (2d time),	O.E.
	Richard Harper,	Sandwich
	Mary Slocum,	
	Thomas Story,	Old England
	John Butler,	Ireland
1705—	Samuel Bownas,	Old England
	("He was imprisoned 11 months 3 weeks & several days on Long Island.")	

DATE	NAME	RESIDENCE
1705—	Mary Banister,	Old England
	Ann Chapman,	Old England
	Hugh Copperthwait (2d time),	Long Island
	Peleg Slocum,	Dartmouth
	William Anthony,	R. I.
1706—	John Fothergill,	} O. Eng.
	William Armistead,	
	John Smith,	Philadelphia
	Susannah Freeborn (3d time),	Rhode Island
	Hope Borden, not publick,	
	Joseph Wanton,	} R. I.
	Ephraim Hicks (2d time),	R. I.
	Mary Lawson,	Old England
	Ester Palmer,	Long Island
1707—	Jacob Mott & Wife,	
1708—	Patrick Henderson,	Ireland
	Ebenezer Slocum (2d time),	Conanicut
	Peleg Slocum,	Dartmouth
	Jacob Mott,	Rhode Island
	Thomas Cornell,	Rhode Island
	William Barker,	Rhode Island
	Eleazer Slocum,	
	Joanna Mott,	
	Rose Tibbits,	} Dover
	Sarah Austin,	
	Note.—"These ten came on at the settling of the Yearly Meeting, which was the 23d of 4th Mo. 1708."	
	Joseph Smith,	Providence
	Alice Anthony,	} Rhode Island
	Dorcas Easton,	
	Ephraim Hicks (3 times),	
1709—	Griffith Owen,	} Philadelphia
	John Saltkill,	
	Thomas Cornell,	Rhode Island
	Ebenezer Slocum,	Conanicut
	Jacob Mott, Junr.,	Dartmouth
	William Baldwin,	Old England
	Hugh Durborow,	Philadelphia

DATE	NAME	RESIDENCE
1709	John Easton,	Rhode Island
	Ruth Smith,	Dartmouth
1710	William Wilkinson,	Providence
	Jacob Mott,	Rhode Island
1711	Anthony Morris, }	Pennsylvania
	Thomas Shakel, }	
	Jacob Mott,	Dartmouth
	Peleg Slocum,	Dartmouth
	Thomas Potts,	Pennsylvania
	William Barker,	
	Peleg Slocum Junr.,	Dartmouth
1712	John Oxley,	Philadelphia
	William Wood, not publick,	Dartmouth
	Joseph Smith,	Providence
	Alice Anthony,	Rhode Island
1713	Jacob Morril,	Hampton
	John Farmer,	Old England
	Thomas Chalkley (3d time),	Old England
	Tristram Allen,	Pennsylvania
	Ann Chapman,	Old England
	Alice Wildman, not publick,	
	Susanna Freeborn,	Rhode Island
	John Lowden, formerly of Ireland, but now from the westward.	
	Francis Swain, Old England, but now from the westward.	
1714	Samuel Gasgel, }	Salem
	Samuel Collins, }	
	James Dickenson,	Old England
	James Cooper,	Ireland
	Jacob Mott,	Rhode Island
	John Giles, }	Old England
	Richard Smith, }	
1715	Richard Seaman,	Long Island
	William Wilkinson (2d time),	Providence
	Mary Bannister,	Old England
	Ann Richardson, not publick,	
	Thomas Thompson,	Old England
	David Irish,	Little Compton
	Benjamin Holme,	Old England
1716	William Barker,	Rhode Island
	Benjamin Holme (2d time),	Old England
	William Baldwin, }	Pennsylvania
	Peter Fearson, }	
	Abraham Booth,	Scituate
	Elizabeth Wartnaby,	O. Eng.

DATE	NAME	RESIDENCE
1716	Lydia Norten,	Hampton
	Rose Tibbits (2d time),	Cocheca
	Mary Slocum,	
	Christopher Blackburn,	Phila.
1717	John Farmer,	Old England
	William Armstrong, }	O. Eng.
	James Graham, }	
	Peleg Slocum,	Dartmouth
	Mary Slocum,	
	Hepzibah Hathaway,	
	Griffith, Owen (2d time) }	Phila.
	John Saltkill (2d time) }	
	Richard Castes,	Lynn
	Jacob Mott,	Rhode Island
	Patience Anthony,	
	John Cadwalader, }	Philadelphia
	John Smith, }	
1718	John Wanton,	Rhode Island
	Nicholas Davis,	Rochester
1719	Mary Brown,	Newberry
	Ann Stanyan,	
	Sarah Norten,	Salisbury
	John Danson, }	Old England
	Isaac Hadwen, }	Old England
	Elizabeth Wartnaby,	Old Eng.
	Rebecca Turner,	O. Eng.
	Elizabeth Rallingson, }	O. Eng.
	Lydia Lancaster, }	
	(Sisters by marriage.)	
	Peleg Slocum,	Dartmouth
	Rose Tibbits (3d time),	
	Nicholas Austin,	
1720	Jacob Mott,	Rhode Island
	Stephen Wilcox,	Dartmouth
	James Stanyan,	Salisbury
	Ann Stanyan (2d time),	
	Mary Brown,	Newberry
	Sarah Norten,	
	Nathaniel Howland,	Dartmouth
	Nicholas Austin, }	Dover
	Ephraim Tibbits, }	
	Joseph Wanton,	Tivertown
1721	John Appleton,	Old England
1722	Jno. Fothergill (2d time), }	O.E.
	Lawrence King, }	
	Moses Aldridge,	Mendam
	Lydia Norton,	Amesbury
	Rose Tibbits (4th time),	Cocheca
	Robert Jordan,	Virginia
	Obadiah Lawrence,	Long Island
	John Kinsey,	New Jersey

DATE	NAME	RESIDENCE
1723	John Hussey,	Woodbridge
	Jacob Mott,	Rhode Island
	Joseph Wanton,	Tivertown
	Samuel Aldridge,	
	Ephraim Tibbits, Junr.,	
	Rose Tibbits (5th time),	
1724	Samuel Gaskill,	Salem
	Benjamin Kidd,	Old England
	John Routledge,	Philadelphia
	Clark Rodman,	
	Daniel Gould,	Rhode Island
	Hannah Rodman,	not publick,
	Patience Rodman	
	John Bound,	Long Island
	Adam Mott,	Dartmouth
	John Wing,	Sandwich
	Samuel Collins,	Lynn
	Mary Clark,	Rhode Island
	Deliverance Smith,	
	Hepzibah Hathaway,	
	Thomas Lightfoot, an aged worthy Friend in the seventieth year of his age,	Philadelphia
	John Easton	
	William Barker	
1725	John Wanton,	Rhode Island
	Nicholas Davis,	Rochester
	Lydia Norten (2d time),	Hampton
	Patience Anthony,	Rhode Island
	Ephraim Hicks,	Rhode Island
	Elizabeth Leviss,	
	Jane Fenn,	
1726	Margret Preston, now of	Philadelphia
	Ann Richardson,	not publick,
	William Anthony,	Rhode Island
	William Barker,	
	John Tucker,	Dartmouth
	Abigail Bowls,	Ireland
	Grace Loyd, not publick,	Philadelphia
1727	William Piggot, of London,	Old England
	James Lord,	New Jersey
	Abraham Chase,	Swanzey
	Rose Tibbits (6th time),	
	Mary Dow, from Eastward,	
1728	Rowland Wilson,	Old England

DATE	NAME	RESIDENCE
1728	Susanna Morris, Mary Folk,	Pennsylvania
	Rose Tibbits (7th time),	Dover
	Joseph Smith,	Providence
	Joseph Edmunds,	Greenwich
	Joseph Taylor,	Old England
	Robert Willsons companion,	
	Evan Evans, John Evans	North Wales, Pa.
1729	Ephraim Tibbits,	Dover
	Rose Tibbits, his wife (8th time),	
	John Burling, not publick,	New York
	Martha Wood,	Abington, R. I.
	Ruth Fish,	Abington, R. I.
	John Cadwalader,	Pennsylvania
	Ebenezer Large,	New Jersey
1730	John Salkild,	Philadelphia
	Joshua Lord,	New Jersey
	Rose Tibbits (9th time),	Dover
	Sarah Norton,	
	Sarah Chase,	Swanzey
	Mary Pennel, Mary Lewis,	Chester Co., Pa.
	Obadiah Lawrence, Thomas Franklin,	Long Island
	Adam Mott,	Dartmouth
1731	Ruth Jones,	Pennsylvania
	Rose Tibbits (10th time), Sarah Kenny,	Dover
	Henery Frankland,	Old England
	Joshua Wixom,	Yarmouth
1732	John Richardson,	Yorkshire, Old England
	Paul Johnston,	Ireland
	Hugh Clifton,	Salem, N. J.
	Richard Wall,	Philadelphia
1733	Hannah Dent,	Yorkshire, O. E.
	Isaac Chase, Job Chase,	Swanzey
	Eliphel Harper,	Seconet
	Mongo Buley, Samuel Stephens,	Ireland
	David Irish,	Little Compton, R.I.
	Rose Tibbits (11th time),	Dover
	Patience Redwood, not publick,	Rhode Island
	Alice Alderson, Margaret Copeland,	O. Eng.
	Eliphel Harper (2d time),	Seconet

DATE	NAME	RESIDENCE
1733—	Jane Fenn, }	Pennsylvania
	Rebecca Minshall, }	
	Martha Pettel,	Boston
1734—	Zacheriah Nixon,	Carolina
	Joseph Russel,	Dartmouth
	Moses Aldrige,	Mendum
	Lydia Norton,	Amesbury
	Hannah Proud,	Rhode Island
	Andrew Cramer,	Philadelphia
	John Tucker,	Dartmouth
1735—	John Burton, }	O. Eng.
	William Backhouse, }	
	Joseph Gill,	Ireland
	Thomas Evans,	New Jersey
	John Easton,	Rhode Island
	Hugh Clifton,	New Jersey
	Eliphel Harper (3d time),	Falmouth
	Edward Tyler, }	Bristol, O. Eng.
	Daniel Stanton, }	Philadelphia
	Edward Tyler (2d time),	O. Eng.
	John Easton,	Rhode Island
1736—	Arthur Jones,	Bucks County
	John Tucker,	Dartmouth
	Adam Mott,	Dartmouth
	Lydia Norton,	Pennsylvania
	Hannah Proud, not publick,	Rhode Island
	John Easton, }	Rhode Island
	John Casey, }	
	Peter Davis,	Westerly
	Ebenezer Woodward,	Taunton
	David Irish,	Little Compton
	Theophilius Shove,	Dighton
	Savory Clifton,	Rochester
	Rachel Seaman, }	Long Island
	Mary Prior, }	
	Lydia Sole,	Dartmouth
	Meribah Slocum, not publick,	
1737—	Thomas Chalkley (4th time),	Philadelphia
	Elijah Collins, not publick.	Boston
	John Casey, }	Rhode Island
	Clark Rodman, }	
	Christopher Townsend,	
	Ebenezer Woodward,	Taunton
	John Fothergill,	Old England
	Samuel Jordan,	Virginia
1738—	Ruth Courtney, }	Ireland
	Susanna Hudson, }	
1739—	Michael Lightfoot,	Pennsylvania
	John Hunt,	Old England
	John Tucker,	Dartmouth
	Hugh Clifton (3d time),	N. J.
1740—	Peter Davis,	Westerly
	Christopher Townsend,	R. I.
	Jane Hoskins, }	Chester
	Mary Folke, }	Philadelphia
	Rose Tibbits (12th time),	Dover
	Ebenezer Woodward,	Taunton
	Joshua Lord, }	New Jersey
	Abraham Moss, }	
	Henry Stanton, Junr.,	N. C.
1741—	Deborah Reed,	Freetown
	William Brown, }	
	John Griffith, }	
	Samuel Hopwood,	Old England
	Obadiah Butler, not publick,	
1742—	Samuel Hopwood (2d time),	Old England
	John Churchman,	Chester, Pa.
	Lydia Dean,	Pennsylvania
	Eliphel Harper (4th time),	
	Abigail Kirby,	Dartmouth
	Hannah Jenkins,	Philadelphia
1743—	John Haslem, }	Yorkshire, O. E.
	Joseph Hoskins, }	Chester, Pa.
	Kezia Baker,	Rye, Long Island
	Hannah Cock,	Long Island
	Edmund Peckover,	Old England
	Thomas Redman,	New Jersey
1744—	Christopher Willson,	O. Eng.
	Eleazer Sheldon,	Dublin, Ireland
1745—	Silas Cerpenter,	Providence
	Adam Mott,	Dartmouth
	Deborah Reed (2d time),	Freetown
	Hannah Hoeg, }	Hampton
	Hannah Sweet, }	
	Lydia Sole, }	Nine Partners
	Kezia Wood, }	
	Susana Gifford,	Dartmouth
	Benjamin Farris, }	Oblong
	Joshua White, }	not publick,
	Stephen Chase,	Freetown
1746—	John Casey,	Rhode Island
	Benjamin Buffington,	
	Stephen Chase (2d time),	Freetown
1747—	Robert Knowls, }	Westerly, R. I.
	Joseph Casey, }	

Visiting Friends.

DATE	NAME	RESIDENCE
1747	John Griffith, David Farris,	Pennsylvania
	Thomas Gawthrop,	Old England
	John Armit, not publick,	Philadelphia
	Samuel Notingham,	Old England
	Henry Tucker, not publick,	
	John Wanton, not publick,	
	Peter Andrews, John Woolman,	New Jersey
	Stephen Wilcox,	Dartmouth
1748	Zacheriah Farris,	New Jersey
	Robert Lewis, not publick,	
	Nathaniel Lewis, not publick,	
1749	John Sykes,	N. J.
	Abraham Farrington,	
	Nicholas Austin,	Abington
	Rose Tibbits (13th time),	Dover
	Lydia Sole,	Nine Partners
1750	Isaac Chase,	Swanzey
	James Luther, not publick,	
	Adam Mott,	Dartmouth
	Lydia Mendenhall,	Chester, Pa.
	Ann Schoolfield,	Bucking in Penna.
	Mary Weston,	London, O. E.
	Grace Fisher,	Philadelphia
1751	Jonah Thompson, James Thornton,	Dorsetshire, O.E.
	Esther Hoeg,	Hampton
	Comfort Hoeg,	Hampton
	Joseph Eastis, Jonathan Wood,	Dartmouth
	Jane Ellis,	Exeter, Pa.
	Rebecca Harvey,	Darby
1752	William Horn,	Darby, Pa.
	Benjamin Buffington (2d time),	Swansy
	Jonathan Wood,	Dartmouth
	Stephen Chase,	Freetown
	Samuel Spencer,	Pennsylvania
	Matthew Franklin,	Long Island
1753	Abraham Farrington (2d time),	
	John Casey,	Rhode Island
	Theophilus Shove (2d time),	Dighton
	Isabel Buffington,	Swanzey
1754	Daniel Stanton, (2d time), Israel Pemberton,	Philadelphia not publick,
1754	Thomas Lightfoot, not publick,	Pennsylvania
	Mary Piesley,	Queen County, Ireland
	Catharine Payton,	Dudly, Old England, in Worcestershire
1755	Comfort Hoeg, Elizabeth Dean,	Hampton
	Samuel Fothergill,	Old England
	William Logan,	Pennsylvania
	Joshua Dixon,	Durham, Old England
	Jacob Barney, not publick,	Rhode Island
	Phebe Phares, Mary Chase,	Oblong
	Benjamin Phares (2d time),	Oblong
	William Rufsel, not publick,	
	Thomas Goodwin,	Goshen, Pa.
1756	Thomas Gawthrop (2d time),	Old England
1757	Peter Davis, James Scriven,	Westerly
	Christopher Wilson (2d time),	Old England
	Matthew Franklin (2d time),	Long Island
	Benjamin Phares (3d time),	Oblong
	James Tasker,	Oxfordshire, O.E.
	Mark Reeve, not publick,	Cohansey, N. J.
1758	Samuel Spavold,	Harford, O. E.
	Matthew Franklin (3d time),	Long Island
	John Casey,	Rhode Island
	Mary Piesly, Comfort Hoeg, Patience Dow,	Hampton
	William Rickett,	Old England
	Robert Willis,	Ratiway, N. J.
	Benjamin Phares (4th time),	Oblong
	Richard Titus,	Westerly, L. I.
1759	John Storer,	Nottingham, O. E.
	Benjamin Andrews,	Mt. Holly, N. J.
	John Casey,	Rhode Island

DATE	NAME	RESIDENCE
1759	Stephen Wilcox,	Dartmouth
	Mary Kirby,	Norfolk, O. Eng.
	Elizabeth Smith,	Burlington
	Isaac Andrews, }	New Jersey
	William Foster, }	
	Timothy Davis,	Rochester
	Peter Davis,	Westerly
	John Casey,	Rhode Island
	Nicholas Austin,	Abington
	Benjamin Buffington,	Swanzy
	Paul Osborn,	
	Christopher Townsend,	R. I.
	Nathaniel Green,	Greenwich
	Thomas Hazard,	S. Kingston
	Mary Kirby (2d time),	O. Eng.
	Elizabeth Smith (2d time),	Burlington
1760	Samuel Eastburn,	Bucks Co., Pa.
	John Woolman,	Mount Holly
	Ann Grant,	Little Egg Harbor
	Mary Redman,	Haddonfield, N.J.
	Comfort Hoeg (4th time),	Hampton
	Mary Bowel, not publick,	Hampton
	Elizabeth Shipley,	Wilmington, Del.
	Hannah Foster,	Evesham, N. J.
1761	Jane Crofsfield,	Westmoreland, Old England
	Lydia Southwarth, not publick,	Dighton
	Samuel Nottingham (ye 2d time),	Tortola
	(Formerly of Old England.)	
	Susanna Hutton (2d time), }	Ireland
	Susanna Brown (2d time), }	Phila.
	Robert Wills (2d time),	Ratiway, N. J.
	Note.—Robert Willis and Robert Wills are doubtless the same man.	
1762	Robert Proud,	Yorkshire, O. Eng.
	Matthew Franklin (4th time),	Long Island
	John Pemberton,	Philadelphia
	Hannah Harris, }	Cumberland, O. E.
	Eliz. Wilkinson, }	
	Comfort Hoeg (5th time),	Hampton

DATE	NAME	RESIDENCE
1762	Alice Hall, }	Old England
	Ann Newlin, }	Concord, Pa.
1763	Peter Davis, }	Westerly
	Joseph Condon, }	Charles Town
1764	John Sleeper,	Mt. Holly, N. J.
	Paul Osborn, not publick,	Dighton
	Henry Stanton (2d time),	N. C.
	Richard Titus,	Long Island
	Jonathan Hussey,	Dartmouth
	Matthew Franklin (5th time),	Long Island
	Henry Stanton (3d time),	N. C.
	Timothy Davis,	Rochester
	Thomas Comstock,	Greenwich
	Hannah Chase,	Swanzey
	Robert Willis (3d time),	N. J.
	James Mitchel, not publick,	Rhode Island
1765	William Ricket (2d time)	Old England
	Paul Osborn, not publick,	Oblong
	Mordecai Yarnal,	Philadelphia
	Robert Willis (4th time),	N. J.
1766	Thomas Gawthrop,	Old England
	Paul Osborn, not publick,	Oblong
	John Griffith (3d time),	O. Eng.
	Thomas Ross,	Bucks Co., Pa.
1767	William Hunt, }	New Garden,
	Zechariah Dicks, }	in N.Car.
	William Hunt (2d time), }	N. Car.
	Thomas Thornbrough, }	
	Aaron Vail,	Nine Partners
	William Hunt (3d time),	N. C.
	Thomas Thornbrough (2d time),	North Carolina
	Aaron Vail (2d time),	Nine Partners
1768	Thomas Carlton,	Kennett, Pa.
	Joshua Shearman, }	Nine Partners
	Aaron Lancaster, }	Marrineck
1769	John Pemberton,	Philadelphia
	Rachel Wilson, }	Kendal, O. E.
	Sarah Hopkins, }	West Jersey
1770	Peter Davis,	Westerly
	Joshua Brown,	Pennsylvania
	David Willits,	Long Island
	Comfort Hoeg,	Hampton
	Matthew Franklin (6th time),	Long Island
	Richard Titus (3d time),	L. I.

Visiting Friends.

DATE	NAME	RESIDENCE
1771	William Hunt (4th time),	N.C.
	Thomas Thornbrough (3d time),	North Carolina
	Joseph Oxley,	Norwich, O. Eng.
	Joshua Thompson, not publick,	New Jersey
	Mary Callender,	Rhode Island
	Amey Thurston, not public,	
	Stephen Comfort, }	Pa.
	Mark Reeves, }	Pa.
	David Pharis,	Pa.
	Samuel Neals,	Old England
1772	Thomas Cumstock (2d time),	Oblong
	Gaus Tallcott,	New Milford
	James Neals,	from Eastward
	Moses Farnum, }	Smithfield
	George Arnold, }	Smithfield
	William Jones,	Mt. Holly, N. J.
1773	William Matthews,	Warwick, Pa.
	John Willis,	Long Island
	Abraham Anthony,	Rhode Island
	David Buffum,	Providence
	Thomas Hazard,	South Kingston
	Abel Thomas, }	Pa.
	Samuel Lee, not publick, }	Pa.
	("Abel was silent in publick while among us except in a Select meeting.")	
	Robert Knowls,	Westerly
1774	Robert Walker,	Leeds, in Yorkshire
	Elizabet Robinson,	Richmond, in Yorkshire
	Susanna Lightfoot (3d time),	Chester County, Pa.
	Samuel Smith,	Philadelphia
	John Simpson,	Bucks Co., Pa.
	Zechariah Dicks (2d time), }	New Garden
	John Carter, }	
	William Coffin, Jr., not publick	
	Morris Birbeck, not publick,	Old England
1774	Benjamin Barney Junr.	
	Zechariah Dicks (3d time),	
	John Carter (2d time),	
	Morris Birbeck (2d time),	
	John Pemberton, }	Philadelphia
	Charles West, }	Philadelphia
	Mary Lever,	Old England
	Rebecca Scattergood,	Phila.
1775	William Jones,	Mount Holly
	Moses Farnum,	Smithfield
	Robert Willis,	Ratiway, N. J.
	Jonathan Farnum,	Smithfield
	Joseph Rotch, not publick,	Dartmouth
	Thomas Gawthrop,	Old England
	Paul Osborn, not publ,	Oblong
1776	David Farris,	Wilmington
	John Perry, not publick,	Wilmington
	Phebe Yarnal,	Concord, Pa.
	Rebecca Wright,	New Jersey
	Rebecca Wright (2d time),	N. J.
	Phebe Yarnall (2d time),	Pa.
	Mary Calender (2d time),	Rhode Island
	Eunice Barney, not publick,	
1777	Mehetible Jenkins,	Dover
	Hannah Hacker, not publick,	Salem
	Richard Holder, not publick,	Salem
	Patience Brayton,	Swanzey
	Aaron Lancaster,* (2d time), }	Oblong / Nine Partners
	David Sands, }	
	Benjamin Jones,	Mount Holly
	George Dilwyn,	Burlington
	Joshua Fulsome,	From Eastward
	James Neals,	From Eastward
	Asa Aldrige,	From Smithfield or thereaway
1778	Aaron Lancaster,† (3d time), }	Oblong
	David Sands (2d time), }	Nine Partners

---

* 1777 (8 mo.)—"These friends were on the Island 3 weeks and 4 or 5 days; they had extraordinary Service among us, in visiting all the families of friends distinctly, also having Select meetings of the heads of families of friends, also with the youth, males by themselves, and females by themselves, also several meetings of other Societies selected from those under the care of friends; may their zeal for the prosperity of truth & our welfare be gratefully remembered."

† "1778 (6 mo.)—Aaron Lancaster 3 times Obl. David Sands 2 time 9 partners these friends have not been home since they were here Last year, but have been visiting to Ye Eastwd. as far as Kennebeck."

DATE	NAME	RESIDENCE
1778	Eliz. Southwick,	Smithfield or thereaway
	Abigail Arnold,	
	Oziah Wilkinson,	
	Aaron Lancaster (4th time),	
	Seth Gardner,	
1779	David Sands (3d time),	
	Isaac Varney, not publick, From Salem	
	David Sands (4th time),	
	Solomon Underhill,	L. I.
	Joseph Walters,	Nine Partners
	Mary Mitchell (formerly Calendar) (3d time),	Greenwich
	Abraham Griffith,	Pens——
	Paul Osborn,	Oblong
1780	Joseph Mitchel,	Greenwich
	John Lloyd,	Pennsylvania
	Benedict Carpenter,	Long Island
	John Allsop, not publick,	
1781	David Brooks,	New Garden
	Seth Coffin, not publick,	
	John Foreman,	Pa.
	Thomas Scattergood,	Pa.
	James Thornton,	Abington, Pa.
	Samuel Smith,	Philadelphia
	Thomas Carrington,	Pa.
	Patience Brayton,	Swanzey
	George Churchman,	Maryland
	David Cooper,	New Jersey
	Warner Mifflin,	Penna.
	("3 worthy Elders who Laboured industriously for a reformation amongst us.")	
	Elizabeth Heighth,	Nine Partners
	Hannah Barker,	Nine Partners
1782	William Jackson,	Pennsylvania
	Mary Mitchel (wife of James),	
	George Dillwin (2d time),	Burlington
	Joseph Pierceall,	Long Island
	Joseph Mitchel,	Rhode Island
	Sarah Hampton,	New Jersey
	Anna Willis,	Long Island
	Patience Brayton,	Swanzey
	NOTE.—"The first Quarterly meeting held at Nantucket, was on ye 1st of 7th mo this present year, 1782."	
1783	Thomas Huszard,	S. Kingston
	Moses Brown,	Providence
	Job Scott,	Smithfield or thereaway

DATE	NAME	RESIDENCE
1783	Caleb Green,	Conanicut
	Mehitable Jenkins,	Dover
	Elizabeth Varney,	Berwick
	Mary Mitchel (wife of Joseph),	
	Mary Mitchel (wife of James),	
	Patience Brayton,	Swanzey
	Abel Thomas (2d time),	Pa.
	Tristram Russel,	Nine Partners
	Joseph Mitchel,	Rhode Island
1784	David Willits (2d time),	
	Samuel Hopkins,	Pennsylvania
	Tedeman Hull,	Nine Partners
	John Willis,	Long Island
	Joseph Willis, not publick,	
	Phineas Buckley, not publick,	
	Hugh Judge,	Wilmington, Del.
	Joseph Tatnall, not publick,	Wilmington, Del.
	John Haighton,	Philadelphia
	James Bringhurst, not publick,	Philadelphia
1785	Zechariah Dicks (4th time),	New Garden, No. Carolina
	John Elliot, Jr.,	Phila.
	Ann Jesop,	No. Carolina
	("After being with us awhile went to London with Zechariah Dicks on a religious visit to Friends in great Britain.")	
	Joseph Mitchel,	Rhode Island
	("Was here awhile then went of and returned again and Visited the familys of Friends among us, being the Last time of his being here.")	
1786	John Storer (2d time),	O. Eng.
	John Townsend,	O. Eng.
	Nicholas Waln,	Philadelphia
	Sarah Lundy (2d time),	N. J.
	Robert Willis (6th time),	N. J.
	John Townsend (2d time),	
	Elihu Kirk,	Pennsylvania
	Thomas Colly,	O. Eng.
	Joseph More,	
	Abraham Gibbons,	
1787	Wm. Savery,	Phila.
1788	Joseph Delaplane,	New York
	Solomon Underhill,	Long Island
	Gideon Seaman Elder,	Long Island
	Samuel Emlin,	Phila.

Visiting Friends.

DATE	NAME	RESIDENCE
1788	Remington Hobby,	Kennebec
1789	Benjamin Worth,	Manmoraneck
	James Mott Elder,	Manmoraneck
	George Martin, }	Pennsylvania
	John Talbert, }	Pennsylvania
	Rebecca Jones,	of Phila., "who taried on the Island some days & visited some familys of Friends among us, having Select meeting with the young men & Young women Separately also a meeting with the Blacks."
	John Simpson, }	Pennsylvania
	Asa Smith, }	Providence
	Zacchariah Faris, }	Pennsylvania
	Robert Johnson, }	Pennsylvania
	Isaac Everet,	of Phila.
	John Stone,	
	Slade Stphen,	Swanzey
	Joseph Austin,	
1790	Daniel Offla,	Philadelphia
	Elisabeth Drinker,	Philadelphia
	Benjamin Worth,	Merionck
	Hugh Judge,	Wilmington
	James Mott,	Long Island
	John Morton,	Philadelphia
	Hannah Yerks,	
	Joshua Brown,	Philadelphia
	Benjamin Swett,	
	Jacob Mott,	Rhode Island
	Jacob Maul,	New Jersey
1791	Samuel Emlen,	Philadelphia
	Thomas Scattergood,	Phila.
	Benjamin Worth,	Vassal
	Caleb Cresson,	Philadelphia
	Mary Ridgeway,	Ireland
	Jane Watson,	Ireland
	Elizabeth Martin,	Long Island
	Sarah Lundy,	
	William Shotwell,	
	Jessa Copeland,	Virginia
1792	John Reeve,	New Jersey
	Benjamin Reeve,	
	George R.,	
1793	Elisha Thornton,	
	Benedict Arnold,	Sfield
	Elias Hicks,	N. Y.
	James Mott,	Long Island
	Sarah Talbot,	
	Ann Ferris,	Pennsylvania

DATE	NAME	RESIDENCE
1793	Stephen Mendenhall,	Pa.
	Peter Yarnall,	Philadelphia
	Jacob Mott,	Long Island
	Thomas Willis,	
1794	Joshua Evans,	New Jersey
	Gardner Earle,	N.
	David Sands,	
	John Wigham,	Scotland
1795	Rebecca Wright,	New Jersey
	Martha Routh,	England
	John Cloud,	N. P.
	James Davis,	
	Joseph Collins,	
	Abigail Robinson,	Rhode Island
	Henry Hull,	
	Paul Upton,	
	Deborah Darby,	
	Rebecca Young,	
	Cornelius Howland,	
	Elizab. & Hannah Mott,	R. I.
1796	Remmington Hobby,	Vassa
	Hannah Barnard,	Hudson
	Elizabeth Varney,	
	John Loyd,	Pennsylvania
	James Davis,	N. B.
	Stephen Buffinton,	
	Phebe Nichols,	
1797	John Wigham,	
	Nathan Allen,	Smithfield
	Aaron Wells,	Philadelphia
	Martha Routh,	England
	Charity Cook,	
	Lydia Haskins,	Carolina
	James Davis,	N. B.
	John M.,	F.
	John Elliot,	
	Richard Jordan,	
	Josiah White,	
	Thomas Comstock,	Hudson
1798	Elisha Thornton, }	Smithfield
	Walter Allen, }	Smithfield
	John Parish,	Philadelphia
	William Jackson,	Pennsylvania
	Silas Downing,	Long Island
	James Mott,	
	Mary Prior,	England
	Elizabeth Foulk,	Philadelphia
	Mehitable Jenkins,	
	Sarah Cartland,	
	Stephen Buffinton,	Dartmouth
	Daniel Haverland,	

DATE	NAME	RESIDENCE
1798—	Tripp Mosher,	
	Roger Haverland,	
	Isaac Osborn,	
	Jeremiah Austin,	
	Thomas Rotch & wife,	
	Jarvis Johnson,	Ireland
	Joseph Whitehall,	
	Richard Mott,	
	Abraham Underhill,	
	Rebecca Jones,	
	Jane Snowden,	
	Ruth Ann Rutter,	
	Sarah Cresson,	Philadelphia
	Jonathan Evans,	
	Chalkley Albertson,	} North Ca.
	Zachariah Nixon,	
1800—	Stephen Buffington,	Dartmouth
	Pennington Hobby,	
	Jacob Taber,	Maine
	Nathan Hunt,	North Ca.
	John Heil,	
	Hugh Judge,	New York
	Willet Hicks,	New York
	Ruth Halleck,	Nine Partners
	Sarah Hull,	Nine Partners
1801—	Joseph Hoeg,	Vermont
	John Hall,	England
	Stephen Grellette,	
	Elizh Coggeshall,	
	Ann Mifflin,	Phila.
	Lot Tripp,	New York
1802—	Joseph Hoeg,	
	John Winslow,	Portland
	Martha Routh,	England
	Betsey Pennington,	Salem
	John Davis,	New Bedford
1803—	James Simpson and Wife,	Pennsylvania
	Micajah Collins,	Lynn
	Elizh Coggeshall,	
	Elizabeth Bud,	New York
	Peter Barker,	Philadelphia
	Lydia Rotch,	New Bedford
1804—	Ann Alexander,	England
	Hannah Fisher,	Philadelphia
	Edward Gallug,	
	Lydia Rotch,	
	James Davis,	
	Stephen Buffington,	
	John R. Davis,	
1805—	Wm. Crotch,	England

DATE	NAME	RESIDENCE
1805—	James Davis,	
	Abel Thomas,	
	Thomas Lea,	Penna.
1806—	John Baily,	
	John R. Davis,	
	Daniel Quimby,	Nine Partners
	Enoch Dorland,	
	Israel Sabins,	Richmond
	Daniel Aldridge,	Uxbridge
1807—	Matthew Franklin,	New York
	Richard Mott,	New York
	William Flanner,	N. C.
	Stephen Gardner,	North Carolina
	John Baily,	
	Benjm Worth & wife,	Me.
1808—	Lydia Rotch,	New Bedford
	John Baily,	
	Stephen Buffington,	
1809—	James Mendenhall,	Vermont
	Ann Merriott,	} Nine Partners
	Esther Griffith,	
	Hannah Field,	
	Gideon Seaman,	
	Stephen Buffinton,	
	Benjamin Percival,	
	James Davis,	
	Lydia Rotch,	New Bedford
	Rowland Green,	
1810—	Thomas Titus,	
	Willet Hicks,	New York
	James Davis,	
	John Baily,	
	Stephen Buffinton,	
	Lydia Rotch,	New Bedford
	Benjamin Worth,	Vassal
	(No doubt meant for Vassalboro', Me.)	
1811—	Edward Brooks,	West Chester
	William Williams,	Tennessee
	Thomas Scattergood,	
	Amos Piesley,	Pittsfield
	John Bailey,	
	Mary Allison,	
	Elisha Thornton,	
	Benjamin Mitchell,	
	Lydia Rotch,	
	" Benjamin F.,"	
	Benjamin Worth,	Vass.
	Nathan Hunt,	} New Garden
	Matthew Coffin,	

Visiting Friends.

DATE	NAME	RESIDENCE
1811—	James Davis,	
	Elizabeth Coggeshall,	New York
	Joseph Douglas, }	Maine
	Edward Cobb, }	Maine
1812—	Amos Piesly,	
	Benjamin Fulsom,	New York
	David Sands,	
	James Hazzard,	
	Benjamin Percival,	
	John R. Davis,	
	Matthew Franklin,	
	Nehemiah Merritt,	New York
	Elisha Thornton,	
1813—	Henry Hull,	Stanford
	Abel Thomas,	
	John Baily,	
	John R. Davis,	
	Avis Keene,	
	Elisha Thornton,	
1814—	Gideon Mollineaux, }	New York
	Jabez Green, }	New York
	Hinchman Haines,	Evesham
	Joseph Hains,	West Jersey
	Mary B. Allen,	
1815—	Elisha Thornton,	
	James Halleck,	Cornwall
	Edward Wing,	
	Daniel Jenkins,	
	Benjamin Mitchell,	
	John R. Davis,	
	John Heald, }	
	James Bolton, }	Ohio
	Benjamin Worth,	
	Mary B. Allen,	
	John Murry, }	New York
	Thomas Eddy, }	
	Isaac Bonsel, }	Phila.
	Samuel W. Fisher, }	Phila.
	Benjamin Faber,	
	Stephen Carpenter,	Vermont
	Tristram Russell,	New York
	Richard Mott,	New York
	Lydia Mott,	New York
1816—	Peter Hovey,	
	Elisha Thornton,	
	Benjamin Percival,	
	Philip Dunham,	
	Anna M. Thorn,	Nine Partners
	Jemima Keys,	Pennsylvania

DATE	NAME	RESIDENCE
1816—	Elizabeth Baldwin,	New York
	Judith Coffin,	
	Rachel Barnard,	
	Benjamin Swain,	
	Ruth Davis,	
	Hannah Dennis, }	
	Jonathan Dennis, }	
	David Harkness,	
	Obed Harkness,	New York
1817—	Isaac Thorn,	Nine Partners
	Reuben House,	
	William Cromwell,	Poughkeepsie
	Mary Naftil,	England
	Hannah Lewis,	Phila.
	Jonathan Taylor,	
	Benjamin Ladd,	Ohio
	Benjamin Mitchell,	
	Eldad Hoxey,	
	John Baily,	
	John R. Davis,	
	Mary B. Allen,	
	Tristram Russell,	
	Phillip Dunham,	
1818—	Henry Post,	Hudson
	Jared* T. Hopkins,	Baltimore
	Benjamin Percival,	
	Russell Davis,	
	Elizabeth Coggeshall,	New York
	Margaret Merriot,	
	Isaac Proctor,	
	Obidih Davis,	
	Avis Keene,	
	John Wilbur,	Hopkinton
	Jonathan Dennis,	Rhode Island
	Matthew Ferris,	
	Sylvester Weeks,	
	Thomas Anthony,	Rhode Island
1819—	John Baily,	
	John R. Davis,	
	Benjamin Mitchell,	
	Elizabeth Walker,	
	Margaret Judge,	Maryland
	Mary New,	
	Benjamin Worth,	
	Browning Swift,	
	William Rickman,	England
	Margaret Brooks,	
	Sarah Sutton,	
	Nathan Spencer &	
	Ruth his wife,	New York

* Christian name in family is Gerard.

DATE	NAME	RESIDENCE
1820	Charles Osborne,	Indiana
	James Pegg,	
	Daniel Haveland,	New York
	Silas Downing,	
	Caleb Macomber & wife,	
	Lydia Dean,	Lynn
	Clark Stephen,	Virginia
	Charles Taber,	
	Dorcas Peckham,	
1821	Stephen Grellette,	New York
	Thomas Williams,	
	Benjamin Percival,	
	Browning Swift,	
	John R. Davis,	
	Experience Sherman,	
	Phillip Dunham,	
1822	Rufsell Davis,	
	Christopher Healy,	Pennsylvania
	Moses Comfort,	
	George Withy,	England
	Isaac W. Morris,	Philadelphia
	Adna Heaton,	New York
	Tristram Rufsell,	Cornwall
	Micajah Collins,	
	Stephen Chase,	Lynn
1823	Isaac Hammer,	Tennessee
	James Hazzard,	New York
	Benjamin Percival,	
	Benjamin Mitchell,	
	Jeremiah Hubbard,	⎫ N.Carolina
	Elijah Coffin,	⎭ N.Carolina
1824	Priscilla Hunt,	Indiana
	Matthew Farris,	
	Isaac Stephenson,	England
	William Foster,	England
	John Paul,	Philadelphia
	Benjamin Percival,	
	Rufsell Davis,	
	John R. Davis,	
	Thomas Jones,	
	Browning Swift,	Falmouth
1825	James Hazzard,	New York
	Huldah Hoeg,	Vermont
	Mehitable Austin,	
	John Knowles,	
	Rufsell Davis,	
	Browning Swift,	
	John R. Davis,	
	Sarah Tucker,	
	Susan Howland,	
	George Hatton,	Indiana

DATE	NAME	RESIDENCE
1826	John Warren,	
	John Dow,	Me.
	Elizabeth Robson,	England
	(Came the second time and visited families Bart. Wistar & Ruth Ely, companions.)	
	Bart. Wistar,	
	Ruth Ely,	
	Samuel Merriot,	New York
	John R. Davis,	
	James Tucker & wife,	
	Matthew Farris,	
1827	Valentine Meader & wife,	Vt.
	John R. Davis,	
	Lydia Mott,	
	Thomas Shillitoe,	England
	Smith Upton & wife,	New York
	Anna Braithwaite, accom. by her husband, Isaac,	England
1828	Hannah Hartshorn,	Penna.
	Mary B. Allen,	
	John R. Davis,	
	Obidiah Davis & wife,	
1829	Daniel Puckett,	⎫
	Charles Lippincott,	⎭ Indiana
	George Jones & wife,	England
	Elizabeth Pitfield,	Philadelphia
	John Wilbur,	⎫
	Andrew Nichols,	⎭
	Mary B. Allen,	
	Avis Keene,	
	Mary Card &	
	Anna Macomber,	
1830	Joseph Bowne,	New York
	Phebe Field,	New York
	Elisha Bates,	Ohio
	Mary B. Allen,	
	Jared Patterson,	Car.
	Henry Stanton,	
1831	William Cary,	New York
	Nathan Hunt,	North Carolina
	Jeremiah Hubbard,	N. Carolina
	Elisha Bates,	Ohio
	Joseph Hoeg,	Vermont
	Lindley M. Hoeg,	Vermont
	Charles Taber,	Vermont
	Jonathan Backhouse and wife,	England
1832	Mahlon Hoggett,	

Visiting Friends.

DATE	NAME	RESIDENCE
1832—	Hannah C. Backhouse,	England
	Eliza P. Kirkbride,*	Phila.
	Joseph Bowne,	New York
	Lindley M. Hoeg,	N. Hampshire
1833—	Royal Southwick,	Uxbridge
	Mildrid Ratcliff,	
	George & Ruth Smith,	Ohio
	Hannah Dennis,	Rhode Island
	Deborah Otis,	New Bedford
	Jabez Greene,	New York
	William Evans,	Philadelphia
1834—	Rebecca Updegraff,	Ohio
	Hannah Collins,	New York
	Benjamin Wright,	Penna.
	Thomas Arnott,	Ohio
	Jonathan Backhouse & wife,	England
	Elizabeth Coggeshall,	New York
	Sarah Upton,	New York
	Dugan & Asenath Clark,	Ohio
	Rowland Greene & daughter,	Conanicut
1835 or 36—	Zaccheus Bowman,	Maine
	Martha Meader & Husband,	
1835—	Huldah Hoeg,	Vermont
	Mead Atwater,	New York
	Matthew Purington & wife,	Providence
	Russell Davis,	
	Zacheus Bowerman & wife,	Me.
1836—	Benjamin Fry and wife,	N. H.
	Joshua Linch,	Ohio
	Samuel Rhodes,	Penna.
	John R. Davis,	
	Mary Card,	New Bedford
	Mary B. Allen,	
	Susan Howland,	New Bedford
	Rachel Thornton,	New York
	Valentine Meader & wife,	Me.
	John Wilbur,	Hopkinton
	Benjamin Buffinton,	Fall River
	Lindley M. Hoeg,	N. Hampshire
1837—	Joanna Meader,	Maine
	Ann Pope,	
	Abigail R. Hoag,	New York
	Joseph Hoag and wife,	Vermont
	William Kennard,	
	Thomas Hall,	Ohio
	Moses Beede,	Lynn

DATE	NAME	RESIDENCE
1837—	John R. Davis,	
	Russell Davis,	
	Susan Howland,	
	Avis Keene,	Lynn
	Joseph Trip & wife	New York
	John Meader & wife,	
	James Jones,	
	Nathaniel Austin,	Maine
	Daniel Clapp,	
	Perez Peck,	
1838—	Joseph Bowne,	New York
	John Scott,	Maryland
	Mahlon Day,	New York
	Anna Cates,	
	Edmund Cates,	Maine
	Mary B. Allen,	Smithfield
	Richard Mott,	New York
	Joseph John Gurney,	England
	Henry Hinsdale,	New York
	Hannah Batty,	Vermont
	Charles F. Coffin,	Maine
	Alton D. Pope,	Maine
	Ruth Davis,	Longplain
	Mary Shove,	Swansey
	Lindley M. Hoeg,	Maine
1839—	Russell M. Davis,	
	Seth Kelley,	Yarmouth
	Daniel Wheeler,	England
	Benjamin Fry,	New Hampshire
	Joseph Edgerton,	Ohio
	William Dewees,	
	Thomas & Elizabeth Robson,	England
	Elizabeth Coggeshall,	
	Rachel Thornton,	New York
	Ruth Davis,	
	Mary Davis,	
	Susan Howland,	
	Isaac Lawrence,	
	Sarah Tucker,	
	Anna Macomber,	
	Mary Taber,	
	John Wilbur,	Hopkinton
	Henry Gould,	Newport
1840—	Charles Osborn,	Indiana
	George Evans,	
	Richard Mott,	New York
	John P. Balderston,	Baltimore
	Mary B. Allen,	Smithfield

---

* Afterwards wife of Joseph John Gurney.

DATE	NAME	RESIDENCE
1840—	Susan Howland,	New Bedford
	Huldah Gifford,	
	Lindley M. Hoeg,	N. H.
1841—	Jeremiah Hubbard,	N. C.
	William Kenworth,	
	Thomas & E. Robson, }	Eng.
	James Brown,	
	Elizabeth Wing,	Rhode Island
	Joseph Bowne,	New York
	Richard Thomas,	Baltimore
	Eli & Phebe Haines,	Penna.
	Ruth Davis,	
	Huldah Gifford,	
	Susan Howland,	
	Mary Davis,	
	Anna Jenkins, }	Providence
	Mary B. Allen,	
	John Osborne,	
1842—	Benoni Sprague,	New York
	Anna Thornburgh,	Indiana
	Thomas Hill,	
	Dinah Gardner,	
	Sybil Jones,	
	Ann Jones,	Maine
	Mary Davis,	
	Susan Howland,	
	Huldah Gifford,	
	Lydia Breed,	Weare
	Huldah B. Hoeg,	N. H.
	Thomas Anthony, }	R. I.
	Perez Peck,	
	Newall Ordway, }	Mass.
	Oliver Rogers,	
1843—	David Dudley,	
	David Douglas,	Maine
	Charles F. Coffin,	Maine
	Susan Howland,	
	Mary Davis,	
	Daniel Clapp,	Rhode Island
	E. Foster,	Rhode Island
	Charles F. Coffin, }	Maine
	Joseph Metcalf,	
	Lindley M. Hoeg,	N. Hampshire
	Stephen Jones, Jr., }	Maine
	Rachel W. Jones,	
1844—	Charles Taber, }	Lower Canada
	Paul Southwick,	Lower Canada

DATE	NAME	RESIDENCE
1844—	David Knowles, }	Lower Canada
	Henry Wood,	New Bedford
	Abigail R. Jones, }	
	Hannah Merrill,	N. H.
	James Canney,	
	Sybil Jones,	
	Augustine &	
	Cynthia Jones,	Maine
	Jared Patterson, }	
	Josiah Morris,	Indiana
	Thomas Evans, }	Penna.
	Samuel Bettle, Jr.,	
	Joseph Bowne,	N. Y.
	Lindley M. Hoeg,	New Hampshire
	James Jones & wife, }	
	Martha Hodges,	Maine
	William Kitchen,	
	Zacheus Bowerman,	Maine
	Harvey Derbyshire, }	Canada
	Jonathan Farris,	
1845—	David Dudley, }	
	David Dougles,	Maine
	Samuel Taylor, Jr., }	Maine
	David Shove,	
	John Pease,	England
	Samuel Hilles,	
	Isabel Casson,	England
	Stephen P. Morris, }	Gtn., Pa.
	Catharine Morris,	
	Rowland Green,	Rhode Island
	Benjamin Fry,	New Hampshire
	Cornelius Douglas, }	
	David Douglas,	Maine
	Susan Smith,	New Jersey
	Abigail R. Hanson,	N.H.
	Susan Howland,	
	Anna Macomber,	
	Ruth Baker,	
	John Wilbur,	Rhode Island
	Mary Davis,	Dartmouth
	Thomas B. Gould,	Rhode Island
	Nathan Page,	Danvers
	Mary Davis (2d time),	Danvers
1846—	Mary Davis,	Dartmouth
	Nathan Page,	

INDEX.

Abbott, Dorothy (Swain), (Mrs. Thomas Abbott), 66.
Abbott, Thomas, 66.
Albertson, Lydia (Mrs. Henry Stanton), 221.
Allen, Ann (Coleman), (Mrs. Edward Allen), 170.
Allen, Edward, 170.
Allen, George, Jr., 77.
Allen, John, 77.
Allen, Matthew, 77.
Allen, Rachel (Mrs. Thomas Starbuck), dau. Edward Allen, 169, 170.
Allen, Ralph, Jr., 77.
Allen, William, 77.
Anthony, Susanna (Mrs. Abraham Barker), 191.
Anti-slavery Society, first in New England, 34.
Associates chosen, 11.
Atkinson, Sarah (Mrs. Stephen Coffin), 235.
Austin, Ann (Mrs. Thomas Austin), 206.
Austin, Deborah (Mrs. Lieutenant John Coffin), dau. Joseph Austin, 31, 143, 144, 145, 161, 181, 182, 212, 214, 217, 218, 219.
Austin, Joseph, 21, 31, 144, 145, 161, 169, 173, 181, 206, 210, 212, 218, 219, 222.
Austin, Lydia (Hussey, Macy), (Mrs. William R. Austin), 210.
Austin, Mary (Mrs. Richard Gardner), dau. Joseph Austin, 169, 217, 218, 221, 222.
Austin, Rose (Mrs. Ephraim Tibbetts), dau. Thomas Austin, 205, 206.
Austin, Sarah (Starbuck), (Mrs. Joseph Austin), 20, 21, 31, 144, 161, 169, 173, 181, 206, 210, 212, 218, 219, 222.
Austin, Thomas, 206.
Austin, William R., 210.
Avent, Phillip, 40.
Ayer, Elizabeth (Hutchins), (Mrs. Thomas Ayer), 233.
Ayer, Mary (Mrs. Samuel Colcord), 227, 231.
Ayer, Thomas, father Mary Ayer, 232.

Bache, Richard, 69.
Bache, Sarah (Franklin), (Mrs. Richard Bache), 69.
Bachelor, Deborah (Smith), (Mrs. Nathaniel Bachelor), 56.

Bachelor, Deborah (Mrs. John Wing), dau. Rev. Stephen Bachelor, 56, 57, 154, 185, 188, 190, 210.
Bachelor, Elizabeth (Mrs. Nathaniel Bachelor), 56.
Bachelor, Francis, son Rev. Stephen Bachelor, 56.
Bachelor, Mary (Wyman), (Mrs. Nathaniel Bachelor), 56.
Bachelor, Nathaniel, son Rev. Stephen Bachelor, 56, 57.
Bachelor, Stephen, Rev., 54, 57, 61, 151, 154, 167, 171, 173, 183, 184, 185, 188, 190, 198, 201, 207, 210, 214, 240, 241.
Bachelor, Stephen, son Rev. Stephen Bachelor, 56.
Bachelor, Theodate (Mrs. Christopher Hussey), dau. Rev. Stephen Bachelor, 52, 56, 150, 151, 153, 154, 166, 167, 171, 173, 183, 185, 197, 198, 201, 206, 207, 210, 213, 214.
Balch, Anice (Mrs. John Balch), 164.
Balch, Benjamin, 80, 164.
Balch, John, 164.
Balch, Ruth, dau. Benjamin Balch, 164.
Balch, Sarah (Gardner), (Mrs. Benjamin Balch), 80, 164.
Barker, Abigail (Keen), (Mrs. Prince Barker), 190.
Barker, Abraham, son Robert Barker, 155.
Barker, Abraham, son Benjamin Barker, 190.
Barker, Abraham, son James3 Barker, 191.
Barker, Ann (Mrs. Benjamin Barker), dau. Abraham Barker, 190, 191.
Barker, Barbara (Dungan), (Mrs. James2 Barker), 191.
Barker, Benjamin, son Prince Barker, 190.
Barker, Bethiah (Folger), (Mrs. Samuel Barker), 74, 155.
Barker, Deborah (Mrs. Benjamin Keen), dau. Robert Barker, 191.
Barker, Deborah (Wing), (Mrs. Samuel Barker, 1st wife), 188.
Barker, Elizabeth (Easton), (Mrs. William Barker), 191.
Barker, Elizabeth (Slocum), (Mrs. Isaac Barker, Jr.), 190.
Barker, Elizabeth (Tucker), (Mrs. James3 Barker), 191.

Barker, Elizabeth (Huntington), (Mrs. Joseph Philbrick Newhall), 189, 190, 191.
Barker Family, 155.
Barker Family, connection with Nantucket, 74.
Barker, Francis, son Robert Barker, 155.
Barker, Isaac, Jr., son Isaac Barker, Sr., 190.
Barker, Isaac, Sr., son Robert Barker, 74, 155.
Barker, Jacob, son Robert Barker, 74, 78, 155.
Barker, James1, from England, 191.
Barker, James2, son James1 Barker, 191.
Barker, James3, son William Barker, 191.
Barker, James, son Robert Barker, 155, 194.
Barker, Jedidah, dau. Robert Barker, 155.
Barker, Jedidah (Chase), (Mrs. Robert Barker), 155, 156, 157, 193, 194.
Barker, Josiah, 117.
Barker, Judith, dau. of Robert, 155.
Barker, Judith (Prence), (Mrs. Isaac Barker), 74, 155, 190.
Barker, Lucy (Williams), (Mrs. Robert Barker), 156, 190, 191.
Barker, Lydia, dau. Robert Barker, 154, 155.
Barker, Lydia (Mrs. Francis Swain, Jr.), 152, 153.
Barker, Margaret, dau. Robert Barker, 155.
Barker, Margaret (Buffum), (Mrs. Abraham Barker), 190.
Barker, Mary, dau. Robert Barker, 155.
Barker, Prince, son Isaac Barker, 190.
Barker, Robert, son Samuel Barker, 74, 78, 155, 156, 157, 159, 190, 191, 193, 194.
Barker, Robert, descendants from, 157, 159.
Barker, Robert, Jr., son Robert Barker, 155, 191.
Barker, Samuel, son Isaac Barker, 74, 155, 187, 188.
Barker, Sarah, dau. Robert Barker, 155.
Barker, Sarah (Gardner), (Mrs. Robert Barker, 2d wife), 74, 155, 158, 159.

Barker, Susanna (Anthony), (Mrs. Abraham Barker), 191.
Barker, William, son James² Barker, 191.
Barnard, Abigail (Mrs. Samuel Fellows), dau. Thomas Barnard, 228.
Barnard, Benjamin, son Nathaniel Barnard, Jr., 211.
Barnard, Bethia (Folger), (Mrs. John Barnard), 64.
Barnard, Eleanor (Mrs. Thomas Barnard), 64, 156, 157, 159, 193, 194, 211, 214, 218, 219, 228, 229, 230, 236.
Barnard, Elizabeth (Macy), (Mrs. Francis Barnard), 211.
Barnard, Elizabeth (Mrs. Nathaniel Barnard, Jr.), 211.
Barnard, Elizabeth (Mrs. Barnabas Coleman), 62.
Barnard, Eunice (Mrs. Elijah Cornell), dau. Reuben Barnard, 211.
Barnard, Francis, son Benjamin Barnard, 211.
Barnard, Hannah (Mrs. Benjamin Stevens), dau. Thomas Barnard, 229.
Barnard, Joannah (Harvey), Mrs. Robert Barnard), 64, 156, 157, 159, 193, 194, 212, 214, 219.
Barnard, John, son Robert Barnard, 64.
Barnard, Joseph, 113.
Barnard, Judith (Gardner), (Mrs. Benjamin Barnard), 211.
Barnard, Mary (Mrs. John Folger), dau. Nathaniel Barnard, 156, 192, 193, 217, 218.
Barnard, Mary (Mrs. Nathaniel Barnard, Sr.), dau. Robert Barnard, 64, 156, 193, 211, 212, 218, 219.
Barnard, Nathaniel, son Thomas Barnard, 64, 65, 156, 193, 211, 218.
Barnard, Nathaniel, Jr., son Nathaniel Barnard, Sr., 211.
Barnard, Phebe (Coleman), (Mrs. Reuben Barnard), 211, 213, 214.
Barnard, Phebe (Coleman), family removed from Nantucket, 215.
Barnard, Reuben, 211, 213, 214.
Barnard, Reuben, descendants from, 214.
Barnard, Robert, 9, 11, 62, 63, 64, 68, 156, 157, 159, 193, 194, 212, 214, 219.
Barnard, Stephen, 65.
Barnard, Thomas, 4, 5, 9, 63, 156, 157, 159, 190, 193, 194, 211, 214, 218, 219, 228, 229, 230, 236.
Barney, Benjamin, 181.
Barney, Elizabeth (Mrs. William Rotch), dau. Benjamin Barney, 180, 181, 182.
Barney, Lydia (Starbuck), (Mrs. Benjamin Barney), 181.
Bartlett, Sarah, 33.

Batchelder, Susanna (Mrs. Ebenezer Webster), 57.
Bates, James, 125.
Bennington, Agnes (Mrs. James Gorham), 197, 203, 229.
Bichford, Robto, 36.
Bicknell, Lydia Spooner (Sherman), (Mrs. Simeon Smith Bicknell), 226.
Biron, an Icelander, 1.
Bishop, John, 9.
Bond, Elizabeth (Powell), (Mrs. Herrick Bond), 202.
Bond, Herrick, 202.
Bradford, Jael (Hobart), (Mrs. Joseph Bradford), 85.
Bradford, Joseph, 85.
Brayton, Judge, 145.
Brayton, Love (Mitchell), (Mrs. Judge Brayton), 145.
Brewster Mary (Mrs. Thomas Prence), dau. William Brewster, 230.
Brewster, Sarah (Collier), (Mrs. Love Brewster), 75.
Brewster, William, 230.
Breed, Keziah (Mrs. Samuel⁴ Newhall), 189.
Bridges, James, 65.
Briggs, Sarah (Mrs. Stephen Wing), 188. 306
Brown, Abial (Mrs. Sylvanus Hussey), dau. John Brown, 150.
Brown, Abigail (Mrs. Hezediah Cartwright), 143.
Brown, Hannah (Hobart), (Mrs. John Brown), 83, 84, 150, 157.
Brown, John, 49, 84.
Brown, John, Jr., 83, 150, 157.
Brown, John, Sr., 150, 157.
Brown, Rachel (Gardner), (Mrs. John Brown), 83, 150, 156, 157.
Brown, Rachel (Mrs. James Chase), 156.
Buffum, David, 192.
Buffum, Hepzibah (Mitchell), (Mrs. David Buffum), 192.
Buffum, Joshua, banished from England, 90.
Buffum, Margaret (Mrs. Abraham Barker), dau. David Buffum, 190, 192.
Bunker, Ann (Mrs. Joseph Coleman), dau. George Bunker, 170.
Bunker, Ann (Mrs. Nathaniel Paddack), dau. William Bunker, 152, 153, 171, 172, 199, 204, 205.
Bunker, Anne, 105.
Bunker, Desire (Gorham), (Mrs. Zecariah Bunker), 238.
Bunker, Elizabeth (Coffin), (Mrs. Jonathan Bunker), 144, 162, 208, 238.
Bunker, Elizabeth Thorne (Clement), (Mrs. Nathan² Bunker), 237, 238, 240, 241.

Bunker, George, son William Bunker, 65, 144, 151, 153, 158, 162, 166, 170, 171, 172, 183, 195, 198, 200, 205, 207, 208, 209, 222.
Bunker, George, son William Bunker, MSS. and family, 237, 238, 239, 240.
Bunker, Jabez, 107.
Bunker, Jabez, son William Bunker, 195.
Bunker, Jane (Godfrey), (Mrs. George Bunker), 65, 144, 151, 153, 158, 162, 166, 170, 171, 172, 183, 195, 198, 200, 205, 207, 208, 209, 222.
Bunker, Hannah (Gardner), (Mrs. Jabez Bunker), 195.
Bunker, Jonathan, son William Bunker, 144, 162, 208, 238.
Bunker, Lydia (Paddack), (Mrs. Shubael Bunker), 238.
Bunker, Martha (Mrs. Stephen Hussey), dau. George Bunker, 53, 150, 151, 166, 167, 171, 183, 197, 198, 206, 207, 210.
Bunker, Mary (Mrs. Stephen Coffin), dau. George and Jane (Godfrey) Bunker, 31, 158, 166, 170, 207, 208, 222.
Bunker, Mary (Macy), (Mrs. William Bunker), 144, 153, 162, 172, 195, 199, 205, 208, 209, 228, 230, 240.
Bunker, Miss (Mrs. Admiral Dahlgren), 237.
Bunker, Nathan, 237, 238, 240.
Bunker, Priscilla (Mrs. Abraham² Macy), dau. Samuel Bunker, 29, 195.
Bunker, Priscilla (Coleman), (Mrs. Samuel Bunker), 195.
Bunker, Ruth (Mrs. Richard Coffin), dau. Jonathan Bunker, 143, 144, 162, 207, 208.
Bunker, Samuel, son Jabez Bunker, 195.
Bunker, Shubael, 238.
Bunker, William (Bon Cœur), 144, 237, 238, 239, 240.
Bunker, William, Sr., 151, 153, 154, 158, 159, 162, 163, 166, 167, 170, 171, 172, 173, 183, 185, 195, 198, 200, 201, 202, 205, 207, 208, 209, 222, 223, 237.
Bunker, William, son George Bunker, 144, 145, 153, 162, 171, 195, 199, 205, 208, 209, 238, 239.
Bunker, Zecariah, 238.
Bursell, Anna (Mrs. Silas Sears), 230.

Capehart, Edward Everett, 227.
Capehart, Sarah (Wadleigh), (Mrs. Edward Everett Capehart), 227.
Cartwright, Abigail (Brown), (Mrs. Hezediah Cartwright), 143.
Cartwright, Bethiah (Pratt), (Mrs. Sampson Cartwright), 143.

Index. 333

Cartwright, Edward, Jr., son Edward Cartwright, 104, 147.
Cartwright, Edward, Sr., 143, 145, 147.
Cartwright, Elizabeth (Trott), (Mrs. Edward Cartwright), 103, 104, 143, 147.
Cartwright, Elizabeth, dau. Edward Cartwright, 147.
Cartwright, Hezediah, son Sampson Cartwright, 143.
Cartwright, James, son Hezediah Cartwright, 142, 143.
Cartwright, John, 113.
Cartwright, Love (Macy), (Mrs. James Cartwright), 142.
Cartwright, Lydia, dau. James Cartwright, 142.
Cartwright, Mary, dau. Edward Cartwright, 104.
Cartwright, Nicholas, son Edward Cartwright, 104, 147.
Cartwright, Sampson, son Edward Cartwright, 104, 143, 147.
Cartwright, Susanna, dau. Edward Cartwright, 104.
Cartwrite, Edward, will of, 103, 143, 145, 147.
Cavender, Charles, son Thomas Cavender, 165.
Cavender, Elizabeth (Mott), (Mrs. Thomas Cavender), 164, 165.
Cavender, Fanny (Mrs. Thomas Parish), 165.
Cavender, Henry, son Thomas Cavender, 165.
Cavender, Mary (Mrs. William J. Wilcox), 165.
Cavender, Thomas S., 164, 165.
Chace, Marcia (Mrs. George T. Powell), 202.
Chalkley, Thomas, his visit to Nantucket, 120.
Challis, Philip, 14, 63, 190.
Challis, Sarah (Mrs. Samuel Johnson), 190.
Chapman, Dorothy (Swain, Abbott), (Mrs. Edward Chapman), 66.
Chapman, Edward, 66.
Charles I. of England, 241.
Chase, Elizabeth (Philbrick), (Mrs. Thomas Chase), 156, 157, 193.
Chase, Isaac, Lieutenant, son Thomas Chase, 156, 193.
Chase, James, son Lieutenant Isaac Chase, 156.
Chase, Jedidah (Mrs. Robert Barker), dau. James Chase, 155, 156, 157, 193, 194.
Chase, Mary (Tilton), (Mrs. Lieutenant Isaac Chase), 156.
Chase, Peter, 192.
Chase, Rachel (Brown), (Mrs. James Chase), 156.

Chase, Thomas, 156, 157, 193.
Chember, Robert, 37.
Christian names of some early settlers, 94.
Christisen, Wenlock, 94.
Church, Sarah (Mrs. Nathan Folger), 158, 162, 207.
Clark, Elizabeth (Somerby), (Mrs. Nathaniel1 Clark), 228.
Clark, Elizabeth (Toppan), (Mrs. Nathaniel2 Clark), 228.
Clark, Nathaniel1, 228.
Clark, Nathaniel2, son Nathaniel1, 228.
Clark, Nathaniel3, son Nathaniel2, 227.
Clark, Sarah (Greenleaf), (Mrs. Nathaniel3 Clark), 227.
Clark, Sarah (Mrs. Benjamin Dole), dau. Nathaniel3 Clark), 227.
Claverly, Nicholas, 148.
Clement, Ann (Harrison), (Mrs. Jacob Clement), 251.
Clement, Elizabeth (Tilly), (Mrs. Jacob Clement), widow Nathaniel Cooper, 241.
Clement, Jacob, son Jacob Clement, 241.
Clement, Jacob, son James Clement, 241.
Clement, James, son Gregory Clement, 241.
Clement, James, son Jacob Clement, 241.
Clement, Mary (Thorne), (Mrs. James Clement), 241.
Clevanger, Bartholomew, 36.
Coffin, Abigail (Starbuck), (Mrs. Peter Coffin), 20, 21, 27, 224, 226, 232.
Coffin, Abigail (Mrs. Nathaniel Gardner), dau. James Coffin, 196, 197, 211.
Coffin, Alexander, 113.
Coffin and its synonym, 25.
Coffin, Ann (Mrs. Batcheldor Hussey), dau. Daniel Coffin, 206, 207.
Coffin, Ann (Folger), (Mrs. Benj. Coffin), 160, 163.
Coffin, Ann (Folger), (Mrs. Thomas Coffin), 43.
Coffin, Anna (Mrs. Solomon Gardner), dau. Stephen Coffin, 169, 221, 222.
Coffin, Benjamin, son Nathaniel Coffin, 160.
Coffin, Damaris (Gayer), (Mrs. Nathaniel Coffin), 106, 161.
Coffin, Daniel, son Peter Coffin, 207.
Coffin, Deborah (Austin), (Mrs. Lieutenant John Coffin), 31, 143, 145, 161, 181, 182, 214, 217, 219.
Coffin, Deborah (Macy), (Mrs. Benjamin Coffin), 160.

Coffin, Deborah (Mrs. Thomas3 Macy), dau. Lieutenant John Coffin, 143, 161, 181, 211.
Coffin, Deborah (Mrs. Tristram Starbuck), dau. Samuel Coffin, 216, 217.
Coffin, Dinah (Mrs. Abishai Folger), widow Benjamin Starbuck, 158.
Coffin, Dinah (Mrs. Nathaniel Starbuck, Jr.), dau. James Coffin, 149, 158, 167, 171, 172, 183, 184, 193, 204, 205, 207, 208, 216, 217, 218.
Coffin, Dionis (Stevens), (Mrs. Tristram Coffin), 24, 142, 143, 144, 145, 149, 151, 158, 159, 160, 161, 162, 163, 167, 169, 170, 172, 173, 181, 184, 185, 190, 193, 194, 197, 198, 200, 201, 202, 204, 205, 206, 207, 208, 209, 212, 214, 217, 218, 219, 222, 223, 224, 225, 226, 229, 230, 232, 235, 236, 239.
Coffin, Eliza (Mrs. Benjamin H. Yarnall), 163.
Coffin, Elizabeth (Mrs. Nathaniel Barnard, Jr.), 211.
Coffin, Elizabeth (Brown, Greenly), (Mrs. Sir Isaac Coffin), 43.
Coffin, Elizabeth (Stratton), (Mrs. Daniel Coffin), 207.
Coffin, Elizabeth (Barnes), (Mrs. Nathaniel Coffin), 42.
Coffin, Elizabeth (Mrs. Jonathan Bunker), dau. James Coffin, 144, 162, 163, 208, 209, 225.
Coffin, Elizabeth (Mrs. Stephen Greenleaf), dau. Tristram Coffin, 28, 47, 228, 229, 230.
Coffin, Enoch, son Joshua and Margaret (Morse) Coffin, 33.
Coffin, Experience (Look), (Mrs. Stephen Coffin, Jr.), 158.
Coffin family, early wills of, 33.
Coffin, first settler of the name, 24.
Coffin, Hepzibah (Harker), (Mrs. Jonathan Coffin, Sr.), 224.
Coffin, Hepzibah (Mrs. Thaddeus Waterman), dau. Jonathan Coffin, 224, 226.
Coffin, Hope (Gardner), (Mrs. John Coffin, Esq.), 143, 145, 162, 163, 207, 210.
Coffin, Isaac, Sir, Admiral, 41, 42.
Coffin, Isaac, Sir, descent from Tristram Coffin, 42.
Coffin, Isaac, Sir, visits Nantucket, 44.
Coffin, James, 9, 11, 30, 103, 105.
Coffin, James, son Tristram Coffin, Sr., 28, 143, 144, 145, 149, 151, 160, 162, 163, 167, 172, 173, 184, 185, 193, 194, 197, 201, 204, 205, 208, 209, 210, 214, 217, 218, 219, 224, 225, 226, 238.
Coffin, James, son James, 225.
Coffin, Jane (Heard), (Mrs. Tristram Coffin, of 4th generation), 232.

Coffin, Joan, 24.
Coffin, John, brother Sir Isaac Coffin, 41.
Coffin, John, son of Tristram Coffin, Sr., died in infancy, 28.
Coffin, John, Esq., son James Coffin, 143, 145, 162, 163, 207, 210.
Coffin, John, Lieutenant, son Tristram Coffin, Sr., 31, 143, 145, 161, 181, 182, 214, 217, 219.
Coffin, John, Lieutenant, his commission, 31.
Coffin, Jonathan, Jr., son Jonathan Coffin, Sr., 224.
Coffin, Jonathan, Sr., son James Coffin, 224.
Coffin, Joshua, 53.
Coffin, Joshua5, 33, 34.
Coffin, Joshua5, children of, 33.
Coffin, Joshua6, son Joshua5 Coffin and Margaret (Morse) Coffin, 33.
Coffin, Judith (Somerby), (Mrs. Tristram Coffin, Jr.), 28, 228.
Coffin, Judith (Mrs. Francis Macy), dau. Richard Coffin, 143.
Coffin, Lucretia (Mrs. James Mott), dau. Thomas Coffin, 163.
Coffin, Margaret (Morse), (Mrs. Joshua Coffin), 33.
Coffin, Martha (Mrs. Peter Pelham), dau. Thomas Coffin, 163.
Coffin, Mary (Mrs. James Coffin), dau. John and Abigail Severance, 28, 143, 144, 149, 151, 160, 162, 163, 167, 172, 173, 184, 193, 194, 197, 201, 204, 205, 208, 209, 210, 214, 217, 218, 219, 224, 225, 226, 238.
Coffin, Mary (Bunker), (Mrs. Stephen Coffin, Sr.), 31, 158, 159, 160, 207, 222.
Coffin, Mary (Mrs. Nathaniel Starbuck, Sr.), dau. Tristram Coffin, Sr., 29, 142, 149, 150, 151, 167, 169, 170, 171, 172, 173, 181, 183, 185, 193, 197, 198, 199, 200, 201, 204, 205, 206, 207, 208, 212, 216, 217, 218, 219, 240.
Coffin, Mary (Mrs. Richard Pinkham), dau. James3 Coffin, 196, 197, 203, 204, 209.
Coffin, Mary, dau. Joshua5 and Margaret (Morse) Coffin, 33.
Coffin, Mary (Mrs. Solomon Temple), dau. Thomas Coffin, 163.
Coffin, Miriam (Gardner), (Mrs. Samuel Coffin), 217.
Coffin, Nathaniel, 41.
Coffin, Nathaniel, son James Coffin, 42, 160.
Coffin, Nathaniel, son William Coffin, 42.
Coffin, Peleg, Esq., 2.
Coffin, Peter, 4, 5, 9, 21.

Coffin, Peter, Hon., son Tristram Coffin, Sr., 27, 68, 232.
Coffin, Peter, son Stephen, 207.
Coffin, Priscilla (Mrs. Jonathan Coffin, Jr., 224.
Coffin, Richard, son John Coffin, Esq., 143, 162, 207.
Coffin, Richard, Sir, 24.
Coffin, Ruth (Bunker), (Mrs. Richard Coffin), 143, 162, 207.
Coffin, Ruth (Gardner), (Mrs. James Coffin), 225.
Coffin, Ruth (Mrs. William Folger), dau. Richard Coffin, 161, 162, 206, 207.
Coffin, Sally, dau. Thomas Coffin, 163.
Coffin, Samuel, son Lieutenant John Coffin, 217.
Coffin, Sarah, dau. Joshua5 and Margaret (Morse) Coffin, 33.
Coffin School on Nantucket, 41, 44.
Coffin, Stephen, Jr., son Stephen Coffin, Sr., 158.
Coffin, Stephen, son Tristram Coffin, Jr., 235.
Coffin, Stephen, son Tristram Coffin, Sr., 31, 158, 159, 160, 207, 222.
Coffin, Thomas, 43.
Coffin, Thomas, son Benjamin Coffin, 160, 163.
Coffin, Thomas M., son Thomas Coffin, 163.
Coffin, Tristram, Jr., son of Tristram Coffin, Sr., 9, 11, 28, 34, 68, 228, 235, 236.
Coffin, Tristram, Sr., 3, 4, 5, 8, 9, 24, 25, 26, 28, 48, 68, 142, 143, 144, 145, 149, 151, 158, 159, 160, 161, 162, 163, 167, 169, 170, 172, 173, 181, 182, 184, 185, 190, 193, 194, 197, 198, 200, 201, 202, 204, 205, 206, 207, 208, 209, 212, 214, 217, 218, 219, 222, 223, 224, 225, 226, 229, 230, 232, 235, 236, 239, 240, 241.
Coffin, Tristram, his commission, 26.
Coffin, Tristram, descendants of, 31.
Coffin, Tristram, of 3d generation, son of Peter Coffin, of 2d generation, 232.
Coffin, Tristram, son Tristram Coffin, of 3d generation, 232.
Coffin, William, son Nathaniel Coffin, 42.
Coffin, word signifies, 24.
Coffing, "An," dau. Nicolas Coffing, 37.
Coffing, Johan, dau. Lionell Coffing, 37.
Coffing, Johan, dau. Nicolas Coffing, 37.
Coffing, John, son Nicolas Coffing, 37.
Coffing, Lionell, 37.

Coffing, Nicolas, son Nicolas, executor, 37.
Coffing, Philip, 37.
Coffing, Richard, son Lionell Coffing, 37.
Coffing, Thomas, 37.
Coffing, Tristram, son Philip Coffing, 37.
Coffyn, Ann, dau. Nicholas Coffyn, 35.
Coffyn, Deborah, dau. Peter Coffyn, 39, 40.
Coffyn, Eunice, dau. Peter Coffyn, 39, 40.
Coffyn, Johan (Mrs. Nicholas Coffyn), 34.
Coffyn, Johan (Mrs. Peter Coffyn), 38, 40.
Coffyn, Johan, dau. Peter Coffyn, 39, 40.
Coffyn, John, son Nicholas Coffyn, 35, 36.
Coffyn, John, son Peter Coffyn, 39, 40.
Coffyn, Mary, dau. Peter Coffyn, 39, 40.
Coffyn, "Nichas," brother Peter Coffyn, 40.
Coffyn, Nicholas, son Nicholas, 34, 35, 36.
Coffyn, Nicholas, grandfather Tristram Coffin, Sr., 33.
"Coffyn, Nicholas," will, 33.
Coffyn, Peter, son Nicholas Coffyn, 34.
Coffyn, Peter, will of, 38.
Coffyn, Tristram, son Peter Coffyn, England, 38, 39.
Coggeshall, Ann (Mrs. Peter Easton), dau. John Coggeshall, 191, 192, 194.
Coggeshall, Caleb, son Joshua Coggeshall, 216.
Coggeshall, Caleb, son Job Coggeshall, 216, 220.
Coggeshall, Deborah (Mrs. Paul Macy), dau. Job Coggeshall, 216.
Coggeshall, Deborah (Starbuck), (Mrs. Job Coggeshall), 216.
Coggeshall, Elizabeth (Hosier), (Mrs. Caleb Coggeshall), 216, 220.
Coggeshall, Giles H., son Caleb Coggeshall, 219.
Coggeshall, Joan (West), (Mrs. Joshua Coggeshall), 216, 219.
Coggeshall, Job, son Caleb Coggeshall, 216.
Coggeshall, John, 192, 194, 216, 219.
Coggeshall, Joshua, son John Coggeshall, 216, 219.
Coggeshall, Marianna (Walters), (Mrs. Giles H. Coggeshall), 219.
Coggeshall, Mary (Stanton), (Mrs. John Coggeshall), 192, 216.
Coggeshall, Mercy (Mitchell), (Mrs. Caleb Coggeshall), 216.

Colcord, Ann (Mrs. Edward Colcord), 227, 230, 231, 232.
Colcord, Deborah (Mrs. Tristram Coffin, of 3d generation), 232.
Colcord, Ebenezer1, son Samuel Colcord, 227.
Colcord, Ebenezer2, son Ebenezer1 Colcord, 227.
Colcord, Edward, 227, 230, 231, 232.
Colcord, Edward, son Jonathan Colcord, 231.
Colcord, Hannah (Fellows), (Mrs. Ebenezer1 Colcord), 227.
Colcord, Jane (Coffin), (Mrs. Edward Colcord), 231, 232.
Colcord, John, son Ebenezer2 Colcord, 227.
Colcord, Jonathan, son Samuel Colcord, 231.
Colcord, Lydia (Morrell), (Mrs. John Colcord), 227.
Colcord, Mary (Ayer), (Mrs. Samuel Colcord), 227, 231.
Colcord, Mary Pennypacker (Walker), (Mrs. Tristram Coffin Colcord), 231.
Colcord, Patience (Stevens), (Mrs. Ebenezer2 Colcord), 227.
Colcord, Peter, son Edward and Jane Colcord, 231.
Colcord, Phebe (Hamilton), (Mrs. Peter Colcord), 231.
Colcord, Samuel, son Edward Colcord, 227, 231, 232, 233.
Colcord, Sarah (Mrs. Dolel Wadley), dau. John Colcord, 227.
Colcord, Tristram Coffin, later Coffin Colket, 231, 232.
Coleman, Andrew, son Enoch Coleman, 73.
Coleman, Ann (Mrs. Edward Allen), dau. Joseph Coleman, 170.
Coleman, Ann (Bunker), (Mrs. Joseph Coleman), 170.
Coleman, Barnabas, son John Coleman, Jr., 62, 150.
Coleman, Benjamin, son Thomas Coleman, 61.
Coleman, Daniel, son Solomon Coleman, 213.
Coleman, Deliverance (Swett), (Mrs. Solomon Coleman), 213.
Coleman, Elihu, 29.
Coleman, Elihu, son Jethro Coleman, 198.
Coleman, Elizabeth (Barnard), (Mrs. Barnabas Coleman), 62.
Coleman, Elizabeth (Mrs. Abraham Macy), 195, 198, 201.
Coleman, Elizabeth (Mooers), (Mrs. Daniel Coleman), 213.
Coleman, Elizabeth (Macy), (Mrs. Elihu Coleman), 198.
Coleman, Enoch, son Jeremiah, 73.

Coleman, Hepzibah (Mrs. John Russell, Jr.), dau. Barnabas Coleman, 149, 150, 151.
Coleman, Hepzibah (Wing), (Mrs. William Coleman, Sr.), 186.
Coleman, Isaac, 17.
Coleman, Isaac, son Thomas Coleman, 61.
Coleman, Jeremiah, son John Coleman, 73.
Coleman, Jethro, son John Coleman, 198.
Coleman, Joanna, dau. Thomas Coleman, 61.
Coleman, Joanna (Folger), (Mrs. John Coleman), 73, 150, 196, 198, 213.
Coleman, John, 8, 73.
Coleman, John, Jr., son John Coleman, Sr., 132, 150, 196, 198, 213.
Coleman, John, Sr., son Thomas Coleman, 8, 150, 196, 198, 213.
Coleman, Joseph, son Thomas Coleman, 61, 170.
Coleman, Lydia (Paddack), (Mrs. Jethro Coleman), 198.
Coleman, Lydia, dau. Andrew Coleman, 73.
Coleman, Lydia Wing, dau. William Coleman, Sr. (Lydia unmarried), 186.
Coleman, Margery (Mrs. Thomas Coleman), 61.
Coleman, Mary (Mrs. Thomas Coleman), 61.
Coleman, Nathaniel, 29.
Coleman, Nathaniel, son of Barnabas Coleman, 61, 62.
Coleman, Phebe (Mrs. Reuben Barnard), 211, 213, 214.
Coleman, Priscilla, 132.
Coleman, Priscilla (Mrs. Samuel Bunker), dau. John Coleman, 195, 196.
Coleman, Priscilla (Starbuck), (Mrs. John Coleman, Jr.), 150, 196, 198.
Coleman, Rachel (Hussey), (Mrs. Barnabas Coleman), 62, 150.
Coleman, Solomon, son John Coleman, 213.
Coleman, Susanna (Mrs. Thomas Coleman), 61, 62, 150, 151, 170, 173, 186, 196, 198, 201, 202, 213, 214.
Coleman, Thomas, 9, 11, 60, 61, 62, 68, 150, 151, 170, 173, 186, 196, 198, 201, 202, 213, 214.
Coleman, Tobias, son Thomas Coleman, 61.
Coleman, Wm., Jr., son William, Sr., 186.
Coleman, William, Sr., 186.
Colket, Coffin, 231, 232.
Colket, Mary Pennypacker (Walker), (Mrs. Coffin Colket), 231.

Collier, Elizabeth, dau. William Collier, 75.
Collier, Jane (Mrs. William Collier), 192.
Collier, Mary (Mrs. Thomas Prence), dau. William Collier, 156, 157, 159, 191, 192, 194, 230.
Collier, Mary, granddaughter William Collier, 75.
Collier, Rebecca, dau. William Collier, 75.
Collier, Sarah, dau. William Collier, 75.
Collier, William, 75, 156, 157, 159, 192, 194.
Conant, Roger, 80.
Contract, a unique, 101.
Cope, Caroline R., dau. Thomas Pim Cope, 164.
Cope, Mary (Drinker), (Mrs. Thomas Pim Cope), 164.
Cope, Thomas Pim, 164.
Copeland, John, 59.
Cornell, Alonzo B., Hon., son Ezra Cornell, 211.
Cornell connection with Nantucket, 211.
Cornell, Elijah, 211.
Cornell, Eunice (Barnard), (Mrs. Elijah Cornell), 211.
Cornell, Ezra, son Elijah Cornell, 211.
Cornell Family, 215.
Cornell, Hannah (Thorne), (Mrs. Richard Cornell), 215.
Cornell, John, 215.
Cornell, Joshua, son John Cornell, 215.
Cornell, Mary (Russell), (Mrs. John Cornell), 215.
Cornell, Mary Ann (Wood), (Mrs. Ezra Cornell), 211.
Cornell, Richard, son John Cornell, 215.
Cornell, Sarah (Thorne), (Mrs. Joshua Cornell), 215.
Coule, James, 37.
Cranston, Mary (Clarke), (Mrs. John Stanton), 221.
Cushman, Robert, 79.
Cuthbertson, Cuthbert, 148.
Cutts, John, 53.

Davis, Anna (Mrs. Richard Price Hallowell), 165.
Davis, Charles, 165.
Davis, Edward Morris, 164, 165.
Davis, Ellen (Bliss, Warner), (Mrs. William Morris Davis), 165.
Davis, Henry Corbit, 165.
Davis intermarriages, 69.
Davis, Maria (Mott), (Mrs. Edward Morris Davis), 164, 165.

Davis, Martha (Mellor), (Mrs. Henry Corbit Davis, 1st wife), 165.
Davis, Naomi (Lawton), (Mrs. Henry Corbit Davis, 2d wife), 165.
Davis, William Morris, 165.
Deeds of purchase, 1, 7.
De Schweinitz, Bernard, 165.
De Schweinitz, Ellen (Lord), (Mrs. Bernard de Schweinitz), 165.
Dewey, Margaret (Mrs. Edmund Hobart), 151, 157.
Dillingham, Deborah (Mrs. Daniel Wing, Jr.), 184.
Dillingham, Edward, 57, 58.
Dole, Benjamin, 227.
Dole, Elizabeth (Mrs. Joseph2 Wadley), dau. Benjamin Dole, 227.
Dole, Sarah (Clark), (Mrs. Benjamin Dole), 227.
Dole, Sarah (Mrs. Edmund Greenleaf), 46, 228, 230.
Drinker Family, 80.
Drinker, Henry, son Joseph Drinker, 164.
Drinker, John, 164.
Drinker, John, son Henry Drinker, 164.
Drinker, Joseph, son John Drinker, 164.
Drinker, Mary (Gottier), (Mrs. Henry Drinker), 164.
Drinker, Mary (Janney), (Mrs. Joseph Drinker), 164.
Drinker, Mary, dau. John Drinker, 164.
Drinker, Rachel (Reynear), (Mrs. John Drinker), 164.
Drinker, Ruth (Balch), (Mrs. John Drinker), 164.
Dungan, Barbara (Mrs. James2 Barker), 191.
Durant, Arthur, 40.
Dyer, Mary, 94.

Earle Family, 166.
Earle, John Milton, 167.
Earle, John Milton, family of, 166.
Earle, Mary (Hussey), (Mrs. Thomas Earle), 167, 168.
Earle, Plimton, 34, 35.
Earle, Sarah (Hussey), (Mrs. John Milton Earle), 167.
Earle, Thomas, 167, 168.
Earle, Thomas, family of, 166.
Easton, Ann (Coggeshall), (Mrs. Peter Easton), 191, 194.
Easton, Elizabeth (Mrs. William Barker), dau. Peter Easton, 191.
Easton, Nicholas, of England, 191, 194.
Easton, Peter, son Nicholas Easton, 191, 194.
Edwards, Nicholas, 36.
Eric, Earl of Norway, 1.

Estes, Hannah (Mrs. Daniel5 Newhall), 189.
Evans, Ann (Thompson, Hodgdon), (Mrs. Robert Evans, 2d wife), 235.
Evans, Elizabeth (Hanson), (Mrs. Joseph Evans), 235.
Evans, Joseph, son Joseph Evans, 235.
Evans, Joseph, son Robert Evans, 235.
Evans, Mercy (Horne), (Mrs. Joseph Evans), 235.
Evans, Robert, 235, 236.
Evelyn, George, 52.
Ewer, Thomas, 77.

Farrar, Susanna (Mrs. Joseph3 Newhall), 189.
Fellows, Abigail (Barnard), (Mrs. Samuel Fellows), 228.
Fellows, Hannah (Mrs. Ebenezer1 Colcord), dau. Samuel Fellows, 227, 228.
Fellows, Samuel, 228.
Fforrett, James, 5.
First Episcopal Church of Lynn, 54.
First ship in British waters after the Revolution, 180.
First vessel built in New Bedford, 180.
Folger, Abiah, dau. Peter Folger, 69.
Folger, Abishai, son Nathan Folger, 114, 155, 158, 161, 206, 207.
Folger, Ann (Mrs. James Mitchell), dau. Jethro Folger, 192, 217.
Folger, Ann (Mrs. Thomas Coffin), 43.
Folger, Ann (Mrs. Benjamin Coffin), dau. William Folger, 160, 161, 163.
Folger, Anna, 167.
Folger, Barzillai, son Nathan Folger, 71.
Folger, Benjamin, 3, 113.
Folger, Benjamin Franklin, 3.
Folger, Bethiah, dau. of Peter Folger, 64.
Folger, Bethiah (Mrs. Samuel Barker), dau. John Folger, 74, 155, 156.
Folger, Charles James, 78.
Folger, Dinah (Starbuck), (Mrs. Abishai Folger, 2d wife), 155, 158.
Folger, Dorcas (Mrs. Joseph Pratt), dau. Peter Folger, 143, 144.
Folger, Eleazer, son Peter Folger, 69, 71, 105, 114, 158, 162, 207, 214.
Folger, Eleazer, Jr., son Eleazer Folger, 69, 107.
Folger, Elezer, 11.
Folger, Elizabeth (Starbuck), (Mrs. Walter Folger), 71.
Folger, Experience (Mrs. John Swain, Jr.), dau. Peter Folger, 152.
Folger Family, 67.
Folger, Frederick, 117.
Folger, Jethro, son John Folger, 192, 217.

Folger, Joanna (Mrs. John Coleman, Sr.), dau. Peter Folger, 73, 150, 196, 198, 213.
Folger, John, son Peter Folger, 156, 192, 217.
Folger, Lydia (Mrs. Zaccheus Hussey), dau. William Folger, 206.
Folger, Mary (Barnard), (Mrs. John Folger), 156, 192, 217.
Folger, Mary (Starbuck), (Mrs. Jethro Folger), 192, 217.
Folger, Mary (Morrell), (Mrs. Peter Folger), 60, 144, 150, 151, 152, 153, 156, 157, 158, 159, 162, 163, 167, 192, 194, 197, 199, 201, 202, 207, 210, 213, 214, 217, 219, 225, 226.
Folger, Nathan, son Eleazer Folger, 71, 114, 158, 162, 207.
Folger, Patience (Mrs. Ebenezer Harker), dau. Peter Folger, 225.
Folger, Peter, 3, 9, 103, 144, 150, 151, 152, 153, 156, 157, 158, 159, 162, 163, 167, 192, 194, 197, 199, 201, 202, 207, 210, 213, 214, 217, 219, 225, 226.
Folger, Peter, son John Folger, 67, 69.
Folger, Phebe, 167.
Folger, Phebe (Mrs. Uriel Hussey), 166, 167.
Folger, Phebe (Coleman), (Mrs. Barzillai Folger), 71.
Folger, Reuben, 113.
Folger, Ruth (Coffin), (Mrs. William Folger), 161, 206.
Folger, Sarah, 167.
Folger, Sarah (Gardner), (Mrs. Eleazer Folger), 71, 158, 162, 207, 214.
Folger, Sarah (Mayhew), (Mrs. Abishai Folger, 1st wife), 161, 206.
Folger, Sarah (Mrs. Tristram Hussey), 166.
Folger, Sarah (Church), (Mrs. Nathan Folger), 158, 162, 207.
Folger, Sarah (Mrs. Hezekiah Gardner), dau. Abishai Folger, 155, 158.
Folger, Sarah (Mrs. Anthony Odar), dau. Eleazer Folger, 213, 214.
Folger, Timothy, 114, 117.
Folger, Timothy, son Abishai Folger, 114.
Folger, Walter, son Barzillai Folger, Sr., 71.
Folger, Walter, Jr., son Walter Folger, 71.
Folger, Walter, clock, 71.
Folger, William, son Abishai Folger, 161, 206.
Foot, Patience, 106.
Foulger, Eleazer, 11.
Foulger, Peter, 11.
Franciscus, Albert H., 174.
Franciscus, Susan (Swift), (Mrs. Albert H. Franciscus), 174.

Index. 337

Franklin, Abiah (Folger), (Mrs. Josiah Franklin), 69.
Franklin, Benjamin, son Josiah Franklin, 69.
Franklin, Deborah (Read), (Mrs. Benjamin Franklin), 69.
Franklin, Josiah, 69.
Freeman, Edward, 58.
Freeman, Joanna (Picket), (Mrs. John4 Freeman), 229.
Freeman, John1, 229, 230.
Freeman, John2, son John1, 229.
Freeman, John3, son John2, 229.
Freeman, John4, son John3, 229.
Freeman, Mercy (Prence), (Mrs. John1 Freeman), 229.
Freeman, Mercy (Watson), (Mrs. John3 Freeman), 229.
Freeman, Sarah (Merrick), (Mrs. John2 Freeman), 229.
Freeman, Sarah (Mrs. Stephen Gorham), dau. John Freeman, 229.
Frier, Margaret (Mrs. Thomas Gardiner), 81, 144, 150, 151, 157, 158, 159, 161, 162, 163, 167, 169, 172, 173, 181, 182, 196, 197, 199, 200, 201, 202, 204, 205, 208, 209, 212, 214, 218, 219, 222, 223, 225, 226.

Gardiner, Damaris (Shattuck), (Mrs. Thomas Gardiner), 81, 86.
Gardiner, Margaret (Frier), (Mrs. Thomas Gardiner), 81, 144, 150, 151, 157, 158, 159, 161, 162, 163, 167, 169, 172, 173, 181, 182, 196, 197, 199, 200, 201, 202, 204, 205, 208, 209, 212, 214, 218, 219, 222, 223, 225, 226, 240.
Gardiner, Sarah (Mrs. Benjamin Balch), 164.
Gardiner, Thomas, 79, 80, 81, 144, 145, 150, 151, 157, 158, 159, 161, 162, 163, 164, 167, 169, 172, 173, 181, 182, 196, 197, 199, 200, 201, 202, 204, 205, 208, 209, 212, 214, 218, 219, 222, 223, 225, 226, 240, 241.
Gardner, Abigail (Coffin), (Mrs. Nathaniel Gardner), 196, 211.
Gardner, Anna (Coffin), (Mrs. Solomon Gardner), 169, 221.
Gardner, Deborah, 18.
Gardner, Deborah (Mrs. John Macy, Sr.), dau. Richard Gardner, 143, 149, 161, 181, 195, 196, 198, 199, 203, 204, 211, 221, 222.
Gardner, Dinah (Mrs. David Macy), dau. Solomon Gardner, 221.
Gardner, Dorcas (Mrs. Dr. Paul Swift), 169, 173, 174.
Gardner, Elizabeth (Mrs. Stephen Gorham), dau. James Gardner, 171, 172, 199, 200, 203, 204, 239.
Gardner, Eunice, 107.
Gardner Family, 79.

Gardner, George, 87.
Gardner, Gideon, 113.
Gardner, Gideon, son Hezekiah, 155.
Gardner, Hannah (Mrs. Jabez Bunker), dau. Nathaniel Gardner, 195.
Gardner, Hezekiah, 155.
Gardner, Hope (Mrs. John Coffin, Esq.), dau. Richard Gardner, 143, 144, 145, 162, 163, 207, 209, 210.
Gardner, James, son Richard, 172, 200, 204, 240.
Gardner, John, son Thomas Gardiner, 79, 82, 83, 84.
Gardner, John, Captain, son Thomas Gardiner, 151, 157, 225, 226.
Gardner, John, Captain, his commission, 83.
Gardner, Joseph, son Richard Gardner, 102.
Gardner, Judith, 107.
Gardner, Judith (Mrs. Benjamin Burnard), dau. Nathaniel Gardner, 211.
Gardner, Lion, 81.
Gardner, Mary, 128.
Gardner, Mary (Austin), (Mrs. Richard2 Gardner), 169, 217, 218, 221.
Gardner, Mary (Gorham), (Mrs. Prince Gardner), 186.
Gardner, Mary (Starbuck), (Mrs. James Gardner), 172, 200, 204, 240.
Gardner, Mary, dau. John Gardner, 225.
Gardner, Mary S. (Mrs. Abraham R. Wing), 186, 187.
Gardner, Miriam (Mrs. John Worth), dau. Richard Gardner, 106, 197, 199, 200, 204, 205, 222.
Gardner, Miriam (Mrs. Samuel Coffin), 217.
Gardner, Nathaniel, son Richard Gardner, 196, 211.
Gardner, Paul, son Solomon Gardner, 169.
Gardner, Prince, 186.
Gardner, Priscilla (Grafton), (Mrs. John Gardner), 151, 157, 225, 226.
Gardner, Rachel (Mrs. John Brown, Jr.), dau. Capt. John Gardner, 83, 150, 151, 157.
Gardner, Rachel (Starbuck), (Mrs. Paul Gardner), 169.
Gardner, Richard, 11, 18, 101, 105, 107, 122.
Gardner, Richard2, son Richard1 Gardner, 144, 169, 217, 218, 221.
Gardner, Richard, son Thomas Gardiner, 79, 81, 82, 86, 143, 144, 145, 149, 150, 151, 158, 159, 161, 162, 163, 167, 169, 172, 173, 181, 182, 196, 197, 199, 200, 201, 202, 204, 205, 208, 209, 211, 212, 214, 218, 219, 221, 222, 223, 240, 241.

Gardner, Ruth (Mrs. James Coffin), dau. John Gardner, 225.
Gardner, Sarah (Mrs. Eleazer Folger), dau. Richard Gardner, 158, 162, 207, 208, 214.
Gardner, Sarah (Mrs. Robert Barker), dau. Abishai Folger and widow Hezekiah Gardner, 74, 155, 159, 159.
Gardner, Sarah (Shattuck), (Mrs. Richard1 Gardner), 18, 81, 86, 143, 144, 149, 151, 158, 159, 161, 162, 163, 167, 169, 172, 173, 181, 182, 196, 197, 199, 200, 201, 202, 204, 205, 208, 209, 211, 212, 214, 218, 219, 221, 222, 223, 240.
Gardner, Sarah, dau. Thomas Gardiner, 80.
Gardner, Solomon, son Richard Gardner, Jr., 169, 221.
Gardner, Susanna (Hussey), (Mrs. Zenas Gardner), 169.
Gardner, Zenas, son Paul Gardner, 169.
Gayer & Bunker, surveyors, 147.
Gayer, Damaris (Mrs. Nathaniel Coffin), dau. William Gayer, 105, 107, 160, 161.
Gayer, Dorcas (Starbuck), (Mrs. William Gayer), 142, 161, 163, 170, 181, 182.
Gayer, Dorcas (Mrs. Jethro Starbuck), dau. William Gayer, 142, 169, 170, 181.
Gayer (or Geare), William, 21, 142, 145, 147, 161, 163, 170, 181, 182.
Gayer, William, Jr., son William Gayer, 105.
Gayer, William, will of, 105.
Gibbons Family, 168.
Gifford, William, 77.
Gillespie, Mrs. E. D., 69.
Godbertson, Godbert, 148.
Godfrey, Jane (Mrs. Richard Swain), widow George Bunker, 151, 153, 158, 162, 166, 170, 171, 172, 183, 195, 198, 200, 205, 207, 208, 209, 222, 238, 239, 240.
Goldsmith, Ralph, 91.
Gorges, Ferdinand, Sir, 4.
Gorham, Agnes (Bennington), (Mrs. James Gorham), 197, 203, 229, 238, 239.
Gorham, Barney, son Stephen, 229.
Gorham, Desire (Howland), (Mrs. John Gorham, Sr.), 171, 173, 196, 199, 201, 202, 203, 209, 229, 238, 239.
Gorham, Desire (Mrs. Zecariah Bunker), 238.
Gorham, Eliza, 29.
Gorham, Elizabeth (Gardner), (Mrs. Stephen Gorham), 171, 199, 203.
Gorham, James, 197, 203, 229, 238, 239.

Gorham, Jane (Johnson), (Mrs. Barney Gorham), 229.
Gorham, John, son John and Desire Gorham, 239.
Gorham, John, Jr., 171, 199, 203, 230.
Gorham, John, Jr., son Ralph Gorham, 171, 173, 196, 199, 201, 202, 203, 209, 229, 238, 239, 241.
Gorham, Joseph, son John Gorham, 229.
Gorham, Josiah, son Joseph Gorham, 229.
Gorham, Lois (Mrs. Jonathan Macy, Sr.), dau. Stephen Gorham, 198, 199, 203.
Gorham, Lydia (Mrs. Joseph Worth), dau. Shubael Gorham, 195, 196.
Gorham, Mary (Otis), (Mrs. John Gorham, Jr.), 171, 199, 203, 230, 239.
Gorham, Mary (Mrs. Prince Gardner), 180.
Gorham, Priscilla (Sears), (Mrs. Josiah Gorham), 229.
Gorham, Puella (Hussey), (Mrs. Shubael Gorham, Sr.), 196, 238.
Gorham, Ralph, son James Gorham, 196, 199, 201, 202, 209, 229, 230, 238, 239, 241.
Gorham, Sarah (Freeman), (Mrs. Stephen Gorham), 229.
Gorham, Sarah Jane (Mrs. Elbridge Gerry Pierce), dau. Barney Gorham, 229.
Gorham, Sarah Sturgis (Mrs. Joseph Gorham), 229.
Gorham, Shubael, son John and Desire Gorham, 196, 238.
Gorham, Stephen, son John Gorham, Jr., 171, 199, 203, 239.
Gorham, Stephen, son Josiah Gorham, 229.
Gorham, Susanna (Mrs. Daniel Paddack), dau. Stephen Gorham, 171.
Gosnold, 2.
Gottier, Mary (Mrs. Henry Drinker), 164.
Grafton, Priscilla (Mrs. John Gardner), 151, 157, 225, 226.
Gray, Alice (Mrs. Sylvanus Hussey, Jr.), 183.
Greenfield, Thomas, 77.
Greenleaf, Edmund, 28, 228, 230, 235, 236.
Greenleaf, Edmund (first to come to America), 46.
Greenleaf, Edmund, will of, 46.
Greenleaf, Elizabeth (Coffin), (Mrs. Captain Stephen Greenleaf), 28, 47, 228, 230, 235, 236.
Greenleaf Family, 46, 47.
Greenleaf, Hester (Weare or Wire), (Mrs. Stephen Greenleaf), 66, 152.

Greenleaf, Judith (Mrs. Tristram Coffin, Jr.), widow Henry Somerby and dau. Edmund and Sarah Greenleaf, 28, 228, 235.
Greenleaf, Judith (Coffin), (Mrs. Nathaniel Greenleaf), 235.
Greenleaf, Margaret (Piper), (Mrs. Tristram Greenleaf), 235.
Greenleaf, Nathaniel, son Tristram Greenleaf, 235.
Greenleaf, Samuel, son Stephen Greenleaf, 228.
Greenleaf, Sarah, 28.
Greenleaf, Sarah (Mrs. Nathaniels Clark), 227.
Greenleaf, Sarah (Dole), (Mrs. Edmund Greenleaf), 46, 228, 230, 235, 236.
Greenleaf, Sarah (Kent), (Mrs. Samuel Greenleaf), 228.
Greenleaf, Sarah, dau. Samuel Greenleaf, 228.
Greenleaf, Stephen, Captain, son Edmund Greenleaf, 4, 5, 9, 28, 46, 47, 48, 49, 66, 68, 152, 228, 230, 235, 236.
Greenleaf, Stephen, Jr., 48.
Greenleaf, Tristram, son Stephen, 235.
Greenleaf's Lane, 49.
Greenly, Elizabeth (Mrs. Sir Isaac Coffin), 43.
Gulf Stream, The, 70.

Hall, Hannah (Mrs. Joseph Sears), 230.
Halloweil, Anna (Davis), (Mrs. Richard Price Hallowell), 165.
Hallowell, Richard Price, 165.
Ham, John, 21.
Hamilton, James, Portsmouth, N. H., 231.
Hamilton, Phebe (Boughton), (Mrs. James Hamilton), 231.
Harker, Ebenezer, 225.
Harker, Hepzibah (Mrs. Jonathan Coffin, Sr), dau. Ebenezer Harker, 224, 225.
Harper, Robert, 77.
Harvey, Joanna (Mrs. Robert Barnard), 156, 157, 159, 193, 194, 212, 214, 219.
Hathaway connection with Nantucket families, 183.
Hathaway, Hepzibah (Mrs. Samuel Wing, Jr.), 184, 186.
Hathaway, Hepzibah (Starbuck), (Mrs. Thomas Hathaway), 184.
Hathaway, Hepzibah, dau. Thomas, 184.
Hathaway, Thomas, 184.
Hazard, Elizabeth (Mrs. George Lawton), dau. Thomas Hazard, 142, 146, 193, 218, 219.

Hazard Family, 146.
Hazard, Martha, 219.
Hazard, Martha (Mrs. Thomas Hazard), 142, 146, 193, 219.
Hazard, Martha (Sheriff), (Mrs. Thomas Hazard, 2d wife), 146.
Hazard, Thomas, 142, 145, 146, 193, 194, 219.
Hazard, Thomas, will of, 146.
Henderson, Patrick, 131.
Herioff, an Icelander, 1.
Hill, James, 47.
Hinchman, Ann (Mrs. John Thorne), 422.
Hinchman, John, 242.
Hinchman, Letitia (Mrs. Thomas Thorne), 241, 242.
Hobart, Abigail, dau. Rev. Peter Hobart, 85.
Hobart, Bathsheba, dau. Rev. Peter Hobart, 84.
Hobart, David, son Rev. Peter Hobart, 85.
Hobart, Edmund, 151, 157.
Hobart, Edmund, father Rev. Peter Hobart, 85.
Hobart, Edmund, Jr., son Edmund Hobart, Sr., 85.
Hobart, Elizabeth, dau. Rev. Peter Hobart, 84.
Hobart, Gershon, son Rev. Peter Hobart, 85.
Hobart, Hannah, dau. Rev. Peter Hobart, died soon, 84.
Hobart, Hannah (Mrs. John Brown, Sr.), dau. Rev. Peter Hobart, 83, 84, 150, 151, 157.
Hobart, Ichabod, son Rev. Peter Hobart, 84.
Hobart, Israel, son Rev. Peter Hobart, 85.
Hobart, Jael, dau. Rev. Peter Hobart, 85.
Hobart, Japhet, son Rev. Peter Hobart, 85.
Hobart, Jeremiah, son Rev. Peter Hobart, 84.
Hobart, Joanna (Quincy), (Mrs. David Hobart), 85.
Hobart, Joshua, son Edmund Hobart, 85.
Hobart, Joshua, son Rev. Peter Hobart, 84.
Hobart, Josiah, son Rev. Peter Hobart, 84.
Hobart, Lydia, dau. Rev. Peter Hobart, 85.
Hobart, Margaret (Dewey), (Mrs. Edmund Hobart), 151, 157.
Hobart, Nehemiah, son Rev. Peter Hobart, 85.
Hobart (or Hubberd), Peter, Rev., son Edmund Hobart, 83, 151, 157.

Index. 339

Hobart, Rebecca, dau. Edmund Hobart, 85.
Hobart, Rebecca, dau. Rev. Peter Hobart, 85.
Hobart, Sarah, dau. Edmund, 85.
Hobart, Sarah (Jackson), (Mrs. Nehemiah Hobart), 85.
Hobart, Sarah (Joyce), (Mrs. David Hobart), 85.
Hobart, Sarah (Wetherall), (Mrs. Israel Hobart), 85.
Hobart, Thomas, son Edmund, 85.
Hodge intermarriage, 69.
Holder, Christopher, 59, 87, 192, 194.
Holder, Mary (Scott), (Mrs. Christopher Holder), 192.
Holder, Mary (Mrs. Peleg Slocum), dau. Christopher Holder, 191, 192.
Holway, Elizabeth (Mrs. Lindley Moore Wing), 186, 187.
Hopcot, Sarah (Mrs. Thomas Macy, Sr.), 143, 144, 145, 149, 151, 153, 154, 161, 163, 167, 172, 173, 181, 182, 195, 196, 197, 198, 200, 201, 202, 203, 206, 209, 211, 214, 221, 222, 223.
Hopkins, Lydia Matilda (Bicknell), (Mrs. Norman Fox Hopkins), 226.
Hopkins, Norman Fox, 226.
Hopper, Ann (Mott), (Mrs. Edward Hopper), 164.
Hopper, Edward, 164.
Hopper, George, son Edward, 165.
Hopper, Isaac, son Edward, 165.
Hopper, James, son Edward, 164.
Hopper, Lucretia, dau. Edward, 164.
Hopper, Maria, dau. Edward, 165.
Hosier, Elizabeth (Mitchell), (Mrs. Giles Hosier), 216, 220.
Hosier, Elizabeth (Mrs. Caleb Coggeshall), dau. Giles Hosier, 216, 220.
Hosier, Giles, 216, 220.
Howland, Ann (Mrs. Sands Wing), 186.
Howland, Arthur, 77.
Howland, Arthur, brother John Howland, 77.
Howland, Arthur, Jr., son Arthur, 78.
Howland, Desire (Mrs. John Gorham, Sr.), 171, 173, 196, 199, 201, 202, 203, 209, 229.
Howland, Desire, dau. John Howland, 172, 198, 200, 205, 230.
Howland, Elizabeth (Tilley), (Mrs. John Howland), 172, 174, 198, 200, 201, 202, 204, 209, 230, 239, 240.
Howland, John, 77, 78, 172, 173, 174, 198, 200, 201, 202, 204, 209, 230, 239, 241.
Howland, Henry, 77.
Hudson, Settling the City of, 113.
Humphrey intermarriage, 69.
Hussey, Abial (Brown), (Mrs. Sylvanus Hussey, Sr.), 150.

Hussey, Abigail, dau. Stephen Hussey, 54.
Hussey, Alice (Gray), (Mrs. Sylvanus Hussey, Jr., 1st wife), 183.
Hussey, Ann (Coffin), (Mrs. Batchelder Hussey), 206.
Hussey, Batchiller, son Stephen Hussey, 54.
Hussey, Batchelder, son Sylvanus Hussey, Sr., 166, 206.
Hussey, Benjamin, 113.
Hussey, Christopher, son John Hussey, 4, 5, 9, 50, 52, 53, 60, 61, 145, 150, 151, 153, 154, 166, 167, 171, 173, 183, 185, 197, 201, 206, 210, 213, 214, 234, 239, 241.
Hussey, Daniel, son Stephen Hussey, 54.
Hussey, Deborah (Paddack), (Mrs. George Hussey), 166, 170.
Hussey, Elizabeth (Robinson), (Mrs. Joseph Hussey), widow Henry Tibbetts, 235.
Hussey, George, son Stephen Hussey, 54.
Hussey, George, son Sylvanus Hussey, Sr., 166, 170.
Hussey, Hepzibah (Starbuck), (Mrs. Sylvanus Hussey, Sr.), 166, 171, 183, 206.
Hussey, Hulda, dau. Christopher Hussey, 53.
Hussey, Jane (Mrs. Richard Hussey), 235.
Hussey, John, 50, 51.
Hussey, John, son Christopher Hussey, 53, 54, 153, 154, 213, 214.
Hussey, John, son John Hussey, 51.
Hussey, John, items concerning, 51.
Hussey, Joseph, son Richard Hussey, 235.
Hussey, Lydia (Macy), (Mrs. Josiah Hussey), 203, 209, 210.
Hussey, Lydia (Wing), (Mrs. Sylvanus Hussey, Jr., 2d wife), 183, 185.
Hussey, Lydia (Folger), (Mrs. Zaccheus Hussey), 206.
Hussey, Lydia, dau. Zaccheus Hussey, 206.
Hussey, Martha (Bunker), (Mrs. Stephen Hussey), 53, 150, 166, 167, 171, 183, 197, 206, 210, 239, 240.
Hussey, Mary (Mrs. Thomas Earle), 167.
Hussey, Mary (Wood), (Mrs. John Hussey), 50, 51.
Hussey, Mary (Mrs. Moses Swett), dau. John Hussey, 152, 153, 213, 214.
Hussey, Mary, dau. Christopher Hussey, 53.
Hussey, Mercy (Evans), (Mrs. Samuel Hussey), 235.

Hussey, Paul, 113.
Hussey, Phebe (Folger), (Mrs. Uriel Hussey), 166, 167.
Hussey, Puella (Mrs. Shubael Gorham, Sr.), dau. Stephen Hussey, 54, 196, 197.
Hussey, Rachel (Mrs. Barnabas Coleman), dau. Sylvanus Hussey, 62, 150.
Hussey, Rebecca (Perkins), (Mrs. John Hussey), 53, 153, 154, 213, 214.
Hussey, Richard, progenitor of Whittier Family, 234, 235, 236.
Hussey, Samuel, son Joseph Hussey, 235.
Hussey, Sarah (Mrs. John Milton Earle), 167.
Hussey, Sarah (Folger), (Mrs. Tristram Hussey), 166.
Hussey, Stephen, 117, 122, 129, 132.
Hussey, Stephen, son Christopher Hussey, 52, 53, 62, 150, 166, 167, 171, 183, 197, 206, 210, 239, 241.
Hussey, Susanna (Mrs. Zenas Gardner), dau. George Hussey, 169, 170.
Hussey, Sylvanus, Sr., son Stephen Hussey, 54, 62, 150, 166, 171, 183, 206.
Hussey, Sylvanus, Jr., 183, 185.
Hussey, Theodate (Bachelor), (Mrs. Christopher Hussey), 52, 56, 150, 151, 153, 154, 166, 167, 171, 173, 183, 185, 197, 201, 206, 210, 213, 214, 239.
Hussey, Theodata, dau. Stephen Hussey, 54.
Hussey, Theodata, dau. Christopher Hussey, 53.
Hussey, Tristram, 166.
Hussey, Tristram, son Batchelder Hussey, 166.
Hussey, Uriel, son George Hussey, 166, 167.
Hussey, Zaccheus, 206.
Hutchins, Frances (Mrs. John Hutchins), 233.
Hutchins, John, 233.

Irwin intermarriage, 60.

Jackson, Sarah (Mrs. Nehemiah Hobart), 85.
Jacob, Mary (Mrs. John Otis), 172, 200, 202, 204, 209.
Janney, Mary (Mrs. Joseph Drinker), 164.
Jenkins, Charles, 113.
Jenkins, John, Jr., 77.
Jenkins, Thomas, 113.
Johnson, Hannah (Mrs. Paul Wing Newhall), 189, 190.
Johnson, Jane (Mrs. Barney Gorham), 229.
Johnson, Mary, widow Edward Johnson, 61.

Johnson, Samuel, 190.
Johnson, Sarah (Challis), (Mrs. Samuel Johnson), 190.

Keen, Abigail (Mrs. Prince Barker), dau. Benjamin Keen, 190, 191.
Keen, Benjamin, 191, 194.
Keen, Deborah (Barker), Mrs. Benjamin Keen), 191.
Kent, Sarah (Mrs. Samuel Greenleaf), 228.
Kimball, Abigail (Mrs. John Severance), dau. Richard Kimball, 184.
Kimball, Richard, 184.
Kimball, Ursula (Scott), (Mrs. Richard Kimball), 184.
Kirby, Richard, Jr., 77.
Knapp, Ann (Mrs. Thomas Philbrick, Jr.), dau. William Knapp, 157, 193.
Knapp, William, 157.
Knight, George, Sir, 5.

Lamson, Edwin, 174.
Lamson, Mary (Swift), (Mrs. Edwin Lamson), 174.
Lawrence, —— (Bunker), (Mrs. Hon. S. Abbott Lawrence), 237.
Lawton, Elizabeth (Hazzard), (Mrs. George Lawton), 142, 146, 193, 218.
Lawton, George, 142, 145, 146, 193, 194, 218, 219.
Lawton, Mercy (Mrs. James Tripp), dau. George Lawton, 142, 146, 192, 193, 194, 217, 218, 219.
Lawton, Naomi (Mrs. Henry Corbit Davis), 165.
Lea & Bunker, 237.
Le Clerc, as connected with the Coffins, 25.
Leddra, William, 91, 94.
Letter to the Magistrates of Salem (1658), 87.
Lincoln, Lydia (Hobart), (Mrs. Thomas Lincoln), 85.
Lincoln, Thomas, Captain, 85.
Linkham, Julian Rumsey, 165.
Linkham, Mary Mott (Lord), (Mrs. Julian Rumsey Linkham), 165.
Little, Eleanor (Barnard), (Mrs. Thomas Little), 64.
Little, George, 64.
Lloyd, Anna (Lord), (Mrs. Herbert M. Lloyd), 165.
Lloyd, Herbert M., 165.
Long, Robert, 48.
Look, Elizabeth (Mrs. Thomas Look), 158.
Look, Experience (Mrs. Stephen Coffin, Jr.), dau. Thomas Look, 158.
Look, Thomas, 11, 158, 159.
Lord, Anna, dau. George W. Lord, 165.

Lord, Bessie, dau. George W. Lord, 165.
Lord, Ellen, dau. George W. Lord, 165.
Lord, George W., 164, 165.
Lord, Lucretia, dau. George W. Lord, 165.
Lord, Martha (Mott), (Mrs. George W. Lord), 164, 165.
Lord, Mary Mott, dau. George W. Lord, 165.
Lovelace, Francis, Esq., 26.
Lovelace, Governor, 12, 81.

McKenzie, Alexander, 224.
McKenzie, Hepzibeth, (Mrs. Martin McKenzie), 224.
McKenzie, Martin, 224.
Macy, Abigail (Mrs. Benjamin Stanton), dau. David Macy, 221, 223.
Macy, Abraham1, son Richard Macy, 195, 201.
Macy, Abraham2, son Abraham1, 195.
Macy, Abraham3, son Abraham Macy2, 195, 198.
Macy, Abraham, Descendants, 201.
Macy, Abraham, Family of, 195.
Macy, Ann Eliza (Macy), (Mrs. Isaac Macy), 210.
Macy, Anna (Worth), (Mrs. Abraham Macy1), 195.
Macy, Catharine C. (Mrs. Townsend Powell), 195, 202.
Macy, David, son John Macy, Jr., 221.
Macy, Deborah (Mrs. Benjamin Coffin), dau. Thomas Macy, Jr., 160, 161.
Macy, Deborah (Coffin), (Mrs. Thomas3 Macy), 143, 161, 181, 211.
Macy, Deborah (Gardner), (Mrs. John Macy, Sr.), 143, 149, 181, 195, 198, 203, 211, 221.
Macy, Deborah (Coggeshall), (Mrs. Paul Macy), 216.
Macy, Deborah (Pinkham), (Mrs. Richard Macy), 195.
Macy, Deborah (Mrs. Daniel Russell), dau. John Macy, 149.
Macy, Deborah, dau. Francis Macy, 102.
Macy, Dinah (Gardner), (Mrs. David Macy), 221.
Macy, Elizabeth (Coleman), (Mrs. Abraham Macy), 195, 198, 201.
Macy, Elizabeth (Mrs. Francis Barnard), dau. Thomas3 Macy, 211.
Macy, Elizabeth (Mrs. Elihu Coleman), dau. Jonathan Macy, 198.
Macy, Francis, son Thomas Macy, 143.
Macy, Francis, extract of will of, 102.
Macy, Francis, Jr., son Francis Macy, 102.

Macy, George, 18.
Macy, Isaac, son Thomas Macy, 210.
Macy, John, 18.
Macy, John, Sr., son Thomas Macy, 143, 149, 161, 181, 195, 198, 203, 211, 221.
Macy, John, Jr., son John Macy, Sr., 198, 203, 221.
Macy, Jonathan, Jr., son Jonathan Macy, Sr., 203.
Macy, Jonathan, Sr., son John Macy, 198, 203.
Macy, Josiah, son Jonathan Macy, 203, 209, 210.
Macy, Josiah, Family of, 203.
Macy, Josiah H., 210.
Macy, Lois (Gorham), (Mrs. Jonathan Macy, Sr.), 198, 203.
Macy, Love (Mrs. James Cartwright), dau. Francis Macy, 142, 143.
Macy, Love, dau. Thomas3 Macy, 181.
Macy, Judith (Coffin), (Mrs. Francis Macy), 143.
Macy, Judith (Worth), (Mrs. John Macy, Jr.), 198, 203, 221.
Macy, Lydia Hussey (Mrs. William R. Austin), widow Jonathan Hasbrouck Stanton, Esq., 210.
Macy, Lydia (Mrs. Josiah Hussey), 203, 209, 210.
Macy, Mary (Mrs. William Bunker), dau. Thomas Macy, 144, 153, 162, 163, 172, 195, 196, 199, 201, 205, 208, 209, 238, 239, 240.
Macy, name signifies, 18.
Macy, Paul, 216.
Macy, Priscilla (Bunker), (Mrs. Abraham2 Macy), 195.
Macy, Richard, son John Macy, 195.
Macy, Rose (Pinkham), (Mrs. Jonathan Macy, Jr.), 203.
Macy, Samuel, 18.
Macy, Sarah (Hopcot), (Mrs. Thomas Macy, Sr.), 18, 143, 144, 145, 149, 151, 153, 154, 161, 163, 167, 172, 173, 181, 182, 195, 196, 197, 198, 200, 201, 202, 203, 206, 209, 211, 214, 221, 222, 223, 239.
Macy, Sarah (Mrs. William Worth), dau. Thomas Macy, 196, 197, 199, 200, 222.
Macy, Thomas, Sr., 3, 4, 5, 8, 9, 14, 15, 20, 26, 60, 63, 68, 143, 144, 145, 149, 151, 153, 154, 161, 163, 167, 172, 173, 181, 182, 190, 195, 196, 197, 198, 200, 201, 202, 203, 206, 209, 211, 214, 221, 222, 223, 240, 241.
Macy, Thomas3, son John Macy, 143, 161, 181, 211.
Macy, Thomas, removes to Nantucket, 17.
Mandamus to the Governors in New England, 90.

Index. 341

Marston, Prudence (Mrs. William Swain), 65, 228.
Mason, Daniel, 85.
Mason, Rebecca (Hobart), (Mrs. Daniel Mason), 85.
Maxfield, Daniel C., 187.
Maxfield, Alice (Rogers, Wing), (Mrs. Daniel C. Maxfield), 187.
Mayhew, Experience, son John Mayhew, 99.
Mayhew, the first known in England, 96.
Mayhew, Jane (Paine), (Mrs. Thomas Mayhew, Jr.), 162, 163, 167, 208, 210.
Mayhew, John, son Thomas Mayhew, Jr., 99.
Mayhew, Jonathan, son Experience Mayhew, 99.
Mayhew, Mary (Rankin), (Mrs. Paine Mayhew), 162, 208.
Mayhew, Mary (Skiffe), (Mrs. Matthew Mayhew), 162, 208.
Mayhew, Matthew, son Thomas Mayhew, Jr., 99, 162, 208.
Mayhew, Paine, son Matthew Mayhew, 162, 208.
Mayhew, Sarah (Mrs. Abishai Folger), dau. Paine Mayhew, 161, 162, 206, 208.
Mayhew, Thomas, Jr., son Thomas Mayhew, Sr., 11, 67, 96, 99, 162, 163, 167, 208, 210.
Mayhew, Thomas, Sr., 3, 5, 6, 9, 68, 96, 97, 162, 163, 167, 208, 210.
Mayhew, Thomas, deed by, 4.
Mayhew, Thomas, son of Thomas, Jr., 99.
Meader, Ann, dau. Eliner Meader, 34.
Meader, Eliner, 34.
Meader, Nicolas, 37.
Mellor, Martha (Mrs. Henry Corbit Davis), 165.
Merrick, Sarah (Mrs. John2 Freeman), 229.
Mitchell, Ann (Folger), (Mrs. James Mitchell), 192, 217.
Mitchell, Elizabeth (Mrs. Giles Hosier), dau. James Mitchell, 216, 217.
Mitchell, Elizabeth (Tripp), (Mrs. Richard2 Mitchell), 141, 192, 217, 219.
Mitchell Family, 141.
Mitchell, Henry, Prof., 73.
Mitchell, Hepzibah, dau. James Mitchell, 192.
Mitchell, James, son Richard Mitchell, Jr., 192, 217.
Mitchell, Love (Mrs. Judge Brayton), 145.
Mitchell, Lydia (Cartwright), (Mrs. Peleg Mitchell, Sr.), 141, 145, 146.
Mitchell, Lydia (Coleman), (Mrs. William Mitchell), 73.

Mitchell, Maria, dau. William Mitchell, 12, 73, 146.
Mitchell, Mary (Starbuck), (Mrs. Richard3 Mitchell), 141.
Mitchell, Mary (Wood), (Mrs. Richard1 Mitchell), 141, 142, 192, 194, 217, 219.
Mitchell, Mercy (Mrs. Caleb Coggeshall), 216.
Mitchell, Peleg, Sr., son Richard3 Mitchell, 141, 145, 146.
Mitchell, Peleg, Sr., descendants of, 145.
Mitchell, Richard1, 141, 145, 192, 194, 217, 219.
Mitchell, Richard2, son Richard1 Mitchell, 141, 192, 217, 219.
Mitchell, Richard3, son Richard2 Mitchell, 141.
Mitchell, William, 73.
Mooer, Edward, 213.
Mooer, Jonathan, 213.
Mooers, Elizabeth (Mrs. Daniel Coleman), dau. Jonathan Mooers, 213.
Mooers, Jonathan, 213.
Moore, Katharine (Swift), (Mrs. Marcus A. Moore), 174.
Moore, Marcus A., 174.
Morrill, Abraham, 228.
Morrill, Eleanor (True), (Mrs. Abraham Morrill), 228.
Morrill, Lydia (Trask), (Mrs. William Morrill), 228.
Morrill, Lydia (Mrs. John Colcord), dau. William Morrill, 227.
Morrill, Mary (Mrs. Peter Folger), 144, 150, 151, 152, 153, 156, 157, 158, 162, 163, 167, 192, 194, 197, 199, 201, 202, 207, 210, 213, 214, 217, 219, 225, 226.
Morrill, William, son Abraham, 228.
Morse, Benjamin, 33.
Morse, Margaret, dau. Benjamin Morse, 33.
Mott, Ann (Mrs. Edward Hopper), dau. James Mott, 164.
Mott, Elizabeth (Mrs. Thomas S. Cavender), 164, 165.
Mott, Emily (Mrs. George R. Shaw), 165.
Mott, Hannah (Mrs. Abraham Tucker), dau. Jacob Mott, 191, 192.
Mott, Isabel (Mrs. Joseph Parish), 165.
Mott, Jacob, 192, 194.
Mott, James, 163, 164.
Mott, Joanna (Slocum), (Mrs. Jacob Mott), 192, 194.
Mott, Lucretia (Coffin), (Mrs. James Mott), 160, 163, 164.
Mott, Lucretia, Family of, 160, 167.
Mott, Lucretia, Letters of, 160.
Mott, Maria (Mrs. Edward Morris Davis), dau. James Mott, 164, 165.

Mott, Maria, dau. Thomas Mott, 165.
Mott, Marianna (Pelham), (Mrs. Thomas Mott), 164, 165.
Mott, Martha (Mrs. George W. Lord), 164, 165.
Mott, Thomas, 164, 165.
Mott, Thomas, son James Mott, 164.
Moulton, " Willm.", 35.
" Mourts Relation," 174.

Nanahumo of Nantucket, 7.
Nantucket, An Impartial Judgment, 133.
Nantucket, Customs, Documents and Incidents of, 100.
Nantucket, Friends' meetings first held, 129.
Nantucket, J. Richardson's meeting at Mary Starbuck's was convened, 124.
Nantucket, losses in Revolutionary War, 118.
Nantucket, ministers visiting the island, 126.
Nantucket, Mr. Arthur Ketchum's sonnet respecting, 118.
Nantucket Monthly Meeting established, 131.
Nantucket, the neutral position of during the Revolutionary War, 111, 114.
Nantucket, oldest house on, 66.
Nantucket, removals from, 113.
Nantucket, rise of the Friends' Society, 120.
Nantucket (Sherburne), 79.
Nantucket, Town Meeting incident, 108.
Nantucket, visit of John Kinsey, 127.
Nantucket, the whale fishery of, 111, 115.
Naumkeag, now Salem, 80.
Newbury, early settlers, 46, 52.
Newhall, Abby, dau. Paul Wing Newhall, 189.
Newhall, Abby W. (Mrs. Micajah Pratt), 189.
Newhall, Barker, son Joseph Philbrick Newhall, 190.
Newhall, Catharine Johnson, dau. Paul Wing Newhall, 189.
Newhall connection with Nantucket families, 189.
Newhall, Daniel5, 189.
Newhall, Elizabeth (" Huntington " Barker), (Mrs. Joseph Philbrick Newhall), 189, 190, 193.
Newhall, Elizabeth (Potter), (Mrs. Thomas2 Newhall), 189.
Newhall, Elizabeth, dau. Paul Wing Newhall, 190.
Newhall, Estes6, 189.

Early Settlers of Nantucket.

Newhall, George, son Paul Wing Newhall, 189.
Newhall, Hannah (Estes), (Mrs. Daniel5 Newhall), 189.
Newhall, Hannah (Johnson), (Mrs. Paul Wing Newhall), 189, 190.
Newhall, Hepzibah (Wing), (Mrs. Estes6 Newhall, 1st wife), 189.
Newhall, Joseph3, 189.
Newhall, Joseph Philbrick, son Estes Newhall, 189, 190, 193.
Newhall, Keziah (Breed), (Mrs. Samuel4 Newhall), 189.
Newhall, Maria, dau. Paul Wing Newhall, 190.
Newhall, Mary, dau. Paul Wing Newhall, 190.
Newhall, Miriam (Philbrick), (Mrs. Estes6 Newhall, 2d wife), 189.
Newhall, Paul Wing, son Estes Newhall, 189, 190.
Newhall, Philena (Marshall, Peterson), (Mrs. William Estes Newhall), 189.
Newhall, Samuel4, 189.
Newhall, Sarah Johnson, dau. Paul Wing Newhall, 189.
Newhall, Susanna (Farrar), (Mrs. Joseph3 Newhall), 189.
Newhall, Thomas1, 189.
Newhall, Thomas2, 189.
Newhall, William Estes, son Paul Wing Newhall, 189.
Newland, William, 77.
Newport, settlement of, 146.
Nickanoose, of Nantucket, 7.
Nine Partners, deed to, 5.
Norman, Lucy Latham (Mrs. David Stanton), 221.
Noyes, Nicholas, 48.
Noyes, Thomas, Captain, 48.

Odar, Anthony, 213, 214.
Odar, Elizabeth (Mrs. Jonathan Mooers), dau. Anthony Odar, 213.
Odar, Sarah Folger (Mrs. Anthony Odar), 213, 214.
Otis, John, 172, 173, 200, 202, 204, 209, 230, 241.
Otis, Mary (Jacob), (Mrs. John Otis), 172, 200, 202, 204, 209, 239.
Otis, Mary (Mrs. John Gorham, Jr.), dau. John Otis, 171, 172, 199, 200, 203, 230.

Paddack, Ann (Bunker), (Mrs. Nathaniel Paddack), 152, 171, 199, 204, 238.
Paddack, Daniel, son Nathaniel, 171, 238.
Paddack, Deborah (Sears), (Mrs. Zechariah Paddack), 152, 153, 166, 171, 173, 199, 202, 204, 209, 238.
Paddack, Deborah (Mrs. George Hussey), dau. Daniel Paddack, 166, 170.
Paddack, Lydia (Mrs. Jethro Coleman), dau. Nathaniel Paddack, 198, 199, 204.
Paddack, Mary (Mrs. Robert Paddack), 152, 171, 199, 204.
Paddack, Mary (Mrs. Francis Swain, Sr.), dau. Nathaniel Paddack, 152.
Paddack, Nathaniel, son Zechariah Paddack, 152, 171, 199, 204, 238.
Paddack, Robert, 152, 171, 173, 199, 204, 238, 240.
Paddack, Stephen, 113.
Paddack, Susanna (Gorham), (Mrs. Daniel Paddack), 171, 238.
Paddack, "Zechariah," son Robert Paddack, 152, 153, 171, 173, 199, 202, 204, 209, 238, 241.
Paige, Anna (Wing), (Mrs. Elwood Paige), 187.
Paige, Elwood, 187.
Paine, Anthony, 142.
Paine, Jane (Mrs. Thomas Mayhew, Jr.), 162, 163, 167, 208, 210.
Paine, Mary (Mrs. John Tripp), 192, 194, 219.
Paine, Mary, dau. Anthony Paine, 142.
Paine, Susanna (Mrs. Anthony Paine), 142.
Parish, Fanny (Cavender), (Mrs. Thomas Parish), 165.
Parish, Isabel Mott (Mrs. Joseph Parish), 165.
Parish, Joseph, 165.
Parish, Thomas, 165.
Paul, Hannah C. (Bunker), (Mrs. James W. Paul), 237.
Peaslee, Joseph, 236.
Peaslee, Ruth (Barnard), (Mrs. Joseph Peaslee), 236.
Pelham, Marianna (Mrs. Thomas Mott), 164, 165.
Pelham, Martha (Coffin), (Mrs. Peter Pelham), 163.
Pelham, Peter, 163.
Pepper intermarriage, 69.
Perry, Edward, 77.
Perry, Elizabeth (Wing), (Mrs. John S. Perry), 187.
Perry intermarriage, 69.
Perry, John S., 187.
Perry, Mary (Mrs. John Wing), 188.
Perkins, Isaac, 214.
Perkins, Rebecca (Mrs. John Hussey), dau. Isaac Perkins, 53, 153, 154, 213, 214.
Perkins, Susanna (Mrs. Isaac Perkins), 214.

Peterson, Philena (Marshall), (Mrs. William Estes Newhall), 189.
Phelps, Nichols, banished from England, 89.
Philbrick, Ann (Knapp), (Mrs. Thomas Philbrick, Jr.), 157, 193.
Philbrick, Elizabeth (Mrs. Thomas Philbrick, Sr.), 193.
Philbrick, Elizabeth (Mrs. Thomas Chase), dau. Thomas Philbrick, 156, 157, 193.
Philbrick, Miriam (Mrs. Estes6 Newhall), 189.
Philbrick, Samuel, son Thomas, Jr., 193.
Philbrick, Thomas, 157.
Philbrick, Thomas, Jr., son Thomas Philbrick, Sr., 193.
Philbrick, Thomas, Sr., from England, 193.
Phillips, Elizabeth (Swift), (Mrs. John E. Phillips), 174.
Phillips, John E., 174.
Pickett, Joanna (Mrs. John4 Freeman), 229.
Pierce, Daniel, 48.
Pierce, David, 48.
Pierce, Elbridge Gerry, 229.
Pierce, Elizabeth Carrol (Mrs. Dole Wudley), dau. Elbridge Gerry Pierce, 227, 229.
Pierce, Elizabeth Carrol, descendants, 230.
Pierce, Sarah Jane (Gorham), (Mrs. Elbridge Gerry Pierce), 229.
Pike Family, 60.
Pike, Robert, 9, 11, 14, 17, 60.
Pike, William, 4, 5.
Pile, William, 68.
Pinkham, Ann (Starbuck), (Mrs. Reuben Pinkham), 203.
Pinkham, Deborah (Mrs. Richard Macy), dau. Richard Pinkham, 195, 196.
Pinkham, Deborah (Paddack), (Mrs. Theophilus Pinkham), 203.
Pinkham, Mary (Coffin), (Mrs. Richard Pinkham), 196, 203, 209.
Pinkham, Reuben, son Theophilus Pinkham, 203.
Pinkham, Richard, 106, 201, 203, 209.
Pinkham, Rose (Mrs. Jonathan Macy, Jr.), dau. Reuben Pinkham, 203.
Pinkham, Theophilus, son Richard, 203.
Plymouth Colony and the Quakers, 77.
Pond, Elizabeth (Wing), (Mrs. Fred Pond), 187.
Potter, Elizabeth (Mrs. Thomas2 Newhall), 189.
Powell, Aaron Macy, son Townsend Powell, 202.

Index. 343

Powell, Catharine C. (Macy), (Mrs. Townsend Powell), 195, 202.
Powell, Elizabeth (Mrs. Herrick Bond), 202.
Powell, George T., son Townsend Powell, 202.
Powell, James, 195.
Powell, Judith Anna (Rice), (Mrs. Aaron Powell), 202.
Powell, Marcia (Chace), (Mrs. George T. Powell), 202.
Powell, Martha (Townsend), (Mrs. James Powell), 195.
Powell, Townsend, son James Powell, 195, 202.
Pratt, Abby W. (Newhall), (Mrs. Micajah Pratt), 189.
Pratt, Bethiah (Mrs. Sampson Cartwright), dau. Joseph Pratt, 143.
Pratt, Dorcas (Folger), (Mrs. Joseph Pratt), 143.
Pratt, Joseph, son Phineas Pratt, 143.
Pratt, Mary (Priest), (Mrs. Phineas Pratt), 143.
Pratt, Micajah, 189.
Pratt, Phineas, 143.
Prence, Elizabeth (Mrs. Arthur Howland), 78.
Prence, Judith (Mrs. Isaac Barker), dau. Governor Thomas Prence, 74, 75, 155, 156, 190.
Prence, Mary (Brewster), (Mrs. Governor Thomas Prence), 230.
Prence, Mary (Collier), (Mrs. Governor Thomas Prence), 75, 156, 157, 159, 191, 194, 230.
Prence, Mercy (Mrs. John Freeman), dau. Governor Thomas Prence, 229, 230.
Prence, Thomas, Governor, 75, 77, 156, 157, 159, 191, 194, 230.
Priest, Degory, 144, 145, 148.
Priest, Mary (Mrs. Phineas Pratt), dau. Degory Priest, 143, 144.
Priest, Sarah (Allerton, Vincent), (Mrs. Degory Priest), 144, 148.
Providence Friends' School, established, 180.

Quakers released by order of court, 93.
Quincy, Edmund, 85.
Quincy, Joanna, dau. Edmund Quincy, 85.

Rankin, Mary (Mrs. Paine Mayhew), 162, 208.
Reynear, Rachel (Mrs. John Drinker), 164.

Reynolds, Katharine (Mrs. Edward Starbuck), 145, 149, 150, 151, 161, 163, 167, 169, 170, 171, 173, 181, 182, 183, 185, 190, 193, 194, 197, 199, 201, 202, 204, 206, 207, 209, 212, 213, 214, 216, 218, 219, 222, 223, 225, 226, 232.
Rhodes, Samuel, 187.
Rhodes, Sophia (Mrs. Asa Shove Wing), 187.
Rice, Judith Anna (Mrs. Aaron Powell), 202.
Richardson, John, his visit to Nantucket, 122.
Ripley, Elizabeth (Hobart), (Mrs. John Ripley), 84.
Robinson, William, 15, 94.
Rocomb, Ebenezer, 131.
Rogers, Anna (Mrs. Samuel Wing), 186.
Rogers, Beulah R. (Wing), (Mrs. Moses Folger Rogers), 186, 187.
Rogers, Moses Folger, 186, 187.
Rolfe, Henry, brother John, 234.
Rolfe, John, 68, 234.
Rotch, Elizabeth Barney (Mrs. William Rotch, Jr.), 160, 182.
Rotch, Elizabeth, dau. Joseph Rotch, 177.
Rotch, Francis, son Joseph Rotch, 177, 180.
Rotch, Hannah (Mrs. William Rotch), 180.
Rotch, Joseph, son William Rotch, 176, 180.
Rotch, Love (Macy), (Mrs. Joseph Rotch), 180.
Rotch, Mary, 176.
Rotch, William, father Joseph Rotch, 180.
Rotch, William, son Joseph Rotch, 114, 117, 176, 177, 179, 180, 182.
Russell, Deborah (Macy), (Mrs. Daniel Russell), 149.
Russell, Daniel, 149.
Russell Family, 149.
Russell, Hepzibah (Coleman), (Mrs. John Russell, Jr.), 149, 151.
Russell, John, 151.
Russell, John, Sr., son Daniel Russell, 149.
Russell, John, Jr., son John Russell, Sr., 149.
Russell, Mary (Mrs. John Cornell), 215.
Russell, Ruth (Starbuck), (Mrs. John Russell, Sr.), 149.

Salisbury and Amesbury, "Old Families," 63.
Salisbury, name changed, 63.
Sandwich Meeting of Friends, 59.
Sandwich, settlement of, 58.

Scott, Martha (Mrs. Henry Scott), 184.
Scott, Mary (Mrs. Christopher Holder), 192.
Scott, Ursula (Mrs. Richard Kimball), 184.
Sears, Anna (Bursell), (Mrs. Silas Sears), 230.
Sears, Rev. Barnes, 154.
Sears, Deborah (Mrs. Zechariah Paddack), dau. Richard Sears, 152, 153, 166, 171, 172, 173, 199, 200, 202, 204, 205, 209.
Sears, Dorothy (Thatcher), (Mrs. David Sears), 153.
Sears, Dorothy (Thatcher), (Mrs. Richard Sears), 154, 172, 173, 200, 202, 205, 209, 230, 239.
Sears, Hannah (Hall), (Mrs. Joseph Sears), 230.
Sears, Joseph, 230.
Sears, Priscilla (Mrs. Josiah Gorham), dau. Joseph Sears, 229, 230.
Sears, Richard, 153, 154, 166, 172, 173, 200, 202, 205, 209, 230, 230, 241.
Sears, Richard, extract from will of 200.
Sears, Silas, 230.
Sears, Thatcher, 200, 230.
Settlement of the island, 1.
Severance, Abigail, 28.
Severance, Abigail (Kimball), (Mrs. John Severance), 184.
Severance, John, 28, 63, 184, 190.
Severance, Mary (Mrs. James Coffin), dau. John Severance, 28, 143, 149, 151, 160, 162, 163, 167, 172, 173, 184, 193, 194, 197, 201, 204, 205, 208, 209, 210, 214, 217, 218, 219, 224, 225, 226.
Shattuck, Damaris (Mrs. Thomas Gardiner), 81, 86, 240.
Shattuck, Hannah (Gardner), (Mrs. George Gardner), 87.
Shattuck, Samuel, 86, 87, 89, 91, 92, 93, 94.
Shattuck, Sarah (Mrs. Richard Gardner), dau. Damaris Shattuck, 81, 86, 143, 144, 149, 150, 151, 158, 159, 161, 162, 163, 167, 169, 172, 173, 181, 182, 196, 197, 199, 200, 201, 202, 204, 205, 208, 209, 211, 212, 214, 218, 219, 221, 222, 223.
Shaw, Emily (Mott), (Mrs. George R. Shaw), 165.
Shaw, George R., 165.
Sheriff, Thomas, 146.
Skiffe, Mary (Mrs. Matthew Mayhew), 162, 208.
Sherburne, original name of Nantucket, 79.
Sherman, Avis (Waterman), (Mrs. John Sherman, Jr.), 226.
Sherman, David, 186.

Early Settlers of Nantucket.

Sherman, Lydia Spooner, dau. John Sherman, Jr., 226.
Sherman, Mary (Shove), (Mrs. David Sherman), 186.
Shove, Elizabeth (Collins), (Mrs. Stephen R. Wing), 186, 187.
Shove, Mary (Mrs. David Sherman), 186.
Slocum, Elizabeth (Mrs. Isaac Barker, Jr.), dau. Peleg Slocum, 190, 191.
Slocum, Giles, 192.
Slocum, Joan (Mrs. Giles Slocum), 192.
Slocum, Mary (Holder), (Mrs. Peleg Slocum), 191.
Slocum, Peleg, 122, 125, 191.
Slocum, Peleg, son Giles Slocum, 192, 194.
Slocum, Joanna (Mrs. Jacob Mott), dau. Giles Slocum, 192, 194.
Smith, Hulda (Hussey), (Mrs. John Smith), 53.
Smith, John, 11.
Smyth, Edw., 20.
Smyth, John, 9, 68.
Somerby, Elizabeth (Mrs. Nathaniel Clark), dau. Henry Somerby, 228.
Somerby, Henry, 28, 228.
Somerby, Judith (Greenleaf), (Mrs. Henry Somerby), 228.
Southwick, Cassandra, banished from England, 89.
Southwick, Josiah, son Laurence, banished from England, 89.
Southwick, Laurence, banished from England, 89.
Southworth, Elizabeth (Collier), (Mrs. Constant Southworth), 75.
Spooner, Lydia (Sherman), (Mrs. Simeon Smith Bicknell), 226.
Spurwill, Thomas, 35.
Standish, Miles, 58.
Stanton, Abigail (Macy), (Mrs. Benjamin Stanton), 221, 223.
Stanton, Avis (Mrs. Robert Stanton), 221.
Stanton, Benjamin, son Henry Stanton, 221, 223.
Stanton connection with Nantucket, 221.
Stanton, David, son Benjamin Stanton, 221.
Stanton, Edwin McMasters, son David Stanton, 216, 221.
Stanton, Henry, son John Stanton, 221.
Stanton, John, son Robert Stanton, 216, 221.
Stanton, Jonathan Hasbrouck, Esq., 210.
Stanton, Lucy Latham (Norman), (Mrs. David Stanton), 221.

Stanton, Lydia (Albertson), (Mrs. Henry Stanton), 221.
Stanton, Lydia Hussey (Macy), (Mrs. Jonathan Hasbrouck Stanton), 210.
Stanton, Mary (Clarke, Cranston), (Mrs. John Stanton), 221.
Stanton, Mary (Mrs. John Coggeshall), dau. John Stanton, 216, 219.
Stanton, Robert, 216, 221.
Starbuck, Abigail (Mrs. Peter1 Coffin), dau. Edward Starbuck, 224, 225, 226.
Starbuck, Ann (Tibbetts), (Mrs. Paul Starbuck), 204.
Starbuck, Ann (Mrs. Reuben Pinkham), dau. Paul Starbuck, 203, 204.
Starbuck, Barnabas, 132.
Starbuck, Benjamin, 113, 158.
Starbuck, Deborah (Mrs. Job Coggeshall), dau. Tristram Starbuck, 216.
Starbuck, Deborah (Coffin), (Mrs. Tristram Starbuck), 216.
Starbuck, Dinah (Mrs. Abishai Folger), 155, 158.
Starbuck, Dinah (Coffin), (Mrs. Nathaniel Starbuck, Jr.), 149, 171, 183, 193, 204, 207, 216, 218.
Starbuck, Dinah (Coffin), (Mrs. Benjamin Starbuck), 158.
Starbuck, Dorcas, 11, 132.
Starbuck, Dorcas (Mrs. William Gayer), dau. Edward Starbuck, 21, 142, 161, 163, 170, 181, 182.
Starbuck, Dorcas (Gayer, Sr.), (Mrs. Jethro Starbuck), 142, 169, 181.
Starbuck, Dorcas, dau. William Gayer, 105, 106, 107.
Starbuck, Edward, Sr., 3, 9, 11, 17, 19, 20, 21, 29, 68, 106, 142, 145, 149, 150, 151, 161, 163, 167, 169, 170, 171, 173, 181, 182, 183, 185, 190, 193, 194, 197, 199, 201, 202, 204, 206, 207, 209, 212, 213, 214, 216, 218, 219, 222, 223, 225, 226, 232, 240, 241.
Starbuck, Elizabeth, dau. Thomas Starbuck, 71.
Starbuck, Hepzibah (Mrs. Thomas Hathaway), dau. Nathaniel Starbuck, Sr., 184, 185.
Starbuck, Hepzibah (Mrs. Sylvanus Hussey, Sr.), dau. Nathaniel Starbuck, Jr., 166, 171, 183, 206, 207.
Starbuck, Jethro, 21, 30, 132.
Starbuck, Jethro, son Nathaniel Starbuck, Sr., 142, 169, 181.
Starbuck, Katharine (Reynolds), (Mrs. Edward Starbuck), 19, 20, 29, 142, 145, 149, 150, 151, 161, 163, 167, 169, 170, 171, 173, 181, 182, 183, 185, 190, 193, 194, 197, 199, 201, 202, 204, 206, 207, 209, 212, 213, 214, 216, 218, 219, 222, 223, 225, 226.

Starbuck, Lydia (Mrs. Benjamin Barney), 181.
Starbuck, Mary (Mrs. James Gardner), dau. Nathaniel Starbuck, Sr., 172, 200, 201, 204, 205.
Starbuck, Mary (Mrs. Jethro Folger), dau. Nathaniel Starbuck, Jr., 192, 193, 217, 218.
Starbuck, Mary (Coffin), (Mrs. Nathaniel Starbuck, Sr.), 21, 29, 30, 123, 126, 132, 142, 149, 150, 169, 171, 172, 181, 183, 185, 193, 197, 199, 201, 204, 205, 207, 212, 216, 218.
Starbuck, Mary, dau. Jethro Starbuck, 142.
Starbuck, name signifies, 23.
Starbuck, Nathaniel, Jr., son Nathaniel Starbuck, Sr., 123, 132, 149, 171, 183, 193, 204, 207, 216, 218.
Starbuck, Nathaniel, Sr., son Edward and Katharine Starbuck, 11, 21, 23, 29, 31, 68, 126, 128, 142, 149, 150, 169, 171, 172, 181, 183, 185, 193, 197, 199, 201, 204, 205, 207, 212, 216, 218, 240.
Starbuck, Paul, 204.
Starbuck, Priscilla (Mrs. John Coleman, Jr.), dau. Nathaniel Starbuck, Sr., 150, 196, 197, 198, 199.
Starbuck, Rachel (Mrs. Paul Gardner), dau. Thomas Starbuck, 169.
Starbuck, Rachel (Allen), (Mrs. Thomas Starbuck), 169.
Starbuck, Ruth (Mrs. John Russell, Sr.), dau. Nathaniel Starbuck, Jr., 149.
Starbuck, Samuel, 114, 117.
Starbuck, Sarah (Mrs. Joseph Austin), dau. Edward Starbuck, 144, 145, 161, 169, 170, 173, 181, 206, 210, 212, 213, 218, 219, 222.
Starbuck, Thomas, 71.
Starbuck, Thomas, son Jethro Starbuck, 169.
Starbuck, Tristram, son Nathaniel Starbuck, Jr., 216.
Stephenson, Marmaduke, 15, 94.
Sterling, William, Earl of, 4.
Stevens, Benjamin, 229.
Stevens, Dionis (Mrs. Tristram Coffin), 144, 145, 149, 151, 158, 159, 160, 161, 162, 163, 167, 169, 170, 172, 173, 181, 184, 185, 190, 193, 194, 197, 198, 200, 201, 202, 204, 205, 206, 207, 208, 209, 212, 214, 217, 218, 219, 222, 223, 224, 225, 226, 229, 230.
Stevens, Eleanor (Mrs. William True), dau. Benjamin Stevens, 229.
Stevens, Hannah (Barnard), (Mrs. Benjamin Stevens), 229.
Stevens, Patience (Mrs. Ebenezer Colcord), 227.
Stevens, Robert, 24.

Stoakes, Jane, referred to as first Friend visiting Nantucket, 130.
Story, Sarah (Starbuck), 21.
Story, Thomas, 126.
Story, William, 21.
Stratton, Elizabeth (Mrs. Daniel Coffin), 207.
Strauss, Albert, 165.
Strauss, Lucretia (Lord), (Mrs. Albert Strauss), 165.
Sturgis, Sarah (Mrs. Joseph Gorham), 229.
Swain, Caleb, son William Swain, 228.
Swain, Dorothy, dau. Richard Swain, Sr., 66, 152.
Swain, Elizabeth (Mrs. Nathaniel Weare), dau. Richard Swain, Sr., 66, 152.
Swain, Experience (Folger), (Mrs. John Swain, Jr.), 152.
Swain Family, 152.
Swain, Francis, Jr., son Francis Swain, Sr., 152, 153.
Swain, Francis, Sr., son John Swain3, 152.
Swain, Francis, son Richard Swain, Sr., 65.
Swain, Hannah (Mrs. Caleb Swain), 228.
Swain, Jane (Godfrey, Bunker), (Mrs. Richard Swain, Sr.), 65, 66.
Swain, John, son Richard Swain, Sr., 4, 9, 66, 68, 122, 129, 152.
Swain, John, Jr., son John Swain, Sr., 152.
Swain, John, 3d, son John Swain, Jr., 152, 153.
Swain, Lydia (Barker), (Mrs. Francis Swain, Jr.), 152, 153.
Swain, Mary (Paddack), (Mrs. Francis Swain, Sr.), 152.
Swain, Mary (Sweet), (Mrs. John Swain, 3d), 152.
Swain, Mary (Webster), (Mrs. William2 Swain), 228.
Swain, Mary (Wier), (Mrs. John Swain, Sr.), 152.
Swain, Prudence (Marston), (Mrs. William1 Swain), 65, 228.
Swain, Richard, Jr., son Richard Swain, 66.
Swain, Richard, Sr., 4, 65, 66, 68, 152, 153, 228, 230, 237.
Swain, Richard3, son Richard2, 66.
Swain, William1, son Richard Swain, Sr., 65, 228.
Swain, William2, son William1 Swain, 228.
Swaine, Anne (Mrs. Joseph1 Wadleigh), dau. Caleb Swain, 227, 228.
Swayne, John, 4, 5.
Swayne, Richard, 5, 9.

Swett, Benjamin, 47, 66, 152, 153, 154, 213, 214.
Swett, Deliverance (Mrs. Solomon Coleman), dau. Moses Swett, 213.
Swett, Esther (Weare), (Mrs. Benjamin Swett), 47.
Swett, Hester (Weare or Wire), (Mrs. Benjamin Swett), 66, 152, 153, 213, 214.
Swett, Mary (Hussey), (Mrs. Moses Swett), 152, 153, 213, 214.
Swett, Mary (Mrs. John Swain, 3d), dau. Moses Swett, 152.
Swett, Moses, son Benjamin Swett, 152, 153, 154, 213, 214.
Swett, Moses, extract from will, 213.
Swift, Content (Mrs. Zaccheus Wing, Jr.), 184.
Swift, Dorcas (Gardner), (Mrs. Dr. Paul Swift), 169, 173, 174.
Swift, Elizabeth (Mrs. John E. Phillips), 174.
Swift, Hannah (Mrs. Daniel Wing, Sr.), 184.
Swift, Katharine (Mrs. Robert Wharton), widow Dr. Marcus A. Moore, 174.
Swift, Mary (Mrs. Edwin Lamson), 174.
Swift, Dr. Paul, 169, 173, 174.
Swift, Susan (Mrs. Albert H. Franciscus), 174.

Taylor, —— (Bunker), (Mrs. Amos Taylor), 237.
Tea thrown into Boston harbor, 180.
Temple, Mary (Coffin), (Mrs. Solomon Temple), 163.
Temple, Solomon, 163.
Thatcher, Dorothy (Mrs. Richard Sears), 154, 172, 173, 200, 202, 205, 200, 230, 239.
Thorne, Elizabeth (Cheeseman), (Mrs. Captain Joseph Thorne), 241.
Thorne Family, 215, 242.
Thorne, Hannah (Mrs. Richard Cornell), 215.
Thorne, John, son Joseph, 242.
Thorne, Joseph, 242.
Thorne, Joseph, Captain, son Thomas, 241.
Thorne, Sarah (Mrs. Joshua Cornell), 215.
Thorne, Thomas, son Joseph, 241, 242.
Tibbetts, Ann (Mrs. Paul Starbuck), dau. Ephraim Tibbetts, 204, 205.
Tibbetts, Ephraim, 205.
Tibbetts, Rose (Austin), (Mrs. Ephraim Tibbetts), 205.
Tilley, Edward, 174.
Tilley, Elizabeth (Mrs. John Howland), dau. John Tilley, 172, 173, 198, 200, 201, 202, 204, 209, 230.

Tilley, John, 80.
Tilley, John, 173, 174, 198, 201, 202, 206, 209, 230, 240, 241.
Tilly, Elizabeth (Mrs. Jacob Clement), 241.
Tilton, Mary (Mrs. Isaac Chase), 156.
Toppan, Elizabeth (Mrs. Nathaniel Clark), 228.
Townsend, Martha (Mrs. James Powell), 195.
Trask, Lydia (Mrs. William Morrill), 228.
Tripp, Elizabeth, dau. James Tripp, 142, 192, 217.
Tripp, Elizabeth (Mrs. Richard Mitchell), 141, 192, 217, 219.
Tripp, Mary (Paine), (Mrs. John Tripp), 142, 192, 194, 217, 219.
Tripp, James, 145.
Tripp, James, son John Tripp, 142, 146, 147, 192, 194, 217, 219.
Tripp, John, 142, 145, 146, 147, 192, 194, 217, 219.
Tripp, Mercy (Lawton), (Mrs. James Tripp), 192, 194, 217, 219.
Trott, Ann, 132.
Trott, John, 147.
True, Eleanor (Mrs. Abraham Morrill), dau. William True, 228, 229.
True, Eleanor (Stevens), (Mrs. William True), 229.
True, William, 229.
Tucker, Abraham, 191, 194.
Tucker, Elizabeth (Mrs. James3 Barker), dau. Abraham Tucker, 191.
Tucker, Hannah (Mott), (Mrs. Abraham Tucker), 191.
Tupper, Benjamin, 114.
Turner, Bathsheba (Hobart), (Mrs. Joseph Turner), 84.

Van der Velde, Bridget, 174.
Van Leer Family, 168.
Varney, Esther (Starbuck), 21.
Varney, Humphrey, 21.
Varney, Sarah (Starbuck), 21.
Vere, family name, 66.
Vincent, John, 148.
Vines, Richard, 5.

Wadleigh, Anne (Swaine), (Mrs. Joseph1 Wadleigh), 227.
Wadleigh, Dole2, son Dole1 Wadley, 227.
Wadleigh, Joseph1, 227.
Wadleigh, Sarah (Mrs. Edward Everett Capehart), 227.
Wadley, Dole1, son Joseph2 Wadley, 227, 230.
Wadley, Elizabeth Carrol (Pierce), (Mrs. Dole Wadley), 227.

Early Settlers of Nantucket.

Wadley, Elizabeth (Dole), (Mrs. Joseph[2] Wadley), 227.
Wadley (or Wadleigh) Family, 227.
Wadley, Joseph[2], 227.
Wadley, Sarah (Colcord), (Mrs. Dole[1] Wadley), 227.
Walker, Mary Pennypacker (Mrs. Coffin Colket), 231.
Walters, Marianna (Mrs. Giles H. Coggeshall), 219.
Wanackmamack, receipt of, 11.
Wanackmanack, deed of, 9.
Warner, Ellen Bliss (Mrs. William Morris Davis), 165.
Waterman, Avis, dau. Thaddeus Waterman, 226.
Waterman Family, connection with Nantucket, 224.
Waterman, Hepzibah (Coffin), (Mrs. Thaddeus Waterman), 224, 226.
Waterman, Hepzibeth (Mrs. Martin McKenzie), dau. Thaddeus Waterman, 224, 226.
Waterman, Robert, son Thaddeus Waterman, 226.
Waterman, Thaddeus, 224, 226.
Watson, Mercy (Mrs. John[3] Freeman), 220.
Weare, Elizabeth (Swain), (Mrs. Nathaniel Weare), 66, 152.
Weare, Hester (Mrs. Benjamin Swett), dau. Nathaniel Weare (or Wire), 47, 66, 152, 153, 213, 214.
Weare, name spelled Weare, Weir, Weyer, Wier, Wire, Wyer, 66.
Weare, Nathaniel, 152.
Weare (or Wire), Nathaniel, Jr., son Nathaniel Weare, Sr., 66.
Weare, Nathaniel, Sr., son Peter Weare, 66.
Weare (or Wire), Peter, son Nathaniel Weare, 66.
Weare, Sarah (Mrs. Nathaniel Weare), 153, 214.
Webb, George, 77.
Webster, Ebenezer, grandfather Daniel Webster, 57.
Webster, Mary (Mrs. William[2] Swain), 228.
West, Joan (Mrs. Joshua Coggeshall), 216, 219.
Wetherill, Sarah, dau. Rev. William Wetherill, 85, 185.
Wetherill, William, Rev., 85.
Weymouth, Captain, 2.
Wharton, Edward, 15, 16.
Wharton, Katharine (Swift), (Mrs. Robert Wharton), 174.
Wharton, Robert, 174.
White Family, 168.
White, John, Rev., 79.
Whittier, Abigail (Hussey), (Mrs. John Whittier), 234, 235.

Whittier, Charles C., 234, 236.
Whittier, John, son Joseph Whittier[2], 234.
Whittier, John Greenleaf, son John Whittier, 234, 236.
Whittier, Joseph[1], son Thomas Whittier, 234, 236.
Whittier, Joseph[2], son Joseph[1] Whittier, 234.
Whittier, Mary (Peaslee), (Mrs. Joseph[1] Whittier), 234, 236.
Whittier, Ruth (Green), (Mrs. Thomas Whittier), 234.
Whittier, Sarah (Greenleaf), (Mrs. Joseph[2] Whittier), 234, 235.
Whittier, Thomas, 234, 236.
Wier, the family name, 66.
Wier (or Weare), Mary (Mrs. John Weare), 66.
Wier (or Weare), Mary (Mrs. John Swain, Sr.), dau. Nathaniel Weare, 66, 152.
Wier (or Wyer or Weare), Nathaniel, 152, 153, 214.
Wiggins, Thomas, 19, 20.
Wilcox, Mary (Cavender), (Mrs. William J. Wilcox), 165.
Wilcox, William J., 165.
Williams, Lucy (Mrs. Robert Barker), 156, 190, 191.
Wing, Abigail (Mrs. Paul Wing), dau. Samuel Wing, 183, 184, 185, 186, 189.
Wing, Abraham R., 186, 187.
Wing, Alice Rogers (Mrs. Daniel C. Maxfield), 187.
Wing, Ann (Howland), (Mrs. Sands Wing), 186.
Wing, Anna (Rogers), (Mrs. Samuel Wing), 186.
Wing, Anna (Mrs. Samuel Rhodes), 187.
Wing, Anna (Mrs. Elwood Paige), 187.
Wing, Asa Shove, son Stephen R. Wing, 187.
Wing, Beulah R. (Mrs. Moses Folger Rogers), 186, 187.
Wing, Charles, son Lindley Moore Wing, 187.
Wing connection with Nantucket families, 183.
Wing, Content (Swift), (Mrs. Zaccheus Wing, Jr.), 184.
Wing, Gonway Phelps, Rev., 56.
Wing, Daniel, 77.
Wing, Daniel, Jr., son Daniel, Sr., 184.
Wing, Daniel, Sr., son John Wing, 59, 184.
Wing, David Shove, died young, 187.
Wing, Deborah (Bachelor), (Mrs. John Wing), 56, 57, 184, 185, 188, 190.
Wing, Deborah (Dillingham), (Mrs. (Mrs Daniel Wing, Jr.), 184.

Wing, Deborah (Mrs. Samuel Barker, 1st wife), 188.
Wing, Dorothy (Mrs. Samuel Wing, Sr.), dau. John Wing, 184, 188.
Wing, Elizabeth (Holway), (Mrs. Lindley Moore Wing), 186, 187.
Wing, Elizabeth (Collins Shove), (Mrs. Stephen R. Wing), 186, 187.
Wing, Elizabeth (Mrs. John S. Perry), widow Fred Pond, 187.
Wing, Hannah (Swift), (Mrs. Daniel Wing, Sr.), 184.
Wing, Hepzibah (Mrs. William Coleman, Sr.), 186.
Wing, Hepzibah (Hathaway), (Mrs. Samuel Wing, Jr.), 184, 186.
Wing, Hepzibah (Mrs. Estes Newhall), 189.
Wing, Hepzibah, dau. Samuel Wing, 186.
Wing, John, 54, 57, 58, 59, 184, 185, 188, 190.
Wing, John, Jr., son Stephen Wing, 188.
Wing, Joseph Rogers, died young, 187.
Wing, Joseph R., 186, 187.
Wing, Lindley Moore, 186, 187.
Wing, Lydia (Mrs. Sylvanus Hussey, Jr., 2d wife), 183, 185.
Wing, Lydia (Renington), (Mrs. Stephen Rogers Wing), 187.
Wing, Lydia, dau. Samuel Wing, 184, 186.
Wing, Mary Ann (Mrs. Joseph R. Wing), dau. Sands Wing, 186, 187.
Wing, Mary Anna, dau. Abraham R. Wing, 187.
Wing, Mary (Perry), (Mrs. John Wing, Jr.), 188.
Wing, Mary H., dau. Joseph R. Wing, 187.
Wing, Mary R., dau. Samuel Wing, 186.
Wing, Mary S. (Gardner), (Mrs. Abraham R. Wing), 186.
Wing, Paul, 186.
Wing, Paul, son Zaccheus Wing, 184, 185, 189.
Wing, Samuel, Jr., son Samuel Wing, Sr., 184, 186.
Wing, Samuel, Sr., son Daniel Wing, Jr., 184.
Wing, Samuel, son Abraham R. Wing, 187.
Wing, Samuel, son Paul Wing, 186.
Wing, Sands, 186.
Wing, Sarah (Briggs), (Mrs. Stephen Wing), 188.
Wing, Sophia (Rhodes), 187.
Wing, Stephen, son John Wing, 188.
Wing, Stephen R., died young, 187.
Wing, Stephen R., 186, 187.
Wing, Stephen Rogers, 187.

Wing, Zaccheus, son Daniel Wing, Jr., 184.
Winslow, Edward, 79.
Winthrop, John, Esq., 5.
Wood, Mary (Mrs. John Hussey), 50, 51.
Wood, Mary (Mrs. Richard1 Mitchell), 192, 194, 217, 219.
Wood, Mary Ann (Mrs. Ezra Cornell), 211.
Woodbridge, Mrs. Mary A., dau. Judge Brayton, 145.

Worth, Anna (Mrs. Abraham1 Macy), 195.
Worth, John, son William Worth, 196, 199, 204, 222.
Worth, Joseph, son John Worth, 196.
Worth, Judith (Mrs. John Macy, Jr.), dau. John Worth, 198, 199, 203, 204, 221, 222.
Worth, Justice, 30.
Worth, Lydia (Gorham), (Mrs. Joseph Worth), 195.
Worth, Miriam (Gardner), (Mrs. John Worth), 196, 199, 204, 222.

Worth, Sarah (Macy), (Mrs. William Worth), 196, 199, 222.
Worth, Shubael, 113.
Worth, William, 196, 199, 222.
Wyer, Robert, 66.
Yarnall, Benjamin H., 163.
Yarnall, Caroline (Cope), (Mrs. Edward Yarnall), 164.
Yarnall, Edward, 164.
Yarnall, Eliza (Coffin), (Mrs. Benjamin H. Yarnall), 163.

www.ingramcontent.com/pod-product-compliance
Lightning Source LLC
Chambersburg PA
CBHW030540080526
44585CB00012B/216